DOCUMENTS S

Arlene M. W. Sindel

University of Central Arkansas

Mary E. Chalmers

Kenyon College

WESTERN CIVILIZATION

A Social and Cultural History

Volume I

MARGARET L. KING

Brooklyn College and the Graduate Center
City University of New York

PRENTICE HALL, UPPER SADDLE RIVER, NEW JERSEY 07458

©2000 by PRENTICE-HALL, INC.
PEARSON EDUCATION
Upper Saddle River, New Jersey 07458

ISBN 0-13-016088-1

Printed in the United States of America

CONTENTS

Part ONE

THE ORIGINS OF THE WEST

From the First Civilizations to Alexander the Great

(Prehistory–300 B.C.E.)

CHAPTER 1

Stone, Bronze, and Word

Prehistory and Early Civilizations

(2 million–500 B.C.E.)

SECTION 1

The Origins of Civilizations

1.1 New Theories about Human Development

Since the 1950s, theories about life among early humans have centered on "traditional" male and female roles, with men responsible for hunting and women for domestic duties and child rearing. In the following excerpt, Barbara Ehrenreich reviews new developments in the theories about the origins of human evolution that challenge these traditional views.

> **Source:** Barbara Ehrenreich, "The Real Truth about the Female," *Time* (March 8, 1999, vol. 153, no. 9).

There were always plenty of prima facie reasons to doubt the Mr. and Mrs. Man-the-Hunter version of our collective biography, such as the little matter of size, or, in science-speak, "sexual dimorphism." If men and women evolved so differently, then why aren't men a whole lot bigger than they are? In fact, humans display a smaller size disparity between the sexes than do many of our ape cousins—suggesting (though not proving) that early men and women sometimes had overlapping job descriptions, like having to drive off the leopards. And speaking of Paleolithic predators, wouldn't it be at least unwise for the guys to go off hunting, leaving the supposedly weak and dependent women and children to fend for themselves at base camp? Odd too, that Paleolithic culture should look so much like the culture of Levittown circa 1955, with the gals waiting at home for the guys to come back with the bacon. In what other carnivorous species is only one sex an actual predator?

Beginning in the '70s, women began to elbow their way into the field and develop serious alternatives to the old, male-centered theory of human evolution. It shouldn't matter, of course, what sex the scientist is, but women had their own reasons for being suspicious of the dominant paradigm. The first revisionist blow came in the mid-'70s, when anthropologists Adrienne Zihlman and Nancy Tanner pointed out that among surviving "hunting" peoples, most of the community's calories—up to 70%—come from plant food patiently gathered by women, not meat heroically captured by men. The evidence for Stone Age consumption of plant foods has mounted since then. In 1994 paleobotanist Sarah Mason concluded that a variety of plant material discovered at the Paleolithic site of Dolni Vestonice in the Czech Republic was in fact edible roots and seeds. At the very least, it seems, the Paleolithic dinner was potluck, and it was probably the women who provided most of the starches, salad and raspberry-mousse desserts. The mother-of-us-all was beginning to look a little peppier and more self-reliant.

Not that even the most efficient gatherer gal doesn't need a little help now and then, especially when she's lactating. Nursing a baby may look pretty effortless, but it can burn up 500 calories a day—the equivalent of running about five miles. Where was the help coming from? Was the female completely dependent on her male significant other, as the prevailing theory has always implied? An alternative possibility lay buried in the mystery of menopause. Nature is no friend of the infertile, and in most primates,

1

the end of childbearing coincides with the end of life, so it was always hard to see why human females get to live for years, even decades, after their ovaries go into retirement. Hence the "grandma hypothesis": maybe the evolutionary "purpose" of the postmenopausal woman was to keep her grandchildren provided with berries and tubers and nuts, especially while Mom was preoccupied with a new baby. If Grandma were still bearing and nursing her own babies, she'd be too busy to baby-sit, so natural selection may have selected for a prolonged healthy and mature, but infertile, stage of the female life cycle.

To test this possibility, anthropologist Kristen Hawkes made quite a nuisance of herself among the hunting-gathering Hadza people of Tanzania, charting the hour-by-hour activities of 90 individuals, male and female, and weighing the children at regular intervals. The results, published in late 1997 and reported by Angier in detail, established that children did better if Grandma was on the case—and, if not her, then a great-aunt or similar grandma figure. This doesn't prove the grandma hypothesis for all times and all peoples, but it does strongly suggest that in the Stone Age family, Dad-the-hunter was not the only provider. The occasional antelope haunch might be a tasty treat, but as Hawkes and her co-workers conclude about the Hadza, "it is women's foraging, not men's hunting, that differentially affects their own families' nutritional welfare." If the grandma hypothesis holds up, we may have to conclude that the male-female pair bond was not quite so central to human survival as the evolutionary psychologists assume. The British anthropologist Chris Knight—who is, incidentally, male—suggests that alliances among females may have been more important in shaping the political economy of Paleolithic peoples.

The thinking that led to man-the-hunter was largely inferential: if you bring the women along on the hunt, the children will have to come too, and all that squalling and chattering would surely scare off the game. This inference was based on a particular style of hunting, familiar from Hemingway novels and common to the New England woods in October, in which a small band of men trek off into the wild and patiently stalk their prey, a deer or two at a time. But there is another way to get the job done known as "communal hunting," in which the entire group—women, men and children—drive the animals over a cliff or into a net or cul-de-sac. The Blackfoot and other Indians hunted bison this way before they acquired the horse—hence all those "buffalo jumps" in the Canadian and American West—and net hunting is the most productive hunting method employed by the Mbuti people of the Congo today. When driving animals into a place where they can be slaughtered, noise is a positive help, whether it's the clashing of men's spears or the squeals of massed toddlers.

But there was only indirect evidence of communal hunting in Paleolithic times until archaeologist Olga Soffer came across the kind of clue that, a gender traditionalist might say, it took a womanly eye to notice. While sifting through clay fragments from the Paleolithic site of Pavlov in what is now the Czech Republic, she found a series of parallel lines impressed on some of the clay surfaces—evidence of woven fibers from about 25,000 years ago. Intrigued to find signs of weaving from this early date, Soffer and her colleagues examined 8,400 more clay fragments from the same and nearby sites, eventually coming across the traces of a likely tool of the communal hunt—a mesh net. The entire theory of man-the-hunter had been based on "durable media," Soffer explains, meaning items like the sharpened stones that can serve as spearheads, rather than softer, biodegradable goods like baskets, fabrics and nets. But in archaeologically well-preserved prehistoric sites, such as those found underwater or in dry caves, the soft goods predominate over the durable by a ratio of about 20 to 1. If the hard stuff was the work of men, then "we've been missing the children, the women, the old people," she asserts. Thanks to Soffer's sharp eye, Paleolithic net hunting is no longer invisible, and in net hunting, Soffer says, "everybody participates."

Furthermore, as Mary Zeiss Stange points out in her 1997 book *Woman the Hunter*, there's no reason to rule out women's hunting with hard-edged weapons too, perhaps even of their own making. Among the Tiwi Aborigines of Australia, hunting is considered women's work, and until the introduction of steel implements, it was done with handmade stone axes the women fashioned for themselves. By putting women's work back into the record, the new female evolutionary scientists may have helped rewrite the biography of the human race. At least we should prepare to welcome our bold and resourceful new ancestor, Xena the hunter princess.

The news of Soffer's discovery . . . will disconcert many feminists as well as sociobiologists. After all, the gratifying thing about man-the-hunter was that he helped locate all the violence and related mischief on the men's side of the campfire: no blood on our hands! But there are other reasons to doubt the eternal equation of masculinity with aggression and violence, femininity with gentleness and a taste for green salads. In ancient Greece and Sumer the deities of the hunt, Artemis and Ninhursag, were female—extremely female, if you will, since these were also the goddesses who presided over childbirth. Even more striking is the association of ancient goddesses with nature's original hunters, the predatory animals. In Anatolia, the predator goddess was Kybele, known as the commander of lions. In Egypt she was Sekhmet, portrayed as a lioness whose "mane smoked with fire [and whose] countenance glowed like the sun."

Images of goddesses tell us nothing about the role of actual women, but they do suggest that about 3,000 years ago, at the dawn of human civilization, the idea of the fearsome huntress, the woman predator, generated no snickers among the pious.

Questions:
1. What are the new theories being suggested?
2. Why are earlier theories being questioned?
3. What kinds of evidence are being used to support the new theories?

1.2   Development of Agricultural Dependence

This chart, while presenting information simply, is the result of multidisciplinary research that often relies on modern technology. It charts the relative importance of four types of food (wild animals, wild plants, agricultural plants, and domesticated animals) in the diet of people living in the Tehuacán Valley in central Mexico, beginning with the development of agriculture in 7000 B.C.E. and ending in 1500 C.E., when Europeans first made contact with the Americas. In answering the questions, refer to the chart and to the introductory material provided as appropriate.

> **Source:** Richard S. MacNeish, "The Development of Agricultural Dependence in the Tehuacán Valley," in ed. Douglas S. Byers, *The Prehistory of the Tehuacan Valley, vol. 1*, (Austin: Robert S. Peabody Foundation/University of Texas Press, 1967), Figure 186: "A Summary of the Subsis-

tence" (p. 301). Copyright 1967 and renewed in 1996 by Robert S. Peabody Museum of Archaeology. Reproduced with an introduction in Russell J. Barber, Lanny B. Fields, Cheryl A. Riggs, *Reading the Global Past, vol. 1*, (Boston: Bedford Books, 1998).

Richard S. MacNeish has studied the rise of agriculture on three continents over an archaeological career that has spanned half a century. He pioneered much of the interdisciplinary research that now is commonplace in archaeology, enlisting botanists, zoologists, geologists, and other scientists to assist an archaeological team that examined the development of agriculture in the Tehuacán Valley of central Mexico. The reports of that research (1967) ran to more than a thousand pages, much of the material very technical, but many of its conclusions can be summarized in the graph in Figure 1.

The width of each bar reflects the relative importance of each category of food source in the Tehuacán Valley at the dates shown; the bars always add up to the same width, since they are calculated on the basis of percentages and have to equal 100 percent at any given time. The calculations began with archaeological fieldwork; during which seeds, bones, shells, and various other biological remains of foodstuffs were recovered and sent back to

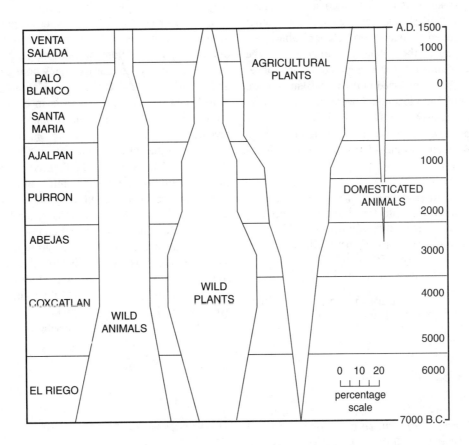

Figure: 1 Changes in Diet in the Tehuacán Valley

the laboratory. There, they were identified and quantified, and calculations were made to convert that information into estimates of the amounts of food represented. Finally, the relative inputs of wild animals, wild plants, agricultural plants, and domesticated animals were totaled for each period represented, and the graph was produced.

Several patterns are obvious in the graph. First, domesticated animals were never a significant source of food in prehistoric Mexico, a fact long recognized. Second, in the earliest times, 7000 to 4200 B.C., there was a rapid falloff in the amount of meat eaten, apparently because of climatic change, as the Tehuacán Valley became dried and there were fewer animals to hunt. Third, in the following period, until about 1200 B.C., agricultural products in the diet increased slowly and gradually; much of this increase in the eating of agricultural plants was offset by comparable decreases in the eating of wild plants. Fourth, about 800 B.C., a final significant change took place: the use of agricultural foods increased sharply, and the use of wild foods (both plant and animal) rapidly decreased. It is at this period that we can truly speak of "agricultural dependence" in the Tehuacán Valley. From 800 B.C. onward, wild foodstuffs had only small importance in subsistence.

The Tehuacán Valley was a provincial area that became dependent on agriculture a bit later than some other parts of Mesoamerica. It is significant that this valley was also behind those other parts of Mesoamerica in urbanization, the development of state governments, and the other elements of civilization. Irrigation and recognizable class distinctions appeared in the Tehuacán Valley during the Santa Maria phase (900–200 B.C.); chiefdom or state-level governments and towns developed in the Palo Blanco phase (200 B.C.–A.D. 700), and clear states were in place during the Venta Salada phase (A.D. 700–1540). This chronology demonstrates the importance of a strong agricultural base prior to the development of other elements of civilization.

Questions:
1. What are some of the disciplines of research used to generate the data for this chart? How might those disciplines have been useful?
2. What does this chart suggest about the development of agriculture? Why might it have taken so many years for it to become predominant?
3. What seems to be the relationship between the development of food sources and of civilization?

Documents 1.3–1.6

In the following four documents, we see how four different civilizations mythologized the beginnings of their civilizations. While these documents do not speak directly to a past that can be documented through archaeological evidence, they can still tell us about what each civilization valued.

1.3   An Egyptian Hymn to the Nile

"Hymn to the Nile" is thought to have been composed for a festival in Thebes celebrating the annual flooding of the Nile River. Its date is unknown.

Source: Adoph Erman, *The Literature of the Ancient Egyptians*, trans. A.M. Blackman (London: Methuen & Co., Ltd., 1927), pp. 146–49, reprinted in John L. Beatty and Oliver A. Johnson, eds., Heritage of Western Civilization, volume 1, 7th edition (Englewood Cliffs, NJ: Prentice Hall, 1991), pp. 19–20).

Praise to thee, O Nile, that issueth from the earth, and cometh to nourish Egypt. Of hidden nature, a darkness in the daytime. . . .

That watereth the meadows, he that Rē[1] hath created to nourish all cattle. That giveth drink to the desert places, which are far from water; it is his dew that falleth from heaven.

Beloved of Kēb,[2] director of the corn-god; that maketh to flourish every workshop of Ptah.[3]

Lord of fish, that maketh the water-fowl to go upstream. . . .

That maketh barley and createth wheat, so that he may cause the temples to keep festivals.

If he be sluggish,[4] the nostrils are stopped up,[5] and all men are impoverished; the victuals of the gods are diminished, and millions of men perish.

If he be niggardly the whole land is in terror and great and small lament. . . . Khnum[6] hath fashioned him. When he riseth, the land is in exultation and every body is in joy. All jaws begin to laugh and every tooth is revealed.

He that bringeth victuals and is rich in food, that createth all that is good. The revered, sweet-smelling. . . . That createth herbage for the cattle, and giveth sacrifice to every god, be he in the underworld, in heaven, or upon earth. . . . That filleth the storehouses, and maketh wide the granaries, that giveth things to the poor.

He that maketh trees to grow according to every wish, and men have no lack thereof; the ship is built by his power, for there is no joinery with stones. . . .

. . . thy young folk and thy children shout for joy over thee, and men hail thee as king. Unchanging of laws, when he cometh forth in the presence of Upper and Lower Egypt. Men drink the water. . . .

---
[1] The sun-god.
[2] The earth-god.
[3] Ptah, the craftsman, who fashions everything, could effect nothing without the Nile.
[4] On the occasion of a deficient inundation.
[5] Men no longer breathe and live.
[6] The ram-headed god, who fashions all that is.

He that was in sorrow is become glad, and every heart is joyful. Sobk,[7] the child of Neith, laugheth, and the divine Ennead, that is in thee, is glorious.

Thou that vomitest forth, giving the fields to drink and making strong the people. He that maketh the one rich and loveth the other. He maketh no distinctions, and boundaries are not made for him.

Thou light, that cometh from the darkness! Thou fat for his cattle. He is a strong one, that createth. . . .

. . . one beholdeth the wealthy as him that is full of care, one beholdeth each one with his implements. . . . None that (otherwise) goeth clad, is clad,[8] and the children of notables are unadorned. . . .

He that establisheth right, whom men love. . . . It would be but lies to compare thee with the sea, that bringeth no corn. . . . no bird descendeth in the desert. . . .

Men begin to play to thee on the harp, and men sing to thee with the hand.[9] Thy young folk and thy children shout for joy over thee, and deputations to thee are appointed.

He that cometh with splendid things and adorneth the earth! That causeth the ship to prosper before men; that quickeneth the hearts in them that are with child; that would fain have there be a multitude of all kinds of cattle.

When thou art risen in the city of the sovereign, then men are satisfied with a goodly list.[10] "I would like lotus flowers," saith the little one, "and all manner of things," saith the . . . commander, "and all manner of herbs," say the children. Eating bringeth forgetfulness of him.[11] Good things are scattered over the dwelling. . . .

When the Nile floodeth, offering is made to thee, cattle are slaughtered for thee, a great oblation is made for thee. Birds are fattened for thee, antelopes are hunted for thee in the desert. Good is recompensed unto thee.

Offering is also made to every other god, even as is done for the Nile, with incense, oxen, cattle, and birds (upon) the flame. The Nile hath made him his cave in Thebes, and his name shall be known no more in the underworld. . . .

All ye men, extol the Nine Gods, and stand in awe of the might which his son, the Lord of All, hath displayed, even he that maketh green the Two River-banks. Thou art verdant, O Nile, thou art verdant. He that maketh man to live on his cattle, and his cattle on the meadow! Thou art verdant, thou art verdant: O Nile, thou art verdant.

1.4   A Mesopotamian King

The Epic of Gilgamesh dates from the third millennium in Mesopotamia, 1500 years older than Homer's Greek epics *The Iliad* and *The Odyssey*

(Chapter 2, Document 2). Several versions of the epic in different languages have been found in such places as Ur, Uruk, the Hittite capital city, Iraq, Assyria, southern Turkey, and Palestine.

Source: *The Epic of Gilgamesh*, trans. N.K. Sandars, (New York: Penguin Books, 1981, © 1972), p. 61.

I will proclaim to the world the deeds of Gilgamesh. This was the man to whom all things were known; this was the king who knew the countries of the world. He was wise, he saw mysteries and knew secret things, he brought us a tale of the days before the flood. He went on a long journey, was weary, worn-out with labour, returning he rested, he engraved on a stone the whole story.

When the gods created Gilgamesh they gave him a perfect body. Shamash the glorious sun endowed him with beauty, Adad the god of the storm endowed him with courage, the great gods made his beauty perfect, surpassing all others, terrifying like a great wild bull. Two thirds they made him god and one third man.

In Uruk he built walls, a great rampart, and the temple of blessed Eanna for the god of the firmament Anu, and for Ishtar the goddess of love. Look at it still today: the outer wall where the cornice runs, it shines with the brilliance of copper; and the inner wall, it has no equal. Touch the threshold, it is ancient. Approach Eanna the dwelling of Ishtar, our lady of love and war, the like of which no latter-day king, no man alive can equal. Climb upon the wall of Uruk; walk along it, I say; regard the foundation terrace and examine the masonry: is it not burnt brick and good? The seven sages laid the foundations.

1.5   The Chinese Sage Kings

"The Canon of Yao and the Canon of Shun" speak of the first two Sage Kings, said to have ruled China in the twenty-third and twenty-second centuries B.C.E. While archaeological evidence only goes back as far as the Shang Dynasty, traditionally the Chinese date the beginnings of their civilization in the twenty-eighth century B.C.E. with the rule of three cultural heroes, followed by the three sage kings. The *Book of History*, from which these Canon come, has been regarded as being the record of these ancient kings, who have been seen throughout the ages as models for all rulers.

Source: "Yao tien and Shun tien," in *Shu ching (Book of History)*; reprinted in *Sources of Chinese Tradition*, compiled by Wm. Theodore de Bary, Wing-tsit Chan, and Burton Watson, (New York: Columbia University, 1960), pp. 10–12.

Examining into antiquity, we find that the Emperor Yao was called Fang-hsün. (He was reverent, intelligent, accom-

---

[7] Sobk has the form of a crocodile and will originally have been a water-god, who rejoices in the inundation.
[8] For hard work, clothes are taken off.
[9] It is an old custom to beat time with the hand while singing.
[10] *I.e.*, a multitude of good things.
[11] The Nile.

plished, sincere, and mild. He was sincerely respectful and capable of modesty.) His light covered the four extremities of the empire and extended to Heaven above and the earth below. He was able to make bright his great virtue, and bring affection to the nine branches of the family. When the nine branches of the family had become harmonious, he distinguished and honored the hundred clans. When the hundred clans had become illustrious, he harmonized the myriad states. The numerous people were amply nourished and prosperous and became harmonious. Then he charged Hsi and Ho with reverence to follow august Heaven and calculate and delineate the sun, the moon, and the other heavenly bodies, and respectfully to give the people the seasons. . . . The emperor said: "Ah, you Hsi and Ho, the year has three hundred and sixty-six days, and by means of an intercalary month you must fix the four seasons and complete the year. If you earnestly regulate all the functionaries, the achievements will all be glorious." The emperor said: "Who will carefully attend to this? I will raise him up and employ him." Fang Ch'i said: "You heir-son Chu is enlightened." The emperor said: "Alas, he is deceitful and quarrelsome; will he do?" . . . The emperor said: "Oh, you Chief of the Four Mountains, I have been on the throne for seventy years. If you can carry out the mandate, I shall resign my position to you." The Chief of the Four Mountains said: "I have not the virtue. I would only disgrace the high position." The emperor said: "Promote someone who is already illustrious, or raise up someone who is humble and mean." They all said to the emperor: "There is an unmarried man in a low position called Shun of Yü." The emperor said: "Yes, I have heard of him. What is he like?" The Chief said: "He is the son of a blind man. His father is stupid, his mother is deceitful, his half brother Hsiang is arrogant. Yet he has been able to live in harmony with them and to be splendidly filial. He has controlled himself and has not come to wickedness." The emperor said: "I will try him; I will wive him and observe his behavior towards my two daughters." He gave orders and sent down his two daughters to the bend of the Kuei River to be wives in the House of Yü. The emperor said: "Be reverent!"

. . . .

The emperor said: "Come, you Shun, in the affairs on which you have been consulted, I have examined your words; your words have been accomplished and capable of yielding fine results for three years; do you ascend to the imperial throne." Shun considered himself inferior in virtue and was not pleased. But in the first month, the first day, he accepted the abdication of Yao in the Temple of the Accomplished Ancestor. . . . Then he made *lei* sacrifice to the Lord-on-High; he made *yin* sacrifice to the six venerable ones; he made *wang* sacrifice to mountains and rivers, and he made comprehensive sacrifices to all the spirits. . . . In the second month of the year he went around the east to the fiefs, and came to the Venerable Tai Mountain where he made burnt offering; he made *wang* sacrifice successively to mountains and rivers and he gave audience to the eastern princes. He

put into accord the seasons, the months, and the proper days. He made uniform the pitchpipes, the measures of length, the measures of capacity, and the weights. . . . He delimited the twelve provinces and raised altars on twelve mountains and he deepened the rivers.

1.6 Indra, an Aryan God

The *Rig Veda* is an Aryan collection of hymns dating from c. 1500 B.C.E., when the Aryans moved through the Khyber Pass and settled into the Indus River Valley long occupied by the Harappan civilization. While the *Rig Veda* celebrates many gods and natural forces, Indra was the most prominent.

Source: *Rig Veda* 2.12. Henotheistic; to Indra; reprinted in *The Beginnings of Indian Philosophy: Selectons from the Rig Veda, Athara Veda, Upanisads, and Mahabharata*, trans. Franklin Edgerton, (Cambridge, MA: Harvard University Press, 1970, © 1965), pp. 53–54.

1. Who as soon as born, first possessor of thought, the god, strengthened the gods by his magic (intellectual) power; of whose fury the two firmaments were afraid because of the greatness of his manliness, he, O folk, is Indra.

. . . .

3. Who slew the dragon and made the seven streams to flow, who drove out the cows (of light) by disclosing Vala (the demon of darkness), who created the fire between two stones, winner of booty in battles, he, O folk, is Indra.

4. By whom all these shatterings were made, who put down the *dāsa* (non-Aryan) race in darkness, who takes the wealth of the enemy as a clever gambler takes the stake when he has won, he, O folk, is Indra.

5. The terrible one, of whom they ask, Where is he? and they even say of him, He is not at all; he diminishes the wealth of the enemy like gambling-stakes. Believe in him! He, O folk, is Indra.

. . . .

7. In whose control are horses, cattle, villages, and all chariots; who created the sun, the drawn, and who guides the waters, he, O folk, is Indra.

. . . .

9. Without whom people do not conquer, whom they invoke for aid while they fight, who has become a match for all, who shakes the unshaken, he, O folks, is Indra.

10. Who slays with his bolt, before they know it, all those that have committed great sin; who does not forgive the insolent his insolence, who slays the *dasyu* (non-Aryan), he, O folk, is Indra.

. . . .

12. The mighty bull of (requiring for control) seven reins, who let loose the seven streams to flow, who,

club in arm, kicked down (presumptuous) Rauhina as he was scaling heaven, he, O folk, is Indra.

. . . .

14. Who helps by his aid him that presses (soma) and cooks (sacrificial food), that chants (hymns) and is busily occupied (with sacrifice); of whom holy utterance is a strengthening, and the soma and this gift (to officiating priests), he, O folk, is Indra.

Questions for Documents 1.3–1.6:
1. What values or elements of civilization do each of the documents highlight?
2. Can you link these elements with what you have learned about each of the respective civilizations?
3. Can you make any comparisons or contrasts among the four civilizations and their own perceptions of their origins?

SECTION 2
Law and Ethical Behavior

Documents 1.7 and 1.8
Although the law code of Hammurabi and the ancient laws of the Hebrews were not the first written law codes, they are the most comprehensive and significant for subsequent civilizations.

1.7 Hammurabi's Law Code

In the twenty-second year of his reign, the Amorite King Hammurabi (d. 1750 B.C.E.), who had made Babylon his capital and conquered Mesopotamia, issued a comprehensive code of laws. He caused them to be inscribed on stones that were erected at crossroads and in marketplaces throughout his kingdom so that all his subjects would know them. A selection of these laws follows.

Source: gopher://gopher.vt.edu: 10010/11/, translated by Leonard W. King [Accessed through http://eawc.evansville.edu/anthology/hammurabi.htm]

When Anu the Sublime, King of the Anunaki, and Bel, the lord of Heaven and earth, who decreed the fate of the land, assigned to Marduk, the over-ruling son of Ea, God of righteousness, dominion over earthly man, and made him great. . . ; then Anu and Bel called by name me, Hammurabi, the exalted prince, who feared God, to bring about the rule of righteousness in the land, to destroy the wicked and the evil-doers; so that the strong should not harm the weak; so that I should rule over the black-headed people like Shamash, and enlighten the land, to further the well-being of mankind. . . .

When Marduk sent me to rule over men, to give the protection of right to the land, I did right and righteousness in. . . , and brought about the well-being of the oppressed.

THE CODE OF LAWS

[to ensure good justice]

3. If any one bring an accusation of any crime before the elders, and does not prove what he has charged, he shall, if it be a capital offense charged, be put to death.

5. If a judge try a case, reach a decision, and present his judgment in writing; if later error shall appear in his decision, and it be through his own fault, then he shall pay twelve times the fine set by him in the case, and he shall be publicly removed from the judge's bench, and never again shall he sit there to render judgement.

[criminal law of property]

8. If any one steal cattle or sheep, or an ass, or a pig or a goat, if it belong to a god or to the court, the thief shall pay thirtyfold therefore; if they belonged to a freed man of the king he shall pay tenfold; if the thief has nothing with which to pay he shall be put to death.

21. If any one break a hole into a house (break in to steal), he shall be put to death before that hole and be buried.

22. If any one is committing a robbery and is caught, then he shall be put to death.

23. If the robber is not caught, then shall he who was robbed claim under oath the amount of his loss; then shall the community, and . . . on whose ground and territory and in whose domain it was compensate him for the goods stolen.

[property laws concerning agriculture and irrigation]

42. If any one take over a field to till it, and obtain no harvest therefrom, it must be proved that he did no work on the field, and he must deliver grain, just as his neighbor raised, to the owner of the field.

45. If a man rent his field for tillage for a fixed rental, and receive the rent of his field, but bad weather come and destroy the harvest, the injury falls upon the tiller of the soil.

46. If he do not receive a fixed rental for his field, but lets it on half or third shares of the harvest, the grain on the field shall be divided proportionately between the tiller and the owner.

48. If any one owe a debt for a loan, and a storm prostrates the grain, or the harvest fail, or the grain does not

grow for lack of water; in that year he need not give his creditor any grain, he washes his debt-tablet in water and pays no rent for this year.

53. If any one be too lazy to keep his dam in proper condition, and does not so keep it; if then the dam break and all the fields be flooded, then shall he in whose dam the break occurred be sold for money, and the money shall replace the corn which he has caused to be ruined.

55. If any one open his ditches to water his crop, but is careless, and the water flood the field of his neighbor, then he shall pay his neighbor corn for his loss.

[laws governing debts and obligations]

108. If a tavern-keeper (feminine form) does not accept corn according to gross weight in payment of drink, but takes money, and the price of the drink is less than that of the corn, she shall be convicted and thrown into the water.

117. If any one fail to meet a claim for debt, and sell himself, his wife, his son, and daughter for money or give them away to forced labor: they shall work for three years in the house of the man who bought them, or the proprietor, and in the fourth year they shall be set free.

121. If any one store corn in another man's house he shall pay him storage at the rate of one gur[1] for every five ka[2] of corn per year.

122. If any one give another silver, gold, or anything else to keep, he shall show everything to some witness, draw up a contract, and then hand it over for safe keeping.

123. If he turn it over for safe keeping without witness or contract, and if he to whom it was given deny it, then he has no legitimate claim.

[laws concerning marriage, family, and inheritance]

128. If a man take a woman to wife, but have no intercourse with her, this woman is no wife to him.

129. If a man's wife be surprised [in a sexually compromising situation] with another man, both shall be tied and thrown into the water, but the husband may pardon his wife and the king his [subjects].

130. If a man violate the wife (betrothed or child-wife) of another man, who has never known a man, and still lives in her father's house, and sleep with her and be surprised, this man shall be put to death, but the wife is blameless.

131. If a man bring a charge against one's wife, but she is not surprised with another man, she must take an oath and then may return to her house.

133. If a man is taken prisoner in war, and there is a sustenance in his house, but his wife leave house and court, and go to another house: because this wife did not keep her court, and went to another house, she shall be judicially condemned and thrown into the water.

134. If any one be captured in war and there is not sustenance in his house, if then his wife go to another house this woman shall be held blameless.

136. If any one leave his house, run away, and then his wife go to another house, if then he return, and wishes to take his wife back: because he fled from his home and ran away, the wife of this runaway shall not return to her husband.

137. If a man wish to separate from a woman who has borne him children, or from his wife who has borne him children: then he shall give that wife her dowry, and a part of the usufruct of field, garden, and property, so that she can rear her children. When she has brought up her children, a portion of all that is given to the children, equal as that of one son, shall be given to her. She may then marry the man of her heart.

138. If a man wishes to separate from his wife who has borne him no children, he shall give her the amount of her purchase money and the dowry which she brought from her father's house, and let her go.

142. If a woman quarrel with her husband, and say: "You are not congenial to me," the reasons for her prejudice must be presented. If she is guiltless, and there is no fault on her part, but he leaves and neglects her, then no guilt attaches to this woman, she shall take her dowry and go back to her father's house.

143. If she is not innocent, but leaves her husband, and ruins her house, neglecting her husband, this woman shall be cast into the water.

145. If a man take a wife, and she bear him no children, and he intend to take another wife: if he take this second wife, and bring her into the house, this second wife shall not be allowed equality with his wife.

148. If a man take a wife, and she be seized by disease, if he then desire to take a second wife he shall not put away his wife, who has been attacked by disease, but he shall keep her in the house which he has built and support her so long as she lives.

149. If this woman does not wish to remain in her husband's house, then he shall compensate her for the dowry that she brought with her from her father's house, and she may go.

154. If a man be guilty of incest with his daughter, he shall be driven from the place (exiled).

157. If any one be guilty of incest with his mother after his father, both shall be burned.

158. If any one be surprised after his father with his chief wife, who has borne children, he shall be driven out of his father's house.

159. If any one, who has brought chattels into his father-in-law's house, and has paid the purchase-money, looks for another wife, and says to his father-in-law: "I do not want your daughter," the girl's father may keep all that he had brought.

160. If a man bring chattels into the house of his father-in-law, and pay the "purchase price" (for his wife): if

---

[1] the basic monetary unit
[2] the basic measurement for volume

then the father of the girl say: "I will not give you my daughter," he shall give him back all that he brought with him.

163. If a man marry a woman and she bear him no sons; if then this woman die, if the "purchase price" which he had paid into the house of his father-in-law is repaid to him, her husband shall have no claim upon the dowry of this woman; it belongs to her father's house.

168. If a man wish to put his son out of his house, and declare before the judge: "I want to put my son out," then the judge shall examine into his reasons. If the son be guilty of no great fault, for which he can be rightfully put out, the father shall not put him out.

170. If his wife bear sons to a man, or his maid-servant have borne sons, and the father while still living says to the children whom his maid-servant has borne: "My sons," and he count them with the sons of his wife; if then the father die, then the sons of the wife and of the maid-servant shall divide the paternal property in common. The son of the wife is to partition and choose.

180. If a father give a present to his daughter—either marriageable or a prostitute (unmarriageable)—and then die, then she is to receive a portion as a child from the paternal estate, and enjoy its usufruct so long as she lives. Her estate belongs to her brothers.

184. If a man do not give a dowry to his daughter by a concubine, and no husband; if then her father die, her brother shall give her a dowry according to her father's wealth and secure a husband for her.

185. If a man adopt a child and to his name as son, and rear him, this grown son can not be demanded back again.

190. If a man does not maintain a child that he has adopted as a son and reared with his other children, then his adopted son may return to his father's house.

[laws concerning physical harm to persons or animals]

195. If a son strike his father, his hands shall be hewn off.

196. If a man put out the eye of another man, his eye shall be put out.

197. If he break another man's bone, his bone shall be broken.

198. If he put out the eye of a freed man, or break the bone of a freed man, he shall pay one gold mina.

199. If he put out the eye of a man's slave, or break the bone of a man's slave, he shall pay one-half of its value.

200. If a man knock out the teeth of his equal, his teeth shall be knocked out.

201. If he knock out the teeth of a freed man, he shall pay one-third of a gold mina.

202. If any one strike the body of a man higher in rank than he, he shall receive sixty blows with an ox-whip in public.

203. If a free-born man strike the body of another free-born man or equal rank, he shall pay one gold mina.

204. If a freed man strike the body of another freed man, he shall pay ten shekels in money.

205. If the slave of a freed man strike the body of a freed man, his ear shall be cut off.

206. If during a quarrel one man strike another and wound him, then he shall swear, "I did not injure him wittingly," and pay the physicians.

207. If the man die of his wound, he shall swear similarly, and if he (the deceased) was a free-born man, he shall pay half a mina in money.

208. If he was a freed man, he shall pay one-third of a mina.

209. If a man strike a free-born woman so that she lose her unborn child, he shall pay ten shekels for her loss.

210. If the woman die, his daughter shall be put to death.

211. If a woman of the free class lose her child by a blow, he shall pay five shekels. . . .

212. If this woman die, he shall pay half a mina.

213. If he strike the maidservant of a man, and she lose her child, he shall pay two shekels. . . .

214. If this maid-servant die, he shall pay one-third of a mina.

[liability laws and fair prices]

219. If a physician make a large incision in the slave of a freed man, and kill him, he shall replace the slave with another slave.

221. If a physician heal the broken bone or diseased soft part of a man, the patient shall pay the physician five shekels in money.

222. If he were a freed man he shall pay three shekels.

223. If he were a slave his owner shall pay the physician two shekels.

224. If a veterinary surgeon perform a serious operation on an ass or an ox, and cure it, the owner shall pay the surgeon one-sixth of a shekel as a fee.

225. If he perform a serious operation on an ass or ox, and kill it, he shall pay the owner one-fourth of its value.

228. If a builder build a house for some one and complete it, he shall give him a fee of two shekels in money for each sar of surface.

229. If a builder build a house for some one, and does not construct it properly, and the house which he built fall in and kill its owner, then that builder shall be put to death.

230. If it kill the son of the owner the son of that builder shall be put to death.

231. If it kill a slave of the owner, then he shall pay slave for slave to the owner of the house.

232. If it ruin goods, he shall make compensation for all that has been ruined, and inasmuch as he did not construct properly this house which he built and it fell, he shall re-erect the house from his own means.

234. If a shipbuilder build a boat of sixty gur for a man, he shall pay him a fee of two shekels in money.

235. If a shipbuilder build a boat for some one, and do not make it tight, if during that same year that boat is sent away and suffers injury, the shipbuilder shall take the boat apart and put it together tight at his own expense. The tight boat he shall give to the boat owner.

239. If a man hire a sailor, he shall pay him six gur of corn per year.

244. If any one hire an ox or an ass, and a lion kill it in the field, the loss is upon its owner.

245. If any one hire oxen, and kill them by bad treatment or blows, he shall compensate the owner, oxen for oxen.

247. If any one hire an ox, and put out its eye, he shall pay the owner one-half of its value.

249. If any one hire an ox, and God strike it that it die, the man who hired it shall swear by God and be considered guiltless.

251. If an ox be a goring ox, and it shown that he is a gorer, and he do not bind his horns, or fasten the ox up, and the ox gore a free-born man and kill him, the owner shall pay one-half a mina in money.

257. If any one hire a field laborer, he shall pay him eight gur of corn per year.

258. If any one hire an ox-driver, he shall pay him six gur of corn per year.

261. If any one hire a herdsman for cattle or sheep, he shall pay him eight gur of corn per [year].

263. If he kill the cattle or sheep that were given to him, he shall compensate the owner with cattle for cattle and sheep for sheep.

267. If the herdsman overlook something, and an accident happen in the stable, then the herdsman is at fault for the accident which he has caused in the stable, and he must compensate the owner for the cattle or sheep.

282. If a slave say to his master: "You are not my master," if they convict him his master shall cut off his ear.

THE EPILOGUE

Laws of justice which Hammurabi, the wise king, established. A righteous law, and pious statute did he teach the land. Hammurabi, the protecting king am I. I have not withdrawn myself from the men, whom Bel gave to me, the rule over whom Marduk gave to me, I was not negligent, but I made them a peaceful abiding-place. . . . That the strong might not injure the weak, in order to protect the widows and orphans, I have in Babylon the city where Anu and Bel raise high their head, in E-Sagil, the Temple, whose foundations stand firm as heaven and earth, in order to bespeak justice in the land, to settle all disputes, and heal all injuries, set up these my precious words, written upon my memorial stone, before the image of me, as king of righteousness.

The king who ruleth among the kings of the cities am I. My words are well considered; there is no wisdom like

unto mine. By the command of Shamash, the great judge of heaven and earth, let righteousness go forth in the land: by the order of Marduk, my lord, let no destruction befall my monument. In E-Sagil, which I love, let my name be ever repeated; let the oppressed, who has a case at law, come and stand before this my image as king of righteousness; let him read the inscription, and understand my precious words: the inscription will explain his case to him; he will find out what is just, and his heart will be glad, so that he will say:

"Hammurabi is a ruler, who is as a father to his subjects, who holds the words of Marduk in reverence, who has achieved conquest for Marduk over the north and south, who rejoices the heart of Marduk, his lord, who has bestowed benefits for ever and ever on his subjects, and has established order in the land."

. . . If a succeeding ruler considers my words, which I have written in this my inscription, if he do not annul my law, nor corrupt my words, nor change my monument, then may Shamash lengthen that king's reign, as he has that of me, the king of righteousness, that he may reign in righteousness over his subjects.

If this ruler do not esteem my words, which I have written in my inscription, if he despise my curses, and fear not the curse of God, if he destroy the law which I have given, corrupt my words, change my monument, efface my name, write his name there, or on account of the curses commission another so to do, that man... may the great God (Anu), the Father of the gods, who has ordered my rule, withdraw from him the glory of royalty, break his scepter, curse his destiny. May Bel, the lord, who fixeth destiny, ... order with his potent mouth the destruction of his city, the dispersion of his subjects, the cutting off of his rule, the removal of his name and memory from the land. ... May Bel curse him with the potent curses of his mouth that can not be altered, and may they come upon him forthwith.

1.8 Laws of the Hebrews

The basis of Hebrew law is the code of moral law known as the Ten Commandments that, according to the account in Genesis, their God Yahweh gave them on Mt. Sinai in the thirteenth century B.C.E. The Hebrews also had other laws and customs they followed that applied those broad principles more specifically.

Source: The Bible, New International Version, © 1973, 1978, 1984, International Bible Society. Ex. 20: 1–17, Ex. 21–23, passim.

EXODUS 20: 1–17

The Ten Commandments

1. And God spoke all these words:
2. "I am the LORD your God, who brought you out of Egypt, out of the land of slavery.

3. "You shall have no other gods before *[besides]* me.

4–6. "You shall not make for yourself an idol in the form of anything in heaven above or on the earth beneath or in the waters below. You shall not bow down to them or worship them; for I, the LORD your God, am a jealous God, punishing the children for the sin of the fathers to the third and fourth generation of those who hate me, but showing love to a thousand [generations] of those who love me and keep my commandments.

7. "You shall not misuse the name of the LORD your God, for the LORD will not hold anyone guiltless who misuses his name.

8–11. "Remember the Sabbath day by keeping it holy. Six days you shall labor and do all your work, but the seventh day is a Sabbath to the LORD your God. On it you shall not do any work, neither you, nor your son or daughter, nor your manservant or maidservant, nor your animals, nor the alien within your gates. For in six days the LORD made the heavens and the earth, the sea, and all that is in them, but he rested on the seventh day. Therefore the LORD blessed the Sabbath day and made it holy.

12. "Honor your father and your mother, so that you may live long in the land the LORD your God is giving you.

13. "You shall not murder.

14. "You shall not commit adultery.

15. "You shall not steal.

16. "You shall not give false testimony against your neighbor.

17. "You shall not covet your neighbor's house. You shall not covet your neighbor's wife, or his manservant or maidservant, his ox or donkey, or anything that belongs to your neighbor."

EXODUS 21

Regarding Slaves and Servants

1. "These are the laws you are to set before them:

2. "If you buy a Hebrew servant, he is to serve you for six years. But in the seventh year, he shall go free, without paying anything.

3. "If he comes alone, he is to go free alone; but if he has a wife when he comes, she is to go with him.

4. "If his master gives him a wife and she bears him sons or daughters, the woman and her children shall belong to her master, and only the man shall go free.

5–6. "But if the servant declares, 'I love my master and my wife and children and do not want to go free,' then his master must take him before the judges. He shall take him to the door or the doorpost and pierce his ear with an awl. Then he will be his servant for life.

7. "If a man sells his daughter as a servant, she is not to go free as menservants do.

Regarding Crimes of Violence

12. "Anyone who strikes a man and kills him shall surely be put to death.

13. "However, if he does not do it intentionally, but God lets it happen, he is to flee to a place I will designate.

17. "Anyone who curses his father or mother must be put to death.

18–19. "If men quarrel and one hits the other with a stone or with his fist *[or tool]* and he does not die but is confined to bed, the one who struck the blow will not be held responsible if the other gets up and walks around outside with his staff however, he must pay the injured man for the loss of his time and see that he is completely healed.

20–21. "If a man beats his male or female slave with a rod and the slave dies as a direct result, he must be punished, but he is not to be punished if the slave gets up after a day or two, since the slave is his property.

22. "If men who are fighting hit a pregnant woman and she gives birth prematurely *[or she has a miscarriage]* but there is no serious injury, the offender must be fined whatever the woman's husband demands and the court allows.

23–25. "But if there is serious injury, you are to take life for life, eye for eye, tooth for tooth, hand for hand, foot for foot, burn for burn, wound for wound, bruise for bruise.

26. "If a man hits a manservant or maidservant in the eye and destroys it, he must let the servant go free to compensate for the eye.

27. "And if he knocks out the tooth of a manservant or maidservant, he must let the servant go free to compensate for the tooth.

Regarding Liability Regarding Property

28. "If a bull gores a man or a woman to death, the bull must be stoned to death, and its meat must not be eaten. But the owner of the bull will not be held responsible.

29. "If, however, the bull has had the habit of goring and the owner has been warned but has not kept it penned up and it kills a man or woman, the bull must be stoned and the owner also must be put to death.

30. "However, if payment is demanded of him, he may redeem his life by paying whatever is demanded.

31. "This law also applies if the bull gores a son or daughter.

32. "If the bull gores a male or female slave, the owner must pay thirty shekels *[about 12 ounces]* of silver to the master of the slave, and the bull must be stoned.

33–34. "If a man uncovers a pit or digs one and fails to cover it and an ox or a donkey falls into it, the owner of the pit must pay for the loss; he must pay its owner, and the dead animal will be his.

35. "If a man's bull injures the bull of another and it dies, they are to sell the live one and divide both the money and the dead animal equally.

36. "However, if it was known that the bull had the habit of goring, yet the owner did not keep it penned up, the owner must pay, animal for animal, and the dead animal will be his.

EXODUS 22

1. "If a man steals an ox or a sheep and slaughters it or sells it, he must pay back five head of cattle for the ox and four sheep for the sheep.

2–3. "If a thief is caught breaking in and is struck so that he dies, the defender is not guilty of bloodshed; but if it happens after sunrise, he is guilty of bloodshed. A thief must certainly make restitution, but if he has nothing, he must be sold to pay for his theft.

5. "If a man grazes his livestock in a field or vineyard and lets them stray and they graze in another man's field, he must make restitution from the best of his own field or vineyard.

6. "If a fire breaks out and spreads into thorn-bushes so that it burns shocks of grain or standing grain or the whole field, the one who started the fire must make restitution.

14. "If a man borrows an animal from his neighbor and it is injured or dies while the owner is not present, he must make restitution.

15. "But if the owner is with the animal, the borrower will not have to pay. If the animal was hired, the money paid for the hire covers the loss.

Regarding Relationships and Ethical Behavior

16. "If a man seduces a virgin who is not pledged to be married and sleeps with her, he must pay the bride-price, and she shall be his wife.

17. "If her father absolutely refuses to give her to him, he must still pay the bride-price for virgins.

18. "Do not allow a sorceress to live.

19. "Anyone who has sexual relations with an animal must be put to death.

20. "Whoever sacrifices to any god other than the LORD must be destroyed.

21. "Do not mistreat an alien or oppress him, for you were aliens in Egypt.

22. "Do not take advantage of a widow or an orphan.

23. "If you do and they cry out to me, I will certainly hear their cry.

24. "My anger will be aroused, and I will kill you with the sword; your wives will become widows and your children fatherless.

25. "If you lend money to one of my people among you who is needy, do not be like a moneylender; charge him no interest.

26–27. "If you take your neighbor's cloak as a pledge, return it to him by sunset, because his cloak is the only covering he has for his body. What else will he sleep in? When he cries out to me, I will hear, for I am compassionate.

31. "You are to be my holy people. . . .

EXODUS 23

1. "Do not spread false reports. Do not help a wicked man by being a malicious witness.

2–3. "Do not follow the crowd in doing wrong. When you give testimony in a lawsuit, do not pervert justice by siding with the crowd, and do not show favoritism to a poor man in his lawsuit.

4. "If you come across your enemy's ox or donkey wandering off, be sure to take it back to him.

5. "If you see the donkey of someone who hates you fallen down under its load, do not leave it there; be sure you help him with it.

6. "Do not deny justice to your poor people in their lawsuits.

7. "Have nothing to do with a false charge and do not put an innocent or honest person to death, for I will not acquit the guilty.

8. "Do not accept a bribe, for a bribe blinds those who see and twists the words of the righteous.

9. "Do not oppress an alien; you yourselves know how it feels to be aliens, because you were aliens in Egypt.

10. "For six years you are to sow your fields and harvest the crops,

11. "But during the seventh year let the land lie unplowed and unused. Then the poor among your people may get food from it, and the wild animals may eat what they leave. Do the same with your vineyard and your olive grove.

Questions for Documents 1.7 and 1.8:
1. What are the authority and principles on which each of these two law codes are based?
2. How are the law codes similar? Different?
3. What do these two law codes reveal about the social structure, family, and the position of women in each society?

1.9   The Instruction of the Ptah-hotep

No Law codes survive from the Egyptian Old Kingdom (2700–2200 B.C.E.). Worldly wisdom and clues to its culture's basic principles and ethics emerge from the texts inscribed in the tombs of the kings and of nobles such as Ptah-hotep, a vizier (chief minister) who lived around 2450 B.C.E. He addressed these instructions to his son, setting forth rules of appropriate behavior. The term "maat" in this text carries with it the meaning of accepted tradition and truth that has always worked and produced harmony.

Source: *Readings in Ancient History: Thought and Experience from Gilgamesh to St. Augustine*, Fifth Edition, ed. Nels M. Bailkey, (Lexington, MA: DC Heath and Company, 1996), pp. 38–42. (Based on a translation by F.L. Griffith in *A Library of the World's Best Literature*, XIII, pp. 5329–40).

PREFACE: ROYAL APPROVAL

The mayor and vizier Ptah-hotep said: "O king, my lord, years come on, old age is here, decrepitude arrives, weakness is renewed. . . . Let it be commanded of your servant to make a staff of old age: let my son be set in my place. Let me tell him the sayings of those who obeyed, the conduct of them of old, of them who listened to the gods. . . .

Said the majesty of this god [the king]: "Instruct him in the sayings of the past. . . . Speak to him, for no one is born wise."

TITLE AND AIM

Beginning of the maxims of good words spoken by the . . . mayor and vizier, Ptah-hotep, teaching the ignorant to know according to the standard of good words, expounding the profit to him who shall listen to it, and the injury to him who shall transgress it. He said to his son:

INTELLECTUAL SNOBBERY

Be not arrogant because of your knowledge, and be not puffed up because you are a learned man. Take counsel with the ignorant as with the learned, for the limits of art cannot be reached, and no artist is perfect in his skills. Good speech is more hidden than the precious greenstone, and yet it is found among slave girls at the millstones. . . .

LEADERSHIP AND "MAAT"

If you are a leader, commanding the conduct of many, seek out every good aim, so that your policy may be without error. A great thing is truth [*maat*], enduring and surviving; it has not been upset since the time of Osiris. He who departs from its laws is punished. It is the right path for him who knows nothing. Wrongdoing has never brought its venture safe to port. Evil may win riches, but it is the strength of truth that it endures long, and a man can say, "I learned it from my father.". . .

CONDUCT AS A GUEST AT TABLE

If you are a guest at the table of one who is greater than you, take what he offers as it is set before you. Fix your gaze upon what is before you, and pierce not your host with many glances, for it is an abomination to force your attention upon him. Speak not to him until he calls, for no one knows what may be offensive; speak when he addresses you, for then your words will give satisfaction. Laugh when he laughs; that will please him, and then whatever you do will please him. . . .

PATIENCE WITH SUPPLIANTS

If you are a leader be kind in hearing the speech of a suppliant. Treat him not roughly until he has unburdened himself of what he was minded to tell you. The compliant sets greater store by the easing of his mind than by the accomplishment of that for which he came. As for him who deals roughly with a petition, men say, "Why, pray, has he ignored it?" Not all that men plead for ever comes to pass, but to listen kindly soothes the heart.

RELATIONS WITH WOMEN

If you wish to prolong friendship in a house into which you enter as master, brother or friend, or any place that you enter, beware of approaching the women. No place in which that is done prospers. There is no wisdom in it. A thousand men are turned aside from their own good because of a little moment, like a dream, by tasting which death is reached. . . . He who . . . lusts after women, no plan of his will succeed.

GREED

If you want your conduct to be good, free from every evil, then beware of greed. It is an evil and incurable sickness. No man can live with it; it causes divisions between fathers and mothers, and between brothers of the same mother; it parts wife and husband; it is a gathering of every evil, a bag of everything hateful. A man thrives if his conduct is right. He who follows the right course wins wealth thereby. But the greedy man has no tomb. . . .

MARRIAGE

If you are prosperous you should establish a household and love your wife as is fitting. Fill her belly and clothe her back. Oil is the tonic for her body. Make her heart glad as long as you live. She is a profitable field for her lord. . . .

CONDUCT IN COUNCIL

If you are a worthy man sitting in the council of his lord, confine your attention to excellence. Silence is more valuable than chatter. Speak only when you know you can resolve difficulties. He who gives good counsel is an artist, for speech is more difficult than any craft. . . .

BEHAVIOR IN CHANGED CIRCUMSTANCES

If you are now great after being humble and rich after being poor in the city that you know, do not boast because of what happened to you in the past. Be not miserly with your wealth, which has come to you by the god's [the king's] gift. You are no different from another to whom the same has happened.

OBEDIENCE TO A SUPERIOR

Bend your back to him who is over you, your superior in the administration; then your house will endure by reason of its property, and your reward will come in due season.

Wretched is he who opposes his superior, for one lives only so long as he is gracious. . . .

EXHORTATION TO LISTEN

If you listen to my sayings, then all your affairs will go forward. They are precious; their memory goes on in the speech of men because of their excellence. If each saying is carried on, they will never perish in this land. . . .

If the son of a man accepts what his father says, no plan of his will fail. . . . Failure follows him who does not listen. He who hears is established; he who is a fool is crushed. . . .

A son who hears is a follower of Horus: there is good for him who listens. When he reaches old age and attains honor, he tells the like to his children, renewing the teaching of his father. Every man teaches as he has acted. He speaks to his children so that they may speak to their children. . . .

CONCLUSION

May you succeed me, may your body be sound, may the king be well pleased with all that is done, and may you spend many years of life! It is no small thing that I have done on earth; I have spent one hundred and ten years of life, which the king gave me, and with rewards greater than those of the ancestors, by doing right for the king until death.

Questions:
1. What are the guiding principles of behavior revealed in these instructions?
2. Keeping in mind that these are a parent's advice rather than enforced law, how do they differ from the ethical principles set forth in Hammurabi's and the Hebrew's laws above?
3. What does this document reveal about Egyptian society during this period?

CHAPTER 2
Armies and Empires
Politics and Power in the Bronze and Iron Ages
(3500–300 B.C.E.)

SECTION 1
Warfare and Diplomacy

Documents 2.1–2.4

These documents illustrate various aspects of war-the diplomacy in its aftermath, the retelling of heroic deeds, historical accounts of battle, and the political debate that often precedes it.

2.1   The Egyptian/Hittite Treaty

Two great empires, the Egyptians and the Hittites, struggled for control of Palestine. In 1290 B.C.E., they fought each other in the Battle of Kadesh, which neither won. The Ramses-Hattusilis Treaty, which ended the fighting, has come down to us in two forms, one from the Egyptian perspective and one from the Hittite perspective. Both versions are reproduced below, allowing one to see how each side understood the terms of the treaty.

> **Source:** James B. Pritchard, Ancient Near Eastern Text Pertaining to the Old Testament, (Princeton: Princeton University Press, 1969), pp. 199–203.

EGYPTIAN TREATY*

Year 21, 1st month of the second season, day 21, under the majesty of the King of Upper and Lower Egypt: User-maat-Re; Son of Re: Ramses Meri-Amon, given life forever, beloved of Amon-Re; Har-akhti Ptah, South-of-His-Wall, Lord of Life of the Two Lands; Mut, the Lady of Ishru; and Khonsu Neferhotep; appearing on the Horus-Throne of the Living like his father Har-akhti forever and ever.

On this day, while his majesty was in the town of Per-Ramses Meri-Amon, doing the pleasure of his father Amon-Re; Har-akhti; Atum, Lord of the Two Lands, the Heliopolitan; Amon of Ramses Meri-Amon; Ptah of Ramses Meri-Amon; and [Seth], the Great of Strength, the Son of Nut, according as they give him an eternity of jubilees and an infinity of years of peace, while all lands and all foreign countries are prostrate under his soles forever—there came the Royal Envoy and Deputy . . . Royal Envoy . . . [User-maat-Re] Setep-en [Re] . . . [Tar]-Teshub, and the Messenger of Hatti, . . .-silis, carrying [the *tablet of silver which*]

the Great Prince of Hatti, Hattusilis [caused] to be brought to Pharaoh—life, prosperity, health!—in order to beg [peace from *the majesty* of User-maat-Re] Setep-en-Re, the Son of Re: Ramses Meri-Amon, [given] life forever and ever, like his father Re every day.

Copy of the tablet of silver which the Great Prince of Hatti, Hattusilis, caused to be brought to Pharaoh—life, prosperity, health!—by the hand of his envoy Tar-Teshub, and his envoy Ra-mose, in order to beg peace from the majesty of [User-maat-Re], Son of Re: Ramses Meri-Amon, the bull of rulers, who has made his frontier where he wished in every land.

Preamble

The regulations which the Great Prince of Hatti, Hattusilis, the powerful, the son of Mursilis, the Great Prince of Hatti, the powerful, the son of the son of Suppi[luliumes, the Great Prince of Hatti, the] powerful, made upon a tablet of silver for User-maat-Re, the great ruler of Egypt, the powerful, the son of Men-maat-Re, the great ruler of Egypt, the powerful, the son of Men-pehti-Re, the great ruler of Egypt, the powerful; the good regulations of peace and of brotherhood, giving peace . . . forever.

Former Relations

Now from the beginning of the limits of eternity, as for the situation of the great ruler of Egypt with the Great Prince of Hatti, the god did not permit hostility to occur between them, through a regulation. But in the time of Muwatallis, the Great Prince of Hatti, my brother, he fought with [Ramses Meri-Amon], the great ruler of Egypt. But here-after, from this day, behold Hattusilis, the Great Prince of Hatti, [is *under*] a regulation for making permanent the situation which the Re and Seth made for the land of Egypt with the land of Hatti, in order not to permit hostility to occur between them forever.

The Present Treaty

Behold, Hattusilis, the Great Prince of Hatti, has set himself in a regulation with User-maat-Re Setep-en-Re, the great ruler of Egypt, beginning from this day, to cause that good peace and brotherhood occur between us forever, while he is in brotherhood with me and he is at peace with me, and I

* Translator: John A. Wilson

15

am in brotherhood with him and I am at peace with him forever.

Now since Muwatallis, the Great Prince of Hatti, my brother, went in pursuit of his fate, and Hattusilis sat as Great Prince of Hatti upon the throne of his father, behold, I have come to be with Ramses Meri-Amon, the great ruler of Egypt, *for we are [together in] our* peace and our brotherhood. It is better than the peace or the brotherhood which was formerly in the land.

Behold, I, as the Great Prince of Hatti, am with [Ramses Meri-Amon], in good peace and in good brotherhood. The children of the children [of] the Great Prince of Hatti *are* in brotherhood and peace with the children of the children of [Ra]mses Meri-[Amon], the great ruler of Egypt, for they are in our situation of brotherhood and our situation [of peace. *The land of Egypt]*, with the land of Hatti, [*shall be*] at peace and in brotherhood like unto us forever. Hostilities shall not occur between them forever.

Mutual Renunciation of Invasion

The great Prince of Hatti shall not trespass against the land of Egypt forever, to take anything from it. And User-maat-Re Setep-en-Re, the great ruler of Egypt, shall not trespass against the land [of Hatti, to take] from it forever.

Reaffirmation of Former Treaties

As to the traditional regulation which had been here in the time of Suppiluliumas, the Great Prince of Hatti, as well as the traditional regulation which had been in the time for Muwatallis, the Great Prince of Hatti, my father, I seize hold of it. Behold, Ramses Meri-Amon, the great ruler of Egypt, seizes hold of [*the regulation which he makes*] together with us, beginning from this day. We seize hold of it, and we act in this traditional situation.

A Defensive Alliance—for Egypt

If another enemy come against the lands of User-maat-Re, the great ruler of Egypt, and he send to the Great Prince of Hatti, saying: "Come with me as reinforcement against him, the Great Prince of Hatti shall [come to him and] the Great Prince of Hatti shall slay his enemy. However, if it is not the desire of the Great Prince of Hatti to go (himself), he shall send his infantry and his chariotry, and he shall slay his enemy. Or, if Ramses Meri-Amon, [the great ruler of Egypt], is enraged against servants belonging to him, and they commit another offence against him, and he go to slay them, the Great Prince of Hatti shall act with him [*to slay*] everyone [against whom] they shall be enraged.

Defensive Alliance—for Hatti

But [if] another enemy [come] against the Great Prince [of Hatti, User]-matt-[Re] Setep-en-Re, [the great ruler of Egypt, shall] come to him as reinforcement to slay his enemy. If it is (not) the desire of Ramses Meri-Amon, the great ruler of Egypt, to come, he shall . . . Hatti, [and he shall send his infantry and his] chariotry, besides returning answer to the land of Hatti. Now if the servants of the Great Prince of Hatti trespass against him, and Ramses Meri-Amon . . .

The Contingency of Death?

. . . the [land] of Hatti and the land [of Egypt] . . . the life. *Should it be that* I shall go [in] pursuit of my fate, *then* Ramses Meri-[Amon], the great ruler of Egypt, living forever, *shall go and come* [*to*] the [land of] Hatti, . . . to cause. . . , to make him lord for them, to make User-maat-Re Setep-en-[Re] the great ruler of Egypt, silent with his mouth forever. Now after he . . . the land of Hatti, and he *returns* . . . the Great Prince of Hatti, as well as the . . .

Extradition of Refugees to Egypt

[If a great man flee from the land of Egypt and come to] the Great Prince of Hatti, or a town belonging to the lands of Ramses Meri-Amon, the great ruler of Egypt, and they come to the Great Prince of Hatti, the Great Prince of Hatti shall not receive them. The Great Prince of Hatti shall cause them to be brought to User-maat-Re Setep-en-Re, the great ruler of Egypt, their lord, [because] of it. Or if a man or two men—no matter who—flee, and they come to the land of Hatti to be servants of someone else, they shall not be left in the land of Hatti; they shall be brought to Ramses Meri-Amon, the great ruler of Egypt.

Extradition of Refugees to Hatti

Or if a great man flee from the land of Hatti and [come to User]-matt-[Re] Setep-en-Re, the [great] ruler of Egypt, or a town or a district or a . . . belonging to the land of Hatti, and they come to Ramses Meri-Amon, the great ruler of Egypt, (then) User-maat-Re Setep-en-Re, the great ruler of Egypt, shall not receive them. Ramses Meri-Amon, the great ruler of Egypt, shall cause them to be brought to the Prince [*of Hatti*]. They shall not be left. Similarly, if a man or two men—[no] matter who—flee, and they come to the land of Egypt to be servants of other people, User-maat-Re Setep-en-Re, the great ruler of Egypt, shall not leave them. He shall cause them to be brought to the Great Prince of Hatti.

The Divine Witnesses to the Treaty

As for these words of the regulation [*which*] the Great Prince of Hatti [*made*] with Ramses [Meri-Amon], the great ruler [of Egypt], in writing upon this tablet of silver—as for these words, a thousand gods of the male gods and of the female gods of them of the land of Hatti, together with a thousand gods of the male gods and of the female gods of them of the land of Egypt, are with me as witnesses [*hearing*] these words: the Re, the lord of the sky; the Re of the town of Arinna; Seth, the lord of the sky; Seth of Hatti; Seth of the town of Arinna; Seth of the town of Zippalanda; Seth of the town of Pe(tt)iyarik; Seth of the town of Hissas(ha)pa; Seth of the town of Sarissa; Seth of the town of Aleppo; Seth of the town of Lihzina; Seth of the town. . . ; . . . ; Seth of the town of *Sahpin*; *Antaret* of the land of Hatti; the god of Zithari(as); the god of *Karzis*; the god of Hapantaliyas; the goddess of the town of Karahna; the goddess of. . . ; the Queen of the Sky; the gods, the lords of oaths; this goddess, the Lady of the Ground; the Lady of the Oath, Ishara; the Lady (*of the*) mountains and the rivers of the land of Hatti; the gods of the land of Kizuwadna; Amon; the Re; Seth; the male gods; the female gods; the mountains; and the rivers of the land of Egypt; the sky; the earth; the great sea; the winds; and the clouds.

Curses and Blessings for this Treaty

As for these words which are on this tablet of silver of the land of Hatti and of the land of Egypt—as for him who shall not keep them, a thousand gods of the land of Hatti, together with a thousand gods of the land of Egypt, shall destroy his house, his land, and his servants. But, as for him who shall keep these words which are on this tablet of silver, whether they are Hatti or whether they are Egyptians, and they are not *neglectful of* them, a thousand gods of the land of Hatti, together with a thousand gods of the land of Egypt, shall cause that he be well, shall cause that he live, together with his houses and his (land) and his servants.

Extradition of Egyptians from Hatti

If a man flee from the land of Egypt—or two or three—and they come to the Great Prince of Hatti, the Great Prince of Hatti shall lay hold of them, and he shall cause that they be brought back to User-maat-Re Setep-en-Re, the great ruler of Egypt. But, as for the man who shall be brought to Ramses Meri-Amon, the great ruler of Egypt, do not cause that his crime be raised against him; do not cause that his house or his wives or his children be destroyed; [do not cause that] he be [slain]; do not cause that injury be done to his eyes, to his ears, to his mouth, or to his legs; do not let any [crime be raised] against him.

Extradition of Hittites from Egypt

Similarly, if men flee from the land of Hatti—whether he be one or two or three—and they come to User-maat-Re Setep-en-Re, the great ruler of Egypt, let Ramses Meri-Amon, the [great] ruler [of Egypt], lay hold [of them and cause] that they be brought to the Great Prince of Hatti, and the Great Prince of Hatti shall not raise their crime against them, and they shall not destroy his house or his wives or his children, and they shall not slay him, and they shall not do injury to his ears, to his eyes, to his mouth, or to his legs, and they shall not raise any crime against him.

Description of the Tablet

What is in the middle of the table of silver. On its front side: figures consisting of an image of Seth embracing an image of the Great Prince [of Hatti], surrounded by a border with the words: "the seal of Seth, the ruler of the sky; the seal of

the regulation which Hattusilis made, the Great Prince of Hatti, the powerful, the son of Mursilis, the Great Prince of Hatti, the powerful." What is within that which surrounds the figures: the seal [*of Seth.* What is on] its other side: figures consisting of a female image of [the] goddess of Hatti embracing a female image of the Princess of Hatti, surrounded by a border with the words: "the seal of the Re of the town of Arinna, the lord of the land; the seal of Putuhepa, the Princess of the land of Hatti, the daughter of the land of Kizuwadna, the [*priestess*] of [*the town of*] Arinna, the Lady of the Land, the servant of the goddess." What is within the surrounding (frame) of the figures: the seal of the Re of Arinna, the lord of every land.

HITTITE TREATY*

Title

Treaty of Rea-mashesha mai Amana, the great king, the king of the land of Egypt, the valiant, with Hattusilis, the great king of the Hatti land, his brother, for establishing [good] peace [and] good brotherhood [worthy of] great [king]ship between them forever.

Preamble

These are the words of Rea-mashesha mai Amana, the great king of the land of Egypt, the valiant of all lands, the son of Min-mua-rea, the great king, the king of the land of Egypt, the valiant, the grandson of Minpakhtarea, the great king, the king of the land of Egypt, the valiant, (spoken) to Hattusilis, the great king, the king of the Hatti land, the valiant, the son of Mursilis, the great king, the king of the Hatti land, the valiant, the grandson of Suppiluliumas, the great king, the king of the Hatti land, the valiant.

Relations up to the Conclusion of the Treaty

Now I have established good brotherhood (and) good peace between us forever. In order to establish good peace (and) good brotherhood in [the relationship] of the land of Egypt with the Hatti land forever (I speak) thus: Behold, as for the relationship between the land of Egypt and the Hatti land, since eternity the god does not permit the making of hostility between them because of a treaty (valid) forever. Behold, Rea-Mashesha mai Amana, the great king, the king of the land of Egypt, in order to bring about the relationship that the Sun-god and the Storm-god have effected for the land of Egypt with the Hatti land finds himself in a relationship valid since eternity which [does not permi]t the making of hostility between [them] until all and everlasting time.

The Present Treaty

Rea-mashesha mai Amana, the great king, the king of the land of Egypt, has entered into a treaty (written) upon a silver tablet with Hattusilis, the great king, the king of the

* Translator: Albrecht Goetze

Hatti land, [his] brother, [from] this [da]y on to establish good peace (and) good brotherhood be[tween us] forever. He is a brother [to me] and I am a brother to him and at peace with him forever. And as for us, our brotherhood and our peace is being brought about and it will be better than the brotherhood and the peace which existed formerly for the land of Egypt with the Hatti land.

Future Relations of the Two Countries

Behold Rea-mashesha mai Amana, the king of the land of Egypt, is in good peace (and) in good brotherhood with [Hattusilis], the great king, the king of the Hatti land.

Behold, the sons of Rea-mashesha mai Amana, the king of the land of Egypt, are in peace with (and) brothers of the sons of Hattusilis, the great king, the king of the Hatti land, forever. They are in the same relationship of brotherhood and peace as we.

And as for (the relationship of) the land of Egypt with the Hatti land, they are at peace and brothers like us forever.

Mutual Renunciation of Aggression

Rea-mashesha mai Amana, the great king, the king of the land of Egypt, shall not tresspass into the Hatti land to take anything therefrom in the future. And Hattusilis, the great king, the king of the Hatti land, shall not tresspass into the land of Egypt to take anything therefrom in the future.

Behold, the holy ordinance (valid) forever which the Sun-god and the Storm-god had brought about for the land of Egypt with the Hatti land (calls for) peace and brotherhood so as not to make hostility between them. Behold, Rea-mashesha mai Amana, the great king, the king of the land of Egypt, has seized hold of it in order to bring about well-being from this day on. Behold, the land of Egypt (in its relation) with the Hatti land—they are at peace and brothers forever.

Defensive Alliance

If an enemy from abroad comes against the Hatti land, and Hattusilis, the great king, the king of the Hatti land, sends to me saying: "Come to me to help me against him," Rea-mashesha mai Amana, the great king, the king of the land of Egypt, shall send his foot soldiers (and) his charioteers and they shall slay [his enemy and] take revenge upon him for the sake of the Hatti land.

And if Hattusilis, the great king, the king of the Hatti land, is angry with servants belonging to him (and it) they have failed against him and sends to Rea-mashesha mai Amana, the great king, the king of the land of Egypt, on their account—lo! Rea-mashesha mai Amana shall send his foot soldiers (and) his charioteers and they shall destroy all those with whom he is angry.

If an enemy from abroad comes against the land of Egypt and Rea-mashesha mai Amana, the king of the land of Egypt, your brother, sends to Hattusilis, the king of the Hatti land, his brother, saying: "Come here to help me against him"—lo! Hattusilis, the king of the Hatti land, shall send his foot soldiers (and) his charioteers and shall slay my enemies.

And if Rea-mashesha ma[i Amana, the king of] the land of Egypt, is angry with servants belonging to him—(and if) they have committed sin again[st him and I send] to Hattusilis the king of the Hatti land, my brother, on his account—lo! Hattusilis, [the king of the Hatti land,] my brother, shall send his foot soldiers (and) his charioteers and they shall destroy all those with whom he is angry.

Succession to the Throne

Behold, the son of Hattusilis, the king of the Hatti land, shall be made king of the Hatti land in place of Hattusilis, his father, after the many years of Hattusilis, the king of the Hatti land. If the noblemen the Hatti land commit sin againt him—lo! [Rea-mashesha mai Amana, the king of Egypt, shall send foot soldiers] (and) charioteers to take revenge upon them [for the sake of the Hatti land. And after they have established order] in the country of the king of the Hatti land, [they shall return] to the country [of Egypt].

(Corresponding provision concerning Egypt lost in a gap.)

Extradition of Fugitives

[If a nobleman flees from the Hatti land and i]f one (such) man comes [to Rea-mashesha mai Amana, the great king, the king of the land of Egypt,] in order to enter his services—[be it a . . . belonging to Ha]ttusilis, the king of the Hatti land, [be it a . . .] or a single town—[Rea-mashesha mai Amana, the great king, the king of the land Egypt, shall seize them and] shall have them brought back to the king of the Hatti land.

(several badly broken lines)

[If a nobleman] flees [from Rea-mashesha mai Amana, the king of the land of Egypt, and if one (such) man] comes to the [Hatti] land, [Ha]ttusilis, [the great king, the king of the Hatti land, shall seize him and] shall have him brought back to R[ea-mashesha mai] Amana, the great king, the king of Egypt, his brother.

If one man flees from the [Hatti land or] two men, [or three men and come to] Rea-mashesha mai [Amana, the great king, the king of the land of Egyp]t, [Rea-mashesha] mai Amana, the great king, [the king of the land of Egypt, shall seize them and have them brought back t]o Hattusilis, his brother. [Rea-mashesha mai Amana and Hattusilis are verily] brothers; hence [let them not *exact punishment for*] their sins, [let them not] tear out [their eyes; let them not *take revenge upon*] their people [. . . together with] their [wives and wi]th their children.

If [one man flees from Egypt] or two men or three men [and come to Hattusilis, the great king, the king of the Hatti land, Hattusilis, the great king], the king of the Hatti land, his brother, shall seize them and have them brought [back to Rea-mashesha mai Amana, the great king, the king of] the land of Egypt, [Hattusilis, the king of the Hatti land], and Rea-mashesha, the great king, the k[ing of the land of Egypt, are verily brothers; hence let them not *exact punishment for* their sins,] [. . .] let them not tear out their eyes; [let them not *take revenge upon* their people . . . together with] their wives (and) with their children.

(After some fragmentary lines that text breaks off altogether. With the end of the treaty the list of the gods who were invoked as witnesses is missing.)

2.2 The Trojan Horse

During his adventurous return journey from the Trojan War (c. 1200 B.C.E.), Odysseus is rescued from the sea by King Alkinoös' daughter Nausikaa. After feasting with the king and his men, Odysseus, who has not revealed his own identity, asks the minstrel to sing the story of the Trojan horse, by which the Greeks finally defeated the Trojans.

Source: Homer, *The Odyssey*, trans. Robert Fitzgerald, (Garden City: Anchor Books, 1963), pp. 140–42.

Now shift your theme, and sing that wooden horse Epeios built, inspired by Athena—the ambuscade Odysseus filled with fighters and sent to take the inner town of Troy. Sing only this for me, sing me this well, and I shall say at once before the world the grace of heaven has given us a song."

The minstrel stirred, murmuring to the god, and soon clear words and notes came one by one, a vision of the Akhaians in their graceful ships drawing away from shore: the torches flung and shelters flaring: Argive soldiers crouched in the close dark around Odysseus: and the horse, tall on the assembly ground of Troy. For when the Trojans pulled it in, themselves, up to the citadel, they sat nearby with long-drawn-out and hapless argument—favoring, in the end, one course of three: either to stave the vault with brazen axes, or haul it to a cliff and pitch it down, or else to save it for the gods, a votive glory—the plan that could not but prevail. For Troy must perish, as ordained, that day she harbored the great horse of timber; hidden the flower of Akhaia lay, and bore slaughter and death upon the men of Troy. He sang, then, of the town sacked by Akhaians pouring down from the horse's hollow cave, this way and that way raping the steep city, and How Odysseus came like Arês to the door of Deïphobos, with Meneláos, and braved the desperate fight there—conquering once more by Athena's power.

The splendid minstrel sang it.

And Odysseus let the bright molten tears run down his cheeks, weeping the way a wife mourns for her lord on the lost field where he has gone down fighting the day of wrath that came upon his

children. At sight of the man panting and dying there, she slips down to enfold him, crying out; then feels the spears, prodding her back and shoulders, and goes bound into slavery and grief. Piteous weeping wears away her cheeks: but no more piteous than Odysseus' tears, cloaked as they were, now, from the company. Only Alkínoös, at his elbow, knew—hearing the low sob in the man's breathing—and when he knew, he spoke:

"Hear me, lords and captains of Phaiákia! And let Demódokos touch his harp no more. His theme has not been pleasing to all hear. During the feat, since our fine poet sang," our guest has never left off weeping. Grief seems fixed upon his heart. Break off the song! Let everyone be easy, host and guest; there's more decorum in a smiling banquet!

2.3 The Battle of Thermopylae

The Battle of Thermopylae was fought between the Persians and the Spartans (also called the Lacedaemonians) in 480 B.C.E. Because the Olympic Games were in session, only advance troops were at the Thermopylae pass when the battle took place. The Spartans lost the battle, delaying and crippling the Persians, but not sufficiently to stop them from crossing the mountains by an alternate route, forcing the Greeks to evacuate Athens. Shortly afterwards, in a naval battle not far from Athens, the Greeks routed the Persians, stopping the Persians' advance into Greek territory. Persia would later help the Spartans against Athens in the Peloponnesian War.

Source: Herodotus, *The Histories*, trans. Aubrey de Sélincourt, (New York: Penguin Books, 1982, © 1954, 1972), pp. 513–19.

The Persian army was now close to the pass, and the Greeks, suddenly doubting their power to resist, held a conference to consider the advisability of retreat. It was proposed by the Peloponnesians generally that the army should fall back upon the Peloponnese and hold the Isthmus; but when the Phocians and Locrians expressed their indignation at this suggestion, Leonidas gave his voice for staying where they were and sending, at the same time, an appeal for reinforcements to the various states of the confederacy, as their numbers were inadequate to cope with the Persians.

During the conference Xerxes sent a man on horseback to ascertain the strength of the Greek force and to observe what the troops were doing. He had heard before he left Thessaly that a small force was concentrated here, led by the Lacedaemonians under Leonidas of the house of Heracles. The Persian rider approached the camp and took a thorough survey of all he could see—which was not, however, the whole Greek army; for the men on the further side of the wall which, after its reconstruction, was now guarded, were out of sight. He did, none the less, carefully observe the troops who were stationed on the outside of the wall. At that moment these happened to be the Spartans, and some of them were stripped for exercise, while others were combing their hair. The Persian spy watched them in astonishment; nevertheless he made sure of their numbers, and of everything else he needed to know, as accurately as he could, and then rode quietly off. No one attempted to catch him, or took the least notice of him.

Back in his own camp he told Xerxes what he had seen. Xerxes was bewildered; the truth, namely that the Spartans were preparing themselves to die and deal death with all their strength, was beyond his comprehension, and what they were doing seemed to him merely absurd. Accordingly he sent for Demaratus, the son of Ariston, who had come with the army, and questioned him about the spy's report, in the hope of finding out what the behaviour of the Spartans might mean. 'Once before,' Demaratus said, 'when we began our march against Greece, you heard me speak of these men. I told you then how I saw this enterprise would turn out, and you laughed at me. I strive for nothing, my lord, more earnestly than to observe the truth in your presence; so hear me once more. These men have come to fight us for possession of the pass, and for that struggle they are preparing. It is the common practice of the Spartans to pay careful attention to their hair when they are about to risk their lives. But I assure you that if you can defeat these men and the rest of the Spartans who are still at home, there is no other people in the world who will dare to stand firm or lift a hand against you. You have now to deal with the finest kingdom in Greece, and with the bravest men.

Xerxes, unable to believe what Demaratus said, asked further how it was possible that so small a force could fight with his army. 'My lord,' Demaratus replied, 'treat me as a liar, if what I have foretold does not take place.' But still Xerxes was unconvinced.

For four days Xerxes waited, in constant expectation that the Greeks would make good their escape; then, on the fifth, when still they had made no move and their continued presence seemed mere impudent and reckless folly, he was seized with rage and sent forward the Medes and Cissians with orders to take them alive and bring them into his presence. The Medes charged, and in the struggle which ensued many fell; but others took their places, and in spite of terrible losses refused to be beaten off. They made it plain enough to anyone, and not least to the king himself, that he had in his army many men, indeed, but few soldiers. All day the battle continued; the Medes, after their rough handling, were at length withdrawn and their place was taken by Hydarnes and his picked Persian troops—the King s. Immortals—who advanced to the attack in full confidence of bringing the business to a quick and easy end. But, once engaged, they were no more successful than the Medes had been; all went as before, the two armies fighting in a confined space, the Persians using shorter spears than the Greeks and having no advantage from their numbers.

On the Spartan side it was a memorable fight; they were men who understood war pitted against an inexperi-

enced enemy, and amongst the feints they employed was to turn their backs on a body and pretend to be retreating in confusion, whereupon the enemy would pursue them with a great clatter and roar; but the Spartans, just as the Persians were on them, would wheel and face them and inflict in the new struggle innumerable casualties. The Spartans had their losses too, but not many. At last the Persians, finding that their assaults upon the pass, whether by divisions or by any other way they could think of, were all useless, broke off the engagement and withdrew. Xerxes was watching the battle from where he sat; and it is said that in the course of the attacks three times, in terror for his army, he leapt to his feet.

Next day the fighting began again, but with no better success for the Persians, who renewed their onslaught in the hope that the Greeks, being so few in number, might be badly enough disabled by wounds to prevent further resistance. But the Greeks never slackened; their troops were ordered in divisions corresponding to the states from which they came, and each division took its turn in the line except the Phocian, which had been posted to guard the track over the mountains. So when the Persians found that things were no better for them than on the previous day, they once more withdrew.

How to deal with the situation Xerxes had no idea; but just then, a man from Malis, Ephialtes, the son of Eurydemus, came, in hope of a rich reward, to tell the king about the track which led over the hills to Thermopylae—and thus he was to prove the death of the Greeks who held the pass.

. . . . The ascent of the Persians had been concealed by the oak-woods which cover all these hills, and it was only when they were up that the Phocians became aware of their approach; for there was no wind, and the marching feet made a loud swishing and rustling in the fallen leaves. Leaping to their feet, the Phocians were in the act of arming themselves when the enemy was upon them. The Persians were surprised at the sight of troops preparing to resist; they had expected no opposition—yet here was a body of men barring their way. Hydames asked Ephialtes who they were, for his first uncomfortable thought was that they might be Spartans; but on learning the truth he prepared to engage them. The Persian arrows flew thick and fast, and the Phocians, supposing themselves to be the main object of the attack, hurriedly withdrew to the highest point of the mountain, where they made ready to face destruction. But the Persians with Ephialtes and Hydarnes paid no further attention to them, but passed on along the descending track with all possible speed.

The Greeks at Thermopylae had their first warning of the death that was coming with the dawn from the seer Megistias, who read their doom in the victims of sacrifice; deserters, too, came in during the night with news of the Persian flank movement, and lastly, just as day was breaking, the look-out men came running from the hills. In council of war their opinions were divided, some urging that they must not abandon their post, others the opposite. The result was that the army split: some dispersed, contingents returning to their various cities, while others made ready to stand by Leonidas.

. . . And indeed by remaining at his post he left a great name behind him, and Sparta did not lose her prosperity, as might otherwise have happened, for right at the outset of the war the Spartans had been told by the Delphic oracle that either their city must be laid waste by the foreigner or a Spartan king be killed. The prophecy was in verse and ran as follows:

> Hear your fate, 0 dwellers
> In Sparta of the wide spaces;
> Either your famed, great town
> must be sacked by Perseus' sons,
> Or, If that be not, the whole Land
> of Lacedaemon
> Shall mourn the death of a king
> of the house of Heracles,
>
> For not the strength of lions or
> of bulls shall hold him,
> Strength against strength;
> for he has the power of Zeus,
> And will not be checked till one
> of these two he has consumed.

I believe it was the thought of this oracle, combined with his wish to lay up for the Spartans a treasure of fame in which no other city should share, that made Leonidas dismiss those troops;* I do not think that they deserted, or went off without orders, because of a difference of opinion. Moreover, I am strongly supported in this view by the case of the seer Megiscias, who was with the army—an Acarnanian said to be of the clan of Melampus—who foretold the coming doom from his inspection of the sacrificial victims. He quite plainly received orders from Leonidas to quit Thermopylae, to save him from sharing the army's fate. He refused to go, but he sent his only son, who was serving with the forces.

. . . In the morning Xerxes poured a libation to the rising sun, and then waited till it was well up before he began to move forward. This was according to Ephialtes' instructions, for the way down from the ridge is much shorter and more direct than the long and circuitous ascent. As the Persian army advanced to the assault, the Greeks under Leonidas, knowing that they were going to their deaths went out into the wider part of the pass much further than they had done before; in the previous days' fighting they had been holding the wall and making sorties from behind it into the narrow neck, but now they fought outside the narrows. Many of the invaders fell; behind them the

---

* Those troops that dispersed before the battle.

company commanders plied their whips indiscriminately, driving the men on. Many fell in to the sea and were drowned, and still more were trampled to death by their friends. No one could count the number of the dead. The Greeks, who knew that the enemy were on their way round by the mountain track and that death was inevitable, put forth all their strength and fought with fury and desperation. By this time most of their spears were broken, and they were killing Persians with their swords.

In the course of that fight Leonidas fell, having fought most gallantly, and many distinguished Spartans with him—their names I have learned, as those of men who deserve to be remembered; indeed, I have learned the names of all the three hundred. Amongst the Persian dead, too, were many men of high distinction, including two brothers of Xerxes, Habrocomes and Hyperanthes, sons of Darius by Artanes' daughter Phratagune.

There was a bitter struggle over the body of Leonidas; four times the Greeks drove the enemy off, and at last by their valour rescued it. So it went on, until the troops with Ephialtes were close at hand; and then, when the Greeks knew that they had come, the character of the fighting changed. They withdrew again into the narrow neck of the pass, behind the wall, and took up a position in a single compact body—all except the Thebans—on the little hill at the entrance to the pass, where the stone lion in memory of Leonidas stands today. Here they resisted to the last, with their swords, if they had them, and, if not, with their hands and teeth, until the Persians, coining on from the front over the ruins of the wall and closing in from behind, finally overwhelmed them with missile weapons.

2.4 The Melian Dialogue

The Athenians used the Delian League, after the Persian threat had ended, to expand their own empire and to rebuild Athens, which had been destroyed in the war. In this manner, Classical Athens blossomed, embracing democracy for its citizens at home and empire abroad. While the dialogue excerpted below does not reproduce an actual debate, Thucydides uses the dialogue to show how the people of Athens and Melos might have argued for their own positions on the eve of battle.

Source: Thucydides, *History of the Peloponnesian War*, trans. Rex Warner, (New York: Penguin Books, 1980, © 1954, 1972), pp. 400–08.

Next summer Alcibiades sailed to Argos with twenty ships and seized 300 Argive citizens who were still suspected of being pro-Spartan. These were put by the Athenians into the nearby islands under Athenian control.

The Athenians also made an expedition against the island of Melos. They had thirty of their own ships, six from Chios, and two from Lesbos; 1,200 hoplites, 300 archers, and twenty mounted archers, all from Athens; and about 1,500 hoplites from the allies and the islanders.

The Melians are a colony from Sparta. They had refused to join the Athenian empire like the other islanders, and at first had remained neutral without helping either side; but afterwards, when the Athenians had brought force to bear on them by laying waste their land, they had become open enemies of Athens.

Now the generals Cleomedes, the son of Lycomedes, and Tisias, the son of Tisimachus, encamped with the above force in Melian territory and, before doing any harm to the land, first of all sent representatives to negotiate. The Melians did not invite these representatives to speak before the people, btu asked them to make the statement for which they had come in front of the governing body and the few. The Athenian representatives then spoke as follows:

'So we are not to speak before the people, no doubt in case the mass of the people should hear once and for all and without interruption an argument from us which is both persuasive and incontrovertible, and should so be led astray. This, we realize, is your motive in bringing us here to speak before the few. Now suppose that you who sit here should make assurance doubly sure. Suppose that you, too, should refrain from dealing with every point in detail in a set speech, and should instead interrupt us whenever we say something controversial and deal with that before going on to the next point? Tell us first whether you approve of this suggestion of ours.'

The Council of the Melians replied as follows:

'No one can object to each of us putting forward our own views in a calm atmosphere. That is perfectly reasonable. What is scarcely consistent with such a proposal is the present threat, indeed the certainty, of your making war on us. We see that you have come prepared to judge the argument yourselves, and that the likely end of it all will be either war, if we prove that we are in the right, and so refuse to surrender, or else slavery.'

Athenians: If you are going to spend the time in enumerating your suspicions about the future, or if you have met here for any other reason except to look the facts in the face and on the basis of these facts to consider how you can save your city from destruction, there is no point in our going on with this discussion. If, however, you will do as we suggest, then we will speak on.

Melians: It is natural and understandable that people who are placed as we are should have recourse to all kinds of arguments and different points of view. However, you are right in saying that we are met together here to discuss the safety of our country and, if you will have it so, the discussion shall proceed on the lines that you have laid down.

Athenians: Then we on our side will use no fine phrases saying, for example, that we have a right to our empire because we defeated the Persians, or that we have come against you now because of the injuries you have done us—a great mass of words that nobody would believe. And we ask you on your side not to imagine that you will influence us by saying that you, though a colony of Sparta, have not joined Sparta in the war, or that you have never done us any harm. Instead we recommend that you should try to get what it is possible for you to get, taking into consideration what we both really do think; since you know as well as we do that, when these matters are discussed by practical people, [the standard of justice depends on the equality of power to compel and that in fact the strong do what they have the power to do and the weak accept what they have to accept.]

Melians: Then in our view (since you force us to leave justice out of account and to confine ourselves to self-interest)—in our view it is at any rate useful that you should not destroy a principle that is to the general good of all men—namely, that in the case of all who fall into danger there should be such a thing as fair play and just dealing, and that such people should be allowed to use and to profit by arguments that fall short of a mathematical accuracy. And this is a principle which affects you as much as anybody, since your own fall would be visited by the most terrible vengeance and would be an example to the world.

Athenians: As for us, even assuming that our empire does come to an end, we are not despondent about what would happen next. One is not so much frightened of being conquered by a power which rules over others, as Sparta does (not that we are concerned with Sparta now), as of what would happen if a ruling power is attacked and defeated by its own subjects. So far as this point is concerned, you can leave it to us to face the risks involved. What we shall do now is to show you that it is for the good of our own empire that we are here and that it is for the preservation of your city that we shall say what we are going to say. We do not want any trouble in bringing you into our empire, and we want you to be spared for the good both of yourselves and of ourselves.

Melians: And how could it be just as good for us to be the slave as for you to be the masters?

Athenians: You, by giving in, would save yourselves from disaster; we, by not destroying you, would be able to profit from you.

Melinas: So you would not agree to our being neutral, friends instead of enemies, but allies of neither side?

Athenians: No, because it is not so much your hostility that injures us; it is rather the case that, if we were on friendly terms with you, our subjects would regard that as a sign of weakness in us, whereas your hatred is evidence of our power.

Melinas: Is that your subjects' idea of fair play—that no distinction should be made between people who are quite unconnected with you and people who are mostly your own colonists or else rebels whom you have conquered?

Athenians: So far as right and wrong are concerned they think that there is no difference between the two, that those who still preserve their independence do so because they are strong, and that if we fail to attack them it is because we are afraid. So that by conquering you we shall increase not only the size but the security of our empire. We rule the sea and you are islanders, and weaker islanders too than the others; it is therefore particularly important that you should not escape.

Melians: But do you think there is no security for you in what we suggest? For here again, since you will not let us mention justice, but tell us to give in to your interests, we, too, must tell you what our interests are and, if yours and ours happen to coincide, we must try to persuade you of the fact. Is it not certain that you will make enemies of all states who are at present neutral, when they see what is happening here and naturally conclude that in course of time you will attack them too? Does not this mean that you are strengthening the enemies you have already and are forcing others to become your enemies even against their intentions and their inclinations?

Athenians: As a matter of fact we are not so much frightened of states on the continent. They have their liberty, and this means that it will be a long time before they begin to take precautions against us. We are more concerned about islanders like yourselves, who are still unsubdued, or subjects who have already become embittered by the constraint which our empire imposes on them. These are the people who are most likely to act in a reckless manner and to bring themselves and us, too, into the most obvious danger.

Melinas: Then surely, if such hazards are taken by you to keep your empire and by your subjects to escape from it, we who are still free would show ourselves great cowards and weaklings if we failed to face everything that comes rather than submit to slavery.

Athenians: No, not if you are sensible. This is no fair fight, with honour on one side and shame on the other. It is rather a question of saving your lives and not resisting those who are far too strong for you.

Melians: Yet we know that in war fortune sometimes makes the odds more level than could be expected from the difference in numbers of the two sides. And if we surrender, then all our hope is lost at once, whereas, so long as we remain in action, there is still a hope that we may yet stand upright.

Athenians: Hope, that comforter in danger! If one already has solid advantages to fall back upon, one can indulge in hope. It may do harm, but will not destroy one. But hope is by nature an expensive commodity, and those who are risking their all on one cast find out what it means only when they are already ruined; it never fails them in the period when such a knowledge would enable them to take precautions. Do not let this happen to you, you who are weak and whose fate depends on a single movement of the scale. And do not be like those people who, as so commonly happens, miss the chance of saving themselves in a human and practical way, and, when every clear and distinct hope has left them in their adversity, turn to what is blind and vague, to prophecies and oracles and such things which by encouraging hope lead men to ruin.

Melians: It is difficult, and you may be sure that we know it, for us to oppose your power and fortune, unless the terms be equal. Nevertheless we trust that the gods will

give us fortune as good as yours, because we are standing for what is right against what is wrong; and as for what we lack in power, we trust that it will be made up for by our alliance with the Spartans, who are bound, if for no other reason, then for honour's sake, and because we are their kinsmen, to come to our help. Our confidence, therefore, is not so entirely irrational as you think.

Athenians: So far as the favour of the gods is concerned, we think we have as much right to that as you have. Our aims and our actions are perfectly consistent with the beliefs men hold about the gods and with the principles which govern their own conduct. Our opinion of the gods and our knowledge of men lead us to conclude that it is a general and necessary law of nature to rule whatever one can. This is not a law that we made ourselves, nor were we the first to act upon it when it was made. We found it already in existence, and we shall leave it to exist for ever among those who come after us. We are merely acting in accordance with it, and we know that you or anybody else with the same power as ours would be acting in precisely the same way. And therefore, so far as the gods are concerned, we see no good reason why we should fear to be at a disadvantage. But with regard to your views about Sparta and your confidence that she, out of a sense of honour, will come to your aid, we must say that we congratulate you on your simplicity but do not envy you your folly. In matters that concern themselves or their own constitution the Spartans are quite remarkably good; as for their relations with others, that is a long story, but it can be expressed shortly and clearly by saying that of all people we know the Spartans are most conspicuous for believing that what they like doing is honourable and what suits their interests is just. And this kind of attitude is not going to be of much help to you in your absurd quest for safety at the moment.

Melians: But this is the very point where we can feel most sure. Their own self-interest will make them refuse to betray their own colonists, the Melians, for that would mean losing the confidence of their friends among the Hellenes and doing good to their enemies.

Athenians: You seem to forget that if one follows one's self-interest one wants to be safe, whereas the path of justice and honour involves one in danger. And, where danger is concerned, the Spartans are not, as a rule, very venturesome.

Melians: But we think that they would even endanger themselves for our sake and count the risk more worth taking than in the case of others, because we are so close to the Peloponnese that they could operate more easily, and because they can depend on us more than on others, since we are of the same race and share the same feelings.

Athenians: Goodwill shown by the party that is asking for help does not mean security for the prospective ally. What is looked for is a positive preponderance of power in action. And the Spartans pay attention to this point even more than others do. Certainly they distrust their own native resources so much that when they attack a neighbour they bring a great army of allies with them. It is hardly likely therefore that, while we are in control of the sea, they will cross over to an island.

Melians: But they still might send others. The Cretan sea is a wide one, and it is harder for those who control it to intercept others than for those who want to slip through to do so safely. And even if they were to fail in this, they would turn against your own land and against those of your allies left unvisited by Brasidas. So, instead of troubling about a country which has nothing to do with you, you will find trouble nearer home, among your allies, and in your own country.

Athenians: It is a possibility, something that has in fact happened before. It may happen in your case, but you are well aware that the Athenians have never yet relinquished a single siege operation through fear of others. But we are somewhat shocked to find that; though you announced your intention of discussing how you could preserve yourselves, in all this talk you have said absolutely nothing which could justify a man in thinking that he could be preserved. Your chief points are concerned with what you hope may happen in the future, while your actual resources are too scanty to give you a chance of survival against the forces that are opposed to you at this moment. You will therefore be showing an extraordinary lack of common sense if, after you have asked us to retire from this meeting, you still fail to reach a conclusion wiser than anything you have mentioned so far. Do not be led astray by a false sense of honour—a thing which often brings men to ruin when they are faced with an obvious danger that somehow affects their pride. For in many cases men have still been able to see the dangers ahead of them, but this thing called dishonour, this word, by its own force of seduction, has drawn them into a state where they have surrendered to an idea, while in fact they have fallen voluntarily into irrevocable disaster, in dishonour that is all the more dishonourable because it has come to them from their own folly rather than their misfortune. You, if you take the right view, will be careful to avoid this. You will see that there is nothing disgraceful in giving way to the greatest city in Hellas when she is offering you such reasonable terms—alliance on a tribute-paying basis and liberty to enjoy your own property. And, when you are allowed to choose between war and safety, you will not be so insensitively arrogant as to make the wrong choice. This is the safe rule—to stand up to one's equals, to behave with deference towards one's superiors, and to treat one's inferiors with moderation. Think it over again, then, when we have withdrawn from the meeting, and let this be a point that constantly recurs to your minds—that you are discussing the fate of your country, that you have only one country, and that its future for good or ill depends on this one single decision which you are going to make.

The Athenians then withdrew from the discussion. The Melians, left to themselves, reached a conclusion which was much the same as they had indicated in their previous replies. Their answer was as follows:

'Our decision, Athenians, is just the same as it was at first. We are not prepared to give up in a short moment the liberty which our city has enjoyed from its foundation for 700 years. We put our trust in the fortune that the gods will send and which has saved us up to now, and in the help of men—that is, of the Spartans; and so we shall try to save ourselves. But we invite you to allow us to be friends of yours and enemies to neither side, to make a treaty which shall be agreeable to both you and us, and so to leave our country.'

The Melians made this reply, and the Athenians, just as they were breaking off the discussion, said:

'Well, at any rate, judging from this decision of yours, you seem to us quite unique in your ability to consider the future as something more certain than what is before your eyes, and to see uncertainties as realities, simply because you would like them to be so. As you have staked most on and trusted most in Spartans, luck, and hopes, so in all these you will find yourselves most completely deluded.'

The Athenian representatives then went back to the army, and the Athenian generals, finding that the Melians would not submit, immediately commenced hostilities and built a wall completely round the city of Melos, dividing the work out among the various states. Later they left behind a garrison of some of their own and some allied troops to blockade the place by land and sea, and with the greater part of their army returned home. The force left behind stayed on and continued with the siege.

· · · ·

Siege operations were not carried on vigorously and, as there was also some treachery from inside, the Melians surrendered unconditionally to the Athenians, who put to death all the men of military age whom they took, and sold the women and children as slaves. Melos itself they took over for themselves, sending out later a colony of 500 men.[41]

Questions for Documents 2.1–2.4
1. According to these documents, what roles do the gods play in war and diplomacy? What impact do they have?
2. What elements of warfare (tactics, strategies, weapons) were employed and to what effect?
3. In each of these documents, what evidence is there that interpretations varied between the two sides? What reasons might there be for these differences? What affects did or might this have had?

---

[41] That there were Melian survivors, who were restored by Lysander at the end of the war, is stated by Xenophon (*Hellenica*, 11, 2, 9).

SECTION 2
How to Rule

Documents 2.5 and 2.6: The Near Eastern Tradition

When a legendary king died, his reign would be eulogized, emphasizing the important concepts of kingship. Sometimes he would pass on advice about ruling to his successor, much as the Vizier Ptah-hotep left instructions for his son (Chapter 1, Document 9).

2.5 Babylonian Concepts of Ruling: "The Death of Gilgamesh"

By explaining the significance of the life of Gilgamesh at his death, *The Epic of Gilgamesh* also explains the principles of Mesopotamian kingship.
Source: *The Epic of Gilgamesh*, trans. N.K. Sandars (New York: Penguin Books, 1981, © 1972), pp. 118–19.

The destiny was fulfilled which the father of the gods, Enlil of the mountain, had decreed for Gilgamesh: "In netherearth the darkness will show him a light: of mankind, all that are known, none will leave a monument for generations to come to compare with his. The heroes, the wise men, like the new moon have their waxing and waning. Men will say, "Who has ever ruled with might and with power like him?" As in the dark month, the month of shadows, so without him there is no light. O Gilgamesh, this was the meaning of your dream. You were given the kingship, such was your destiny, everlasting life was not your destiny. Because of this do not be sad at heart, do not be grieved or oppressed; he has given you power to bind and to loose, to be the darkness and the light of mankind. He has given unexampled supremacy over the people, victory in battle from which no fugitive returns, in forays and assault from which there is no going back. But do not abuse this power, deal justly with your servants in the palace, deal justly before the face of the Sun."

> The king has laid himself down
> and will not rise again,
> The Lord of Kullah will not rise again;
> He overcame evil, he will not come again;
> Though he was strong of arm he will not rise again;
>
> He had wisdom and a comely face,
> he will not come again;
> He is gone into the mountain,
> he will not come again;

> On the bed of fate, he will not rise again,
> From the couch of many colours
> he will not come again.

2.6 The Ideal of Hebrew Kingship: David and Solomon

The greatest king in Hebrew history is King David who lived in the tenth century B.C.E. Here are two versions of his final advice to his son and successor Solomon, followed by Solomon's reaction to assuming the throne of the Kingdom of Israel.
Source: The Bible, New International Version, © 1973, 1978, 1984, International Bible Society. 2 Sam 23, 1 Kings 3: 3–14.

2 Samuel 23

1 These are the last words of David: "The oracle of David son of Jesse, the oracle of the man exalted by the Most High, the man anointed by the God of Jacob, Israel's singer of songs.

2 "The Spirit of the LORD spoke through me; his word was on my tongue.

3–4 The God of Israel spoke, the Rock of Israel said to me: "When one rules over men in righteousness, when he rules in the fear of God, he is like the light of morning at sunrise on a cloudless morning, like the brightness after rain that brings the grass from the earth.'

5 "Is not my house right with God? Has he not made with me an everlasting covenant, arranged and secured in every part? Will he not bring to fruition my salvation and grant me my every desire?

6–7 But evil men are all to be cast aside like thorns, which are not gathered with the hand. Whoever touches thorns uses a tool of iron or the shaft of a spear; they are burned up where they lie."

SOLOMON BECOMES KING

1 Kings 3:3–14

3 Solomon showed his love for the LORD by walking according to the statutes of his father David, except that he offered sacrifices and burned incense on the high places.

4 The king went to Gibeon to offer sacrifices, for that was the most important high place, and Solomon offered a thousand burnt offerings on that altar.

5 At Gibeon the LORD appeared to Solomon during the night in a dream, and God said, "Ask for whatever you want me to give you."

6 Solomon answered, "You have shown great kindness to your servant, my father David, because he was faithful to you and righteous and upright in heart. You have continued this great kindness to him and have given him a son to sit on his throne this very day.

7 "Now, 0 LORD my God, you have made your servant king in place of my father David. But I am only a little child and do not know how to carry out my duties.

8 Your servant is here among the people you have chosen, a great people, too numerous to count or number.

9 So give your servant a discerning heart to govern your people and to distinguish between right and wrong. For who is able to govern this great people of yours?"

10 The Lord was pleased that Solomon had asked for this.

11 So God said to him, "Since you have asked for this and not for long life or wealth for yourself, nor have asked for the death of your enemies but for discernment in administering justice,

12 I will do what you have asked. I will give you a wise and discerning heart, so that there will never have been anyone like you, nor will there ever be.

13 Moreover, I will give you what you have not asked for—both riches and honor—so that in your lifetime you will have no equal among kings.

14 And if you walk in my ways and obey my statutes and commands as David your father did, I will give you a long life."

Questions for Documents 2.5 and 2.6:
1. In these selections, what are the qualities of good kingship?
2. How do the principles of kingship differ between the two societies?
3. What comfort is given to those who mourn Gilgamesh's and David's deaths?

Documents 2.7 and 2.8: Chinese Traditions
The Ancient Near East has given us the oldest documentation of government and society, but civilizations flourished also in the Indus and Yellow Valleys in South and East Asia. Out of these societies emerged other concepts of government and kingship. Here are selections from the Chinese traditions.

2.7   The *Analects* of Confucius

The followers of Confucius recorded his teachings from the fifth century B.C.E. that synthesized important elements in Chinese tradition and society. Neither laws nor a religion, the *Analects* focused on producing harmony and good government during an "era of warring states."

Source: Arthur Waley, trans., *The Analects of Confucius*, (New York: Vintage Books, 1938), pp. 21–27, passim.

BOOK I

1. The Master said, To learn and at due times to repeat what one has learnt, is that not after all a pleasure? That friends should come to one from afar, is that not after all delightful? To remain unsoured even though one's merits are unrecognized by others, is that not after all what is expected of a gentleman?

2. Master Yu said, Those who in private life behave well towards their parents and elder brothers, in public life seldom show a disposition to resist the authority of their superiors. And as for such men starting a revolution, no instance of it has ever occurred. It is upon the trunk that a gentleman works. When that is firmly set up, the Way grows. And surely proper behaviour towards parents and elder brothers is the trunk of Goodness?

4. Master Tsêng said, Every day I examine myself on these three points: in acting on behalf of others, have I always been loyal to their interests? In intercourse with my friends, have I always been true to my word? Have I failed to repeat the precepts that have been handed down to me?

5. The Master said, A country of a thousand war-chariots cannot be administered unless the ruler attends strictly to business, punctually observes his promises, is economical in expenditure, shows affection towards his subjects in general, and uses the labour of the peasantry only at the proper times of year.

6. The Master said, A young man's duty is to behave well to his parents at home and to his elders abroad, to be cautious in giving promises and punctual in keeping them, to have kindly feelings towards everyone, but seek the intimacy of the Good. If, when all that is done, he has any energy to spare, then let him study the polite arts.

9. Master Tsêng said, When proper respect towards the dead is shown at the End and continued after they are far away, the moral force of a people has reached its highest point.

10. Tzu-Ch'in said to Tzu-kung, When our Master arrives in a fresh country he always manages to find out about its policy. Does he do this by asking questions, or do people tell him of their own accord? Tzukung said, Our Master gets things by being cordial, frank, courteous, temperate, deferential. That is our Master's way of enquiring—a very different matter, certainly, from the way in which enquiries are generally made.

14. The Master said, A gentleman who never goes on eating till he is sated, who does not demand comfort in his home, who is diligent in business and cautious in speech, who associates with those that possess the Way and thereby corrects his own faults—such a one may indeed be said to have a taste for learning.

16. The Master said, (the good man) does not grieve that other people do not recognize his merits. His only anxiety is lest he should fail to recognize theirs.

BOOK II

1. The Master said, He who rules by moral force is like the pole-star, which remains in its place while all the lesser stars do homage to it.

3. The Master said, Govern the people by regulations, keep order among them by chastisements, and they will flee from you, and lose all self-respect. Govern them by moral force, keep order among them by ritual and they will keep their self-respect and come to you of their own accord.

7. Tzu-yu asked about the treatment of parents. The Master said, "Filial sons" nowadays are people who see to it that their parents get enough to eat. But even dogs and horses are cared for to that extent. If there is no feeling of respect, wherein lies the difference?

14. The Master said, A gentleman can see a question from all sides without bias. The small man is biased and can see a question only from one side.

15. The Master said, 'He who learns but does not think, is lost.' He who thinks but does not learn is in great danger.

16. The Master said, He who sets to work upon a different strand destroys the whole fabric.

17. The Master said, Yu, shall I teach you what knowledge is? When you know a thing, to recognize that you know it, and when you do not know a thing, to recognize that you do not know it. That is knowledge.

18. Tzu-chang was studying the *Song* Han-lu. The Master said, Hear much, but maintain silence as regards doubtful points and be cautious in speaking of the rest; then you will seldom get into trouble. See much, but ignore what it is dangerous to have seen, and be cautious in acting upon the rest; then you will seldom want to undo your acts. He who seldom gets into trouble about what he has said and seldom does anything that he afterwards wishes he had not done, will be sure incidentally to get his reward.

20. Chi K'ang-tzu asked whether there were any form of encouragement by which he could induce the common people to be respectful and loyal. The Master said, Approach them with dignity, and they will respect you. Show piety towards your parents and kindness toward your children, and they will be loyal to you. Promote those who are worthy, train those who are incompetent; that is the best form of encouragement.

BOOK IV

5. Wealth and rank are what every man desires; but if they can only be retained to the detriment of the Way he professes, he must relinquish them. Poverty and obscurity are what every man detests; but if they can only be avoided to the detriment of the Way he professes, he must accept them. The gentleman who ever parts company with Good-ness does not fulfil that name. Never for a moment does a gentleman quit the way of Goodness. He is never so harried but that he cleaves to this; never so tottering but that he cleaves to this.

11. The Master said, Where gentlemen set their hearts upon moral force the commoners set theirs upon the soil. Where gentlemen think only of punishments, the commoners think only of exemptions.

12. The Master said, Those whose measures are dictated by mere expediency will arouse continual discontent.

16. The Master said, A gentleman takes as much trouble to discover what is right as lesser men take to discover what will pay.

17. The Master said, In the presence of a good man, think all the time how you may learn to equal him. In the presence of a bad man, turn your gaze within!

18. The Master said, In serving his father and mother a man may gently remonstrate with them. But if he sees that he has failed to change their opinion, he should resume an attitude of deference and not thwart them; may feel discouraged, but not resentful.

24. The Master said. A gentleman covets the reputation of being slow in word but prompt in deed.

BOOK VIII

2. The Master said, Courtesy not bounded by the prescriptions of ritual becomes tiresome. Caution not bounded by the prescriptions of ritual becomes timidity, daring becomes turbulence, inflexibility becomes harshness.

The Master said, When gentlemen deal generously with their own kin, the common people are incited to Goodness. When old dependents are not discarded, the common people will not be fickle.

6. Master Tsêng said, The man to whom one could with equal confidence entrust an orphan not yet fully grown or the sovereignty of a whole State, whom the advent of no emergency however great could upset—would such a one be a true gentleman? He, I think, would be a true gentleman indeed.

9. The Master said, The common people can be made to follow it; they cannot be made to understand it.

10. The Master said, One who is by nature daring and is suffering from poverty will not long be law-abiding. Indeed, any men, save those that are truly Good, if their sufferings are very great, will be likely to rebel.

24. The Master said, First and foremost, be faithful to your superiors, keep all promises, refuse the friendship of all who are not like you; and if you have made a mistake, do not be afraid of admitting the fact and amending your ways.

2.8 "Legalism: An Alternative System"

One Confucian scholar, dissatisfied with the continual warfare that plagued the Chinese states, came to the conclusion that stronger measures than those advocated by Confucius were necessary to bring peace. Han Fei-Tzu was the principal theoretician of Legalism, a political ideology that promoted authoritarian power over the people. He became chief minister to the King of Q'in who put this philosophy of government into practice by conquering all other Chinese states and forcing them to unify under his rule as the First Emperor of China.

Source: Han Fei-Tzu, *The Complete Works*, 2 vols., trans. W.K. Liao (London: Arthur Probsthain, 1959), Vol. II, pp. 322–33. Reprinted in *Documents in World History, Volume I: The Great Traditions: From Ancient Times to 1500*, edited by Peter N. Stearns, et. Al. (New York: Harper Collins Publishers, 1988), pp. 41–45.

If orders are made trim, laws never deviate; if laws are equable, there will be no culprit among the officials. Once the law is fixed, nobody can damage it by means of virtuous words. If men of merit are appointed to office, the people will have little to say; if men of virtue are appointed to office the people will have much to talk about. The enforcement of laws depends upon the method of judicial administration. Who administers judicial affairs with ease attains supremacy. . . . Whoever procrastinates in creating order, will see his state dismembered.

Govern by penalties; wage war by rewards; and enlarge the bounties so as to put the principles of statecraft into practice. If so, there will be no wicked people in the state nor will there by any wicked trade at the market. If things are many and trifles are numerous, and if farming is relaxed and villainy prevails, the state will certainly be dismembered.

If the people have a surplus of food, make them receive rank by giving grain to the state. If only through their own effort they can receive rank, then farmers will not idle.

If a tube three inches long has no bottom, it can never be filled. Conferring office and rank or granting profit and bounty without reference to merit, is like a tube having no bottom.

. . . The affairs of the government, however small, should never be abandoned. For instance, office and rank are always obtained according to the acquired merit; though there may be flattering words, it will be impossible thereby to make any interference in the state affairs. This is said to be "government by figures." For instance, in attacking with force, ten points are taken for every point given out; but in attacking with words, one hundred are lost for every one marched out. If a state is fond of force, it is called hard to attack; if a state is fond of words, it is called easy to attack.

If the ability of the official is equal to his post, if his duty is lightened and he never reserves any surplus energy in mind, and if he does not shift any responsibility of additional offices back to the ruler, then there will be no hidden grudge inside. If the intelligent ruler makes the state affairs never mutually interfere, there will be no dispute; if he allows no official to hold any kind of additional post, everybody will develop his talent or skill; and if he allows no two persons to share the same meritorious achievement, there will be no quarrel.

If penalties are heavy and rewards are few, it means that the superior loves the people, wherefore the people will die for rewards. If rewards are many amid penalties are light, it means that the superior does not love the people, wherefore the people will never die for rewards.

. . . .

In inflicting penalties light offences should be punished severely; if light offences do not appear, heavy offences will not come. This is said to be to abolish penalties by means of penalties. And the state will certainly become strong. If crimes are serious but penalties are light, light penalties breed further troubles. This is said to create penalties through penalties, and such a state will infallibly be dismembered.

The sage in governing the people considers their springs of action, never tolerates their wicked desires, but seeks only for the people's benefit. Therefore, the penalty he inflicts is not due to any hatred for the people but to his motive of loving the people. If penalty triumphs, the people are quiet; if reward overflows, culprits appear. Therefore the triumph of penalty is the beginning of order; the overflow of reward, the origin of chaos.

Indeed, it is the people's nature to delight in disorder and detach themselves from legal restraints. Therefore, when the intelligent sovereign governs the state, if he makes rewards clear, the people will be encouraged to render meritorious services; if he makes penalties severe, the people will attach themselves to the law. If they are encouraged to render meritorious services, public affairs will not be obstructed; if they attach themselves to the law, culprits will not appear. Therefore, he who governs the people should nip the evil in the bud; he who commands troops, should inculcate warfare in the people's mind. If prohibitions can uproot causes of villainy, there will always be order; if soldiers can imagine warfare in mind, there will always be victory. When the sage is governing the people, he attains order first, wherefore he is strong; he prepares for war first, wherefore he wins.

. . . Indeed, the strength of the state is due to the administration of its political affairs; the honour of the sovereign is due to his supreme power. Now, the enlightened ruler possesses the supreme power and the administrative organs; the ignoble ruler possesses both the supreme power and the administrative organs, too. Yet the results are not the same, because their standpoints are different. Thus, as the enlightened ruler has the supreme power in his grip, the superior is held in high esteem; as he unifies the administrative organs, the state is in order. Hence law is the origin of supremacy and penalty is the beginning of love.

Indeed, it is the people's nature to abhor toil and enjoy ease. However, if they pursue ease, the land will waste; if the land wastes, the state will not be in order. If the state is not orderly, it will become chaotic. If reward and penalty take no effect among the inferiors, government will come to a deadlock. Therefore, he who wants to accomplish a great achievement but hesitates to apply his full strength, can not hope for the accomplishment of the achievement; he who wants to settle the people's disorder but hesitates to change their traditions, can not hope to banish the people's disorder.

Hence there is no constant method for the government of men. The law alone leads to political order. If laws are adjusted to the time, there is good government. If government fits the age, there will be great accomplishment. Therefore, when the people are naive, if you regulate them with fame, there will be good government; when everybody in the world is intelligent, if you discipline them with penalties, they will obey. While time is moving on, if laws do not shift accordingly, there will be misrule; while abilities are diverse, if prohibitions are not changed, the state will be dismembered, therefore, the sage in governing the people makes laws move with time and prohibitions change with abilities. Who can exert his forces to land-utilization, will become rich; who can rush his forces at enemies, will become strong. The strong man not obstructed in his way will attain supremacy.

Therefore, the way to supremacy lies in the way of shutting culprits off and the way of blocking up wicked men. Who is able to block up wicked men, will eventually attain supremacy. The policy of attaining supremacy relies not on foreign states' abstention from disturbing your state, but on their inability to disturb your state. Who has to rely on foreign powers' abstention from disturbing his state before he can maintain his own independence, will see his state dismembered; who relies on their inability to disturb his state and willingly enacts the law, will prosper.

Therefore, the worthy ruler in governing the state follows the statecraft of invulnerability. When rank is esteemed, the superior will increase his dignity. He will accordingly bestow rewards on men of merit, confer ranks upon holders of posts, and appoint wicked men to no office. Who devotes himself to practical forces, gets a high rank. If the rank is esteemed, the superior will be honoured. The superior, if honoured, will attain supremacy. On the contrary, if the state does not strive after practical forces but counts on private studies, its rank will be lowered. If the rank is lowered, the superior will be humbled. If the superior is humbled, the state will be dismembered. Therefore, if the way of founding the state and using the people can shut off foreign invaders and block up self-seeking subjects, and if the superior relies on himself, supremacy will be attained.

. . . Indeed, if the state is orderly, the people are safe; if affairs are confused, the country falls into peril. Who makes laws strict, hits on the true nature of mankind; who makes prohibitions lenient, misses the apparent fact. Moreover, everybody is, indeed, gifted with desperate courage. To exert desperate courage to get what one wants, is human nature. Yet everybody's likes and dislikes should be regulated by the superior. Now the people like to have profit and bounty and hate to be punished; if the superior catches their likes and dislikes and thereby holds their desperate courage under control he will not miss the realities of affairs.

. . . For this reason, the state at the height of order is able to take the suppression of villainy for its duty. Why? Because its law comprehends human nature and accords with the principles of government.

If so, how to get rid of delicate villainy? By making the people watch one another in their hidden affairs. Then how to make them watch one another? By implicating the people of the same hamlet in one another's crime. When everyone knows that the penalty or reward will directly affect him, if the people of the same hamlet fail to watch one another, they will fear they may not be able to escape the implication, and those who are evil-minded, will not be allowed to forget so many people watching them. Were such the law, everybody would mind his own doings, watch everybody else, and disclose the secrets of any culprit. For, whosoever denounces a criminal offence, is not held guilty but is given a reward; whosoever misses any culprit, is definitely censured and given the same penalty as the culprit. Were such the law, all types of culprits would be detected. If the minutest villainy is not tolerated, it is due to the system of personal denunciation and mutual implication.

Indeed, the most enlightened method of governing a state is to trust measures and not men. For this reason, the tactful state is never mistaken if it does not trust the empty fame of men. If the land within the boundary is always in order it is because measures are employed. If any falling state lets foreign soldiers walk all over its territory and can neither resist nor prevent them, it is because that state trusts men and uses no measures. Men may jeopardize their own country, but measures can invade others' countries. Therefore, the tactful state spurns words and trusts laws.

Questions for Documents 2.7 and 2.8
1. What are the basic principles of government and rule in each of these documents?
2. How does each regard the nature of society?
3. How do they compare with the principles of the peoples of Mesopotamia? The Hebrews? The Egyptians of the Old Kingdom?

CHAPTER 3
The Greek *Polis*
The New Politics of Ancient Greece
(1000–300 B.C.E.)

SECTION 1
Forming the *Polis*

Documents 3.1 and 3.2

The following two selections were written by the second century C.E. Roman historian Plutarch, who used sources that have long since disappeared. He describes the work of the legendary founders of two Greek city-poleis, Sparta and Athens. The early history of the two city-states were quite similar, but social, political and economic crises led the two societies down radically different paths.

3.1 Lycurgus the Law-giver

Whether the Spartan state owes its form to one man's vision is questionable, but the Spartans themselves had always regarded the legendary figure Lycurgus as the lawgiver who founded the institutions of their society and government.

> **Source:** *Plutarch's Lives*, trans. John Dryden, revised by A.H. Clough, Vol. 1. (New York: Little, Brown and Company, 1909), pp. 83–100, 120–22.

There is so much uncertainty in the accounts which historians have left us of Lycurgus, the lawgiver of Sparta, that scarcely any thing is asserted by one of them which is not called into question or contradicted by the rest. Their sentiments are quite different as to the family he came or the voyages he undertook, the place and manner of his death, but most of all when they speak of the laws he made and the commonwealth which he founded. They cannot, by any means, be brought to an agreement as to the very age in which he lived; . . .

Amongst the many changes and alterations which Lycurgus made, the first and of greatest importance was the establishment of the senate, which, having a power equal to the kings' in matters of great consequence, and, as Plato expresses it, allaying and qualifying the fiery genius of the royal office, gave steadiness and safety to the commonwealth. . .

After the creation of the thirty senators, his next task, and, indeed, the most hazardous he ever undertook, was the making of a new division of their lands. For there was an extreme inequality amongst them, and their state was overloaded with a multitude of indigent and necessitous persons, while its whole wealth had centered upon a very few. To the end, therefore, that he might expel from the state arrogance and envy, luxury and crime, and those yet more inveterate diseases of want and superfluity, he obtained of them to renounce their properties, and to consent to a new division of the land, and that they should live all together on an equal footing; merit to be their only road to eminence, and the disgrace of evil, and credit of worthy acts, their one measure of difference between man and man.

Upon their consent to these proposals, proceeding at once to put them into execution, he divided the country of Laconia in general into thirty thousand equal shares, and the part attached to the city of Sparta into nine thousand; these he distributed among the Spartans, as he did the others to the country citizens. Some authors say that he made but six thousand lots for the citizens of Sparta, and that king Polydorus added three thousand more. Others say that Polydorus doubled the number Lycurgus had made, which, according to them, was but four thousand five hundred. A lot was so much as to yield, one year with another, about seventy bushels of grain for the master of the family, and twelve for his wife, with a suitable proportion of oil and wine. And this he thought sufficient to keep their bodies in good health and strength; superfluities they were better without. It is reported, that, as he returned from a journey shortly after the division of the lands, in harvest time, the ground being newly reaped, seeing the stacks all standing equal and alike, he smiled, and said to those about him, "Methinks all Laconia looks like one family estate just divided among a number of brothers."

Not contented with this, he resolved to make a division of their movables too, that there might be no odious distinction or inequality left amongst them; but finding that it would be very dangerous to go about it openly, he took another course, and defeated their avarice by the following stratagem: he commanded that all gold and silver coin should be called in, and that only a sort of money made of iron should be current, a great weight and quantity of which was but very little worth; so that to lay up twenty or thirty pounds there was required a pretty large closet, and, to remove it, nothing less than a yoke of oxen. With the diffusion of this money, at once a number of vices were banished from

Lacedæmon; for who would rob another of such a coin? Who would unjustly detain or take by force, or accept as a bribe, a thing which it was not easy to hide, nor a credit to have, nor indeed of any use to cut in pieces? For when it was just red hot, they quenched it in vinegar, and by that means spoilt it, and made it almost incapable of being worked.

In the next place, he declared an outlawry of all needles and superfluous arts; . . . So there was now no more means of purchasing foreign goods and small wares; merchants sent no shiploads into Laconian ports; no rhetoric-master, no itinerant fortune-teller, no harlot-monger, or gold or silversmith, engraver, or jeweller, set foot in a country which had no money; so that luxury, deprived little by little of that which fed and fomented it, wasted to nothing, and died away of itself. For the rich had no advantage here over the poor, as their wealth and abundance had no road to come abroad by, but where shut up at home doing nothing. And in this way they became excellent artists in common, necessary things; bedsteads, chairs, and tables, and such like staple utensils in a family, were admirably well made there; . . .

The third and most masterly stroke of this great lawgiver, by which he struck a yet more effectual blow against luxury and the desire of riches, was the ordinance he made, that they should all eat in common, of the same bread and same meat, and of kinds that were specified, and should not spend their lives at home, laid on costly couches at splendid tables, delivering themselves up into the hands of their tradesmen and cooks, to fatten them in corners, like greedy brutes, and to ruin not their minds only but their very bodies, which, enfeebled by indulgence and excess, would stand in need of long sleep, warm bathing, freedom from work, and, in a word, of as much care and attendance as if they were continually sick. It was certainly an extraordinary thing to have brought about such a result as this, but a greater yet to have taken away from wealth, as Theophrastus observes, not merely the property of being coveted, but its very nature of being wealth. For the rich, being obliged to go to the same table with the poor, could not make use of or enjoy their abundance, nor so much as please their vanity by looking at or displaying it. So that the common proverb, that Plutus, the god of riches, is blind, was nowhere in all the world literally verified but in Sparta. There, indeed, he was not only blind, but like a picture, without either life or motion. Nor were they allowed to take food at home first, and then attend the public tables, for every one had an eye upon those who did not eat and drink like the rest, and reproached them with being dainty and effeminate.

. . . They used to send their children to these tables as to schools of temperance; here they were instructed in state affairs by listening to experienced statesmen; here they learnt to converse with pleasantry, to make jests without scurrility, and take them without ill humor.

After drinking moderately, every man went to his home without lights, for the use of them was, on all occasions, forbid, to the end that they might accustom themselves to march boldly in the dark. Such was the common fashion of their meals.

Lycurgus would never reduce his laws into writing; nay, there is a Rhetra expressly to forbid it. For he thought that the most material points, and such as most directly tended to the public welfare, being imprinted on the hearts of their youth by a good discipline, would be sure to remain, and would find a stronger security, than any compulsion would be, in the principles of action formed in them by their best lawgiver, education. And as for things of lesser importance, as pecuniary contracts, and such like, the forms of which have to be changed as occasion requires, he thought it the best way to prescribe no positive rule or inviolable usage in such cases, willing that their manner and form should be altered according to the circumstances of time, and determinations of men of sound judgment. Every end and object of law and enactment it was his design education should effect.

One, then, of the Rhetras was, that their laws should not be written; another is particularly levelled against luxury and expensiveness, for by it it was ordained that the ceilings of their houses should only be wrought by the axe, and their gates and doors smoothed only by the saw. . . .

A third ordinance of Rhetra was, that they should not make war often, or long, with the same enemy, lest that they should train and instruct them in war, by habituating them to defend themselves. And this is what Agesilaus was much blamed for, a long time after; it being thought, that, by his continual incursions into Beotia, he made the Thebans a match for the Lacedamonians; and therefore Antalcidas, seeing him wounded one day, said to him, that he was very well paid for taking such pains to make the . . . Thebans good soldiers, whether they would or no. These laws were called the Rhetras, to intimate that they were divine sanctions and revelations. . . .

Hitherto I, for my part, see no sign of injustice or want of equity in the laws of Lycurgus, though some who admit them to be well contrived to make good soldiers, pronounce them defective in point of justice. The Cryptia, perhaps (if it were one of Lycurgus's ordinances, as Aristotle says it was), gave both him and Plato, too, this opinion alike of the lawgiver and his government. By this ordinance, the magistrates [dispatched] privately some of the ablest of the young men into the country, from time to time, armed only with their daggers, and taking a little necessary provisions with them; in the daytime, they hid themselves in out-of-the-way places, and there lay close, but, in the night, issued out into the highways, and killed all the Helots they could light upon; sometimes they set upon them by day, as they were at work in the fields, and murdered them. As, also, Thucydides, in his history of the Peloponnesian war, tells us, that a good number of them[1] after being singled out for their bravery by the Spartans, garlanded, as enfranchised persons, and led about to all the temples in token of honors, shortly after disappeared all of a sudden, being about the number of two thousand; and no man either then or since could give an account how they came by their deaths. And Aristotle, in particular, adds, that the ephori, so soon as they were entered into their office, used to declare war against them, that they might be massacred without a breach of religion. It is confessed, on all hands, that the Spartans dealt with them very hardly; for it was a common thing to force them to drink to excess, and to lead them in that condition into their public halls, that the children might see what a sight a drunken man; . . .

When he perceived that his more important institutions had taken root in the minds of his countrymen, that Custom had rendered them familiar and easy, that his commonwealth was now grown up and able to go alone, then, as, Plato somewhere tells us, the Maker of the world, when first he saw it existing and beginning its motion, felt joy, even so Lycurgus, viewing with joy and satisfaction the greatness and beauty of his political structure, now fairly at work and in motion, conceived the thought to make it immortal too, and, as far as human forecast could reach, to deliver it down unchangeable to posterity. He called an extraordinary assembly of all the people, and told them that he now thought every thing reasonably well established, both for the happiness and the virtue of the state; but that there was one thing still behind, of the greatest importance, which he thought not fit to impart until he had consulted the oracle; in the mean time, his desire was that they would observe the laws without any the least alteration until his return, and then he would do as the god should direct him. They all consented readily, and bade him hasten his journey; but, before he departed, he administered an oath to the two kings, the senate, and the whole commons, to abide by and maintain the established form of polity until Lycurgus should be come back. This done, he set out for Delphi, and, having sacrificed to Apollo, asked him whether the laws he had established were good, and sufficient for a people's happiness and virtue. The oracle answered that the laws were excellent, and that the people, while it observed them, should live in the height of renown. Lycurgus took the oracle in writing, and sent it over to Sparta; and, having sacrificed the second time to Apollo, and taken leave of his friends and his son, he resolved that the Spartans should not be released from the oath they had taken, and that he would, of his own act, close his life where he was. He was now about that age in which life was still tolerable, and yet might be quitted without regret.

---
[1] Helots.

3.2 Solon: Shaping Athenian Democracy

The Athenians selected Solon as their sole magistrate (archon) at the end of the seventh century B.C.E. to reform the government in order to prevent political and social revolution. His reform measures began the process of creating a democracy in Athens.

Source: *Plutarch's Lives*, trans. John Dryden, revised by A.H. Clough, Vol. 1. (New York: Little, Brown and Company, 1909), pp. 179–90.

The Athenians . . . fell into their old quarrels about the government. . . . The Hill quarter favored democracy, the Plain oligarchy, and those that lived by the Seaside stood for a mixed sort of government, and so hindered either of the other parties from prevailing. And the disparity of fortune between the rich and the poor, at that time, also reached its height; so that the city seemed to be in a truly dangerous condition, and no other means for freeing it from disturbances and settling it, to be possible but a despotic power. All the people were indebted to the rich; and either they tilled their land for their creditors, paying them a sixth part of the increase, and were, therefore, called Hectemorii ["Sixth-parters"] and Thetes, or else they engaged their body for the debt, and might be seized, and either sent into slavery at home, or sold to strangers; some (for no law forbade it) were forced to sell their children, or fly their country to avoid the cruelty of their creditors; *but* the most part and the bravest of them began to combine together and encourage one another to stand to it, to choose a leader, to liberate the condemned debtors, divide the land, and change the government.

Then the wisest of the Athenians, perceiving Solon was of all men the only one not implicated in the troubles, that he had not joined in the exactions of the rich, and was not involved in the necessities of the poor, pressed him to succor the commonwealth and compose the differences. Though Phanias the Lesbian affirms, that Solon, to save his country, put a trick upon both parties, and privately promised the poor a division of the lands, and the rich, security for their debts. Solon, however, himself says that it was reluctantly at first that he engaged in state affairs, being afraid of the pride of one party and the greediness of the other; he was chosen archon, however, after Philombrotus, and empowered to be an arbitrator and lawgiver; the rich consenting because he was wealthy, the poor because he was honest. There was a saying of his current before the election, that when things are *even* there never can be war, and this pleased both parties, the wealthy and the poor; the one conceiving him to mean, when all have their fair proportion; the others, when all are absolutely equal. Thus, there being great hopes on both sides, the chief men pressed Solon to take the government into his own hands, and, when he was once settled, manage the business freely and according to his pleasure; and many of the commons, perceiving it would be a difficult change to be effected by law and reason, were willing to have one wise and just man set over the affairs; and some say that Solon had this oracle from Apollo

> Take the mid-seat, and be the vessel's guide;
> Many in Athens are upon your side.

But chiefly his familiar friends chid him for [rejecting] monarchy only because of the name, as if the virtue of the ruler could not make it a lawful form; . . . yet this could not shake Solon's resolution; but, as they say, he replied to his friends, that it was true a tyranny was a very fair spot, but it had no way down from it; and in a copy of verses to Phocus he writes;

> —that I spared my land,
> And withheld from usurpation and
> from violence my hand,
> And forbore to fix a stain and a disgrace
> on my good name,
> I regret not; I believe that it will
> be my chiefest fame.

From which it is [made clear] that he was a man of great reputation before he gave his laws. The [ridicule] put upon him for refusing the power, he records in these words;

> Solon surely was a dreamer,
> and a man of simple mind;
> When the gods would give him fortune,
> he of his own will declined;
> When the net was full of fishes,
> over-heavy thinking it,
> He declined to haul it up, through
> want of heart and want of wit.
> Had but I that chance of riches and
> of kingship, for one day,
> I would give my skin for flaying,
> and my house to die away.

Thus he makes the many and the low people speak of him. Yet, though he refused the government, he was not too mild in the affair; he did not show himself mean and submissive to the powerful, nor make his laws to pleasure those that chose him. For where it was well before, he applied no remedy, nor altered any thing, for fear lest,

> Overthrowing altogether and disordering the state,

he should be too weak to new-model and recompose it to a tolerable condition; but what he thought he could effect by persuasion upon the pliable, and by force upon the stubborn, this he did, as he himself says;

> With force and justice working both in one.

And, therefore, when he was afterwards asked if he had left the Athenians the best laws that could be given, he replied, "The best they could receive." The way which, the moderns say, the Athenians have of softening the badness of a thing, b~ ingeniously giving it some pretty and innocent [name], calling harlots, for example, 'mistresses,' tributes 'customs,' a garrison 'a guard,' and the jail 'the chamber,' seems originally to have been Solon's contrivance, who called cancelling debts *Seisacthea*, a relief, or disencumbrance. For the first thing which he settled was, that what debts remained should be forgiven, and no man, for the future, should engage the body of his debtor for security. Though some, as Androtion, affirm that the debts were not cancelled, but the interest only lessened, which sufficiently pleased the people; so that they named this benefit the Seisacthea, together with the enlarging their measures, and raising the value of their money; for he made a pound, which before passed for seventy-three drachmas, go for a hundred; so that, though the number of pieces in the payment was equal, the value was less; which proved a considerable benefit to those that were to discharge great debts, and no loss to the creditors. But most agree that it was the taking off the debts that was called Seisacthea, which is confirmed by some places in his poem, where he takes honor to himself that—

> The mortgage-stones that covered her, by me
> Removed,—the land that was a slave is free;

that some who had been seized for their debts he had brought back from other countries, where—

> so far their lot to roam,
> They had forgot the language of their home;

and some he had set at liberty,

> —Who here in shameful servitude were held.

While he was designing this, a most vexatious thing happened; for when he had resolved to take off the debts, and was considering the proper form and fit beginning for it, he told some of his friends, Conon, Clinias, and Hipponicus, in whom he had a great deal of confidence, that he would not meddle with the lands, but only free the people from their debts; upon which, they, using their advantage, made haste and borrowed some considerable sums of money, and purchased some large farms; and when the law was enacted, they kept the possessions, and would not return the money; which brought Solon into great suspicion and dislike, as if he himself had not been abused, but was concerned in the contrivance. But he presently stopped this suspicion, by releasing his debtors [who owed him] five talents (for he had lent so much), according to the law. . . .

In this he pleased neither party, for the rich were angry for their money, and the poor that the land was not divided. . . .

When he had constituted the Areopagus of those who had been yearly archons, of which he himself was a member . . . observing that the people, now free from their debts, were unsettled and imperious, he formed another council of four hundred, a hundred out of each of the four tribes, which was to inspect all matters before they were propounded to the people, and to take care that nothing but what had been first examined should be brought before the general assembly. The upper council, or Areopagus, he made inspectors and keepers of the laws, conceiving that the commonwealth, held by these two councils, like anchors, would be less liable to be tossed by tumults, and the people be more at quiet. Such is the general statement, that Solon instituted the Areopagus; which seems to be confirmed, because Draco makes no mention of the Areopagites. . . .

Amongst his other laws, one is very peculiar and surprising, which disfranchises all who stand neutral in a sedition; for it seems he would not have any one remain insensible and regardless of the public good, and, securing his private affairs, glory that he has no feeling of the distempers of his country; but at once join with the good party and those that have the right upon their side, assist and venture with them, rather than keep out of harm's way and watch who would get the better. It seems an absurd and foolish law which permits an heiress, if her lawful husband fail her, to take his nearest kinsman; yet some say this law was well contrived against those, who, conscious of their own unfitness, yet, for the sake of the portion, would match with heiresses, and make use of law to put a violence upon nature; for now, since she can quit him for whom she pleases, they would either abstain from such marriages, or continue them with disgrace, and suffer for their covetousness and designed affront; it is well done, moreover, to confine her to her husband's nearest kinsman, that the children may be of the same family. Agreeable to this is the law that the bride and bridegroom shall be shut into a chamber, and eat a quince together; and that the husband of an heiress shall consort with her thrice a month; for though there be no children, yet it is an honor and due affection which a husband ought to pay to a virtuous, chaste wife; it takes off all petty differences, and will not permit their little quarrels to proceed to a rupture . . .

He is likewise much commended for his law concerning wills; for before him none could be made, but all the wealth and estate of the deceased belonged to his family; but he, by permitting them, if they had no children, to bestow it on whom they pleased, showed that he esteemed friendship a stronger tie than kindred, and affection than necessity; and made every man's estate truly his own. Yet he allowed not all sorts of legacies, but those only which were not extorted by the frenzy of a disease, charms, imprisonment, force, or the persuasions of a wife; with good reason thinking that being seduced into wrong was as bad as being forced, and that between deceit and necessity, flattery and compulsion, there was little difference, since both may equally suspend the exercise of reason.

. . . Observing the city to be filled with persons that flocked from all parts into Attica for security of living, and that most of the country was barren and unfruitful, and that traders at sea import nothing to those that could give them nothing in exchange, he turned his citizens to trade, and made a law that no son should be obliged to relieve a father who had not bred him up to any calling. It is true, Lycurgus, having a city free from all strangers, and land, according to Euripides,

Large for large hosts, for twice their number much,

and, above all, an abundance of laborers around Sparta, who should not be left idle, but be kept down with continual toil and work, did well to take off his citizens from laborious and mechanical occupations, and keep them to their arms, and teach them only the art of war. But Solon, fitting his laws to the state of things, and not making things to suit his laws, and finding the ground scarce rich enough to maintain the husbandmen, and altogether incapable of feeding an unoccupied and leisurely multitude, brought trades into credit, and ordered the Areopagites to examine how every man got his living, and chastise the idle.

Questions for Documents 3.1 and 3.2
1. What problems did both Sparta and Athens have in common?
2. Comparing the two city-states, how did the role of the family differ?
3. Why did each believe they had the better society?
4. What was Plutarch's opinion of each culture?

SECTION 2
Governing the *Polis*

Documents 3.3 and 3.4

This section examines differing principles on how one should govern the polis. On this topic, as on so many others, Plato and Aristotle (originally teacher and student) took remarkably different approaches. In these selections, the philosophers address the proper roles of men, women, and slaves in the polis. When reading these selections, it is useful to remember that women had no political role in Athens and were rarely even seen outside the family compound.

3.3. Plato: Envisioning Women's Equality in the *Polis*

Plato's account takes the form of a dialogue between Socrates and his students on what is the role of women in his ideal republic, where the guardians are to be specially chosen and educated for their roles as rulers.

> **Source:** Plato, *The Republic of Plato*, trans. Francis MacDonald Cornford, (New York: Oxford University Press, 1972), pp. 148–55.

We must go back, then, to a subject which ought, perhaps, to have been treated earlier in its proper place; though, after all, it may be suitable that the women should have their turn on the stage when the men have quite finished their performance, especially since you are so insistent. In my judgement, then, the question under what conditions people born and educated as we have described should possess wives and children, and how they should treat them, can be rightly settled only by keeping to the course on which we started them at the outset. We undertook to put these men in the position of watch-dogs guarding a flock. Suppose we follow up the analogy and imagine them bred and reared in the same sort of way. We can then see if that plan will suit our purpose.

How will that be?

In this way. Which do we think right for watch-dogs: should the females guard the flock and hunt with the males and take a share in all they do, or should they be kept within doors as fit for no more than bearing and feeding their puppies, while all the hard work of looking after the flock is left to the males?

They are expected to take their full share, except that we treat them as not quite so strong.

Can you employ any creature for the same work as another, if you do not give them both the same upbringing and education?

No.

Then, if we are to set women to the same tasks as men, we must teach them the same things. They must have the same two branches of training for mind and body and also be taught the art of war, and they must receive the same treatment.

That seems to follow.

Possibly, if these proposals were carried out, they might be ridiculed as involving a good many breaches of custom.

They might indeed.

The most ridiculous—don't you think?—being the notion of women exercising naked along with the men in the wrestling-schools; some of them elderly women too, like the old men who still have a passion for exercise when they are wrinkled and not very agreeable to look at.

Yes, that would be thought laughable, according to our present notions.

Now we have started on this subject, we must not be frightened of the many witticisms that might be aimed at such a revolution, not only in the matter of bodily exercise but in the training of women's minds, and not least when it comes to their bearing arms and riding on horseback. Having begun upon these rules, we must not draw back from the harsher provisions. The wits may be asked to stop being witty and try to be serious; and we may remind them that it is not so long since the Greeks, like most foreign nations of the present day, thought it ridiculous and shameful for men to be seen naked. When gymnastic exercises were first introduced in Crete and later at Sparta, the humorists had their chance to make fun of them; but when experience had shown that nakedness is better uncovered than muffled up, the laughter died down and a practice which the reason approved ceased to look ridiculous to the eye. This shows how idle it is to think anything ludicrous but what is base. One who tries to raise a laugh at any spectacle save that of baseness and folly will also, in his serious moments, set before himself some other standard than goodness of what deserves to be held in honour.

Most assuredly.

The first thing to be settled, then, is whether these proposals are feasible; and it must be open to anyone, whether a humorist or serious-minded, to raise the question whether, in the case of mankind, the feminine nature is capable of taking part with the other sex in all occupations, or in none at all, or in some only; and in particular under which of these heads this business of military service falls.

· · · ·

Shall we take the other side in this debate and argue against ourselves? We do not want the adversary's position to be taken by storm for lack of defenders.

I have no objection.

Let us state his case for him. 'Socrates and Glaucon,' he will say, 'there is no need for others to dispute your position; you yourselves, at the very outset of founding your commonwealth, agreed that everyone should do the one work for which nature fits him.' Yes, of course; I suppose we did. 'And isn't there a very great difference in nature between man and woman?' Yes, surely. 'Does not that natural difference imply a corresponding difference in the work to be given to each?' Yes. 'But if so, surely you must be mistaken now and contradicting yourselves when you say that men and women, having such widely divergent natures, should do the same things?' What is your answer to that, my ingenious friend?

It is not easy to find one at the moment. I can only appeal to you to state the case on our own side, whatever it may be.

This, Glaucon, is one of many alarming objections which I foresaw some time ago. That is why I shrank from touching upon these laws concerning the possession of wives and the rearing of children.

It looks like anything but an easy problem.

True, I said; but whether a man tumbles into a swimming-pool or into mid-ocean, he has to swim all the same. So must we, and try if we can reach the shore, hoping for some Arion's dolphin or other miraculous deliverance to bring us safe to land.[1]

I suppose so.

Come then, let us see if we can find the way out. We did agree that different natures should have different occupations, and that the natures of man and woman are different; and yet we are now saying that these different natures are to have the same occupations. Is that the charge against us?

Exactly.

It is extraordinary, Glaucon, what an effect the practice of debating has upon people.

Why do you say that?

Because they often seem to fall unconsciously into mere disputes which they mistake for reasonable argument, through being unable to draw the distinctions proper to their subject; and so, instead of a philosophical exchange of ideas, they go off in chase of contradictions which are purely verbal.

I know that happens to many people; but does it apply to us at this moment?

Absolutely. At least I am afraid we are slipping unconsciously into a dispute about words. We have been strenuously insisting on the letter of our principle that different natures should not have the same occupations, as if we were scoring a point in a debate; but we have altogether neglected to consider what sort of sameness or difference we meant and in what respect these natures and occupations were to be defined as different or the same. Consequently, we might very well be asking one another whether there is

not an opposition in nature between bald and long-haired men, and, when that was admitted, forbid one set to be shoemakers, if the other were following that trade.

That would be absurd.

Yes, but only because we never meant any and every sort of sameness or difference in nature, but the sort that was relevant to the occupations in question. We meant, for instance, that a man and a woman have the same nature if both have a talent for medicine; whereas two men have different natures if one is a born physician, the other a born carpenter.

Yes, of course.

If, then, we find that either the male sex or the female is specially qualified for any particular form of occupation, then that occupation, we shall say, ought to be assigned to one sex or the other. But if the only difference appears to be that the male begets and the female brings forth, we shall conclude that no difference between man and woman has yet been produced that is relevant to our purpose. We shall continue to think it proper for our Guardians and their wives to share in the same pursuits.

And quite rightly.

The next thing will be to ask our opponent to name any profession or occupation in civic life for the purposes of which woman's nature is different from man's.

That is a fair question.

He might reply, as you did just now, that it is not easy to find a satisfactory answer on the spur of the moment, but that there would be no difficulty after a little reflection.

Perhaps.

Suppose, then, we invite him to follow us and see if we can convince him that there is no occupation concerned with the management of social affairs that is peculiar to women. We will confront him with a question: When you speak of a man having a natural talent for something, do you mean that he finds it easy to learn, and after a little instruction can find out much more for himself; whereas a man who is not so gifted learns with difficulty and no amount of instruction and practice will make him even remember what he has been taught? Is the talented man one whose bodily powers are readily at the service of his mind, instead of being a hindrance? Are not these the marks by which you distinguish the presence of a natural gift for any pursuit?

Yes, precisely.

Now do you know of any human occupation in which the male sex is not superior to the female in all these respects? Need I waste time over exceptions like weaving and watching over saucepans and batches of cakes, though women are supposed to be good at such things and get laughed at when a man does them better?

It is true, he replied, in almost everything one sex is easily beaten by the other. No doubt many women are better at many things than many men; but taking the sexes as a whole, it is as you say.

To conclude, then, there is no occupation concerned with the management of social affairs which belongs

---

[1] The musician Arion, to escape the treachery of Corinthian sailors, leapt into the sea and was carried ashore at Taenarum by a dolphin, Herod. i. 24.

either to woman or to man, as such. Natural gifts are to be found here and there in both creatures alike; and every occupation is open to both, so far as their natures are concerned, though woman is for all purposes the weaker.

Certainly.

Is that a reason for making over all occupations to men only?

Of course not.

No, because one woman may have a natural gift for medicine or for music, another may not.

Surely.

Is it not also true that a woman may, or may not, be warlike or athletic?

I think so.

And again, one may love knowledge, another hate it; one may be high-spirited, another spiritless?

True again.

It follows that one woman will be fitted by nature to be a Guardian, another will not; because these were the qualities for which we selected our men Guardians. So for the purpose of keeping watch over the commonwealth, woman has the same nature as man, save in so far as she is weaker.

So it appears.

It follows that women of this type must be selected to share the life and duties of Guardians with men of the same type, since they are competent and of a like nature, and the same natures must be allowed the same pursuits.

Yes.

We come round, then, to our former position, that there is nothing contrary to nature in giving our Guardians' wives the same training for mind and body. The practice we proposed to establish was not impossible or visionary, since it was in accordance with nature. Rather, the contrary practice which now prevails turns out to be unnatural.

So it appears.

Well, we set out to inquire whether the plan we proposed was feasible and also the best. That it is feasible is now agreed; we must next settle whether it is the best.

Obviously.

Now, for the purpose of producing a woman fit to be a Guardian, we shall not have one education for men and another for women, precisely because the nature to be taken in hand is the same.

True.

What is your opinion on the question of one man being better than another? Do you think there is no such difference?

Certainly I do not.

And in this commonwealth of ours which will prove the better men—the Guardians who have received the education we described, or the shoemakers who have been trained to make shoes?[1]

It is absurd to ask such a question.

Very well. So these Guardians will be the best of all the citizens?

By far.

And these women the best of all the women?

Yes.

Can anything be better for a commonwealth than to produce in it men and women of the best possible type?

No.

And that result will be brought about by such a system of mental and bodily training as we have described?

Surely.

We may conclude that the institution we proposed was not only practicable, but also the best for the commonwealth.

Yes.

The wives of our Guardians, then, must strip for exercise, since they will be clothed with virtue, and they must take their share in war and in the other social duties of guardianship. They are to have no other occupation; and in these duties the lighter part must fall to the women, because of the weakness of their sex. The man who laughs at naked women, exercising their bodies for the best of reasons, is like one that 'gathers fruit unripe,' for he does not know what it is that he is laughing at or what he is doing. There will never be a finer saying than the one which declares that whatever does good should be held in honour, and the only shame is in doing harm.

That is perfectly true.

3.4 Aristotle: An Argument for Subordination

Aristotle explains his view of male and female principles first in a segment on fertilization and then in an excerpt on slavery.

Source: Aristotle, *De Generatione Animalium and Politics* in *Aristotle Selections*, ed. W.D. Ross, (New York: Charles Scribner's Sons, 1955), pp. 291–93.

Now semen is a secretion and is moved with the same movement as that in virtue of which the body increases (this increase being due to subdivision of the nutriment in its last stage). When it has entered the uterus it puts into form the corresponding secretion of the female and moves it with the same movement wherewith it is moved itself. For the female's contribution also is a secretion, and has all the parts in it potentially though none of them actually; it has in it potentially even those parts which differentiate the female from the male, for just as the young of mutilated parents are sometimes born mutilated and sometimes not, so also the young born of a female are sometimes female and sometimes male instead. For the female is, as it were, a mutilated male, and the catamenia are semen, only not pure; for there is only one thing they have not in them, the principle of

---

[1] The elementary education of Chap. IX will be open to all citizens, but presumably carried further (to the age of 17 or 18, see p. 259) in the case of those who show special promise.

soul. For this reason, whenever a wind-egg is produced by any animal, the egg so forming has in it the parts of both sexes potentially, but has not the principle in question, so that it does not develop into a living creature, for this is introduced by the semen of the male. When such a principle has been imparted to the secretion of the female it becomes an embryo.

. . . .

For that some should rule and others be ruled is a thing not only necessary, but expedient; from the hour of their birth, some are marked out for subjection, others for rule.

And there are many kinds both of rulers and subjects (and that rule is the better which is exercised over better subjects—for example, to rule over men is better than to rule over wild beasts; for the work is better which is executed by better workmen, and where one man rules and another is ruled, they may be said to have a work); for in all things which form a composite whole and which are made up of parts, whether continuous or discrete, a distinction between the ruling and the subject element comes to light. Such a duality exists in living creatures, but not in them only; it originates in the constitution of the universe; even in things which have no life there is a ruling principle, as in a musical mode. But we are wandering from the subject. We will therefore restrict ourselves to the living creature, which, in the first place, consists of soul and body: and of these two, the one is by nature the ruler, and the other the subject. But then we must look for the intentions of nature in things which retain their nature, and not in things which are corrupted. And therefore we must study the man who is in the most perfect state both of body and soul, for in him we shall see the true relation of the two; although in bad or corrupted natures the body will often appear to rule over the soul, because they are in an evil and unnatural condition. At all events we may firstly observe in living creatures both a despotical and a constitutional rule; for the soul rules the body with a despotical rule, whereas the intellect rules the appetites with a constitutional and royal rule. And it is clear that the rule of the soul over the body, and of the mind and the rational element over the passionate, is natural and expedient; whereas the equality of the two or the rule of the inferior is always hurtful. The same holds good of animals in relation to men; for tame animals have a better nature than wild, and all tame animals are better off when they are ruled by man; for then they are preserved. Again, the male is by nature superior, and the female inferior; and the one rules, and the other is ruled; this principle, of necessity, extends to all mankind.

Where then there is such a difference as that between soul and body, or between men and animals (as in the case of those whose business is to use their body, and who can do nothing better), the lower sort are by nature slaves, and it is better for them as for all inferiors that they should be under the rule of a master. For he who can be, and therefore is, another's, and he who participates in rational principle enough to apprehend, but not to have, such a principle, is a slave by nature. Whereas the lower animals cannot even apprehend a principle; they obey their instincts. And indeed the use made of slaves and of tame animals is not very different; for both with their bodies minister to the needs of life. Nature would like to distinguish between the bodies of freemen and slaves, making the one strong for servile labour, the other upright, and although useless for such services, useful for political life in the arts both of war and peace. But the opposite often happens—that some have the souls and others have the bodies of freemen. And doubtless if men differed from one another in the mere forms of their bodies as much as the statues of the Gods do from men, all would acknowledge that the inferior class should be slaves of the superior. And if this is true of the body, how much more just that a similar distinction should exist in the soul? but the beauty of the body is seen, whereas the beauty of the soul is not seen. It is clear, then, that some men are by nature free, and others slaves, and that for these latter slavery is both expedient and right.

Questions for Documents 3.3 and 3.4

1. Compare and contrast Plato's and Aristotle's views on what is the nature of men and women.
2. What consequences do these perspectives have, according to Plato and Aristotle, and in your own thinking?
3. What is Aristotle's view of slavery?
4. How does Aristotle link slavery and the question of gender (male/female) difference?
5. What do you think of Plato's and Aristotle's views on these topics?

SECTION 3
Life in the *Polis*

Documents 3.5–3.8

Studying the writings and lives of great political leaders or philosophers does not necessarily reveal how the rest of the people lived in the society. The following selections not only describe the laws and customs affecting women, children and slaves in Greek society, but show how they actually fared at the hands of the law and society.

3.5   Aristotle's Will

The great fourth-century Athenian philosopher Aristotle left this will when he died in 322 B.C.E.

Source: Diogenes Laertius, *Lives of Eminent Philosophers*, trans. R.D. Hicks, Vol. 1. (Cambridge, MA: Harvard University Press, 1959), pp. 455–59.

"All will be well; but, in case anything should happen, Aristotle has made these dispositions. Antipater is to be executor in all matters and in general; but, until Nicanor shall arrive, Aristomenes, Timarchus, Hipparchus, Dioteles and (if he consent and if circumstances permit him) Theophrastus shall take charge as well of Herphyllis and the children as of the property. And when the girl shall be grown up she shall be given in marriage to Nicanor; but if anything happen to the girl (which heaven forbid and no such thing will happen) before her marriage, or when she is married but before there are children, Nicanor shall have full powers, both with regard to the child and with regard to everything else, to administer in a manner worthy both of himself and of us. Nicanor shall take charge of the girl and of the boy Nicomachus as he shall think fit in all that concerns them as if he were father and brother. And if anything should happen to Nicanor (which heaven forbid!) either before he marries the girl, or when he has married her but before there are children, any arrangements that he may make shall be valid. And if Theophrastus is willing to live with her, <he shall have> the same rights as Nicanor. Otherwise the executors in consultation with Antipater shall administer as regards the daughter and the boy as seems to them to be best. The executors and Nicanor, in memory of me and of the steady affection which Herpyllis has borne towards me, shall take care of her in every other respect and, if she desires to be married, shall see that she be given to one not unworthy; and besides what she has already received they shall give her a talent of silver out of the estate and three handmaids whomsoever she shall choose besides the maid she has at present and the man-servant Pyrrhaeus; and if she chooses to remain at Chalcis, the lodge by the garden, if in Stagira, my father's house. Whichever of these two houses she chooses, the executors shall furnish with such furniture as they think proper and as Herpyllis herself may approve. Nicanor shall take charge of the boy Myrmex, that he be taken to his own friends in a manner worthy of me with the property of his which we received. Ambracis shall be given her freedom, and on my daughter's marriage shall receive 500 drachmas and the maid whom she now has. And to Thale shall be given, in addition to the maid whom she has and who was bought, a thousand drachmas and a maid. And Simon, in addition to the money before paid to him towards another servant, shall either have a servant purchased for him or receive a further sum of money. And Tycho, Philo, Olympius and his child shall have their freedom when my daughter is married. None of the servants who waited upon me shall be sold but they shall continue to be employed; and when they arrive at the proper age they shall have their freedom if they deserve it. My executors shall see to it, when the images which Gryllion has been commissioned to execute are finished, that they be set up, namely that of Nicanor, that of Proxenus, which it was my intention to have executed, and that of Nicanor's mother; also they shall set up the bust which has been executed of Arimnestus, to be a memorial of him seeing that he died childless, and shall dedicate my mother's statue to Demeter at Nemea or wherever they think best. And wherever they bury me, there the bones of Pythias shall be laid, in accordance with her own instructions. And to commemorate Nicanor's safe return, as I vowed on his behalf, they shall set up in Stagira stone statues of life size to Zeus and Athena the Saviours."

Such is the tenor of Aristotle's will. It is said that a very large number of dishes belonging to him were found, and that Lyco mentioned his bathing in a bath of warm oil and then selling the oil. Some relate that he placed a skin of warm oil on his stomach, and that, when he went to sleep, a bronze ball was placed in his hand with a vessel under it, in order that, when the ball dropped form his hand into the vessel, he might be waked up by the sound.

3.6   Laws Relating to Women: Excerpts from the Gortyn Law Code

These laws that date from the fifth century B.C.E. provide the women of Gortyn in Crete with more independent legal rights in property and marriage than Athenian women enjoyed.

Source: *Women's Life in Greece and Rome. A Source Book in Translation*, ed. Mary R. Lefkowitz and Maureen B. Fant. 2nd ed., (Baltimore: Johns Hopkins University Press, 1992). This selection was found at their internet site: [http://www.uky.edu/ArtsSciences/Classics/wlgr/wlgr-greeklegal76.html]

SEXUAL OFFENCES

If a person rapes a free person, male or female, he shall pay 100 staters, and if [the victim] is from the house of an *apetarios*,[1] 10 staters; and if a slave rapes a free person, male or female, he shall pay double. If a free man rapes a serf, male or female, he shall pay 5 drachmas. If a male serf rapes a serf, male or female, he shall pay five staters.

If a person deflowers a female household serf, he shall pay 2 staters. If she has already been deflowered, 1 obol if in day-time, 2 obols if at night. The female slave's oath takes precedence.[2]

If anyone makes an attempt to rape a free woman under the guardianship of a relative, he shall pay 10 staters, if a witness testifies.

If someone is taken in adultery with a free woman in her father's house, or her brother's or her husband's, he is to pay 10 staters; if in another man's house, 50 staters; if with the wife of an apetairos, 10 staters. But if a slave is taken in adultery with a free woman, he must pay double. If a slave is taken in adultery with a slave, 5 staters.

DISPOSITION OF PROPERTY IN DIVORCE

If a husband and wife divorce, she is to keep her property, whatever she brought to the marriage, and one-half the produce (if there is any) from her own property, and half of whatever she has woven within the house; also she is to have 5 staters if her husband is the cause of the divorce. If the husband swears that he is not the cause of the divorce, the judge is to take an oath and decide. If the wife carries away anything else belonging to the husband, she must pay 5 staters and whatever she carries away from him, and whatever she has stolen she must return to him. About what she denies [having taken], the judge is to order that she must swear by Artemis before the statue of [Artemis] Archeress in the Amyclean temple. If anyone takes anything from her after she has made her denial, he is to pay 5 staters and return the thing itself. If a stranger helps her to carry anything away, he must pay 10 staters and double the amount of whatever the judge swears that he helped her to take away.

WIDOWHOOD

If a man dies and leaves children behind, if the wife wishes, she may marry, keeping her own property and whatever her husband gave her according to an agreement written in the presence of three adult free witnesses. If she should take anything away that belongs to her children, that is grounds for a trial. If the husband leaves her without issue, she is to have her own property and half of whatever she has woven within the house, and she is to get her portion of the produce in the house along with the lawful heirs, and whatever her husband may have given her according to written agreement. But if she should take away anything else, it is grounds for a trial.

If a woman dies without issue the husband is to give her property back to her lawful heirs and half of what she has woven within and half of the produce if it comes from her property. If the husband or wife wishes to pay for its transport, it is to be in clothing or twelve staters or something worth 12 staters, but not more.

If a female serf is separated from a male serf while he is alive or if he dies, she is to keep what she has. If she takes anything else away, it is grounds for a trial.

PROVISIONS FOR CHILDREN IN CASE OF DEATH OR DIVORCE

If a wife who is separated from her husband should bear a child, it is to be brought to the husband in his house in the presence of three witnesses. If he does not receive it, it is up to the mother to raise or expose the child. The oath of relatives and witnesses is to have preference, if they brought it.

If a female serf should bear a child while separated [from her husband], she is to bring it to the master of the man who married her, in the presence of two witnesses. If he does not receive the child, it is to belong to the master of the female serf, but if she marries the same man again before the end of the year, the child shall belong to the master of the male serf. The oaths of person who brought the child and of the witnesses shall have preference.

If a divorced woman should expose her child before presenting it according to the law, she shall pay 50 staters for a free child, and 5 for a slave, if she is convicted. If the man to whom she brings the child has no house, or she does not see him, she shall not pay a penalty if she exposes the child.

If a female serf who is not married conceives and bears a child, the child shall belong to the master of her father. If the father is not alive then to the masters of her brothers.

The father has power over the children and division of property, and the mother over her own possessions. So long as [the father and mother] are alive, the property is not to be divided. But if one of them is fined, the person who is fined shall have his share reduced proportionately according to the law.

If a father dies, the city dwellings and whatever is inside the houses in which a serf who lives in the country does not reside, and the cattle which do not belong to a serf, shall belong to the sons. The other possessions shall be divided fairly, and the sons shall each get two parts, however many they are, and the daughters each get one part, however many they are.

The mother's property shall also be divided if she dies, in the same way as prescribed for the father's. But if there is no property other than the house, the daughters shall

---

[1] A free man, but not a citizen, perhaps roughly equivalent in status to the Attic *metoikos*, 'resident alien,' who had more rights than a slave but fewer than a citizen.

[2] Here and elsewhere in the Code, if oaths are sworn by both sides, the oath that has precedence wins by default; presumably, the oath was not merely an asseveration that one is telling the truth, but a solemn demand that the gods punish the swearer for lying.

receive their share as prescribed. If the father during his lifetime should give to a married daughter, let him give her share as prescribed, but not more. The daughter to whom he gave or promised her share shall have it, but no additional possessions from her father's property.

If any woman does not have property either from a gift by her father or brother or from a pledge or from an inheritance given when the Aithalian clan consisting of Cyllus and his colleagues [where in power], these women are to have a portion, but it will not be lawful to take away gifts given previously.

If a mother dies leaving children, the father has power over the mother's estate, but he should not sell or mortage it, unless the children are of age and give their consent. If he marries another wife, the children are to have power over their mother's estate.

DETERMINATION OF SOCIAL STATUS

If a slave goes to a free woman and marries her, the children shall be free. If a free woman goes to a slave, the children shall be slaves.

HEIRESSES[3]

The heiress is to marry the oldest of her father's living brothers. If her father has no living brothers but there are sons of the brothers, she is to marry the oldest brother's son. If there are more heiresses and sons of brothers, the [additional heiress] is to marry the next son after the son of the oldest. The groom-elect is to have one heiress, and not more.

If the heiress is too young to marry, she is to have the house, if there is one, and the groom-elect is to have half of the revenue from everything.

If he does not wish to marry her as prescribed by law, the heiress is to take all the property and marry the next one in succession, if there is one. If there is no one, she may marry whomever she wishes to of those who ask her from the same phratry.[4] If the heiress is of age and does not wish to marry the intended bridgeroom, or the intended groom is too young and the heiress is unwilling to wait, she is to have the house, if there is one in the city, and whatever is in the house, and taking half of the remaining property she is to marry another of those from the phratry who ask her, but she is to give a share of the property to the groom [whom she rejected].

If there are no kinsmen as defined for the heiress, she is to take all the property and marry from the phratry whomever she wishes.

If no one from the phratry wishes to marry her, her relations should announce to the tribe 'does anyone want to marry her?' If someone wants to, it should be within thirty days of the announcement. If not, she is free to marry another man, whomever she can.

---

[3] Special provisions were made for daughters when no brothers were available to inherit.

[4] The father's kinship group, sometimes translated 'tribe' or 'clan.'

RESTRICTIONS CONCERNING ADOPTION

A woman is not to adopt [a child] nor a man under age.

3.7 On the Murder of Eratosthenes: A Husband's Defense

This is a transcript of a trial before the citizen's assembly at Athens around 400 B.C.E. Euphiletus defends himself on a charge of murdering Eratosthenes, his wife's lover.

Source: W.R.M. Lamb, trans., Lysias, (Cambridge: Harvard University Press, 1960), pp. 5–21, 27.

. . . When I, Athenians, decided to marry, and brought a wife into my house, for some time I was disposed neither to vex her nor to leave her too free to do just as she pleased; I kept a watch on her as far as possible, with such observation of her as was reasonable. But when a child was born to me, thence-forward I began to trust her, and placed all my affairs in her hands, presuming that we were now in perfect intimacy. It is true that in the early days, Athenians, she was the most excellent of wives; she was a clever, frugal housekeeper, and kept everything in the nicest order. But as soon as I lost my mother, her death became the cause of all my troubles. For it was in attending her funeral that my wife was seen by this man [Eratosthenes], who in time corrupted her. He looked out for the servant-girl who went to market, and so paid addresses to her mistress by which he wrought her ruin.

Now in the first place I must tell you, sirs (for I am obliged to give you these particulars), my dwelling is on two floors, the upper being equal in space to the lower, with the women's quarters above and the men's below. When the child was born to us, its mother suckled it; and in order that, each time that it had to be washed, she might avoid the risk of descending by the stairs, I used to live above, and the women below. By this time it had become such an habitual thing that my wife would often leave me and go down to sleep with the child, so as to be able to give it the breast and stop its crying. Things went on in this way for a long time, and I never suspected, but was simple-minded enough to suppose that my own was the chastest wife in the city.

Time went on, sirs; I came home unexpectedly from the country, and after dinner the child started crying in a peevish way, as the servant-girl was annoying it on purpose to make it so behave; for the man was in the house,—I learnt it all later. So I bade my wife go and give the child her breast, to stop its howling. At first she refused, as though delighted to see me home again after so long; but when I began to be angry and bade her go,

"Yes, so that you," she said, "may have a try here at the little maid. Once before, too, when you were drunk, you pulled her about." At that I laughed, while she got up, went out of the room, and closed the door, feigning to make fun, and she turned the key in the lock. I, without giving a thought to the matter, or having any suspicion, went to sleep in all content after my return from the country.

Towards daytime she came and opened the door. I asked why the doors made a noise in the night; she told me that the child's lamp had gone out, and she had lit it again at our neighbour's. I was silent and believed it was so. But it struck me, sirs, that she had powdered her face, though her brother had died not thirty days before; even so, however, I made no remark on the fact, but left the house in silence.

After this, sirs, an interval occurred in which I was left quite unaware of my own injuries; I was then accosted by a certain old female, who was secretly sent by a woman with whom that man was having an intrigue, as I heard later. This woman was angry with him and felt herself wronged, because he no longer visited her so regularly, and she kept a close watch on him until she discovered what was the cause. So the old creature accosted me where she was on the look-out, near my house, and said, "Euphiletus, do not think it is from any meddlesomeness that I have approached you; for the man who is working both your and your wife's dishonour happens to be our enemy. If, therefore, you take the servant-girl who goes to market and waits on you, and torture her, you will learn all. It is," she said, "Eratosthenes of Oë who is doing this; he has debauched not only your wife, but many others besides; he makes an art of it."

With these words, sirs, she took herself off; I was at once perturbed; all that had happened came into my mind, and I was filled with suspicion,—reflecting first how I was shut up in my chamber, and then remembering how on that night the inner and outer doors made a noise, which had never occurred before, and how it struck me that my wife had put on powder. All these things came into my mind, and I was filled with suspicion. Returning home, I bade the servant-girl follow me to the market, and taking her to the house of an intimate friend, I told her I was fully informed of what was going on in my house.

"So it is open to you," I said, "to choose as you please between two things,—either to be whipped and thrown into a mill, never to have any rest from miseries of that sort, or else to speak out the whole truth and, instead of suffering any harm, obtain my pardon for your transgressions. Tell no lies, but speak the whole truth."

The girl at first denied it, and bade me do what I pleased, for she knew nothing; but when I mentioned Eratosthenes to her, and said that he was the man who visited my wife, she was dismayed, supposing that I had exact knowledge of everything. At once she threw herself down at my knees, and having got my pledge that she should suffer no harm, she accused him, first, of approaching her after the funeral, and then told how at last she became his messenger; how my wife in time was persuaded, and by what means she procured his entrances, and how at the Thesmophoria,[1]

while I was in the country, she went off to the temple with his mother. And the girl gave an exact account of everything else that had occurred.

When her tale was all told, I said, "Well now, see that nobody in the world gets knowledge of this; otherwise, nothing in your arrangement with me will hold good. And I require that you show me their guilt in the very act; I want no words, but manifestation of the fact, if it really is so."

She agreed to do this. Then came an interval of four or five days. . .[2]. But first I wish to relate what took place on the last day. I had an intimate friend named Sostratus. After sunset I met him as he came from the country. As I knew that, arriving at that hour, he would find none of his circle at home, I invited him to dine with me ; we came to my house, mounted to the upper room, and had dinner. When he had made a good meal, he left me and departed ; then I went to bed. Eratosthenes, sirs, entered, and the maidservant roused me at once, and told me that he was in the house. Bidding her look after the door, I descended and went out in silence; I called on one friend and another, and found some of them at home, while others were out of town. I took with me as many as I could among those who were there, and so came along. Then we got torches from the nearest shop, and went in; the door was open, as the girl had it in readiness.

We pushed open the door of the bedroom, and the first of us to enter were in time to see him lying down by my wife; those who followed saw him standing naked on the bed. I gave him a blow, sirs, which knocked him down, and pulling round his two hands behind his back, and tying them, I asked him why he had the insolence to enter my house. He admitted his guilt; then he besought and implored me not to kill him, but to exact a sum of money.

To this I replied, "It is not I who am going to kill you, but our city's law, which you have transgressed and regarded as of less account than your pleasures, choosing rather to commit this foul offence against my wife and my children than to obey the laws like a decent person."

Thus it was, sirs, that this man incurred the fate that the laws ordain for those who do such things; he had not been dragged in there from the street, nor had he taken refuge at my hearth, as these people say.[3] For how could it be so, when it was in the bedroom that he was struck and fell down then and there, and I pinioned his arms, and so many persons were in the house that he could not escape them, as he had neither steel nor wood nor anything else with which he might have beaten off those who had entered? But, sirs, I think you know as well as I that those whose acts are against justice do not acknowledge that their enemies speak the truth, but lie themselves and use other such devices to foment anger in their hearers against those whose acts are just. So, first read the law.

He did not dispute it, sirs: he acknowledged his guilt, and besought and implored that he might not be killed,

---

[1] A festival in honour of Demeter, celebrated by Athenian matrons in October

[2] Some words are missing here in the text.

[3] Witnesses for the prosecution. To kill someone on the hearth, the center of the family religion, would be sacrilege.

and was ready to pay compensation in money. But I would not agree to his estimate, as I held that our city's law should have higher authority; and I obtained that satisfaction which you deemed most just when you imposed it on those who adopt such courses. Now, let my witnesses come forward in support of these statements.

• • • •

[Witnesses are called and heard supporting his statements.]

I therefore, sirs, do not regard this requital as having been exacted in my own private interest, but in that of the whole city. For those who behave in that way, when they see the sort of prizes offered for such transgressions, will be less inclined to trespass against their neighbours, if they see that you also take the same view. Otherwise it were better far to erase our established laws, and ordain others which will inflict the penalties on men who keep watch on their own wives, and will allow full immunity to those who would debauch them. This would be a far juster way than to let the citizens be entrapped by the laws; these may bid a man, on catching an adulterer, to deal with him in whatever way he pleases, but the trials are found to be more dangerous to the wronged parties than to those who, in defiance of the laws, dishonour the wives of others. For I am now risking the loss of life, property and all else that I have, because I obeyed the city's laws.

3.8   Education and the Family in Sparta

By the fifth century B.C.E. in Athens, young men of respectable family were educated at schools and by tutors to be good citizens and daughters were rarely educated beyond their domestic duties in the household. All children's lives and their educations remained under the control of their fathers. Sparta developed an entirely different system for raising their next generation of citizens.

Source: *Plutarch's Lives*, trans. John Dryden, revised by A.H. Clough, Vol. 1. (New York: Little, Brown and Company, 1909), pp. 100–119.

In order to the good education of their youth (which, as I said before, he thought the most important and noblest work of a lawgiver), [Lycurgus] went so far back as to take into consideration their very conception and birth, by regulating their marriages. For Aristotle is wrong in saying, that, after he had tried all ways to reduce the women to more modesty and sobriety, he was at last forced to leave them as they were, because that, in the absence of their husbands, who spent the best part of their lives in the wars, their wives, whom they were obliged to leave absolute mistresses at home, took great liberties and assumed the superiority; and were treated with overmuch respect and called by the title of lady or queen. The truth is, he took in their case, also, all the care that was possible; he ordered the maidens to exercise themselves with wrestling, running, throwing the quoit, and casting the dart, to the end that the fruit they conceived might, in strong and healthy bodies, take firmer root and find better growth, and withal that they, with this greater vigor, might be the more able to undergo the pains of child-bearing. And to the end he might take away their over-great tenderness and fear of exposure to the air, and all acquired womanishness, he ordered that the young women should go naked in the processions, as well as the young men, and dance, too, in that condition, at certain solemn feasts, singing certain songs, whilst the young men stood around, seeing and hearing them. On these occasions, they now and then made, by jests, a befitting reflection upon those who had misbehaved themselves in the wars; and again sang encomiums upon those who had done any gallant action, and by these means inspired the younger sort with an emulation of their glory. Those that were thus commended went away proud, elated, and gratified with their honor among the maidens; and those who were rallied were as sensibly touched with it 'As if they had been formally reprimanded; and so much the more, because the kings and the elders, as well as the rest of the city, saw and heard all that passed. Nor was there any thing shameful in this nakedness of the young women; modesty attended them, and all wantonness was excluded. It taught them simplicity and a care for good health, and gave them some taste of higher feelings, admitted as they thus were to the field of noble action and glory. Hence it was natural for them to think and speak as Gorgo, for example, the wife of Leonidas, is said to have done, when -some foreign lady, as it would seem, told her that the women of Lacedæmon were the only women of the world who could rule men; "With good reason," she said, "for we are the only women who bring forth men."

These public processions of the maidens, and their appearing naked in their exercises and dancings, were incitements to marriage, operating upon the young with the rigor and certainty, as Plato says, of love, if not of mathematics. But besides all this, to promote it yet more effectually, those who continued bachelors were in a degree disfranchised by law; for they were excluded from the sight of those public processions in which the young men and maidens danced naked, and, in wintertime, the officers compelled them to march naked themselves round the market-place, singing as they went a certain song to their own disgrace, that they justly suffered this punishment for disobeying the laws. Moreover, they were denied that respect and observance which the younger men paid their elders; and no man, for example, found fault with what was said to Dercyllidas, though so eminent a commander; upon whose approach one day, a young man, instead of rising, retained his seat, remarking, "No child of yours will make room for me."

In their marriages, the husband carried off his bride by a sort of force; nor were their brides ever small and of tender years, but in their full bloom and ripeness. After this, she who superintended the wedding comes and clips the hair of the bride close round her head, dresses her up in man's clothes, and leaves her upon a mattress in the dark; afterwards comes the bridegroom, in his every-day clothes, sober and composed, as having supped at the common table, and, entering privately into the room where the bride lies, unties her virgin zone, and takes her to himself; and, after staying some time together, he returns composedly to his own apartment, to sleep as usual with the other young men. And so he continues to do, spending his days, and, indeed, his nights with them, visiting his bride in fear and shame, and with circumspection, when he thought he should not be observed; she, also, on her part, using her wit to help and find favorable opportunities for their meeting, when company was out of the way. In this manner they lived a long time, insomuch that they sometimes had children by their wives before ever they saw their faces by daylight. Their interviews, being thus difficult and rare, served not only for continual exercise of their self-control, but brought them together with their bodies healthy and vigorous, and their affections fresh and lively, unsated and undulled by easy access and long continuance with each other; while their partings were always early enough to leave behind unextinguished in each of them some remainder fire of longing and mutual delight. After guarding marriage with this modesty and reserve, he was equally careful to banish empty and womanish jealousy. For this object, excluding all licentious disorders, he made it, nevertheless, honorable for men to give the use of their wives to those whom they should think fit, that so they might have children by them; ridiculing those in whose opinion such favors are so unfit for participation as to fight and shed blood and go to war about it. Lycurgus allowed a man who was advanced in years and had a young wife to recommend some virtuous and approved young man, that she might have a child by him, who might inherit the good qualities of the father, and be a son to himself. On the other side, an honest man who had love for a married woman upon account of her modesty and the wellfavoredness of her children, might, without formality, beg her company of her husband, that he might raise, as it were, from this plot of good ground, worthy and well-allied children for himself. And, indeed, Lycurgus was of a persuasion that children were not so much the property of their parents as of the whole commonwealth, and, therefore, would not have his citizens begot by the first comers, but by the best men that could be found; the laws of other nations seemed to him very absurd and inconsistent, where people would be so solicitous for their dogs and horses as to exert interest and pay money to procure fine breeding, and yet kept their wives shut up, to be made mothers only by themselves, who might be foolish, infirm, or diseased; as if it were not apparent that children of a bad breed would prove their bad qualities first upon those who kept and were rearing them, and well-born children, in like manner, their good qualities.

. . . Nor was it in the power of the father to dispose of the child as he thought fit; he was obliged to carry it before certain triers at a place called Lesche ; these were some of the elders of the tribe to which the child belonged; their business it was carefully to view the infant, and, if they found it stout and well made, they gave order for its rearing, and allotted to it one of the nine thousand shares of land above mentioned for its maintenance, but, if they found it puny and ill-shaped, ordered it to be taken to what was called the Apothetæ, a sort of chasm under Taygetus; as thinking it neither for the good of the child itself; nor for the public interest, that it should be brought up, if it did not, from the very outset, appear made to be healthy and vigorous. Upon the same account, the women did not bathe the new-born children with water, as is the custom in all other countries, but with wine, to prove the temper and complexion of their bodies; from a notion they had that epileptic and weakly children faint and waste away upon their being thus bathed, while, on the contrary, those of strong and vigorous habit acquire firmness and get a temper by it, like steel. There was much care and art, too, used by the nurses; they had no swaddling bands; the children grew up free and unconstrained in limb and form, and not dainty and fanciful about their food; not afraid in the dark, or of being left alone; without any peevishness or ill humor or crying. . . .

. . . Nor was it lawful, indeed, for the father himself to breed up the children after his own fancy; but as soon as they were seven years old they were to be enrolled in certain companies and classes, where they all lived under the same order and discipline, doing their exercises and taking their play together. Of these, he who showed the most conduct and courage was made captain; they had their eyes always upon him, obeyed his orders, and underwent patiently whatsoever punishment he inflicted; so that the whole course of their education was one continued exercise of a ready and perfect obedience. The old men, too, were spectators of their performances, and often raised quarrels and disputes among them, to have a good opportunity of finding out their different characters, and of seeing which would be valiant, which a coward, when they should come to more dangerous encounters. Reading and writing they gave them, just enough to serve their turn; their chief care was to make them good subjects, and to teach them to endure pain and conquer in battle. To this end, as they grew in years, their discipline was proportionally increased; their heads were close-clipped, they were accustomed to go bare-foot, and for the most part to play naked.

After they were twelve years old, they were no longer allowed to wear any under-garment; they had one coat to serve them a year; their bodies were hard and dry, with but little acquaintance of baths and unguents; these human indulgences they were allowed only on some few particular days in the year. They lodged together in little bands upon beds made of the rushes which grew by the banks of the river Eurotas, which they were to break off with their hands without a knife; if it were winter, they mingled some thistle-down with their rushes, which it was thought had the property of giving warmth. By the time they were come to this age, there was not any of the more hopeful boys who had not a lover to bear him company. The old men, too, had an eye upon them, coming often to the grounds to hear and see them contend either in wit or strength with one another, and this as seriously and with as much concern as if they were their fathers, their tutors, or their magistrates; so that there scarcely was any time or place without some one present to put them in mind of their duty, and punish them if they had neglected it.

Besides all this, there was always one of the best and honestest men in the city appointed to undertake the charge and governance of them; he again arranged them into their several bands, and set over each of them for their captain the most temperate and boldest of those . . . who were usually twenty years old. . . . This young man, therefore, was their captain when they fought, and their master at home, using them for the offices of his house; sending the oldest of them to fetch wood, and the weaker and less able, to gather salads and herbs, and these they must either go without or steal; which they did by creeping into the gardens, or conveying themselves cunningly and closely into the eating-houses; if they were taken in the fact, they were whipped without mercy, for thieving so ill and awkwardly. They stole, too, all other meat they could lay their hands on, looking out and watching all opportunities, when people were asleep or more careless than usual. If they were caught, they were not only punished with whipping, but hunger, too, being reduced to their ordinary allowance, which was but very slender, and so contrived on purpose, that they might set about to help themselves, and be forced to exercise their energy and address. This was the principal design of their hard fare; there was another not inconsiderable, that they might grow taller; for the vital spirits, not being overburdened and oppressed by too great a quantity of nourishment, which necessarily discharges itself into thickness and breadth, do, by their natural lightness, rise; and the body, giving and yielding because it is pliant, grows in height. The same thing seems, also, to conduce to beauty of shape; . . .

They taught them, also, to speak with a natural and graceful raillery, and to comprehend much matter of thought in few words. For Lycurgus, who ordered, as we saw, that a great piece of money should be but of an inconsiderable value, on the contrary would allow no discourse to be current which did not contain in few words a great deal of useful and curious sense; children in Sparta, by a habit of long silence, came to give just and sententious answers; for, indeed, as loose and incontinent livers are seldom fathers of many children, so loose and incontinent talkers seldom originate many sensible words. King Agis, when some Athenian laughed at their short swords, and said that the jugglers on the stage swallowed them with ease, answered him, "We find them long enough to reach our enemies with;" and as their swords were short and sharp, so, it seems to me, were their sayings. . . .

. . . Nor was their instruction in music and verse less carefully attended to than their habits of grace and good breeding in conversation. And their very songs had a life and spirit in them that inflamed and possessed men's minds with an enthusiasm and ardor for action; the style of them

was plain and without affectation; the subject always serious and moral; most usually, it was in praise of such men as had died in defence of their country, or in derision of those that had been cowards; the former they declared happy and glorified; the life of the latter they described as most miserable and abject. There were also vaunts of what they would do and boasts of what they had done. . .

Their discipline continued still after they were fullgrown men. No one was allowed to live after his own fancy; but the city was a sort of camp, in which every man had his share of provisions and business set out, and looked upon himself not so much born to serve his own ends as the interest of his country. Therefore, if they were commanded nothing else, they went to see the boys perform their exercises, to teach them something useful, or to learn it themselves of those who knew better. And, indeed, one of the greatest and highest blessings Lycurgus procured his people was the abundance of leisure, which proceeded from his forbidding to them the exercise of any mean and mechanical trade. Of the money-making that depends on troublesome going about and seeing people and doing business, they had no need at all in a state where wealth obtained no honor or respect. The Helots tilled their ground for them, and paid them yearly in kind the appointed quantity, without any trouble of theirs. . . . So much beneath them did they esteem the frivolous devotion of time and attention to the mechanical arts and to money-making.

. . . To conclude, he bred up his citizens in such a way that they neither would nor could live by themselves; they were to make themselves one with the public good, and, clustering like bees around their commander, be by their zeal and public spirit carried all but out of themselves, and devoted wholly to their country. . . .

He filled Lacedæmon all through with roofs and examples of good conduct; with the constant sight of which from their youth up, the people would hardly fail to be gradually formed and advanced in virtue.

And this was the reason why he forbade them to travel abroad, and go about acquainting themselves with foreign rules of morality, the habits of ill-educated people, and different views of government. . . . He was as careful to save his city from the infection of foreign bad habits, as men usually are to prevent the introduction of a pestilence.

Questions for Documents 3.5 to 3.8
1. What rights did husbands and fathers have over their families in Athens, Crete, and Sparta?
2. How do these documents illustrate the difference in the lives of women and the institution of marriage in these Greek city-states?
3. What do these documents reveal about the lives of servants or slaves in these societies?
4. Compare Athenian and Spartan society. Which appears to be the most successful society? Why?

CHAPTER 4
School of Hellas
Poetry, Ideas, and the Arts
in Ancient Greece
(800–300 B.C.E.)

SECTION 1
Development in Literature

Documents 4.1 and 4.2

Poetry flourished and was valued by the Greeks. In the centuries following the composition of the lengthy heroic epics of Homer, poets like Sappho turned from glorifying mighty deeds to the expression of individual experience. Great deeds were still praised, however, but in odes, celebrating the accomplishements of Olympic athletes.

4.1 Poetry: Sappho

Sappho, believed to have been born about 612 B.C.E., wrote exquisite poetry praised throughout the ages for its perfection. Mother, wife, poet, dancer, teacher, Sappho's character has long been a subject for debate. In her sixth century B.C.E. society, respectable women attended school and enjoyed far more freedoms than their nearly cloistered fifth century Athenian sisters.

Source: Sappho, *Poems: Containing nearly all the Fragments printed from the restored Greek texts*, trans. P. Maurice Hill, (London: Staples, 1953), pp. 9, 19, 25, 43, 55, 63.

24 REVERENCE FOR BEAUTY

For when I look upon you face to face, then I see in you
such beauty as not even Hermione possessed,
but I compare you with auburn-haired Helen,
rather than with mortal maids—though even
that is only a guess.

But understand this, that I am so struck with
your beauty that I can only render honour to it with the
sacrifice of my mind, and reverence you with my desire
for your company.

77 SOCIAL CLIMBING (A LETTER TO HER BROTHER, CHARAXOS)

If you crawl round the feet of the great instead of the beautiful and the good, and bid your friends farewell, and in the swollen pride of your heart say that I have become a dis-

grace to you—with such things you can flatter your heart. Feed your fill! For my mind is not so softly moved by the petulance of a child! But make no mistake. The snare never catches the old bird. I have put two and two together and know well the depth of your former villainy, and what sort of enemy I am up against. So turn your mind to better thoughts.

For, assuredly, I know that having been brought up to be kindly of heart, I have the Blessed Ones on my side.

35 TO HER PUPILS

You slight the fair gifts of the
deep-bosomed Muses, children,
when you say 'We will crown
you, dear [Sappho], as first of
singers with the clear sweet
voice'.

Do you not realise that age has
wrinkled all my skin, that my
hair has become white from
being black, and that I have
hardly any teeth left; or that my
knees can no longer carry my body back
again to the old days when
I joined in the dance, like
the fawns, the nimblest
of living things?

But what can I do? Not even
God himself can do what
cannot be done. And, for us, as
unfailingly as starry
night follows rosy-armed
morning, and brings darkness to the
furthest ends of the earth, so
death tracks down and
overtakes every living thing;
and as he himself would not
give Orpheus his dearest wife,
so is he ever used to keep

prisoner every woman whom
he overtakes, even if he should
make her follow her spouse with
his singing and piping.

But listen now—I love
delicate living, and for me
brightness and beauty and a longing
for the sunlight have been
given me as a protection.
And, therefore, I have no
intention of departing to the
Grace of God before I need,
but will lovingly pursue my
life with you who love me.

And now this is enough
for me that I have your
love, and I desire no more.

51 THE APPLE

As the sweet apple reddens on
the top of the bough,
On the very topmost twig,
Which the apple-pickers had forgotten—
No, not forgotten, but
they could not reach it!

52 THE BLUEBELLS

As on the slopes, shepherd-men
trampled the bluebells underfoot,
and the flowers stain the earth with
colour.

60 THE GIRDLE

She wore an embroidered leather
girdle, the ends of which reached
down to her feet, a beautiful
piece of Lydian workmanship.

61 LOVE-SICKNESS

Sweet Mother, I cannot play the loom,
For I am overcome by my desire for a boy;
And all the fault of tender Aphrodite!

62 SELF RESTRAINT

When anger spread through your
breast, guard your tongue
from nagging.

65 THE FISHERMAN

On the grave of Pelagon, the
fisherman, his father Meniscos placed
a net and oar—witnesses to his life
of toil.

66 EPITAPH

Here lies the dust of Timas, who died
upon her wedding eve; Persephone took
her into her sea-dark chamber.
And when she died, all her companions
sheared their lovely locks with the
sharp steel
And placed them on her tomb.

67 DEATH

Death is an evil. The gods have judged
it so. For otherwise they had died themselves.

68 THE PHILISTINE

Thou shalt be dead for ever,
Nor shall anything be remembered
of thee either now or at any time.
For thou hast scorned the roses of Poetry;
Therefore shalt thou go wandering about
among the feeble ghosts in the halls of Death.

4.2 Poetry: Pindar

Pindar wrote his odes in honor of the victors in the great pan-Hellenic athletic contests: the Olympic Games, the Pythian Games at Delphi, the Isthmian Games in Corinth, and the Nemean Games. This ode praises the victor (Pytheas from Aegina, the winner of the Youths' Pankration, a form of wrestling), his trainer (Menaner, an Athenian) and both their city-states with many allusions from Greek mythology. Pindar was born in 519 B.C.E. near Thebes in Boetia where he lived most of his life, although he spent several years of his youth in Athens studying music and poetry.

Source: Pindar, *The Odes of Pindar*, trans. Geoffrey S. Conway, (London: J.M. Dent and Sons, 1972), pp. 191–95.

str. 1 No sculptor I, to carve an image standing
Idle upon its step. But every craft and sail
Speed, lovely song, from Aegina
To tell abroad that Lampon's son,
Broad-shouldered Pytheas,
Has won at Nemea the Pankratiast crown,
Though not yet on his cheek is seen the dower
Of rich-flown summer, mother of the vine-bloom.

ant. 1 The clan of Aeacus, warrior heroes sprung
From Zeus and Cronos and
the glorious Nereids, share his honour,
And his own motherland, those meadows
Loved by her guests. That she might breed
Brave men and noble ships
A prayer went up long since beside the altar
Of Zeus Hellenius, where the far-famed sons
Of Endais stood and stretched their hands to heaven,

ep. 1 With Phocus in his lordly might,
Whom divine Psamatheia bore
Beside the crested wave.
Of a dread act, a deed maybe
Unrightly dared, my heart forebodes to tell,
Wherefore these warriors left his famous isle,
What fate of heaven drove them from Oenone.
Be still my tongue: here profits not
To tell the whole truth with clear face unveiled.
Often is man's best wisdom to be silent.

str. 2 But if of fortune's wealth my praise is due
Of strength of hand or armoured war, rake a long landing-pit
Straightway for me; my limbs can muster
A nimble spring; even o'er the main
Eagles can wing their way.
Yet for these men the Muses' peerless choir
Glad welcome sang on Pelion, and with them
Apollo's seven-stringed lyre and golden quill

ant. 2 Led many a lovely strain. To Zeus a prelude,
Then sang they first divine Thetis, and Peleus, whom with guile
Fair-faced Hippolyta, Cretheus' daughter,
Sought to ensnare, as helpmate duping
Magnetes' chief, Acastus

Her husband, with deceit-embroidered counsel,
And false-wrought tales, that Peleus made to force her
There in her marriage bed. False tale indeed!

ep. 2 For it was she conjured and begged him
With many a full-hearted prayer.
Her reckless words but chafed
His wrath, and he fearing the Father,
Protector of the law of host and guest,
Straightway denied her. Then from heaven beholding
The king of the high gods, cloud-gathering Zeus,
With nodding brow forthwith ordained
A sea-nymph of the golden-spindled Nereids
His bride should be, and to accept this kinship,
Comes now Themistius in your path of praise?
Hence chill reserve; sing out full-throated, hoist
Your sail to the mast's topyard, cry him for valour
Twice crowned at Epidaurus, boxer
Pankratiast, and at Aeacus' city gate
Wreathed with fresh flowers, gift of the fair-haired Graces.

Questions for Documents 4.1 and 4.2

1. What are the themes and topics of Sappho's poetry? What do they reveal about her life?
2. How do both Pindar's and Sappho's poetry reflect what people valued in Greek society and culture?
3. How do these poems compare to Homer's epic poetry (see Chapter 2, Document 2)?

4.3 Drama: *Antigone* by Sophocles

Antigone, written in the fifth century B.C.E. by Sophocles, deals with the children of Oedipus, the king who could not escape his fate. Antigone focuses on the meaning of honor and duty. Gender issues are also involved. Before the play begins, the sons of Oedipus, cursed by their father, have quarreled over royal power in Thebes. Eteocles drove his brother Polyneices from Thebes to the city-state of Argos where he married the daughter of the king. Polyneices then marched on Thebes to recover the throne. During the battle, the two

---

ant. 1 *Cronos:* father of Zeus who was the father of Aeacus.
Nereids: sea-nymphs, daughters of Nereus, a sea-god. Thetis wife of Peleus and mother of Achilles was one of them.
Zeus Hellenius: a cult of Zeus under this title is believed to have been set up by the Myrmidons, the earliest inhabitants of Aegina.
Sons of Endais: Telamon and Peleus, sons of Aeacus by his wife Endais.
ep. 1 *Phocus:* son of Aeacus by Psamatheia, a sea-nymph.
A dread act: owing to jealousy of their half-brother Phocus, who was the favourite son of their father, Telamon and Peleus killed him while they were practising hurling the discus. For this the two brothers had to leave Aegina. Telamon went to Salamis and Peleus to Thessaly. Pindar's language in these lines, part of a passage devoted to the praise of the clan of Aeacus, seems to aim at not incriminating the brothers too deeply. Phocus was killed by a blow from a discus, and one version of the story is that it was an accident.
Oenone: the original name of the island of Aegina. Oenone was the mother of Aeacus by Zeus.
str. 2 *Landing-pit:* metaphor from the long-jump, which was a regular athletic event.
Eagles: by a quick change of metaphor, Pindar identifies himself or his art as often in other Odes with an eagle, the king of birds.
These men: Telamon and Peleus.
Pelion: Mount Pelion, where the marriage feast of Peleus and Thetis was held, attended by all the gods (see Nem. III. ant. 2 and 3, and Nem. IV. str. 8)
ant. 2 *Magnetes:* the tribe inhabiting the area of Mount Pelion and Mount Ossa in eastern Thessaly where Acastus was king.

ep. 2 *The Father:* Zeus. A breach of the laws of hospitality was regarded as a serious sacrilege, as it still is in Eastern and near-Eastern countries.
Golden-spindled: an epithet applied more than once to the Nereids by Pindar. Its origin is perhaps that, as the Nereids move about the sea, their spindles, used as they are today by the peasant women of Greece as they go about the country-side, were seen as the whirling spray of the sea-waves. Unbleached wool has a golden tinge in Greece, but this Greek epithet can equally well mean glorious-, bright- or shining-spindled.
This kinship: the wife of Poseidon was Amphitrite, also a Nereid, so that Peleus on his marriage to Thetis would become the brother-in-law of Poseidon.
Themistius: Pytheas' grandfather.
Fresh flowers: on his return to Aegina from his victories at Epidaurus, Themistius seems to have been welcomed with 'wreaths', perhaps floral wreaths, but possibly—'gift of the fair-haired Graces'—poems in his honour.

brothers meet and kill each other. Their uncle, Creon, became king and immediately forbid the burial of Polyneices.

Source: Dudley Fitts, *Greek Plays in Modern Translation*, (New York: Dial Press, 1947), pp. 459–62, 464–65, 469–77.

Scene: Before the palace of Creon, King of Thebes. . . . Time: dawn of the day after the repulse of the Argive army from the assault of Thebes.

PROLOGUE

[ANTIGONE and ISMENE enter from the central door of the Palace.

ANTIG.   Ismenê, dear sister,
You would think that we had already suffered enough
For the curse on Oedipus:
I cannot imagine any grief
That you and I have not gone through. And now—
Have they told you the new decree of our King Creon?

ISMENE   I have heard nothing: I know
That two sisters lost two brothers, and double death
In a single hour; and I know that the Argive army
Fled in the night; but beyond this, nothing.

ANTIG.   I thought so. And that is why I wanted you To come out here with me. There is something we must do.

ISMENE   Why do you speak so strangely?

ANTIG.   Listen, Ismenê:
Creon buried our brother Eteoclês
With military honours, gave him a soldier's funeral,
And it was right that he should; but Polyneicês,
Who fought as bravely and died as miserably,—
They say that Creon has sworn
No one shall bury him, no one mourn for him,
But his body must lie in the fields, a sweet treasure
For carrion birds to find as they search for food.
That is what they say, and our good Creon is coming here
To announce it publicly; and the penalty—
Stoning to death in the public square!
There it is,
And now you can prove what you are:
A true sister, or a traitor to your family.

ISMENE   Antigonê, you are mad! What could I possibly do?

ANTIG.   You must decide whether you will help me or not.

ISMENE   I do not understand you. Help you in what?

ANTIG.   Ismenê, I am going to bury him. Will you come?

ISMENE   Bury him! You have just said the new law forbids it.

ANTIG.   He is my brother. And he is your brother, too.

ISMENE   But think of the danger! Thank what Creon will do!

ANTIG.   Creon is not strong enough to stand in my way.

ISMENE   Ah sister!
Oedipus died, everyone hating him
For what his own search brought to light, his eyes
Ripped out by his own hand; and Iocastê died,
His mother and wife at once: she twisted the cords
That strangled her life; and our two brothers died,
Each killed by the other's sword. And we are left:
But oh, Antigonê,
Think how much more terrible than these
Our own death would be if we should go against Creon
And do what he has forbidden! We are only women,
We cannot fight with men, Antigonê!
The law is strong, we must give in to the law
In this thing, and in worse. I beg the Dead
To forgive me, but I am helpless: I must yield
To those in authority. And I think it is dangerous business
To be always meddling.

ANTIG.   If that is what you think,
I should not want you, even if you asked to come.
You have made your choice, you can be what you want to be.
But I will bury him; and if I must die,
I say that this crime is holy: I shall lie down
With him in death, and I shall be as dear
To him as he to me.
It is the dead,
Not the living, who make the longest demands:
We die for ever . . .
You may do as you like,
Since apparently the laws of the gods mean nothing to you.

ISMENE   They mean a great deal to me; but I have no strength
To break laws that were made for the public good.

ANTIG.   That must be your excuse, I suppose. But as for me,
I will bury the brother I love.

ISMENE   Antigonê,
I am so afraid for you!

ANTIG.   You need not be:
You have yourself to consider, after all.

ISMENE But no one must hear of this, you must tell no one!
I will keep it a secret, I promise!

ANTIG. Oh tell it! Tell everyone!
Think how they'll hate you when it all comes out
If they learn that you knew about it all the time!

ISMENE So fiery! You should be cold with fear.

ANTIG. Perhaps. But I am doing only what I must.

ISMENE But can you do it? I say that you cannot.

ANTIG. Very well: when my strength gives out, I shall do
no more.

ISMENE Impossible things should not be tried at all.

ANTIG. Go away, Ismenê:
I shall be hating you soon, and the dead will too,
For your words are hateful. Leave me my foolish
plan:
I am not afraid of the danger; if it means death,
It will not be the worst of deaths—death without
honour.

ISMENE Go then, if you feel that you must.
You are unwise,
But a loyal friend indeed to those who love you.

[Exit into the Palace. ANTIGONE goes off, L.
Enters the Chorus.

SCENE I

CHORAG. But now at last our new King is coming:
Creon of Thebes, Menoiceus' son.
In this auspicious dawn of his reign
What are the new complexities
That shifting Fate has woven for him?
What is his counsel? Why has he summoned
The old men to hear him?
[Enter Creon from the Palace. He addresses the
Chorus from the top step.

CREON Gentlemen: I have the honour to inform you that
our Ship of State, which recent storms have
threatened to destroy, has come safely to har-
bour at last, guided by the merciful wisdom of
Heaven. I have summoned you here this morning because I know that I can depend upon
you: your devotion to King Laïos was
absolute; you never hesitated in your duty to
our late ruler Oedipus; and when Oedipus
died, your loyalty was transferred to his children. Unfortunately, as you know, his two
sons, the princes Eteoclês and Polyneicês,
have killed each other in battle; and I, as the
next in blood, have succeeded to the full
power of the throne.

I am aware, of course, that no Ruler can expect
complete loyalty from his subjects until he has
been tested in office. Nevertheless, I say to
you at the very outset that I have nothing but
contempt for the kind of Governor who is
afraid, for whatever reason, to follow the
course that he knows is best for the State; and
as for the man who sets private friendship
above the public welfare,—I have no use for
him, either. I call God to witness that If I saw
my country headed for ruin, I should not be
afraid to speak out plainly; and I need hardly
remind you that I would never have any deal-
ings with any enemy of the people. No one
values friendship more highly than I; but we
must remember that friends made at the risk
of wrecking our Ship are not real friends at all.

These are my principles, at any rate, and that is
why I have made the following decision concerning the sons of Oedipus: Eteoclês, who
died as a man should die, fighting for his
country, is to be buried with full military honours, with all the ceremony that is usual when
the greatest heroes dies; but his brother
Polyneicês, who broke his exile to come back
with fire and sword against his native city and
the shrines of his father's god, whose one idea
was to spill the blood of his blood and sell his
own people into slavery—Polyneicês, I say, is
to have no burial: no man is to touch him or
say the least prayer for him; he shall lie on the
plain, unburied; and the birds and the scaveng-
ing dogs can do with him whatever they like.

This is my command, and you can see the
wisdom behind it. As long as I am king, no
traitor is going to be honoured with the loyal
man. But whoever shows by word and deed
that he is on the side of the State,—he shall
have my respect while he is living, and my
reverence when he is dead.

CHORAG. If that is your will, Creon son of Menoiceus,
You have the right to enforce it; we are yours.

CREON That is my will. Take care that you do your part.

CHORAG. We are old men: let the younger ones carry it out.

CREON I do not mean that: the sentries have been appointed.

CHORAG. Then what is it that you would have us do?

CREON You will give no support to whoever breaks the law.

CHORAG. Only a crazy man is in love with death!

CREON   And death it is; yet money talks, and the wisest
        Have sometimes been known to count a few
            coins too many.

A sentry discovers Antigone burying her brother's body and
brings her to King Creon.

SCENE II

> [Re-enter Sentry leading Antigone.

CHORAG. What does this mean? Surely this captive woman
         Is the Princess, Antigonê. Why should she be
             taken?

SENTRY   Here is the one who did it! We caught her
         In the very act of burying him.—Where is Creon?

CHORAG. Just coming from the house.

> [Enter Creon, C.

CREON   What has happened?
        Why have you come back so soon?

· · · ·

SENTRY   . . . Here is this woman. She is the guilty one:
         We found her trying to bury him.
         Take her, then; question her; judge her as you
             will.
         I am though with the whole thing now, and glad
             of it.

CREON   But this is Antigonê! Why have you brought her
            here?

SENTRY   She was burying him, I tell you!

> [Severely.

CREON   Is this the truth?

SENTRY   I saw her with my own eyes. Can I say more?

· · · ·

> [Slowly, dangerously.

CREON   And you, Antigonê,
        You with your head hanging,—do you confess
            this thing?

ANTIG. I do. I deny nothing.

> [To Sentry:

CREON   You may go.

> [Exit Sentry.

> [To Antigone:
Tell me, tell me briefly:
Had you heard my proclamation touching this
    matter?

ANTIG. It was public. Could I help hearing it?

CREON   And yet you dared defy the law.

ANTIG.   I dared.
        It was not God's proclamation. That final Justice
        That rules the world below makes no such laws.
        Your edict, King, was strong,
        But all your strength is weakness itself against
        The immortal unrecorded laws of God.
        They are not merely now: they were, and shall be,
        Operative for ever, beyond man utterly.
        I knew I must die, even without your decree:
        I am only mortal. And if I must die
        Now, before it is my time to die,
        Surely this is no hardship: can anyone
        Living, as I live, with evil all about me,
        Think Death less than a friend? This death of mine
        Is of no importance; but if I had left my brother
        Lying in death unburied, I should have suffered.
        Now I do not.
                        You smile at me. Ah Creon,
        Think me a fool, if you like; but it may well be
        That a fool convicts me of folly.

CHORAG. Like father, like daughter: both headstrong, deaf
            to reason!
         She has never learned to yield.

CREON   She has much to learn.
        The inflexible heart breaks first, the toughest iron
        Cracks first, and the wildest horses bend their
            necks
        At the pull of the smallest curb.
                                         Pride? In a slave?
        This girl is guilty of a double insolence,
        Breaking the given laws and boasting of it.
        Who is the man here,
        She or I, if this crime goes unpunished?
        Sister's child, or more than sister's child,
        Or closer yet in blood—she and her sister
        Win bitter death for this!

> [To servants:
                                         Go, some of you,
        Arrest Ismenê. I accuse her equally.
        Bring her: you will find her sniffling in the house
            there.
        Her mind's a traitor: crimes kept in the dark
        Cry for light, and the guardian brain shudders;
        But how much worse than this
        Is brazen boasting of barefaced anarchy!

ANTIG. Creon, what more do you want than my death?

CREON   Nothing.
        That gives me everything.

ANTIG.   Then I beg you: kill me.
        This talking is a great weariness: your words

Are distasteful to me, and I am sure that mine
Seem so to you. And yet they should not seem so:
I should have praise and honour for what I have
   done.
All these men here would praise me
Were their lips not frozen shut with fear of you.
                                        [Bitterly.
Ah the good fortune of kings,
Licensed to say and do whatever they please!

CREON   You are alone here in that opinion.

ANTIG.   No, they are with me. But they keep their tongues
           in leash.

CREON   Maybe. But you are guilty, and they are not.

ANTIG.   There is no guilt in reverence for the dead.

CREON   But Eteoclês—was he not your brother too?

ANTIG.   My brother too.

CREON   And you insult his memory?
                                               [Softly.

ANTIG.   The dead man would not say that I insult it.

CREON   He would: for you honour a traitor as much as
           him.

ANTIG.   His own brother, traitor or not, and equal in
           blood.

CREON   He made war on his country. Eteoclês defended it.

ANTIG.   Nevertheless, there are honours due all the dead.

CREON   But not the same for the wicked as for the just.

ANTIG.   Ah Creon, Creon,
           Which of us can say what the gods hold wicked?

CREON   An enemy is an enemy, even dead.

ANTIG.   It is my nature to join in love, not hate.
                                 [Finally losing patience.

CREON   Go join them, then; if you must have your love,
           Find it in hell!

CHORAG.   But see, Ismenê comes:
                                 [Enter Ismene, guarded.
           Those tears are sisterly, the cloud
           That shadows her eyes rains down gentle sorrow.

CREON   You too, Ismenê,
           Snake in my ordered house, sucking my blood
           Stealthily—and all the time I never knew
           That these two sisters were aiming at my throne!
                                               Ismenê,
           Do you confess your share in this crime, or deny
               it?
           Answer me.

ISMENE   Yes, if she will let my say so. I am guilty.
                                               [Coldly.

ANTIG.   No, Ismenê. You have no right to say so.
           You would not help me, and I will not have you
               help me.

ISMENE   But now I know what you meant; and I am here
           To join you, to take my share of punishment.

ANTIG.   The dead man and the gods who rule the dead
           Know whose act this was. Words are not friends.

ISMENE   Do you refuse me, Antigonê? I want to die with
               you:
           I too have a duty that I must discharge to the
               dead.

ANTIG.   You shall not lessen my death by sharing it.

ISMENE   What do I care for life when you are dead?

ANTIG.   Ask Creon. You're always hanging on his opinions.

ISMENE   You are laughing at me. Why, Antigonê?

ANTIG.   It's a joyless laughter, Ismenê.

ISMENE   But can I do nothing?

ANTIG.   Yes. Save yourself. I shall not envy you.
           There are those who will praise you; I shall have
               honour, too.

ISMENE   But we are equally guilty!

ANTIG.   No, more, Ismenê.
           You are alive, but I belong to Death.

CREON   [To the Chorus:
           Gentlemen, I beg you to observe these girls:
           One has just now lost her mind; the other
           It seems, has never had a mind at all.

ISMENE   Grief teaches the steadiest minds to waver, King.

CREON   Yours certainly did, when you assumed guilt with
               the guilty!

ISMENE But how could I go on living without her?

CREON You are.
She is already dead.

ISMENE But your own son's bride!

CREON There are places enough for him to push his plow.
I want no wicked women for my sons!

ISMENE O dearest Haimon, how your father wrongs you!

CREON I've had enough of your childish talk of marriage!

CHORAG. Do you really intend to steal this girl from your
son?

CREON No; Death will do that for me.

CHORAG. Then she must die?

CREON You dazzle me.
—But enough of this talk!

[To Guards:
You, there, take them away and guard them well:
For they are but women, and even brave men run
When they see Death coming.

[Exeunt Ismente, Antigone, and Guards.

Questions:
1. Why is Antigone willing to defy the king's decree and give her brother burial?
2. What arguments to Ismene and Creon use to oppose her action?
3. What can you conclude about the way men and women were regarded in this society?

SECTION 2
Development in Philosophy and History

Documents 4.4–4.6

The fifth century B.C.E. in Greece, and in Athens particularly, was a period of great achievement intellectually, artistically, and politically. The three selections in this section all describe new ways of thinking in philosophy and history that have affected intellectual development through the millenia.

4.4   The Socratic Method

Plato's *Dialogues* are our chief source for understanding the personality and philosophy of Socrates (469 - 399 B.C.E.) who left nothing in writing himself. They imitate the question-and-answer method that Socrates used in leading his students to recognize fundamental truths about themselves and their world.

> **Source:** *Plato: Selected Passages*. Trans. Benjamin Jowett, and ed. R.W. Livingstone, (The World's Classics 1940), pp. 19–21. Reprinted by permission of The Clarendon Press in Readings in Ancient History: Thought and Experience form Gilgamesh to St. Augustine, Fifth Edition, ed. Nels M. Bailkey, (Lexington, MA: DC Heath and Co., 1996), pp. 244–46.

There is a rough and a smooth method in intellectual education. There is a time-honored mode which our fathers commonly practiced towards their sons, and which is still adopted by many—either of roughly reproving their errors, or of gently advising them; these two methods may be correctly described as admonition. But some thinkers appear to have arrived at the conclusion that all ignorance is involuntary, and that no one who thinks himself wise is willing to learn anything in the subjects in which he believes himself clever, and that the admonitory sort of instruction gives much trouble and does little good. So they set to work to eradicate the spirit of conceit in another way. They cross-examine a man's words, when he thinks that he is talking sense but really is not, and easily convict him of inconsistencies in his opinions; these they then place side by side, and show that they contradict one another. He, seeing this, is angry with himself, and grows gentle toward others, and thus is entirely delivered from great prejudices and harsh notions, in a way which is most amusing to the hearer, and produces the most lasting good effect on the person who is the subject of the operation. For as the physician considers that the body will receive no benefit from taking food until internal obstacles have been removed, so the purifier of the soul is conscious that his patient will receive no benefit from the application of knowledge until he is refuted, and from refutation learns modesty; he must be purged of his prejudices first and made to think that he knows only what he knows, and no more. For all these reasons, Theaetetus, we must admit that refutation is the greatest and chiefest of purifications, and he who has not been refuted, though he be the King of Persia himself, is in an awful state of impurity; he is uneducated and ugly just where purity and beauty are essential to happiness

My art is like that of midwives, but differs from theirs, in that I attend men and not women, and I look after their souls when they are in labor, and not after their bodies: and the triumph of my art is in thoroughly examining whether the thought which the mind of a young man brings forth is a phantom and a lie, or a fruitful and true birth. And like the midwives, I am barren, and the reproach often made against me, that I ask questions of others and have not the wit to answer them myself, is very just—the reason is, that the god compels me to be a midwife, but does not allow me to have children. So I myself am not at all wise, nor have I any invention or child of my own soul to show, but those who talk with me profit. Some of them appear dull enough at first, but afterwards, as our acquaintance ripens, if God is gracious to them, they all make astonishing progress; and this in the opinion of others as well as in their own. It is quite clear that they never learned anything from me; all that they master and discover comes from themselves. But to me and the god they owe their delivery. And the proof of my words is, that many of them in their ignorance, either in their self-conceit despising me, or falling under the influence of others, have gone away too soon; and have not only lost by an ill upbringing the children of whom I had previously delivered them, but have had subsequent miscarriages owing to evil associates, prizing lies and shams more than the truth; and they have at last ended by seeing themselves, as others see them, to be great fools. Dire are the pangs which my art is able to arouse and to allay in those who consort with me, just like the pangs of women in childbirth; night and day they are full of perplexity and travail which is even worse than that of the women. So much for them. And there are others, Theaetetus, who come to me apparently having nothing in them; and as I know that they have no need of my art, I coax them into marrying some one, and by the grace of God I can generally tell who is likely to do them good. Many of them I have given away to Prodicus, and many to other inspired sages. I tell you this long story, friend Theaetetus, because I suspect, as indeed you seem to think yourself, that you are in labor—great with some conception. Come then to me, who am a midwife's son and myself a midwife, and do your best to answer the questions which I will ask you. And if I expose your first-born, because I discover upon inspection that the conception which you have formed is a blind shadow, do not quarrel with me on that account, as women do when their first children are taken from them. For I have actually known some who were ready to bite me when I deprived them of a darling folly, they did not see that I acted from goodwill, not knowing that no god is the enemy of man; neither am I their enemy in all this, but it would be wrong for me to admit falsehood, or to stifle the truth of Socrates.

4.5 Historical Methods: Herodotus

Herodotus (ca. 484 - ca. 425 B.C.E.) well deserves the title, "the father of history." His predecessors were mere story-tellers compared to Herodotus, who eyed the old tales more critically and sought to determine why the events in the stories occurred the way they did.

> **Source:** Herodotus, *The Histories,* trans. Aubrey de Selincourt. (New York: Penguin Books, 1972), pp. 1–8, passim.

Herodotus of Halicarnassus, his *Researches* are here set down to preserve the memory of the past by putting on record the astonishing achievements both of our own and of other peoples; and more particularly, to show how they came into conflict.

Learned Persians put the responsibility for the quarrel on the Phoenicians. These people came originally from the so-called Red Sea; and as soon as they had penetrated to the Mediterranean and settled in the country where they are today, they took to making long trading voyages. Loaded with Egyptian and Assyrian goods, they called at various places along the coast, including Argos, in those days the most important place in the land, now called Hellas.

Here in Argos they displayed their wares, and five or six days later when they were nearly sold out, a number of women came down to the beach to see the fair. Amongst these was the king's daughter, whom Greek and Persian writers agree in calling Io, daughter of Inachus. These women were standing about near the vessel's stern, buying what they fancied, when suddenly the Phoenician sailors passed the word along and made a rush at them. The greater number got away; but Io and some others were caught and bundled aboard the ship, which cleared at once and made off for Egypt.

This, according to the Persian account (the Greeks have a different story), was how Io came to Egypt; and this was the first in a series of provocative acts.

Later on some Greeks, whose name the Persians fail to record—they were probably Cretans—put into the Phoenician port of Tyre and carried off the king's daughter Europa, thus giving them tit for tat.

For the next outrage it was the Greeks again who were responsible. They sailed in an armed merchantman to Aea in Colchis on the river Phasis, and, not content with the regular business which had brought them there, they abducted the king's daughter Medea. The king sent to Greece demanding reparations and his daughter's return; but the only answer he got was that the Greeks had no intention of offering reparation, having received none themselves for the abduction of Io from Argos.

The accounts go on to say that some forty or fifty years afterwards Paris, the son of Priam, was inspired by these stories to steal a wife for himself out of Greece, being confident that he would not have to pay for the venture any more than the Greeks had done. And that was how he came to carry off Helen.

The first idea of the Greeks after the rape was to send a demand for satisfaction and for Helen's return. The demand was met by a reference to the seizure of Medea and the injustice of expecting satisfaction from people to whom they themselves had refused it, not to mention the fact that they had kept the girl.

Thus far there had been nothing worse than woman-stealing on both sides; but for what happened next the Greeks, they say, were seriously to blame; for it was the Greeks who were, in a military sense, the aggressors. Abducting young women, in their opinion, is not, indeed, a lawful act; but it is stupid after the event to make a fuss about it. The only sensible thing is to take no notice; for it is obvious that no young woman allows herself to be abducted if she does not wish to be. The Asiatics, according to the Persians, took the seizure of the women lightly enough, but not so the Greeks: the Greeks, merely on account of a girl from Sparta, raised a big army, invaded Asia and destroyed the empire of Priam. From that root sprang their belief in the perpetual enmity of the Grecian world towards them—Asia with its various foreign-speaking peoples belonging to the Persians, Europe and the Greek states being, in their opinion, quite separate and distinct from them.

Such then is the Persian story. In their view it was the capture of Troy that first made them enemies of the Greeks. . . .

As to Io, the Phoenicians do not accept the Persians' account; they deny that they took her to Egypt by force. On the contrary, the girl while she was still in Argos went to bed with the ship's captain, found herself pregnant, and, ashamed to face her parents, sailed away voluntarily to escape exposure.

So much for what Persians and Phoenicians say; and I have no intention of passing judgement on its truth or falsity. I prefer to rely on my own knowledge, and to point out who it was in actual fact that first injured the Greeks; then I will proceed with my history, telling the story as I go along of small cities no less than of great. For most of those which were great once are small today; and those which used to be small were great in my own time. Knowing, therefore, that human prosperity never abides long in the same place, I shall pay attention to both alike. . . .

This, then, is the version the Egyptian priests gave me of the story of Helen, and I am inclined to accept it for the following reason: had Helen really been in Troy, she would have been handed over to the Greeks with or without Paris' consent; for I cannot believe that either Priam or any other kinsman of his was mad enough to be willing to risk his own and his children's lives and the safety of the city, to let Paris continue to live with Helen. If, moreover, that had been their feeling when the troubles began, surely later on, when the Trojans had suffered heavy losses in every battle they fought, and there was never an engagement (if we may believe the epic poems) in which Priam himself did not lose two of his sons, or three, or even more; surely, I repeat, in such circumstances as these, there can be little doubt that, even if Helen had been the wife of Priam the king, he would have given her back to the Greeks, if to do so offered a chance of relief from the suffering which the war had caused. Again, Paris was not heir to the throne, and so could not have been acting as regent for his aged father; for it was Hector, his elder brother and a better man than he, who was to have succeeded on Priam's death, and it was not likely that Hector would put up with his brother's lawless behaviour, especially as it was the cause of much distress both to himself and to every other Trojan besides. The fact is, they did not give Helen up because they had not got her; what they told the

Greeks was the truth and I do not hesitate to declare that the refusal of the Greeks to believe it came of divine volition in order that their utter destruction might plainly prove to mankind that great sins meet with great punishments at the hands of God. That, at least, is my own belief.

4.6 Historical Methods: Thucydides

Thucydides' great historical work was his *History of the Peloponnesian Wars* that he experienced first-hand. Here he explains his reason for writing about them and the method he pursued in the task.

Source: Thucydides, *History of the Peloponnesian Wars*, trans. Rex Warner, (New York: Penguin, 1954, revised 1972), pp. 35–39, 45–48.

BOOK ONE: INTRODUCTION

Thucydides the Athenian wrote the history of the war fought between Athens and Sparta, beginning the account at the very outbreak of the war, in the belief that it was going to be a great war and more worth writing about than any. of those which had taken lace in the past. My belief was based on the fact that the two sides were at the very height of their power and preparedness and I saw, too, that the rest of the Hellenic world was committed to one side or the other; even those who were not immediately engaged were deliberating on the courses which they were to take later. This was the greatest disturbance in the history of the Hellenes,[1] affecting also a large part of the non-Hellenic world, and indeed, I might almost say, the whole of mankind. For though I have found it impossible, because of its remoteness in time, to acquire a really precise knowledge of the distant past or even of the history preceding our own period, yet, after looking back into it as far as I can, all the evidence leads me to conclude that these periods were not great periods either in warfare or in anything else.

It appears, for example, that the country now called Hellas had no settled population in ancient times; instead there was a series of migrations, as the various tribes, being under the constant pressure of invaders who were stronger than they were, were always prepared to abandon their own territory. There was no commerce, and no safe communication either by land or sea; the use they made of their land was limited to the production of necessities; they had no surplus left over for capital, and no regular system of agriculture, since they lacked the protection of fortifications and at any moment an invader might appear and take their land away from them. Thus, in the belief that the day-to-day necessities of life could be secured just as well in one place as in another, they showed no reluctance in moving from

---

[1] In the Greek language, ancient as well as modern, the name of the country is Hellas, of the people 'Hellenes. Hellas' included all Greek communities, wherever they were established, but here Thucydides is referring more narrowly to the Greek peninsula

their homes, and therefore built no cities of any size or strength, nor acquired any important resources. . . .

In investigating past history, and in forming the conclusions which I have formed, it must be admitted that one cannot rely on every detail which has come down to us by way of tradition. People are inclined to accept all stories of ancient times in an uncritical way—even when these stories concern their own native countries. Most people in Athens, for instance, are under the impression that Hipparchus, who was killed by Harmodius and Aristogiton, was tyrant at the time, not realizing that it was Hippias who was the eldest and the chief of the sons of Pisistratus, and that Hipparchus and Thessalus were his younger brothers. What happened was this; on the very day that had been fixed for their attempt, indeed at the very last moment, Harmodius and Aristogeiton had reason to believe that Hippias had been informed of the plot by some of the conspirators. Believing him to have been forewarned, they kept away from him, but, as they wanted to perform some daring exploit before they were arrested themselves, they killed Hipparchus when they found him by the Leocorium organizing the Panathenaic procession.

The rest of the Hellenes, too, make many incorrect assumptions not only about the dimly remembered past, but also about contemporary history. For instance, there is a general belief that the kings of Sparta are each entitled to two votes, whereas in fact they have only one; and it is believed, too, that the Spartans have a company of troops called 'Pitanate'. Such a company has never existed. Most people in fact, will not take trouble in finding out the truth, but are much more inclined to accept the first story they hear.

However, I do not think that one will be far wrong in accepting the conclusions I have reached from the evidence which I have put forward. It is better evidence than that of the poets, who exaggerate the importance of their themes, or of the prose chroniclers, who are less interested in telling the truth than in catching the attention of their public, whose authorities cannot be checked, and whose subject-matter, owing to the passage of time, is mostly lost in the unreliable streams of mythology. We may claim instead to have used only the plainest evidence and to have reached conclusions which are reasonably accurate, considering that we have been dealing with ancient history. As for

this present war, even though people are apt to think that the war in which they are fighting is the greatest of all wars and, when it is over, to relapse again into their admiration of the past, nevertheless, if one looks at the facts themselves, one will see that this was the greatest war of all.

In this history I have made use of set speeches some of which were delivered just before and others during the war. I have found it difficult to remember the precise words used in the speeches which I listened to myself and my various informants have experienced the same difficulty; so my method has been, while keeping as closely as possible to the general sense of the words that were actually used, to make the speakers say what in my opinion, was called for by each situation. . . .

And with regard to my factual reporting of the events of the war I have made it a principle not to write down the first story that came my way, and not even to be guided by my own general impressions; either I was present myself at the events which I have described or else I heard of them from eye-witnesses whose reports I have checked with as much thoroughness as possible, Not that even so the truth was easy to discover: different eye-witnesses give different accounts of the same events, speaking out of partiality for one side or the other or else from imperfect memories. And it may well be that my history will seem less easy to read because of the absence in it of a romantic element. It will be enough for me, however, if these words of mine are judged useful by those who want to understand clearly the events which happened in the past and which (human nature being what it is) will, at some time or other and in much the same ways, be repeated in the future. My work is not a piece of writing designed to meet the taste of an immediate public, but was done to last forever.

Questions for Documents 4.4–4.6:

1. What is the goal of each of these men and what are their methods to reach it?
2. What do all three of these new methods of thought have in common?
3. If Socrates, Herodotus, and Thucydides were to apply their methods of examination to our own state and history, how do you think they would be regarded by the public?

SECTION 3
Defining the Political World

Documents 4.7–4.9

Greece was never a single political entity, but a group of antagonistic, quarreling city-states who did not even all unite against their common enemy, Persia. The fifty years following the defeat of the Athenian Empire in the Peloponnesian Wars was marked by almost continuous warfare (encouraged by Persia) between Greek city-states. Meanwhile, a new power arose to the north of Greece in Macedon whose king was creating a formidable military force.

4.7 Demonsthenes: "Philip is Our Enemy"

Demonsthenes of Athens (384–322 B.C.E.) feared the energetic and ambitious Philip, who had unified the mounted warrior nobles and the peasants of Macedon into an effective monarchy supported by a powerful military machine. In a series of speeches Demonsthenes implored the Athenians to defend their state against possible threat of Macedonian "domination of Greece and the end of the honors and rights of our ancestors."

Source: *Readings in Ancient History: Thought and Experience from Gilgamesh to St. Augustine*, Fifth Edition, ed. Nels M. Bailkey, (Lexington, MA: DC Heath and Company, 1996), pp. 285–88. (Based on the translation by Charles R. Kennedy of *First Philippic*, Chs. 2–12, 38–45, 48–50.)

First I say, you must not despair, men of Athens, under your present circumstances, wretched as they are; for that which is worst in the days that are past provides the best hope for the future. What do I mean? That your affairs are amiss, men of Athens, because you do nothing that is needed; for surely if you came into your present predicament while doing all that you should do, we could not then hope for any improvement.

Consider next, what some of you know by report and others know from experience, how powerful the Spartans were not long ago, yet how nobly and patriotically you did what was worthy of Athens and undertook the war [378–371 BC] against them for the rights of Greece. Why do I remind you of this? To show and convince you, men of Athens, that nothing, if you are on your guard, is to be feared, nothing, if you are negligent, goes as you desire. Take for example the strength of the Spartans then, which you overcame by attention to your duties, and the insolence of this man now, by which through neglect of our interests we are confounded. But if there are any among you, men of Athens, who think Philip hard to be conquered in view of the magnitude of his existing power and the loss by us of all our strongholds, they reason rightly. But they should remember that once we held Pydna and Potidaea and Methone and all the region round about Macedonia as our own, and that many of the tribes now leagued with him were then independent and free and preferred our friendship to his. Had Philip then concluded that it was difficult to contend with Athens, when she had so many strong outposts on his borders and he was destitute of allies, he would never have gained his recent successes nor acquired his present power. But he saw clearly, men of Athens, that all these outposts were the open prizes of war, that by natural right the possessions of the absent belong to those on the spot and the possessions of the negligent to those who will venture and toil. Acting on this principle, he has won these places and holds them, either by right of conquest or by means of friendship and alliance—for all men will side with and respect those whom they see prepared and willing to take action.

Men of Athens, if you will adopt this principle now, though you did not do so before, and if each citizen who can and ought to give his service to the state is ready to give it without excuse, the rich to contribute, the able-bodied to enlist; if, put bluntly, you will become your own masters and each cease expecting to do nothing himself while his neighbor does everything for him, then, God willing, you will recover your own, get back what has been frittered away, and turn the tables on Philip. Do not imagine that his power is everlasting like that of a god. There are those who hate and fear and envy him, men of Athens, even among those who now seem most friendly. We can assume that all the feelings that are in other men belong also to his adherents. But now they are all cowed, having no refuge because of your apathy and indolence, which I urge you to abandon at once. For you see, men of Athens, to what pitch of arrogance the man has advanced: he leaves you not even the choice of action or inaction, he threatens and uses outrageous language, he cannot rest content in possession of his conquests but continually widens their circle, and, while we dally and delay, he throws his net around us.

When, then, Athenians, when will you act as becomes you? What are you waiting for? When it is necessary, I suppose. And how should we regard what is happening now? Surely, to free men the strongest necessity is the disgrace of their condition. Or tell me, do you like walking about and asking one another, "Is there any news?" Could there be more startling news than that a Macedonian is subduing Athenians and directing the affairs of Greece? "Is Philip dead?" you ask. "No, but he is sick." What difference does it make? Should anything happen to this man, you will soon create a second Philip if that is the way you attend to affairs. For this Philip has grown great not so much by his own strength as by our negligence. . . .

Shameful it is, men of Athens, to delude ourselves, and by putting off everything unpleasant to miss the time for action and be unable even to understand that skillful makers of war should not follow circumstances, but be in advance of them; for just as a general may be expected to lead his armies, so statesmen must guide circumstances if they are to carry out their policies and not be forced to follow at the heels of events. Yet you, men of Athens, with greater resources than any people—ships, infantry, cavalry, revenue—have never up to this day made proper use of them; instead, your war with Philip differs in no respect from the boxing of barbarians. For among them the party struck moves his hands to the spot; strike him somewhere else, there go his hands again. He neither can nor will parry a blow or look his opponent in the face. So you, if you hear of Philip in the Chersonese, vote to send relief there, if at Thermopylae, the same; if anywhere else, you run up and down after his heels. You take your orders from him; no plan have you devised, no event do you forsee, until you learn that something has happened or is about to happen. Formerly perhaps this was tolerable; now it is come to a crisis and is tolerable no longer. It seems to me, men of Athens, as if some god, ashamed for us because of our conduct, has inspired this activity in Philip. For if he were willing to remain at peace in possession of his conquests and prizes, attempting nothing further, some of you, I think, would be satisfied with a state of things which brands our nation with shame, cowardice, and deep disgrace. But by continually encroaching and grasping after more, he may possibly rouse you, if you have not completely abandoned hope. . . .

One thing is clear: he will not stop, unless someone stops him. Are we to wait for this? Do you think all is well if you dispatch empty ships and the vague hope of some deliverer? Shall we not man the fleet? Shall we not sail with at least a part of our troops, now if never before? Shall we not make a landing on his coast? "Where, then, shall we land?" someone asks. The war itself, men of Athens, will uncover the weak parts of his empire, if we make the effort; but if we sit at home listening to the orators accuse and malign one another, no good can ever be achieved. I believe that wherever you send a force of our own citizens—or even partly ours—there Heaven will bless us and Fortune will aid our struggle; but where you send out a general and an empty decree and high hopes from the debate, nothing that you desire is achieved; your enemies scoff, and your allies die of fright. . . .

Some of us go about saying that Philip is negotiating with Sparta for the destruction of Thebes and the dissolution of the free states; some say that he has sent envoys to the king [of Persia]; others say that he is fortifying cities in Illyria—thus do we wander about, each inventing his own story. For my part, men of Athens, I solemnly believe that Philip is intoxicated with the magnitude of his exploits and has many such dreams in his mind, for he sees the absence of opponents and is elated by his successes. But most certainly he has no such plan of action as to let the most foolish among us know what his intentions are, and the most foolish are these newsmongers. Let us dismiss such talk and remember only that Philip is our enemy, that he has long been robbing and insulting us, that wherever we have expected aid from others we have found hostility, that the future depends on ourselves, and that unless we are willing to fight him there we shall perhaps be forced to fight here. This let us remember, and then we shall decide wisely and be done with idle conjectures. You need not speculate about the future except to assure yourselves that it will be disastrous unless you face the facts and are willing to do your duty.

4.8 Isocrates: "Philip, Be Our Benefactor"

Isocractes supported the unification of Greece as a realistic necessity. When a voluntary union of Greek city-states appeared hopeless, he finally turned to King Philip of Macedon in 346 B.C.E., urging him to take the lead in organizing a free and peaceful Greece.

Source: Based on the translation by J.H. Freese in *Orations of Isocrates*, Vol. 1, reprinted by permission of G. Bell & Sons, Ltd. In *Readings in Ancient History: Thought and Experience from Gilgamesh to St. Augustine*, Fifth Edition, ed. Nels M. Bailkey, (Lexington, MA: DC Heath and Company, 1996), pp. 289–93.

Rejoicing at the resolutions which were adopted concerning peace, and thinking that they would be to your advantage and to that of all the rest of Hellas as well as to us, I was unable to divert my thoughts from the possibilities connected with it and was in a frame of mind to set to work immediately to consider how to give permanence to what we had achieved and to prevent our state from again, after a short interval, desiring other wars. An examination of these questions in my own mind led me to the conclusion that there was no other way for her to remain at peace except by the determination of the leading states of Hellas to put an end to mutual quarrels and carry the war into Asia, resolving to win from the barbarians the selfish advantages which they now look for at the expense of Hellenes. This was, indeed, the policy I had already advised in the *Panegyric* oration.

To trouble the great festivals with oratory, addressing the crowds that come there, is really to speak without an audience; speeches of that kind are as ineffectual as laws and constitutions drawn up by the sophists. Those who wish, on the contrary, to do some practical good instead of idly chattering, and who think they have formed ideas of value to the community, must leave it to others to orate at the festivals while they seek a champion for their cause from among those who are powerful in speech and action and have great reputations—if, that is to say, anyone is to pay attention to them.

With this in mind, I chose to address my discourse to you, not making this choice to win your favor, although it is true that I should consider it of great importance to speak in a manner acceptable to you, but it was not to this end that I came to this decision. It was because I saw that all the other men of high repute were living under the rule of states and laws, without power to do anything but obey orders, and besides were far too weak for the enterprise which I shall propose, while to you alone had Fortune granted full power to send ambassadors to whomsoever you chose and to receive them from whomever you pleased, and to say whatever you thought it expedient to say, and besides this, that you were the possessor to a greater degree than any man in Hellas of wealth and power, the only two things in existence which can both persuade and compel—things which I think will also be required by the enterprise which I am going to propose. For my intention is to advise you to take the lead both in securing the harmony of Hellas and in conducting a campaign against the barbarians; and as persuasion is expedient in dealing with the Greeks, so force is useful in dealing with the barbarians. Such, then, is the general scope of my discourse. . . .

I will now direct my remarks to the subject at hand. I say that, while neglecting none of your own interests, you ought to try to reconcile Argos, Sparta, Thebes, and our state; for if you are able to bring these together you will have no difficulty in uniting the others as well, for they are all under the influence of those that I have mentioned and when alarmed take refuge with one or the other of those states and depend on their aid. So if you can persuade four states only to act wisely, you will also release the rest from many evils. . . .

And you have a good opportunity, for . . . it is a good thing to appear as the benefactor of the leading states and at the same time to be furthering your own interests no less than theirs. Besides this, you will remove any unpleasant relations that you have had with any of them, for services rendered in the present crisis will cause all of you to forget the wrongs you have committed against each other in the past. Moreover, it is also beyond question that there is nothing which all men remember so well as benefits received in times of trouble. And you can see how they have been reduced to distress by war. . . .

Now perhaps someone will venture to oppose what I have said on the ground that I am endeavoring to persuade you to undertake an impossible task. He may say that the Argives can never be friends with the Spartans, or the Spartans with the Thebans, nor, in a word, can those who have been accustomed always to seek their selfish interests ever cast their lot with one another. I think that nothing of this kind could have been accomplished when our state, or again when Sparta, was supreme in Hellas, for either of them could easily have blocked the attempt; but now I no longer have the same opinion of them. For I know that they have all been brought down to the same level by their misfortunes, so that I think they will much prefer the benefits of union to the selfish advantages of their former policy.

Now I am surprised that those who consider it impossible that any such policy could be carried out do not know from their own experience, or have not heard from others, that there have been indeed many terrible wars after which the participants have been reconciled and done each other great services. What could exceed the enmity between Xerxes and the Hellenes? Yet everyone knows that both we and the Spartans were more pleased with the friendship of Xerxes than of those who helped us to found our respective empires. And need we refer to ancient history or to our relations with the barbarians? . . . When the Spartans made war against the Thebans with the intention of ravaging Boeotia and breaking up its league of cities, we gave our help and thwarted their desires; and when fortune changed again and the Thebans and all the Peloponnesians attempted to lay Sparta in ruins, we alone in Hellas made an alliance even with our ancient foes and contributed to their preservation. A man then would be full of folly who could observe such great reversals and see that states care nothing for former enmities or oaths or anything else save what they suppose to be for their advantage, caring only for what is expedient and devoting all their energies to that end, and still suppose that they would be of the same mind now as they always have been, especially with you to preside over the settlement of their disputes, which expediency recommends and present necessity compels. For I think that with these influences fighting on your side everything will turn out as it should.

I should be satisfied with what I have already said on this subject had I not omitted one point, not from forgetfulness, but from a certain unwillingness to mention it. However, I think I ought to disclose it now, for I am of the opinion that it is as much to your advantage to hear what I have to say concerning it as it is becoming to me to speak with my accustomed freedom. I perceive that you are being slandered by those who are jealous of you and are accustomed to throw their own cities into confusion—men who regard the peace which is for the good of all as a war against their own selfish interests. Unconcerned about everything else, they speak of nothing but your power, asserting that its growth is not for the interests of Hellas but against them, and that you have been already for a long time plotting against us all, and that, while you pretend to be anxious to assist the Messenians as soon as you have settled with the Phocians, you are in reality endeavoring to get the Peloponnesus into your power. . . . By talking such nonsense and pretending that they possess an accurate knowledge of affairs, and by predicting a speedy overthrow of the whole world, they persuade many. . . .

On these points no sensible man would venture to contradict me. And I think that it would occur to any others who should propose to advise in favor of the expedition to Asia to point out that all whose lot it has been to undertake war against the Persian king have risen from obscurity to renown, from poverty to wealth, and from low estate to the ownership of many lands and cities. . . .

What opinion must we think all will have of you if you actually do this; above all, if you endeavor to conquer the whole Persian Empire, or at least to take from it a vast territory, what some call "Asia from Cilicia to Sinope," and in addition to build cities throughout this region and send there as colonists those who are now wanderers from want of their daily bread and who harass all whom they meet? For if we do not stop these men from joining together by providing them with sufficient to live upon, they will before we realize it become so numerous that they will be as great a cause of alarm to the Hellenes as to the barbarians. We, however, pay no attention to them; we ignore the existence of a terrible menace that threatens us all and is increasing day by day.

CONCLUSION

When Fortune honorably leads the way, it is a disgrace to lag behind and show yourself unready to advance in whatever direction she wishes. I think that, while you ought to honor all those who speak well of what you have done, you ought to consider that the most honorable eulogy is that of those who consider your talents worthy of still greater deeds than those which you have already accomplished, great as they are, and who express themselves grateful to you, not only in the present, but who will cause posterity to admire your acts beyond those of all who have lived in former times.

It remains to summarize what I have said in this discourse in order that, in as few words as possible, you may understand the chief point of my advice. I say that you ought to be the benefactor of the Hellenes, the king of Macedonia, and the ruler over as many barbarians as possible. If you succeed in this, all will be grateful to you—the Hellenes by reason of advantages enjoyed; the Macedonians, if you govern them like a king and not like a tyrant; and the rest of mankind, if they are freed by you from barbarian despotism and gain the protection of Hellas. How far my composition is well proportioned in style and in expression, I may

Questions for Documents 4.7 and 4.8
1. Why did Demonsthenes and Isocrates view Philip so differently?
2. What arguments did each assemble to persuade the Athenians to their course of action?
3. Can you see any situations producing similar debate in the present political discourse in our own nation? In global politics?

4.9 Herodotus on the Persians: Defining the Other

The great theme of Herodotus' *Histories* is the age-old conflict between East and West, beginning with the Trojan War and culminating in the defeat of the Persian invasion of Greece in the early fifth century B.C.E. by the tiny disunited Greek city-states when Herodotus himself was just a small child. (As

we know, this was not the end of the Greek-Persian conflict, and the Persians continued to be the great enemy for the Greek states for the next 150 years.) Herodotus investigated the Persians and their culture in an effort to understand the reason for this conflict.

Source: Herodotus, *The Histories*, trans. Aubrey de Selincourt, (New York: Penguin Books, 1972), pp. 96–99.

The following are certain Persian customs which I can describe from personal knowledge. The erection of statues, temples, and altars is not an accepted practice amongst them, and anyone who does such a thing is considered a fool, because, presumably, the Persian religion is not anthropomorphic like the Greek. Zeus, in their system, is the whole circle of the heavens, and they sacrifice to him from the tops of mountains. They also worship the sun, moon, and earth, fire, water, and winds, which are their only original deities: it was later that they learned from the Assyrians and Arabians the cult of Uraniami Aphrodite. The Assyrian name for Aphrodite is Mylitta, the Arabian Alilat, the Persian Mitra.'

As for ceremonial, when they offer sacrifice to the deities I mentioned, they erect no altar and kindle no fire; the libation, the flute music, the garlands, the sprinkled meal—all these things, familiar to us, they have no use for; but before a ceremony a man sticks a spray of leaves, usually myrtle leaves, into his headdress, takes his victim to some open place and invokes the deity to whom he wishes to sacrifice. The actual worshipper is not permitted to pray for any personal or private blessing, but only for the king and for the general good of the community, of which he is himself a part. When he has cut up the animal and cooked it, he makes a little heap of the softest green stuff he can find, preferably clover, and lays all the meat upon it. This done, a Magus (a member of this caste is always present at sacrifices) utters an incantation over it in a form of words which is supposed to recount the Birth of the Gods. Then after a short interval the worshipper removes the flesh and does what he pleases with it.

Of all days in the year a Persian most distinguishes his birthday, and celebrates it with a dinner of special magnificence. A rich Persian on his birthday will have an ox or a horse or a camel or a donkey baked whole in the oven and served up at table, and the poor some smaller beast. The main dishes at their meals are few, but they have many sorts of dessert, the various courses being served separately. It is this custom that has made them say that the Greeks leave the table hungry, because we never have anything worth mentioning after the first course: they think that if we did, we should go on eating. They are very fond of wine, and no one is allowed to vomit or relieve himself in the presence of another person.

If an important decision is to be made, they discuss the question when they are drunk, and the following day the master of the house where the discussion was held submits their decision for reconsideration when they are sober. If they still approve it, it is adopted; if not, it is abandoned. Conversely, any decision they make when they are sober, is reconsidered afterwards when they are drunk.

When Persians meet in the streets one can always tell by their mode of greeting whether or not they are of the same rank; for they so nor speak but kiss their equals upon the mouth, those somewhat superior on the cheeks. A man of greatly inferior rank prostrates himself in profound reverence. After their own nation they hold their nearest neighbours most in honour, then the nearest but one, and so on, their respect decreasing as the distance grows, and the most remote being the most despised. Themselves they consider in every way superior to everyone else in the world, amid allow other nations a share of good qualities decreasing according to distance, the furthest off being in their view the worst. By a similar sort of principle the Medes extended their system of administration and government during the period of their dominance: the various nations governed each other, the Medes being the supreme authority and concerning themselves specially with their nearest neighbours; these in their turn ruling *their* neighbours, who were responsible for the next, and so on.

No race is so ready to adopt foreign ways as the Persian; for instance, they wear the Median costume because they think it handsomer than their own, and their soldiers wear the Egyptian corselet. Pleasures, too, of all sorts they are quick to indulge in when they get to know about them—a notable instance is pederasty, which they learned from the Greeks. Every man has a number of wives, and a much greater number of concubines. After prowess in fighting, the chief proof of manliness is to be the father of a large family of boys. Those who have most sons receive an annual present from the king—on the principle that there is strength in numbers. The period of a boy's education is between the ages of five and twenty, and they are taught three things only: to ride, to use the bow, and to speak the truth. Before the age of five a boy lives with the women and never sees his father, the object being to spare the father distress if the child should die in the early stages of its upbringing. In my view this is a sound practice. I admire also the custom which forbids even the king himself to put a man to death for a single offence, and any Persian under similar circumstances to punish a servant by an irreparable injury. Their way is to balance faults against services, and then, if the faults are greater and more numerous, anger may take its course. They declare that no man has ever yet killed his father or mother; in the cases where this has apparently happened, they are quite certain that inquiry would reveal that the son was either a changeling or born out of wedlock, for they insist that it is most improbable that the actual parent should be killed by his child. What they are forbidden to do, they are forbidden also to mention. They consider telling lies more disgraceful than anything else, and, next to that, owing money. There are many reasons for their horror of debt, but the chief is their conviction that a man who owes money is bound also to tell lies. Sufferers from the scab or from leprosy are isolated and forbidden in the city. They say these diseases are punishments for offending the sun, and they expel any stranger who catches them: many Persians drive away even white doves, as if they, too, were guilty of the same offence. They have a profound reverence for rivers: they will never pollute a river with urine or spittle, or even wash their hands in one, or allow anyone else to do so. There is one other peculiarity which one notices about them, though they themselves are unaware of it: all their names, which express magnificence or physical qualities, end in the letter S. . . . Inquiry will prove this in every case without exception.'

All this I am able to state definitely from personal knowledge. There is another practice, however, concerning the burial of the dead, which is not spoken of openly and is something of a mystery: it is that a male Persian is never buried until the body has been torn by a bird or a dog. I know for certain that the Magi have this custom, for they are quite open about it. The Persians in general, however, cover a body with wax and then bury it. The Magi are a peculiar caste, quite different from the Egyptian priests and indeed from any other sort of person. The Egyptian priests make it an article of religion to kill no living creature except for sacrifice, but the Magi not only kill anything, except dogs and men, with their own hands but make a special point of doing so; ants, snakes, animals, birds—no matter what, they kill them indiscriminately. Well, it is an ancient custom, so let them keep it.

Questions:

1. What characteristics of the Persians does Herodotus feel are most different from the Greeks?
2. What practices and customs does Herodotus view favorably?
3. What does he seem to believe are their greatest weaknesses?

Part TWO

THE ORIGINS OF THE WEST

From Roman Dominion
to the New Peoples of Europe
(300 B.C.E.–1300 C.E.)

CHAPTER 5

Our Sea

The Mediterranean World in the Hellenistic
and Early Roman Eras
(300–27 B.C.E.)

SECTION 1
Creating a New World

5.1 Alexander Addresses His Troops

Alexander the Great, ruler of Macedonia (356–323 B.C.E.), conquered the Persian Empire in the fourth century B.C.E. In less than ten years he conquered a vast empire and enabled the exchange of knowledge, culture, and technology between East and West that created a new Hellenistic world.

Alexander's personal charisma and leadership abilities shine through as he rallies his troops to fight against the larger Persian army. The source is Arrian, who wrote his biography of Alexander in the second century C.E. He carefully relied upon eyewitness accounts and thus provides us with access to primary sources that no longer exist.

Source: Arrian, *The Campaign of Alexander*, trans. Aubrey de Selincourt (New York: Penguin Books, 1958; revised, 1971), pp. 112–14.

Alexander now sent for his infantry and cavalry commanders and all officers in charge of allied troops and appealed to them for confidence and courage in the coming fight. "Remember," he said, "that already danger has often threatened you and you have looked it triumphantly in the face; this time the struggle will be between a victorious army and an enemy already once vanquished. God himself, moreover, by suggesting to Darius to leave the open ground and cram his great army into a confined space, has taken charge of operations in our behalf. We ourselves shall have room enough to deploy our infantry, while they, no match for us either in bodily strength or resolution, will find their superiority in numbers of no avail. Our enemies are Medes and Persians, men who for centuries have lived soft and luxurious lives; we of Macedon for generations past have been trained in the hard school of danger and war. Above all, we are free men, and they are slaves. There are Greek troops, to be sure, in Persian service—but how different is their cause from ours! They will be fighting for pay—and not much of it at that; we, on the contrary, shall fight for Greece, and our hearts will be in it. As for our foreign troops—Thracians, Paeonians, Illyrians, Agrianes—they are the best and stoutest soldiers in Europe, and they will find as their opponents the slackest and softest of the tribes of Asia. And what, finally, of the two men in supreme command? You have Alexander, they—Darius!"

Having thus enumerated the advantages with which they would enter the coming struggle, Alexander went on to show that the rewards of victory would also be great. The victory this time would not be over mere underlings of the Persian King, or the Persian cavalry along the banks of Granicus, or the 20,000 foreign mercenaries; it would be over the fine flower of the Medes and Persians and all the Asiatic peoples which they ruled. The Great King was there in person with his army, and once the battle was over, nothing would remain but to crown their many labours with the sovereignty of Asia. He reminded them, further, of what they had already so brilliantly accomplished together, and mentioned any act of conspicuous individual courage, naming the man in each case and specifying what he had done, and alluding also, in such a way as to give least offence, to the risks to which he had personally exposed himself on the field. He also, we are told, reminded them of Xenophon and his Ten Thousand, a force which, though not to be compared with their own either in strength or reputation—a force without the support of cavalry such as they had themselves, from Thessaly, Boeotia, the Peloponnese, Macedon, Thrace, and elsewhere, with no archers or slingers except a small contingent from Crete and Rhodes hastily improvised by Xenophon under pressure of immediate need—nevertheless defeated the King of Persia and his army at the gates of Babylon and successfully repelled all the native troops who tried to bar their way as they marched down to the Black Sea. Nor did Alexander omit any other words of encouragement such as brave men about to risk their lives might expect from a brave commander; and in response to his address his officers pressed forward to clasp his hand and with many expressions of appreciation urged him to lead them to battle without delay.

Questions:
1. How does Alexander encourage his troops before this battle with the Persians?
2. What advantages does Alexander point out that the Greeks possess?
3. What does this speech show about Alexander's leadership abilities?

5.2   Archimedes: Hellenistic Science and Technology

Archimedes (ca. 287–212 B.C.E.) had studied at the Museum in Alexandria, the famous library founded by the Ptolemies, rulers of Egypt. There the combination of ancient Babylonian, Egyptian, and Greek learning raised science and mathematics to their highest point of development in the ancient world. Archimedes, the most famous Hellenistic scientist in physics and mathematics, was killed during the Second Punic War when the Romans under the command of Marcellus besieged and sacked Syracuse. Plutarch records his death as well as accounts testifying to his scientific genius.

Source: *Plutarch's Lives*, trans. John Dryden, revised by A.H. Clough, Vol II, (New York: Little, Brown and Company, 1909), pp. 252–60.

... Appius Marcellus, with sixty galleys, each with five rows of oars, furnished with all sorts of arms and missiles, and a huge bridge of planks laid upon eight ships chained together, upon which was carried the engine to cast stones and darts, assaulted the walls, relying on the abundance and magnificence of his preparations, and on his own previous glory; all which, however, were, it would seem, but trifles for Archimedes and his machines.

These machines he had designed and contrived, not as matters of any importance, but as mere amusements in geometry; in compliance with King Hiero's desire and request, some little time before, that he should reduce to practice some part of his admirable speculations in science, and by accommodating the theoretic truth to sensation and ordinary use, bring it more within the appreciation of people in general. Eudoxus and Archytas had been the first originators of this far-famed and highly prized art of mechanics, which they employed as an elegant illustration of geometrical truths, and as a means of sustaining experimentally, to the satisfaction of the senses, conclusions too intricate for proof by words and diagrams. . . . So it was that mechanics came to be separated from geometry, and, repudiated and neglected by philosophers, took its place as a military art. Archimedes, however, in writing to king Hiero, whose friend and near relation he was, had stated, that given the force, any given weight might be moved, and even boasted, we are told, relying on the strength of demonstration, that if there were another earth, by going into it he could remove this. Hiero being struck with amazement at this, and entreating him to make good this problem by actual experiment, and show some great weight moved by a small engine, he fixed accordingly upon a ship of burden out of the king's arsenal, which could not be drawn out of the dock without great labor and many men; and, loading her with many passengers and a full freight, sitting himself the while far off, with no great endeavor, but only holding the head of the pulley in his hand and drawing the cord by degrees, he drew the ship in a straight line, as smoothly and evenly, as if she had been in the sea. The king, astonished at this, and convinced of the power of the art, prevailed upon Archimedes to make him engines accommodated to all the purposes, offensive and defensive, of a siege. These the king himself never made use of, because he spent almost all his life in a profound quiet, and the highest affluence. But the apparatus was, in a most opportune time, ready at hand for the Syracusans, and with it also the engineer himself.

When, therefore, the Romans assaulted the walls in two places at once, fear and consternation stupefied the Syracusans, believing that nothing was able to resist that violence and those forces. But when Archimedes began to ply his engines, he at once shot against the land forces all sorts of missile weapons, and immense masses of stone that came down with incredible noise and violence, against which no man could stand; for they knocked down those upon whom they fell, in heaps, breaking all their ranks and files. In the meantime huge poles thrust out from the walls over the ships, sunk some by the great weights which they let down from on high upon them; others they lifted up into the air by an iron hand or beak like a crane's beak, and, when they had drawn them up by the prow, and set them on end upon the poop, they plunged them to the bottom of the sea; or else the ships, drawn by engines within, and whirled about, were dashed against steep rocks that stood jutting out under the walls, with great destruction of the soldiers that were aboard them. A ship was frequently lifted up to a great height in the air (a dreadful thing to behold), and was rolled to and fro, and kept swinging, until the mariners were all thrown out, when at length it was dashed against the rocks, or let fall. At the engine that Marcellus brought upon the bridge of ships, which was called Sambuca from some resemblance it had to an instrument of music, while it was as yet approaching the wall, there was discharged a piece of a rock of ten talents' weight, then a second and a third, which, striking upon it with immense force and with a noise like thunder, broke all its foundation to pieces, shook out all its fastenings, and completely dislodged it from the bridge. So Marcellus, doubtful what counsel to pursue, drew off his ships to a safer distance, and sounded a retreat to his forces on land. They then took a resolution of coming up under the walls, if it were possible, in the night; thinking that as Archimedes used ropes stretched at length in playing his engines, the soldiers would now be under the shot, and the darts would, for want of sufficient distance to throw them, fly over their heads without effect. But he, it appeared, had long before framed for such occasion engines accommodated to any distance, and shorter weapons; and had made numerous small openings in the walls, through which, with engines of a shorter range, unexpected blows were inflicted on the assailants. Thus, when they who thought to deceive the defenders came close up to the walls, instantly a shower of darts and other missile weapons was again cast upon them. And when stones came tumbling down perpendicularly upon their heads, and, as it were, the whole wall shot out arrows at them, they retired. And now, again, as they were going off, arrows and darts of a longer range indicted a great slaughter among them, and their ships were driven one against another; while they themselves were not able to retaliate in any way. For Archimedes had provided and fixed most of his engines immediately under the wall; whence the Romans, seeing that infinite mischiefs overwhelmed them from no visible means, began to think they were fighting with the gods.

Yet Marcellus escaped unhurt, and, deriding his own artificers and engineers, "What," said he, "must we give up fighting with this geometrical Briareus, who plays pitch and toss with our ships, and, with the multitude of darts which he showers at a single moment upon us, really outdoes the hundred-handed giants of mythology?" And, doubtless, the rest of the Syracusans were but the body of Archimedes' designs, one soul moving and governing all; for, laying aside all other arms, with his alone they infested the Romans, and protected themselves. In fine, when such terror had seized upon the Romans, that, if they did but see a little rope or a piece of wood from the wall, instantly crying out, that there it was again, Archimedes was about to let fly some engine at them, they turned their backs and fled, Marcellus desisted from conflicts and assaults, putting all his hope in a long siege. Yet Archimedes possessed so high a spirit, so profound a soul, and such treasures of scientific knowledge, that though these inventions had now obtained him the renown of more than human sagacity, he yet would not deign to leave behind him any commentary or writing on such subjects; but, repudiating as sordid and ignoble the whole trade of engineering, and every sort of art that lends itself to mere use and profit, he placed his whole affection and ambition in those purer speculations where there can be no reference to the vulgar needs of life; studies, the superiority of which to all others is unquestioned, and in which the only doubt can be, whether the beauty and grandeur of the subjects examined, or the precision and cogency of the methods and means of proof, most deserve our admiration. It is not possible to find in all geometry more difficult and intricate questions, or more simple and lucid explanations. Some ascribe this to his natural genius; while others think that incredible effort and toil produced these, to all appearance, easy and unlabored results. No amount of investigation of yours would succeed in attaining the proof, and yet, once seen, you immediately believe you would have discovered it; by so smooth and so rapid a path he leads you to the conclusion required. And thus it ceases to be incredible that (as is commonly told of him), the charm of his familiar and domestic Siren made him forget his food and neglect his person, to that degree that when he was occasionally carried by absolute violence to bathe, or have his body anointed, he used to trace geometrical figures in the ashes of the fire, and diagrams in the oil on his body, being in a state of entire preoccupation, and, in the truest sense, divine possession with his love and delight in science. His discoveries were numerous and admirable; but he is said to have requested his friends and relations that when he was dead, they would place over his tomb a sphere containing a cylinder, inscribing it with the ratio which the containing solid bears to the contained.

Such was Archimedes, who now showed himself, and, so far as lay in him, the city also, invincible. While the siege continued, . . . he had opportunity to notice a tower into which a body of men might be secretly introduced, as the wall near to it was not difficult to surmount, and it was itself carelessly guarded. Coming often thither, and entertaining conferences about the release of Damippus, he had pretty well calculated the height of the tower, and got ladders prepared. The Syracusans celebrated a feast to Diana; this juncture of time, when they were given up entirely to wine and sport, Marcellus laid hold of, and, before the citizens perceived it, not only possessed himself of the tower, but, before the break of day, filled the wall around with soldiers, and made his way into the Hexapylum. . . . For it is related, that no less prey and plunder was taken here, than afterward in Carthage. For not long after, they obtained also the plunder of the other parts of the city, which were taken by treachery; leaving nothing untouched but the king's money, which was brought into the public treasury. But nothing afflicted Marcellus so much as the death of Archimedes; who was then, as fate would have it, intent upon working out some problem by a diagram, and having fixed his mind alike and his eyes upon the subject of his speculation, he never noticed the incursion of the Romans, nor that the city was taken. In this transport of study and contemplation, a soldier, unexpectedly coming up to him, commanded him to follow to Marcellus; which he declining to do before he had worked out his problem to a demonstration, the soldier, enraged, drew his sword and ran him through. Others write, that a Roman soldier, running upon him with a drawn sword, offered to kill him; and that Archimedes, looking back, earnestly besought him to hold his hand a little while, that he might not leave what he was then at work upon inconclusive and imperfect; but the soldier, nothing moved by his entreaty, instantly killed him. Others again relate, that as Archimedes was carrying to Marcellus mathematical instruments, dials, spheres, and angles, by which the magnitude of the sun might be measured to the sight, some soldiers seeing him, and thinking that he carried gold in a vessel, slew him. Certain it is, that his death was very afflicting to Marcellus; and that Marcellus ever after regarded him that killed him as a murderer; and that he sought for his kindred and honored them with signal favors.

Questions:
1. How did Archimedes, a scientist, become so instrumental in the defense of Syracuse?
2. How did he feel about his practical war machines? How is this separation between engineering and science still evident today, or is it?

Documents 5.3 and 5.4

The following two selections illustrate how Roman women, although receiving limited freedom and even less public recognition, played crucial roles in both familial and political unions.

5.3   The Rape of Lucretia

Rome was ruled by kings until 509, when an oligarchic revolution ended monarchy and established the Republic. After Rome was conquered by the Etruscans about 600 B.C.E. the kings were Etruscan. This is the story of how the Romans abolished the monarchy by expelling King Tarquin the Proud and his dishonorable son who raped the noble and virtuous Roman matron, Lucretia.

> **Source:** *The Early History of the Rome, Books I–V of The History of Rome from its Foundation,* trans. Aubrey de Selincourt, (Baltimore: Penguin Books, 1960), pp. 33–34, 96–101, 114–16. Reprinted by permission in *Readings in Ancient History: Thought and Experience from Gilgamesh to St. Augustine,* Fifth Edition, ed. Nels M. Bailkey, (Lexington, MA: DC Heath and Company, 1996), pp. 325–328.

[The young princes and nobles of Rome] were drinking one day in the quarters of Sextus Tarquinius—Collatinus, son of Egerius, was also present—when someone chanced to mention the subject of wives. Each of them, of course, extravagantly praised his own; and the rivalry got hotter and hotter, until Collatinus suddenly cried: "Stop! What need is there of words, when in a few hours we can prove beyond doubt the incomparable superiority of my Lucretia? We are all young and strong: why shouldn't we ride to Rome and see with our own eyes what kind of women our wives are? There is no better evidence, I assure you, than what a man finds when he enters his wife's room unexpectedly."

They had all drunk a good deal, and the proposal appealed to them; so they mounted their horses and galloped off to Rome. They reached the city as dusk was falling; and there the wives of the royal princes were found enjoying themselves with a group of young friends at a dinner-party, in the greatest of luxury. The riders then went on to Collatia, where they found Lucretia very differently employed: it was already late at night, but there, in the hall of her house, surrounded by her busy maid-servants, she was still hard at work by lamplight upon her spinning. Which wife had won the contest in womanly virtue was no longer in doubt.

With all courtesy Lucretia rose to bid her husband and the princes welcome, and Collatinus, pleased with his success, invited his friends to sup with him. It was at that fatal supper that Lucretia's beauty, and proven chastity, kindled in Sextus Tarquinius the flame of lust, and determined him to debauch her.

Nothing further occurred that night. The little jaunt was over, and the young men rode back to camp.

A few days later Sextus, without Collatinus's knowledge, returned with one companion to Collatia, where he was hospitably welcomed in Lucretia's house, and, after supper, escorted, like the honored visitor he was thought to be, to the guest-chamber. Here he waited till the house was asleep, and then, when all was quiet, he drew his sword and made his way to Lucretia's room determined to rape her. She was asleep. Laying his left hand on her breast, "Lucretia," he whispered, "not a sound! I am Sextus Tarquinius, I am armed—if you utter a word, I will kill you." Lucretia opened her eyes in terror; death was imminent, no help at hand. Sextus urged his love, begged her to submit, pleaded, threatened, used every weapon that might conquer a woman's heart. But all in vain; not even the fear of death could bend her will. "If death will not move you," Sextus cried, "dishonor shall. I will kill you first, then cut the throat of a slave and lay his naked body by your side. Will they not believe that you have been caught in adultery with a servant—and paid the price?" Even the most resolute chastity could not have stood against this dreadful threat.

Lucretia yielded. Sextus enjoyed her, and rode away, proud of his success.

The unhappy girl wrote to her father in Rome and to her husband in Ardea, urging them both to come at once with a trusted friend—and quickly, for a frightful thing had happened. Her father came with Valerius, Volesus's son, her husband with Brutus, with whom he was returning to Rome when he was met by the messenger. They found Lucretia sitting in her room, in deep distress. Tears rose to her eyes as they entered, and to her husband's question, "Is it well with you?" she answered, "No. What can be well with a woman who has lost her honor? In your bed, Collatinus, is the impress of another man. My body only has been violated. My heart is innocent, and death will be my witness. Give me your solemn promise that the adulterer shall be punished—he is Sextus Tarquinius. He it was who last night came as my enemy disguised as my guest, and took his pleasure of me. That pleasure will be my death—and his, too, if you are men."

The promise was given. One after another they tried to comfort her. They told her she was helpless, and therefore innocent; that he alone was guilty. It was the mind, they said, that sinned, not the body: without intention there could never be guilt.

"What is due to *him*," Lucretia said, "is for you to decide. As for me I am innocent of fault, but I will take my punishment. Never shall Lucretia provide a precedent for unchaste women to escape what they deserve." With these words she drew a knife from under her robe, drove it into her heart, and fell forward, dead.

Her father and husband were overwhelmed with grief. While they stood weeping helplessly, Brutus drew the bloody knife from Lucretia's body, and holding it before him cried: "By this girl's blood—none more chaste till a tyrant wronged her—and by the gods, I swear that with sword and fire, and whatever else can lend strength to my arm, I will pursue Lucius Tarquinius the Proud, his wicked wife, and all his children, and never again will I let them or any other man be King in Rome."

He put the knife into Collatinus's hands, then passed it to Lucretius, then to Valerius. All looked at him in astonishment: a miracle had happened—he was a changed man. Obedient to his command, they swore their oath. Grief was forgotten in the sudden surge of anger, and when Brutus called upon them to make war, from that instant, upon the tyrant's throne, they took him for their leader.

5.4 Women in Roman Politics: Manipulators or Manipulated?

Cleopatra (d. 31 B.C.E.), the most famous woman in Roman politics, was not even Roman, but was the last Ptolemy to rule Egypt. Some historians have argued that the liaison between Cleopatra and Antony was purely for political advantage, but contemporaries and ancient historians did not. Antony's passion for Cleopatra was obvious to them. Although Roman women did not have an official role in public life, they were often used as the cement in political alliances, such as when Antony married Octavia, the sister of Caesar [Octavian, later known as Augustus].

Source: Plutarch, *Parallel Lives*, trans. John Dryden and modernized by A.H. Clough, Vol. V, (New York: Little, Brown and Company, 1909), pp. 189–213.

Antony first entertained Caesar, this also being a concession on Caesar's part to his sister; and when at length an agreement was made between them, that Caesar should give Antony two of his legions to serve him in the Parthian war, and that Antony should in return leave with him a hundred armed galleys, Octavia further obtained of her husband, besides this, twenty light ships for her brother, and of her brother, a thousand foot for her husband. So, having parted good friends, Caesar went immediately to make war with Pompey to conquer Sicily. And Antony, leaving in Caesar's charge his wife and children, and his children by his former wife Fulvia set sail for Asia.

But the mischief that thus long had lain still, the passion for Cleopatra, which better thoughts had seemed to have lulled and charmed into oblivion, upon his approach to Syria, gathered strength again, and broke out into a flame. And, in fine, like Plato's restive and rebellious horse of the human soul, flinging off all good and wholesome counsel, and breaking fairly loose, he sends Fonteius Capito to bring Cleopatra into Syria. To whom at her arrival he made no small or trifling present, Phoenicia, Coele-Syria, Cyprus, great part of Cilicia, that side of Judaea which produces balm, that part of Arabia where the Nabathaeans extend to the outer sea; profuse gifts, which much displeased the Romans.

. . . But Octavia, in Rome, being desirous to Antony, asked Caesar's leave to go to him; which he gave her, not so much, say most authors, to gratify his sister, as to obtain a fair pretence to begin the war upon her dishonorable reception. She no sooner arrived at Athens, but by letters from Antony she was informed of his new expedition, and his will that she should await him there. And, though she were much displeased, not being ignorant of the real reason of this usage, yet she wrote to him to know of what place he would be pleased she should send the things she had brought with her for his use; for she had brought clothes for his soldiers, baggage, cattle, money, and presents for his friends and officers, and two thousand chosen soldiers sumptuously armed, to form praetorian cohorts. This message was brought from Octavia to Antony by Niger, one of his friends, who added to it the praises she deserved so well. Cleopatra, feeling her rival already, as it were, at hand, was seized with fear, lest if to her noble life and her high alliance, she once could add the charm of daily habit and affectionate intercourse, she should become irresistible, and be his absolute mistress for ever. So she feigned to be dying for love of Antony, bring her body down by slender diet; when he entered the room, she fixed her eyes upon him in a rapture, and when he left, seemed to languish and half faint away. She took great pains that he should see her in tears, and, as soon as he noticed it, hastily dried them up and turned away, as if it were her wish that he should know nothing of it. All this was acting while he prepared for Media; and Cleopatra's creatures were not slow to forward the design, upbraiding Antony with his unfeeling, hard-hearted temper, thus letting a woman perish whose soul depended upon him and him alone. Octavia, it was true, was his wife, and had been married to him because it was found convenient for the affairs of her brother that it should be so, and she had the honor of the title; but Cleopatra, the sovereign queen of many nations, had been contented with the name of his mistress, nor did she shun or despise the character whilst she might see him, might live with him, and enjoy him; if she were bereaved of this, she would not survive the loss. In fine, they so melted and unmanned him, that, fully believing she would die if he forsook her, he put off the war and returned to Alexandria, deferring his Median expedition until next summer, though news came of the Parthians being all in confusion with intestine disputes. Nevertheless, he did some time after go into that country, and made an alliance with the king of Media, by marriage of a son of his by Cleopatra to the king's daughter, who was yet very young; and so returned, with his thoughts taken up about the civil war.

When Octavia returned from Athens, Caesar, who considered she had been injuriously treated, commanded her to live in a separate house; but she refused to leave the house of her husband, and entreated him, unless he had already resolved, upon other motives, to make war with Antony, that he would on her account let it alone; it would be intolerable to have it said of the two greatest commanders in the world, that they had involved the Roman people in a civil war, the one out of passion for the other out of resentment about, a woman. And her behavior proved her words to be sincere. She remained in Antony's house as if he were at home in it, and took the noblest and most generous care, not only of his children by her, but of those by Fulvia also. She received all the friends of Antony that came to Rome to seek office or upon any business, and did her utmost to prefer their requests to Caesar; yet this her honorable deportment did but, without her meaning it, damage the reputation of Antony; the wrong he did to such a woman made him hated. Nor was the division he made among his sons at Alexandria less unpopular; it seemed a theatrical piece of insolence and contempt of his country. For, assembling the people in the exercise ground, and causing two golden thrones to be placed on a platform of silver, the one for him and the other for Cleopatra, and at their feet lower thrones for their children, he proclaimed Cleopatra queen of Egypt, Cyprus, Libya, and Coele-Syria, and with her conjointly Caesarion, the reupted son of the former Caesar, who left Cleopatra with child. His own sons by Cleopatra were to have the style of kings of kings; to Alexander he gave Armenia and Media, with Parthia, so soon as it should be overcome; to Ptolemy, Phoenicia, Syria, and Cilicia. Alexander was brought out before the people in the Median costume, the tiara and upright peak, and Ptolemy, in boots and mantle and Macedonian cap done about with the diadem; for this was the habit of the successors of Alexander, as the other was of the Medes and Armenians. And, as soon as they had saluted their parents, the one was received by a guard of Macedonians, the other by one of Armenians. Cleopatra was then, as at other times when she appeared in public, dressed in the habit of the goddess Isis, and gave audience to the people under the name of the New Isis.

Caesar, relating these things in the senate, and often complaining to the people, excited men's minds against Antony. And Antony also sent messages of accusation against Caesar. The principal of his charges were these: first, that he had not made any division with him of Sicily, which was lately taken from Pompey; secondly, that he had retained the ships he had lent him for the war; thirdly, that after deposing Lepidus, their colleague, he had taken for himself the army, governments, and revenues formerly appropriated to him; and, lastly, that he had parcelled out almost all Italy amongst his own soldiers, and left nothing for his. Caesar's answer was as follows: that he had put Lepidus out of government because of his own misconduct; that what he had got in war he would divide with Antony, so soon as Antony gave him a share of Armenia; that Antony's soldiers had no claims in Italy, being in possession of Media and Parthia, the acquisitions which their brave actions under their general had added to the Roman empire.

Antony was in Armenia when this answer came to him, and immediately sent Canidius with sixteen legions towards the sea; but he, in the company of Cleopatra, went to Ephesus, whither ships were coming in from all quarters to form the navy, consisting, vessels of which Cleopatra furnished two hundred, together with twenty thousand talents, and provision for the whole army during the war. Antony, on the advice of Domitius and some others, bade Cleopatra return into Egypt, there to expect the event of the war; but she, dreading some new reconciliation by Octavia's means, prevailed with Canidius, by a large sum of money, to speak in her favor with Antony, pointing out to him that it was not just that one that bore so great a part in the charge of the war should be robbed of her share of glory in the carrying it on; nor would it be politic to disoblige the Egyptians, who were so considerable a part of his naval forces; nor did he see how she was inferior in prudence to any one of the kings that were serving with him; she had long governed a great kingdom by herself alone, and long lived with him, and gained experience in public affairs. These arguments (so the fate that destined all to Caesar would have it), prevailed; and when all their forces had met, they sailed together to Samos, and held high festivities. . . .

This over, he gave Priene to his players for a habitation, and set sail for Athens, where fresh sports and play-acting employed him. Cleopatra, jealous of the honors Octavia had received at Athens (for Octavia was much beloved by the Athenians), courted the favor of the people with all sorts of attentions. The Athenians, in requital, having decreed her public honors, deputed several of the citizens to wait upon her at her house; amongst whom went Antony as one, he being an Athenian citizen, and he it was that made the speech. He sent orders to Rome to have Octavia removed out of his house. She left it, we are told, accompanied by all his children, except the eldest by Fulvia, who was then with his father, weeping and grieving that she must be looked upon as one of the causes of the war. But the Romans pitied, not so much her, as Antony himself, and more particularly those who had seen Cleopatra, whom they could report to have no way the advantage of Octavia either in youth or in beauty.

The speed and extent of Antony's preparations alarmed Caesar, who feared he might be forced to fight the decisive battle that summer. For he wanted many necessaries, and the people grudged very much to pay the taxes; freemen being called upon to pay a fourth part of their incomes, and freed slaves an eighth of their property, so that there were loud outcries against him, and disturbances throughout all Italy. And this is looked upon as one of the greatest of Antony's oversights, that he did not then press the war. For he allowed time at once for Caesar to make his preparations, and for the commotions to pass over. For while people were having their money called for, they were mutinous and violent; but, having paid it, they held their peace. Titius and Plancus, men of consular dignity and friends to Antony, having been ill used by Cleopatra, whom they had most resisted in her design of being present in the war came over to Caesar, and gave information of the contents of Antony's will, with which they were acquainted. It was deposited in the hands of the vestal virgins, who refused to deliver it up, and sent Caesar word, if he pleased, he should come and seize it himself, which he did. And, reading it over to himself, he noted those places that were most for his purpose, and, having summoned the senate, read them publicly. Many were scandalized at the proceeding, thinking it out of reason and equity to call a man to account for what was not to be until after his death. Caesar specially pressed what Antony said in his will about his burial; for he had ordered that even if he died in the city of Rome, his body, after being carried in state through the forum, should be sent to Cleopatra at Alexandria. Calvisius, a dependent of Caesar's, urged other charges in connection with Cleopatra against Antony; that he had given her the library of Pergamus, containing two hundred thousand distinct volumes; that at a great banquet, in the presence of many guests, he had risen up and rubbed her feet, to fulfil some wager or promise; that he had suffered the Ephesians to salute her as their queen; that he had frequently at the public audience of kings and princes received amorous messages written in tablets made of onyx and crystal, and read them openly on the tribunal; that when Furnius, a man of great authority and eloquence among the Romans, was pleading, Cleopatra happening to pass by in her chair, Antony started up and left

them in the middle of their cause, to follow at her side and attend her home.

Calvisius, however, was looking upon as the inventor of most of these stories. Antony's friends went up and down the city to gain him credit, and sent one of themselves, Geminius, to him, to beg him to take heed and not allow himself to be deprived by vote of his authority, and proclaimed a public enemy to the Roman state. But Geminius no sooner arrived in Greece but he was looked upon as one of Octavia's spies; at their suppers he was made a continual butt for mockery, and was put to sit in the least honorable places; all which he bore very well, seeking only an occasion of speaking with Antony. So, at supper, being told to say what business he came about, he answered he would keep the rest for a soberer hour, but one thing he had to say, whether full or fasting, that all would go well if Cleopatra would return to Egypt. And on Antony showing his anger at it, "You have done well, Geminius," said Cleopatra, "to tell your secret without being put to the rack." So Geminius, after a few days, took occasion to make his escape and go to Rome. Many more of Antony's friends were drive from him by the insolent usage they had from Cleopatra's flatterers, amongst whom were Marcus Silanus and Dellius the historian. And Dellius says he was afraid of his life, and that Glaucus, the physician, informed him of Cleopatra's design against him. She was angry with him for having said that Antony's friends were served with sour wine, while at Rome Sarmentus, Caesar's little page (his *delicia*, as the Romans call it), drank Falernian.

As soon as Caesar had completed his preparations, he had a decree made, declaring war on Cleopatra, and depriving Antony of the authority which he had let a woman exercise in his place. Caesar added that he had drunk potions that had bereaved him of his senses, and that the generals they would have to fight with would be Mardion the eunuch, Pothinus, Iras, Cleopatra's hairdressing girl, and Charmion, who were Antony's chief state-councillors.

Questions for Documents 5.3 and 5.4:
1. What did Lucretia represent in this story about the relationship of the Roman Republic?
2. What is Plutarch's interpretation of the relationships between Antony, Cleopatra and Octavia?
3. How do Octavia and Lucretia each typify the ideal Roman woman?
4. How could one argue that these women were both manipulators or manipulated in this political/personal situation?

70   *Chapter 5*

SECTION 2
Living in a New World

5.5   The Twelve Tables

The Law of the Twelve Tables, reflecting the agricultural and pastoral character of the Roman community of small landowners in the first century of the Republic, is the primary source for the social and economic conditions of Rome in the fifth century B.C.E. Recording them in writing was a concession to the Plebeians in 449 B.C.E., curbing the arbitrary power of the Patrician magistrates and marking their first step in eventually achieving equality before the law.

> **Source:** Naphtali Lewis and Meyer Reinhold, ed., *Roman Civilization: Sourcebook I: The Republic*, (New York: Harper Torchbooks, 1966), pp. 102–9.

TABLE I: *PRELIMINARIES TO AND RULES FOR A TRIAL*

If plaintiff summons defendant to court . . . he shall go. If he does not go, plaintiff shall call witness thereto. Then only shall he take defendant by force.

If defendant shirks or takes to his heels, plaintiff shall lay hands on him.

If disease or age is an impediment, he [who summons defendant to court] shall grant him a team; he shall not spread with cushions the covered carriage if he does not so desire.

. . . .

When parties make a settlement of the case, the judge shall announce it. If they do not reach a settlement, they shall state the outline of their case in the meeting place or Forum before noon.

They shall plead it out together in person. After noon, the judge shall adjudge the case to the party present. If both be present, sunset shall be the time limit [of proceedings].

TABLE II: *FURTHER ENACTMENTS ON TRIALS*

. . . Whoever is in need of evidence, he shall go on every third day to call out loudly before witness' doorway.

TABLE III: *EXECUTION; LAW OF DEBT*

When a debt has been acknowledged, or judgment about the matter has been pronounced in court, thirty days must be the legitimate time of grace. After that, the debtor may be arrested by laying on of hands. Bring him into court. If he does not satisfy the judgment, or no one in court offers himself as surety in his behalf, the creditor may take the defaulter with him. He may bind him either in stocks or in fetters; he may bind him with a weight no more than fifteen pounds, or with less if he shall so desire. . . .

Unless they make a settlement, debtors shall be held in bonds for sixty days. During that time they shall be brought before the praetor's court in the meeting place on three successive market days, and the amount for which they are judged liable shall be announced; on the third market day they shall suffer capital punishment or be delivered up for sale abroad, across the Tiber. . . .

TABLE IV. *PATRIA POTESTAS: RIGHTS OF HEAD OF FAMILY*

Quickly kill . . . a dreadfully deformed child.

If a father thrice surrender a son for sale, the son shall be free from the father.

A child born ten months after the father's death will not be admitted into a legal inheritance.

TABLE V: *GUARDIANSHIP; SUCCESSION*

Females shall remain in guardianship even when they have attained their majority . . . except Vestal Virgins.

. . . .

If a person dies intestate, and has no self-successor[1], the nearest agnate[2] kinsman shall have possession of deceased's household.

If there is no agnate kinsman, deceased's clansmen shall have possession of his household.

To persons for whom a guardian has not been appointed by will, to them agnates are guardians.

A spendthrift is forbidden to exercise administration over his own goods. . . . A person who, being insane or a spendthrift, is prohibited from administering his own goods shall be under trusteeship of agnates.

The inheritance of a Roman citizen-freedman shall be made over to his patron if the freedman has died intestate and without self-successor.

. . . .

Debt bequeathed by inheritance is divided proportionally amongst each heir with automatic liability when the details have been investigated.

TABLE V: *ACQUISITION AND POSSESSION*

When a party shall make bond or conveyance, the terms of the verbal declaration are to be held binding.

. . . .

---

[1] A person under the legal power of the same head of household.
[2] from the father's side

Usucapio[3] of movable things requires one year's possession for its completion; but *usucapio* of an estate and buildings two years.

Any woman who does not wish to be subjected in this manner to the hand of her husband should be absent three nights in succession every year, and so interrupt the *usucapio* of each year. . . .

TABLE VII: *RIGHTS CONCERNING LAND*

Ownership within a five-foot strip [between two pieces of land] shall not be acquired by long usage.

The width of a road [extends] to eight feet where it runs straight ahead, sixteen round a bend.

Persons shall mend roadways. If they do not keep them laid with stone, a person may drive his beasts where he wishes.

. . . .

If a water course directed through a public place shall do damage to a private person, he shall have right of suit to the effect that damage shall be repaired for the owner.

Branches of a tree may be lopped off all round to a height of more than 15 feet. . . . Should a tree on a neighbor's farm be bent crooked by a wind and lean over your farm, action may be taken for removal of that tree.

It is permitted to gather up fruit falling down on another man's farm.

TABLE VIII: *TORTS OR DELICTS*

If any person has sung or composed against another person a song such as was causing slander or insult to another, he shall be clubbed to death.

If a person has maimed another's limb, let there be retaliation in kind unless he makes agreement for settlement with him.

If he has broken or bruised a freeman's bone with his hand or a club, he shall undergo penalty of 300 *as*[4] pieces; if a slave's, 150.

If he has done simple harm [to another], penalties shall be 25 *as* pieces.

If a four-footed animal shall be said to have caused loss, legal action . . . shall be either the surrender of the thing which damaged, or else the offer of assessment for the damage.

For pasturing on, or cutting secretly by night, another's crops acquired by tillage, there shall be capital punishment in the case of an adult malefactor . . . he shall be hanged and put to death as a sacrifice to Ceres.[5] In the case of a person under the age of puberty, at the discretion of the praetor either he shall be scourged or settlement shall be made for the harm done by paying double damages.

Any person who destroys by burning any building or heap of corn deposited alongside a house shall be bound, scourged, and put to death by burning at the stake, provided that he has committed the said misdeed with malice aforethought; but if he shall have committed it by accident, that is, by negligence, it is ordained that he repair the damage, or, if he be too poor to be competent for such punishment, he shall receive a lighter chastisement.

Any person who has cut down another person's trees with harmful intent shall pay 25 *as* pieces for every tree.

If theft has been done by night, if the owner kill the thief, the thief shall be held lawfully killed.

It is forbidden that a thief be killed by day . . . unless he defend himself with a weapon; even though he has come with a weapon, unless he use his weapon and fight back, you shall not kill him. And even if he resists, first call out.

In the case of all other thieves caught in the act, if they are freemen, they should be flogged and adjudged to the person against whom the theft has been committed, provided that the malefactors have committed it by day and have not defended themselves with a weapon; slaves caught in the act of theft should be flogged and thrown from the Rock;[6] boys under the age of puberty should, at the praetor's discretion, be flogged, and the damage done by them should be repaired.

If a person pleads on a case of theft in which the thief has not been caught in the act, the thief must compound for the loss by paying double damages.

A stolen thing is debarred from *usucapio*.

No person shall practice usury at a rate more than one twelfth.

. . . .

If a patron shall have defrauded his client, he must be solemnly forfeited.[7]

. . . .

Penalty . . . for false witness . . . a person who has been found guilty of giving false witness shall be hurled down from the Tarpeian Rock. . . .

No person shall hold meetings by night in the city. . . .

TABLE IX: *PUBLIC LAW*

Laws of personal exception [i.e., bills of attainder] must not be proposed; cases in which the penalty affects the person of a citizen must not be decided except through the greatest assembly and through those whom the censors have placed upon the register of citizens.

The penalty shall be capital punishment for a judge or arbiter legally appointed who has been found guilty of receiving a bribe for giving a decision. . . .

---

[3] *Usucapio* is the right of ownership established by long term possession.

[4] The *as* was a Roman bronze monetary unit, originally pound ingots of copper divided into 12 pieces.

[5] Roman goddess with dominion over all plant life. She presided over the interplay of life and death, and she provided food.

[6] The Tarpeian Rock on Capitoline Hill, commonly used as a place of execution.

[7] The man thus adjudged was placed outside human law by being dedicated to a divinity for destruction. This original death by sacrifice was later transformed into outlawry and confiscation of property.

Putting to death . . . of any man who has not been convicted, whosoever he might be, is forbidden.

TABLE X: *SACRED LAW*

A dead man shall not be buried or burned within the city. One must not do more than this [at funerals]; one must not smooth the pyre with an axe, three veils, one small purple tunic, and ten flute-players.

Women must not tear cheeks or hold chorus of "Alas!" on account of funeral. . . .

TABLE XI: *SUPPLEMENTARY LAWS*

Intermarriage shall not take place between plebeians and patricians.

TABLE XII: *SUPPLEMENTARY LAWS*

. . . Arising from delicts committed by children and slaves of a household establishment . . . actions for damages are appointed whereby the father or master could be allowed either to undergo "assessment for damages," or hand over the delinquent to punishment. . . .

. . . .

Whatever the people has last ordained shall be held as binding by law.

Questions:
1. How do the Twelve Tables compare to Hammurabi's or Hebrew laws in regard to the origin of law? Capital punishment? Liability? The rights of women? Usury?
2. What evidence of clients and patrons, patrician and plebeian does the Twelve Tables contain?
3. How does motivation and age matter in determining punishment?

5.6 Slaves in the Roman Countryside

Slaves were an integral part of Roman society and economy. The number of slaves increased drastically in the last century of the Republic and during the early Empire as Roman territory expanded. Below are instructions and advice from three famous Roman writers about how to manage slaves used in agriculture.

Source: Columella, *On Agriculture* 1.8.1, 2, 5, 6, 9, 10, 11, 16, 18, 19; Cato the Elder, *On Agriculture*, 56, 57, 58, 59; Varro, On Agriculture 1.17.1, 3–5, 7, printed in *As the Romans Did: A Sourcebook in Roman Social History*, Jo-Ann Shelton ed., (New York: Oxford University Press, 1998), pp. 169–72.

FROM COLUMBELLA, *ON AGRICULTURE*

A landowner must be concerned about what responsibility it is best to give each slave and what sort of work to assign to each. I advise that you not appoint a foreman from that type of slave who is physically attractive, and certainly not from the type who has been employed in the city, where all skills are directed toward increasing pleasure. This lazy and sleepy type of slave is accustomed to having a lot of time on his hands, to lounging around the Campus Martius, the Circus Maximus, the theaters, the gambling dens, the snack bars, and the brothels, and he is always dreaming of these same foolish pleasures. If a city slave continues to daydream when he has been transferred to a farm, the landowner suffers the loss not just of the slave but actually of his whole estate. You should therefore choose someone who has been hardened to farm work from infancy, and who has been tested by experience.

The foreman should be given a female companion both to keep him in bounds and also to assist him in certain matters. . . . He should not be acquainted with the city or the weekly market, except in regard to matters of buying and selling produce, which is his duty.[1]

The foreman should choose the slaves' clothing with an eye to utility rather than fashion, and he should take care to protect them from the wind, cold, and rain with long-sleeved leather tunics, patchwork cloaks, or hooded capes. All of these garments ward off the elements and thus no day is so unbearable that no out-of-doors work can be done. The foreman should not only be skilled in agricultural operations, but also be endowed with such strength and virtue of mind (at least as far as his slave's personality permits) that he may oversee men neither with laxity nor with cruelty.

There is no better method of maintaining control over even the most worthless of men than demanding hard labor. . . . After their exhausting toil, they will turn their attention to rest and sleep rather than to fun and games.

It should be an established custom for the landowner to inspect the slaves chained in the prison, to examine whether they are securely chained, whether their quarters are safe and well guarded, whether the foreman has put anyone in chains or released anyone from chains without his master's knowledge.

A diligent master investigates the quality of his slaves' food and drink by tasting it himself. He examines their clothing, hand-coverings, and foot-coverings. He should even grant them the opportunity of registering complaints against those who have harmed them either through cruelty or dishonesty. . . . I have given exemption from work and sometimes even freedom to very fertile female slaves when they have borne many children, since bearing a certain number of offspring ought to be rewarded. For a woman who has three sons, exemption from work is the reward; for a woman who has more, freedom.[2]

---

[1] The foreman obviously had some freedom of movement and could travel back and forth to the market, but was not to linger there to enjoy the attractions of the city.

[2] Although the mother might be set free, her children remained as slaves. We do not know whether Columella's willingness to free fertile female slaves was unusual among slave-owners.

CATO THE ELDER, *ON AGRICULTURE*

When the master has arrived at his villa and has paid his respects to the household *lar*[3], he should walk around the whole farm, on the same day if possible; if not, on the next day. When he has learned how the farm is being looked after, what work has been done, and what has not been done, he should summon his foreman the next day and ask how much of the work has been completed, how much remains, whether the completed work was done pretty much on time, whether the remaining work can be finished, and how much wine, grain, and other products were produced. When he has received this information, he should calculate what was done in how many days, by how many workers. When the figures are not encouraging, the foreman usually claims that he has worked diligently but "the slaves have been ill," "the weather has been bad," the slaves have run away," etc., etc. When he has given these and many other excuses, call his attention again to your calculation of the work done and the workers used. If the weather has been rainy, remind him of the chores that could have been done on rainy days: washing out wine vats, sealing them with pitch, cleaning the villa, moving grain, hauling out manure, making a manure pit, cleaning seed, mending ropes, and making new ones. The slaves might also have repaired their cloaks and hats. On festival days, old ditches might have been cleaned out, the road repaired, brambles cut down, gardens dug, the meadow cleared, twigs bundled, thorn bushes uprooted, spelt ground, and general cleaning done. When the slaves were sick, he should not have given them so much food. When these things have been calmly pointed out, give orders for the remaining work to be completed. Look over his account books for ready cash, grain, fodder supplies, wine, oil—what has been sold, what payments have been collected, how much is left, and what remains to be sold. Order him to collect outstanding debts and to sell what remains. Order him to provide whatever is needed for the current year, and to sell off whatever is superfluous. . . . Tell him to scrutinize the herd and hold an auction. Sell your oil, if the price is right, and the surplus wine and grain. Sell off the old oxen, the blemished cattle and sheep, wool, hides, old wagons, old tools, old slaves, sick slaves, and whatever else is superfluous.

Food rations for the slaves: For those who do hard labor, four measures of wheat in winter, four and one-half in the summer. For the foreman, the foreman's wife, the taskmaster, and the shepherd, three measures. For slaves working in chains, four pounds of bread in the winter, five when they begin to dig the vineyard, and back to four again when the figs appear.

. . . .

Clothing for the slaves: Provide a tunic weighing three and one-half pounds and a cloak every other year. Whenever you give a tunic or cloak to any of the slaves, first get the old one back; from it, patchwork coverings can be made. You ought to give the slaves sturdy wooden shoes every other year.

FROM VARRO, *ON AGRICULTURE*

The instruments by which the soil is cultivated: Some men divide these into three categories: (1) articulate instruments, i.e., slaves; (2) inarticulate instruments, i.e., oxen; and (3) mute instruments, i.e. carts. . . .

Slaves should be neither timid nor brazen. They ought to have as overseers men who have knowledge of basic reading and writing skills and of some learning. . . . It is very important that the overseer be experienced in farming operations, for he must not only give orders but also perform the work, so that the other slaves may imitate him and understand that he has been made their overseer for good reason—he is superior to them in knowledge. However, overseers should not be allowed to force obedience with whips rather than words, if words can achieve the same result. Don't buy too many slaves of the same nationality, for this is very often accustomed to cause domestic quarrels. You should make your foremen more eager to work by giving them rewards and by seeing that they have [*monetary* rewards] and female companions from among their fellow slaves, who will bear them children. . . . Slaves become more eager to work when treated generously with respect to food or more clothing or time off or permission to graze some animal of their own on the farm, and other things of this kind. The result is that, when some rather difficult task is asked of them or some rather harsh punishment is meted out, their loyalty and good will toward their master is restored by the consolation of these former generosities.

Questions:
1. How well or badly were slaves regarded and treated in Roman culture?
2. What differences can you see in the three writers' attitude toward slaves?
3. What differences appear between slaves who worked in the countryside on villas and those who lived in city households?

5.7   A Marriage Contract

The following marriage contract was drawn up in Egypt in 13 B.C.E. Since Egypt had only become a Roman province in 30 B.C.E., it is likely that it was as much [or more] influenced by Egyptian and Greek-Hellenistic procedure as by Roman practice.

Source: *As the Romans Did: A Sourcebook in Roman Social History*, Jo-Ann Shelton ed., (New York: Oxford University Press, 1998), p 43.

To Protarchus, from Thermion daughter of Apion, accompained by her guardian Apollonius son of Chaereas, and from Apollonius son of Ptolemaeus:—

---

[3] The *Lars Familiaris* was the spirit or deity who protected the household and its members. There was a shrine to this deity in the home, and sacrifices were made to it regularly.

Thermion and Apollonius son of Ptolemaeus agree that they have come together for the purpose of sharing their lives with one another. The above-mentioned Apollonius son of Ptolemaeus agrees that he has received from Thermion, handed over from her household as a dowry, a pair of gold earrings. . . . From now on he will furnish Thermion, as his wedded wife, with all necessities clothing according to his means, and he will not mistreat her or cast her out or insult her or bring in another wife; otherwise he must at once return the dowry and in addition half again as much.

And Thermion will fulfill her duties toward her husband and her marriage, and will not sleep away from the house or be absent one day without the consent of Apollonius son of Ptolemaeus and will not damage or injure their common home and will not consort with another man; otherwise she, if judged guilty of these actions, will be deprived of her dowry, and in addition the transgressor will be liable to the prescribed fine. Dated the 17th year of Caesar [Augustus].

Questions:
1. How does this marriage contract compare to Greek and Roman laws regarding women and marriage?
2. What is expected of the man and the woman in marriage?
3. What do these expectations tell us about the nature of marriage in Hellenistic/Roman Alexandria?

Documents 5.8 and 5.9
The following two selections demonstrate the changes in Roman politics and government in a span of about twenty years. The first is a communication between two brothers of how best to obtain votes in an election while the second is a record of sweeping reforms implemented by Caesar during his reign.

5.8   How to Run for Political Office

In 63 B.C.E. the great Roman lawyer and orator Marcus Cicero was elected consul after a lively political election. Quintus Cicero, his brother, had written him a letter full of advice in seeking votes during the days before the election by the comitia.

> **Source:** William Stearns Davis, ed., *Readings in Ancient History: Illustrative Extracts from the Sources, Volume II: Rome and the West*, (New York: Allyn and Bacon, 1913), pp. 130–34.

Almost every day as you go down to the Forum you must say to yourself, "I am a *novus homo*" [*i.e.* without noble ancestry]. "I am a candidate for the consulship." "This is Rome." For the "newness" of your name you will best compensate by the brilliance of your oratory. This has ever car-

ried with it great political distinction. A man who is held worthy of defending ex-consuls, cannot be deemed unworthy of the consulship itself. Wherefore approach each individual case with the persuasion that on it depends as a whole your entire reputation. See that all those aids to natural ability, which I know are your special gifts are ready for use . . . and finally take care that both the number and rank of your friends are unmistakable. For you have, as few *novi homines*[1] have had,—all the tax-syndicate promoters, nearly the whole equestrian order, and many municipal towns, especially devoted to you, many people who have been defended by you, many trade guilds, and beside these a large number of the rising generation, who have become attached to you in their enthusiasm for public speaking, and who visit you daily in swarms, and with such constant regularity!

See that you retain these advantages by reminding these persons, by appealing to them, and by using every means to make them understand that this, and this only, is the time for those who are in your debt now, to show their gratitude,[2] and for those who wish for your services in the future, to place you under an obligation. It also seems possible that a "new man" may be much aided by the fact that he has the good wishes of men of high rank, and especially of ex-consuls. It is a point in your favor that you should be thought worthy of this position and rank by the very men to whose position you are wishing to attain.

All these men must be canvassed with care, agents must be sent to them, and they must be convinced that we have always been at one with the Optimates (Aristocratic Party), that we have never been dangerous demagogues in the very least; that if we seem ever to have said anything in the spirit of the other party, we did it with a view of attracting Pompey, that we might have that man of the greatest influence either actively on our side of the canvass, or at least neutral.[3] Also takes pains to get on your side the young men of high rank, and keep the friendship of those whom you already have. They will contribute much to your political position. You have many already: make them feel how much you think depends on them; if you rouse to zeal those who are now only lukewarm friends, that will be a vast gain.

[The writer then goes on to analyze the weak points in Cicero's leading rivals: their vile characters, their numerous personal crimes, their blunders as officials, etc.,—all of which facts Cicero must take advantage.[4] He must also try to make "friends" of every kind of citizen.] "Whosoever gives any sign of inclination to you, or regularly visits your house, you must put down in the category of friends. But yet the most advantageous thing is to be

---

[1] Men, like Cicero, who had no ancestors who had held the upper ("curule") offices.
[2] Theoretically Roman advocates did not receive regular fees, but enjoyed the often substantial "gratitude" of their clients.
[3] Cicero's brother evidently fears he may be suspected of party irregularity—of having favored the rival *Populares* (Catiline's party).
[4] Politics in Cicero's day seem to have been on a fearfully scurrilous and personal basis.

beloved and pleasant in the eyes of those who are friends on the more regular grounds of relationship by blood or marriage, the membership in the same club, or some close tie or other. You must take great pains that [these men] should love you and desire your highest honor—as, for example, your tribesmen, neighbors, clients, and finally your freedmen, yes even your slaves: for nearly all the gossip that forms public opinion emanates from your own servants' quarters.

In a word, you must secure friends of every class, magistrates, consuls and their tribunes to win you the vote of the centuries [that elect the consuls]: men of wide popular influence. Those who either have gained or hope to gain the vote to a tribe or a century, or any other advantage, through *your* influence [for them], take all pains to collect and to secure.

[Cicero must not be squeamish about making friends; he can "without loss of dignity" affect familiarity with about any one and must by all means do so.] . . .

So you see that you will have the votes of all the centuries secured for you by the number and variety of your friends. The first and obvious thing is that you embrace the Roman senators and equites, and the active and popular men of all the other orders. There are many city men of good business habits, there are many freedmen engaged in the Forum who are popular and energetic: these men try with all your might, both personally and by common friends, to make eager in your behalf. Seek them out, send agents to them, show them that they are putting you under the greatest possible obligation. After that, review the entire city, all guilds, districts, neighborhoods. If you can attach to yourself the leading men in these, you will by their means easily keep a hold upon the multitude.

When you have done that, take care to have in your mind a chart of all Italy laid out according to the tribes in each town, and learn it by heart, so that you may not allow any chartered town, colony, praefecture, in a word, any spot in Italy to exist, in which you have not a firm foothold. Trace out also individuals in every region, inform yourself about them, seek them out, secure that in their own districts they shall canvass for you, and be, as it were, candidates in your interest. Men in country towns think themselves in the position of friends if we of the city know them by name; if, however, they think they are besides getting some protection [by your legal talent] for themselves, they will not miss the chance of proving obliging.

[After having thus worked for the "rural vote"], the centuries of the equites too seem capable of being won over if you are careful. And you should be strenuous in seeing as many people as possible every day of every possible class and order, for from the mere numbers of these [who greet you] you can make a guess of the amount of support you will get on the balloting. Your visitors are of three kinds: one consists of morning callers who come to your house, a second of those who escort you to the Forum, the third of those who attend you [constantly] on your canvass. In the case of the mere morning callers, who are less select, and according to

present-day fashion, are decidedly numerous, you must contrive to think that you value even this slight attention [of a call] very highly. It often happens that people when they visit a number of candidates, and observe the one that pays special heed to their attentions, leave off visiting the others, and little by little become real supporters of this man.

Secondly, to those who escort you to the Forum: Since this is a much greater attention than a mere morning call, indicate clearly that they still more gratifying to you; and [with them], as far as it shall lie in your power, go down to the Forum at fixed times, for the daily escort [of a candidate] by its numbers produces a great impression and confers great personal distinction.

The third class is that of people who continually attend you upon your canvass. See that those who do so spontaneously understand that you regard yourself as forever obliged by their extreme kindness; from these on the other hand, who *owe* you the attention [for services rendered] frankly demand that so far as their age and business allow they should be constantly in attendance, and that those who are unable to accompany you in person, should find relatives to substitute in performing this duty. I am very anxious and think it most important that you should always be surrounded with numbers. Besides, it confers a great reputation, and great distinction to be accompanied by those whom you have defended and saved in the law courts. Put this demand fairly before them—that since by your means, and without any fee,—some have retained property, others their honor, or their civil rights, or their entire fortunes,—and since there will never be any other time when they can show their gratitude, they now should reward you by this service.

5.9 Caesar's Reforms

Julius Caesar was dictator and controlled the Roman State for less than four years, from 48 to 44 B.C.E. Yet, during that short period, he not only waged war in Egypt, Asia Minor, Africa, and Spain, but he also executed numerous reforms in a wide array of Roman institutions.

Source: William Stearns David, ed., *Readings in Ancient History: Illustrative Extracts from the Sources, Volume II: Rome and the West*, (New York: Allyn and Bacon, 1913), pp. 150–54. (From Suetonius, *Life of Julius Caesar*, chaps. 31–33, Bohn translation.)

Turning his attention to the regulation of the Republic, he corrected the calendar[1] which had for some time been direfully confused through the unwarrantable liberty which the pontiffs had taken in the matter of intercalation.[1] To such a

---

[1] The old calendar was so unscientific it was necessary to insert arbitrarily extra months to make the years of something like equal length.

height had this abuse proceeded that neither the festivals designed for the harvest fell in the summer, nor those for the vintage fell in autumn. He accommodated the year to the course of the sun, ordaining that in the future it should consist of 365 days without any intercalary month; and that every fourth year an extra day should be inserted.

He filled up the vacancies in the Senate by advancing divers plebeians to the rank of patricians, and also he increased the number of praetors, aediles, quaestors, and lesser magistrates. The method he used in those cases was to recommend such persons as he had pitched upon, by notices distributed among the several [Roman] tribes, thus, "Caesar Dictator to such a tribe [name given], I recommend to you—[the persons are named], that by the favor of your votes, they may obtain the honors which they are seeking." He likewise admitted to office the sons of those who had been proscribed.

The trial of lawsuits he restricted to the two orders of judges,—the equestrian and the senatorial,—excluding the "tribunes of the treasury"[2] who had formerly made up a third class. The revised census of the people he ordered to be taken neither in the usual manner or place, but street by street, by the leading inhabitants of the several quarters of the city; and he reduced the number of those who received corn at the public cost[3] from 320,000 to 120,000. To prevent any tumults on account of the census, he ordered that the praetor should every year fill up by lot the vacancies occasioned by death, from those who were not enrolled for the corn doles.

After having distributed 80,000 citizens among foreign colonies,[4] he enacted,—to halt the drain on the population,—that no freeman of the city, above the age of twenty or under forty, who was not in the army, should absent himself from Italy for more than three years running; also no Senator's son was to go abroad, save in the retinue of some high officer. As to those who tended flocks and herds [he required] that no less than one third of their free-born shepherds should be youths.[5] He bestowed on all physicians and professors of liberal arts the "freedom of the city" in order to fix them [at Rome] and induce others to settle there.

With respect to debts he disappointed the expectation that was generally entertained, that they would be totally canceled. He ordered that debtors should satisfy their creditors according to the value of their estates, at the rate at which they were purchased before the Civil War began. However, from the debt was to be deducted everything that had been paid as interest, either in money or in bonds; as a result of this about one fourth of the [average] debt was lost. He dissolved all the guilds save such as were of ancient foundation.[6] Crimes [under him] were punished with extreme severity; and since the rich were more prone to commit them, because they were [hitherto] liable to banishment without loss of property, he stripped murderers—as Cicero remarks—of their whole estates, and other offenders of a half.

He was extremely constant and strict in the administration of justice. He expelled from the Senate such members as had been convicted of bribery. He dissolved the marriage of a man of praetorian rank who had married a lady two days after her divorce from a former husband, although there was no suspicion of any illicit [previous] connection. He imposed custom duties on foreign goods. The use of litters for traveling, of purple robes, and of jewels he allowed only to persons of a certain age and rank, and on particular days. He enforced rigid execution of the sumptuary laws, placing officers about the markets to seize upon all meats offered for sale contrary to the rules, and to bring them to him. Sometimes he actually sent his lictors and soldiers to carry away such viands as had escaped the notice of his officers, even when they were upon the table.

His thoughts were now fully employed from day to day in a great variety of projects, for the beautifying and improvement of Rome, as well as for guarding and extending the bonds of the Empire. [He planned a magnificent temple of Mars, and also a splendid theater near to the Tarpeian Rock.] He proposed to reduce the civil law to a reasonable compass, and out of that immense and undigested mass of statutes to abridge the best and most necessary parts into a few books; also to make as large a collection of books as possible in the Greek and Latin languages, for the public use—the province of providing and putting them in proper order being assigned to [the noted savant] Marcus Varro.

Then too he intended to drain the pontine marshes, to cut a channel for the discharge of the waters of the Fucine lake, to form a road from the Upper Sea [Adriatic] through the ridge of the Apennines, to make a canal through the Isthmus of Corinth, to drive the Dacians—who had overrun Pontus and Thrace, within their proper limits, and then to make war upon the Parthians, [marching] through Lesser Armenia, but not risking a general engagement [with the Parthians] until he had made some trial of their prowess in war. But in the midst of all his undertakings and projects he was carried off by death.

Questions for Documents 5.8 and 5.9:
1. What appears to be the important qualifications for consular office when appealing to the electorate?
2. What advice and activities in these documents would still be useful in a political campaign today?
3. What problems did Caesar's reforms attempt to correct?
4. What do these selections tell you about politics and government in Rome?

---

[2] The exact nature of these "tribunes of the treasury" is very uncertain.
[3] A prolific source of pauperism and general abuse.
[4] Mostly at Corinth and Carthage, which cities he rebuilt.
[5] The object was to "keep the young men on the farm," to prevent them from flocking to Rome.
[6] The guilds were probably dangerous centers of political agitation.

CHAPTER 6
Pax Romana
Society, State, and Culture
in Imperial Rome
(27 B.C.E.–500 C.E.)

SECTION 1
Establishing the Pax Romana

6.1 Augustus' Moral Legislation: Family Values

In 18 B.C.E. Augustus launched his program of social and moral reform. Concerned about public morality and worried about the continued domination of Italians in the Empire, he enacted laws curbing adultery, promoting marriage, and encouraging childbearing.

> **Source:** Naphtali Lewis and Meyer Reinhold, ed., *Roman Civilization: Sourcebook I: The Republic*, (New York: Harper Torchbooks, 1966), pp. 48–52.

VARIOUS LEGAL SOURCES, COLLECTED IN REGIA ACADEMIA ITALICA, *ACTA DIVI AUGUSTI*, PARS PRIOR (ROME. 1945) *PP. 112–28* (ABRIDGED).

"No one shall hereafter commit debauchery or adultery knowingly and with malice aforethought." These words of the law apply to him who abets as well as to him who commits debauchery or adultery.

The Julian Law on Curbing Adultery punishes not only defilers of the marriages of others . . . but also the crime of debauchery when anyone without the use of force violates either a virgin or a widow of respectable character.

By the second section [of the law] a father, if he catches an adulterer of his daughter . . . in his own home or that of his son-in-law, or if the latter summons him in such an affair, is permitted to kill that adulterer with impunity, just as he may forthwith kill his daughter.

A husband also is permitted to kill an adulterer of his wife, but not anyone at all as is the father's right. For this law provides that a husband is permitted to kill [a procurer, actor, gladiator, convicted criminal, freedman, or slave] caught in the act of adultery with his wife in his own home (but not in that of his father-in-law). And it directs a husband who has killed any one of these to divorce his wife without delay. Moreover, he must make a report to the official who has jurisdiction in the place where the killing has occurred and he must divorce his wife; if he does not do this, he does not slay with impunity.

The law punishes as a procurer a husband who retains his wife after she has been caught in adultery and lets the adulterer go (for he ought to be enraged at his wife, who violated his marriage). In such a case the husband should be punished since he cannot claim the excuse of ignorance or feign patience on the pretext of not believing it.

He by whose aid or advice with malice aforethought it is made possible for a man or woman caught in adultery to evade punishment through bribe or any other collusion is condemned to the same penalty as is fixed for those who are convicted of the crime of procuring.

He who makes a profit from the adultery of his wife is scourged.

If a wife receives any profit from the adultery of her husband she is liable under the Julian Law as if she were an adultress. . . . Anyone who marries a woman convicted of adultery is liable under this law.

• • • •

It was enacted that women convicted of adultery be punished by confiscation of half of their dowry and a third of their property and by relegation to an island, and that the male adulterers be punished by like relegation to an island and by confiscation of half of their property, with the proviso that they be relegated to different islands.

SUETONIUS *LIFE OF AUGUSTUS* XXXIV

Among the laws which he revised or enacted were a sumptuary law and laws on adultery and chastity, on bribery, and on classes permitted to marry. The last of these he amended somewhat more severely than the others, but in the face of the clamor of opposition he was unable to push it through until he had withdrawn or mitigated some of the penalties and increased the rewards. . . . And when he saw that the intent of the law was being evaded by betrothal with immature girls and by frequent changes of wives, he shortened the duration of betrothals[1] and set a limit on divorces.

---
[1] He ordered that girls might not be bethrothed before the age of ten, and he limited the duration of bethrothals to a maximum of two years. Tacitus adds (*Annals*, xxviii) that the rewards offered for successful prosecution of evaders of these laws stimulated the rise of professional spies and informers.

DIO CASSIUS *ROMAN HISTORY* LIV. XV5. I–A

He laid heavier assessments upon the unmarried men and women and on the other hand offered prizes for marriage and the begetting of children. And since among the nobility there were far more males than females, he allowed all [free men] who wished, except senators, to marry freedwomen, and ordered that their offspring should be held legitimate.

TACITUS *ANNALS* III. XXV

Augustus in his old age supplemented the Julian Laws with the Papian-Poppaean Law in order to increase the penalties on celibacy and enrich the treasury. But people were not driven thereby to marriage and the rearing of children in any great numbers, so powerful were the attractions of the childless state. Instead the number of persons courting danger grew steadily greater, for every household was undermined by the denunciations of informers; and now the country suffered from its laws, as it had previously suffered from its vices.

VARIOUS LEGAL SOURCES, COLLECTED IN REGIA ACADEMIA ITALICA, *ACTA DIVI AUGUSTI*, PARS PRIOR (ROME, 1945) *PP. 112–28* (ABRIDGED IN THE COLLECTION CITED ABOVE).

The Julian Law provides as follows:

No one who is or shall be a senator, or a son, grandson born of a son, or great-grandson born of a son's son of any one of these, shall knowingly and with malice aforethought have as betrothed or wife a freedwoman or any woman who herself or whose father or mother is or has been an actor.

And no daughter of a senator or granddaughter born of a son or great-granddaughter born of a grandson (a son's son) shall knowingly and with malice aforethought be betrothed or married to a freedman or to a man who himself or whose father or mother is or has been an actor, and no such man shall knowingly and with malice aforethought have her as betrothed or wife.

Freeborn men are forbidden to marry a prostitute, a procuress, a woman manumitted by a procurer or procuress, one caught in adultery, one convicted in a public action, or one who has been an actress.

Conditions added contrary to laws and imperial decrees or to morality—such as, "if you do not marry," or "if you have no children"—carry no weight.

In the seventh section of the Julian Law priority in assuming the fasces[2] is given not to the consul who is older but to the one who has more children than his colleague either in his power[3] or lost in war.

. . . . But if both are married and the fathers of the same number of children, then the time-honored practice is restored and the one who is older assumes the *fasces* first.

• • • •

A freedwoman who is married to her patron shall not have the right of divorce . . . as long as the patron wants her to be his wife.

A man or wife can, by virtue of marriage, inherit a tenth of the other's estate. But if they have living children from a previous marriage, in addition to the tenth which they take by virtue of marriage they receive as many tenths as the number of children. Likewise a common son or daughter lost after the day of naming adds one tenth, and two lost after the ninth day add two tenths. Besides the tenth they can receive also the usufruct of a third part of the estate, and whenever they have children the ownership of the same part.

Sometimes a man or wife can inherit the other's entire estate, for example, if both or either are not yet of the age at which the law requires children—that is, if the husband is under twenty-five and the wife under twenty; or if both have while married past the age prescribed by the Papian Law-that is, the man sixty, the woman fifty . . .

• • • •

Sometimes they inherit nothing from each other, that is, if they contract a marriage contrary to the Julian and Papian-Poppaean Law (for example if anyone marries a woman of ill repute or a senator marries a freedwoman).

Bachelors also are forbidden by the Julian Law to receive inheritances or legacies. . . . Likewise by the Papian Law childless persons, precisely because they have no children, lose one half of inheritances and legacies.

The Julian Law exempted women from marriage for one year after the death of a husband and six months after a divorce; the Papian Law [raised these to] two years after the death of a husband and a year and six months after a divorce.

In keeping with the thirty-fifth section of the Julian Law, those who without just cause prevent any children in their power from marrying or refuse to give a dowry . . . are compelled to give them in marriage and bestow dowry.

• • • •

If there is no one entitled to the possession of an estate, or if there is someone but he has failed to exercise his right, the estate passes to the public treasury.

Questions:
1. How were men and women treated differently under this legislation?
2. From the opinions expressed in the readings, how effective do you think these laws were in achieving Augustus' goals?

Documents 6.2 and 6.3

These selections are two views of the emperor Augustus, the first from the Roman poet Vergil (70–19 B.C.E.), and the second from the famed Roman historian Tacitus.

---

[2] The ancient symbols of Roman imperium, power.
[3] That is, minors or unmarried females.

6.2 Vergil's *The Aeneid*

Vergil's Aeneid is an epic glorifying Rome, its founders, and its greatness in the "Golden" Augustan age (31 B.C.E.–14 C.E.). The poet voices the Roman public's approval of Augustus' stable government and the general prosperity. Few rulers have been more popular than Augustus during his reign.

> **Source:** *Readings in Ancient History, II, Rome and the West*, ed. William Stearns Davis, (Boston: Allyn and Bacon, 1913), pp. 178–79. (Aeneid, book VI, II. 789–800, 847–853, H.H. Ballard trans.)

[Anchises, in the realms of the dead, is reciting to his son Æneas the future glories of the Roman race.]

> Lo! Caesar and all the Julian
> Line, predestined to rise to the infinite
> spaces of heaven.
> This, yea, this is the man, so often foretold thee
> in promise, Caesar Augustus, descended
> from God, who again shall a golden
> Age in Latium found, in fields
> once governed by Saturn
> Further than India's hordes, or the
> Garymantian peoples
> He shall extend his reign; there's a land beyond
> all of our planets
> 'Yond the far track of the year and the sun,
> where sky-bearing Atlas
> Turns on his shoulders the firmament studded with bright
> constellations;
> Yea, even now, at his coming, foreshadowed
> by omens from heaven,
> Shudder the Caspian realms, and the barbarous Scythian
> kingdoms,
> While the disquieted harbors of Nile are affrighted!

[Anchises now points out the long line of worthies and conquerors who are to precede Augustus, and adds these lines.]

> Others better may fashion the breathing bronze with more
> delicate fingers;
> Doubtless they also will summon more lifelike features
> from marble:
> They shall more cunningly plead at the bar;
> and the mazes of heaven
> Draw to the scale and determine the march
> of the swift constellations.
> Thine be the care, 0 Rome, to subdue
> the whole world for thine empire!
> These be the arts for thee,—the order
> of peace to establish,
> Them that are vanquished to spare, and them
> that are haughty to humble!'

6.3 Tacitus on Augustus

Tacitus (ca. 120 C.E.), hailed as the greatest Roman writer of history, is outstanding for his ability to evaluate critically his carefully gathered facts. He sought to discover the moral lessons that he believed history provided. Idealizing the old Republic, he nevertheless claims to be impartial in his estimate of Augustus.

> **Source:** *Readings in Ancient History: Thought and Experience from Gilgamesh to St. Augustine*, Fifth Edition, ed. Nels M. Bailkey, (Lexington, MA: DC Heath and Company, 1996), pp. 423–26. (From Book I, based on a translation by A.J. Church and W.J. Brodribb.)

Rome at the beginning was ruled by kings. Freedom and the consulship were established by Lucius Brutus [See "The Rape of Lucretia" in Chapter 5] Dictatorships were held for a temporary crisis. The power of the decemvirs did not last beyond two years, nor was the consular jurisdiction of the military tribunes of long duration. The despotisms of Cinna and Sulla were brief; the rule of Pompey and of Crassus soon yielded before Caesar; the arms of Lepidus and Antony yielded before Augustus who, when the world was wearied by civil strife, subjected it to his command under the title of *princeps*. The successes and reverses of the old Roman people have been recorded by famous historians; and fine intellects were not wanting to describe the times of Augustus, till growing sycophancy scared them away. The histories of Tiberius, Germanicus, Claudius, and Nero, while they were in power, were falsified through terror, and after their death were written under the irritation of a recent hatred. Hence my purpose is to relate a few facts about Augustus—more particularly his last acts, then the reign of Tiberius, and all which follows, without either bitterness or partiality, from any motives to which I am far removed.

When after the destruction of Brutus and Cassius there was no longer any army of the Republic, . . . then, dropping the title of triumvir, and giving out that he was a consul, and was satisfied with a tribune's authority for the protection of the people, Augustus won over the soldiers with gifts, the populace with cheap grain, and all men with the allurements of peace, and so grew greater by degrees, while he concentrated in himself the functions of the Senate, the magistrates, and the laws. He was wholly unopposed, for the boldest spirits had fallen in battle, or in the proscription, while the remaining nobles, the readier they were to be slaves, were raised the higher by wealth and promotion, so that, profited by revolution, they preferred the safety of the present to the dangerous past. Nor did the provinces dislike that condition of affairs, for they distrusted the government of the Senate and the people, because of the rivalries between the leading men and the rapacity of the officials, while the protection of the laws was unavailing, as they were continually deranged by violence, intrigue, and finally by corruption.

Augustus meanwhile, as supports to his despotism, raised to the pontificate and curule aedileship Marcellus, his sister's son, while a mere stripling, and Marcus Agrippa, of humble birth, a good soldier, and one who had shared his victory, to two consecutive consulships, and as Marcellus soon afterwards died, he also accepted him as his son-in-law. Tiberius and Drusus, his stepsons, he honored with imperial titles, although his own family was yet undiminished. For he had admitted the children of Agrippa, Caius and Lucius, into the house of the Caesars; and before they had yet laid aside the dress of boyhood he had most fervently desired, with an outward show of reluctance, that they should be entitled "Leaders of the Youth," and be consuls-elect. When Agrippa died, and Lucius Caesar as he was on his way to our armies in Spain, and Caius while returning from Armenia, still suffering from a wound, were prematurely cut off by destiny—or by their step-mother Livia's treachery - Drusus too having long been dead, Tiberiis alone remained alone of the stepsons, and in him everything tended to center. He was adopted as a son, as a colleague in command and a partner in the tribunician power, and paraded through all the armies, no longer through his mother's [Livia] secret intrigues, but at her open suggestion. For she had gained such a hold on the aged Augustus that he drove out as an exile into the island of Planasia his only grandson, Agrippa Postumus, who, though devoid of worthy qualities, and having only the brute courage of physical strength, had not been convicted of any gross offense. And yet Augustus had appointed Germanicus, Drusus's offspring, to the command of eight legions on the Rhine, and required Tiberius to adopt him, although Tiberius had a son, now a young man, in his house; but he did it that he might have several safeguards to rest on. He had no war at the time on his hands except against the Germans, which was rather to wipe out the disgrace of the loss of Quintilius Varus and his army [of three legions destroyed by the Germans east of the Rhine River in 9 C.E.] than out of an ambition to extend the empire, or for any adequate recompense. At home all was tranquil, and there were magistrates with the same title as before; there was a younger generation, sprung up since the victory of Actium, and even many of the older men had been born during the civil wars. How few were left who had seen the Republic!

Thus the state had been revolutionized, and there was not a vestige left of the old sound morality. Stripped of equality, all looked up to the commands of the *princeps* without the least apprehension for the present, while Augustus in the vigor of life, could maintain his own position, that of his house, and the general tranquility. When in advanced old age, he was worn out by a sickly frame, and the end was near and new prospects opened, a few voices began idly to discuss the blessings of freedom.

. . . On the day of the funeral [of Augustus] soldiers stood round as a guard, amid much ridicule from those who had either themselves witnessed or who had heard from their parents of the famous day when slavery was still something fresh, and freedom had been resought in vain by the slaying of Caesar, the dictator—to some the vilest, to others the most glorious of deeds. Now, they said, an aged dictator, whose power has lasted long, who has provided his heirs with abundant means to coerce the state, seems to require the defense of soldiers that his burial may be undisturbed.

Then followed much talk about Augustus himself, and many expressed an idle wonder that the same day marked the beginning of his assumption of power and the close of his life, and, again, that he had ended his days at Nola in the same house and room as his father Octavius. People extolled too the number of his consulships, in which he had equalled Valerius Corvus and Caius Marius combined, the continuance for thirty-seven years of the tribunician power, the title of Imperator twenty-one times earned, and his other honors which had been either frequently repeated or were wholly new. Sensible men, however, spoke variously of his life with praise and censure. Some said that dutiful feeling towards a father [Julius Caesar], and the necessities of the state in which laws had then no place, drove him into civil war, which can neither be planned nor conducted on any right principles . . . the only remedy for his distracted country was the rule of a single man. Yet the state had been organized under neither the name of a kingdom nor a dictatorship, but under that of a *princeps*. The ocean and remote rivers were the boundaries of the empire; the legions, provinces, fleets, all things were linked together; there was law for the citizens; there was respect shown to the allies. The capital had been embellished on a grand scale; only in a few instances had he resorted to force, simply to secure general tranquility.

It was said, on the other hand that filial duty and state necessity were merely assumed as a mask. It was really from a lust for power that he had excited the veterans by bribery, had, when only a youth and without official status, raised an army, tampered with the consul's legions, and feigned an attachment to the faction of Sextus Pompey. Then, when by a decree of the Senate he had usurped the high functions and authority of praetor, . . . he wrested the consulate from a reluctant Senate, and turned against the state the arms with which he had been intrusted against Antony. Citizens were proscribed and lands distributed—distasteful even to those who carried out these deeds. Even granting that the deaths of Cassius and Brutus were sacrifices to an inherited feud (though duty requires us to waive private animosities for the sake of the public welfare), still Sextus Pompey had been deluded by the phantom of peace, and Lepidus by the mask of friendship. Subsequently, Antony had been lured on by the treaties of Tarentum and Brundisium, and by the marriage to his sister, and had paid by his death the penalty of a treacherous alliance. No doubt, there was peace after all this, but it was a peace stained with blood. . . .

The domestic life too of Augustus was not spared—how he had abducted Nero's wife . . . Livia, terrible to the state as a mother, terrible to the house of a step-mother. No honor was left for the gods when Augustus chose to be himself worshipped with temples and statues, like those of the deities, and with flamens and priests. He had not even adopted Tiberius as his successor out of affection or any regard to the state, but, having thoroughly seen his arrogant and savage temper, he had sought glory for himself by a contrast of extreme wickedness

However, after the funeral rites had been duly performed, a temple and divine worship was decreed him.

Questions:
1. Compare Vergil's and Tacitus' opinions of Augustus. How and why are there differences?
2. According to Tacitus, how did Augustus achieve his power?
3. How valid are Tacitus' criticisms of Augustus?

SECTION 2
Living in the Pax Romana

Documents 6.4–6.6

The following three documents reveal much about society under the Pax Romana—Juvenal's (satirical) view of women, his view of the plight of those living in the capital city of Rome, and Domitian's attempts to placate this same urban population with "Bread and Circuses."

6.4 A Satirical View of Women

Juvenal (ca. 55–ca. 130 C.E.), called "the greatest satiric poet who ever lived," wrote sixteen Satires which luridly reveal the glaring vices and follies of Roman society at the end of the first century C.E. In his Sixth Satire, Juvenal denounces the emancipated upper-class women of Rome for breaching social conventions and moral standards.

Source: Peter Green, trans., *Juvenal: The Sixteen Satires*, (New York: Penguin Classics, 1967), pp. 142–44.

Yet a musical wife's not so bad as some presumptuous
Flat-chested busybody who rushes around the town
Gate-crashing all-male meetings, talking back straight-faced
To a uniformed general—and in her husband's presence.
She knows all the news of the world, what's cooking in
Thrace
Or China, just what the stepmother did with her stepson
Behind closed doors, who's fallen in love, which gallant
Is all the rage. She'll tell you who got the widow
Pregnant, and in which month; she knows each woman's
Pillow endearments, and all the positions she favors.
She's the first to spot any comet presaging trouble
For some eastern prince, in Armenia, maybe,
or Parthia.
She's on to the latest gossip and rumors as soon as
They reach the city-gates, or invents her own, informing
Everyone she meets that Niphates has overflowed
And is inundating whole countries—towns are cut off,

She says, and the land is sinking: flood and disaster! Yet
even this is not so insufferable
As her habit, when woken up, of grabbing some poor-class
Neighbor and belting into him with a whip. If her precious
Sleep is broken by barking, 'Fetch me the cudgels,'
She roars, 'and be quick about it!' The dog gets a
thrashing,
But its master gets one first. She's no joke to cross,
And her face is a grisly fright. Not till the evening
Does she visit the baths: only then are her oil-jars and
The rest of her clobber transferred there. First she works
out
With the weights and dumb-bells. Then, when her arms
are aching,
The masseur takes over, craftily slipping one hand
Along her thigh, and tickling her up till she comes.
Lastly she makes for the sweat-room. She loves to sit
there
Amid all that hubbub, perspiring. Meanwhile at home
Her unfortunate guests are nearly dead with hunger.
At last she appears, all flushed, with a three-gallon thirst,
Enough to empty the brimming jar at her feet
Without assistance. She knocks back two straight pints
On an empty stomach, to sharpen her appetite: then
Throws it all up again, souses the floor with vomit
That flows in rivers across the terrazzo. She drinks
And spews by turns, like some big snake that's tumbled
Into a wine-vat, till her gilded jordan brims
Right over with sour and vinous slops. Quite sickened,
Eyes shut, her husband somehow holds down his bile.
Worse still is the well-read menace, who's hardly settled
for dinner
Before she starts praising Virgil, making a moral case
For Dido (death justifies all), comparing, evaluating
Rival poets, Virgil and Homer suspended
In opposite scales, weighed up one against the other.
Critics surrender, academics are routed, all
Fall silent, not a word from lawyer or auctioneer—
Or even another woman. Such a rattle of talk,
You'd think all the poets and bells were being clashed
together

6.5 The Problems of City Life

Life in Rome, the capital and largest city in the empire, was full of hazards, poverty, and discomforts as well as extravagant entertainment and great wealth and power. In his third satire, Juvenal turns his jaundiced eye on the less attractive aspects of Roman life.

Source: Juvenal, Satires 3.232–248, 254–261, 268–314, in Jo-Ann Shelton, ed., As the Romans Did: A Sourcebook in Roman Social History, Second Edition, (New York: Oxford University Press, 1998), pp. 69–70.

Here in Rome many sick people die from lack of sleep. Noise deprives them of sleep, and they develop indigestion and burning ulcers which in turn produce illness. But what rented rooms ever allow sleep? In this city, sleep comes only to the wealthy. This is the source of the disease: carts creaking through the narrow and winding streets and the curses of drivers caught in traffic jams will rob even a deaf man of sleep.

If social duty calls, the rich man will be carried above the heads of the crowd by his tall Ligurian litter bearers. As people give way he will be swiftly transported to his destination, and, inside the litter, he will read or write or sleep, for a litter with the windows closed induces sleep. Without any personal strain, he will arrive before us. Whereas we, although we hurry, are blocked by a wave of people in front of us. And the great crowd behind crushes us. One man hits me with his elbow, another with a hard pole; one man strikes me on the head with a wood beam, another with a wine jar. My legs are covered with thick mud. Then, on all sides, big feet step on me, and a nail from a soldier's boot pierces my toe.

One wagon carries fir-wood timber, another carries pine. They are piled high and they sway, posing for the crowd a threat of danger. For if a wagon carrying marble should tip over and dump its load of mountain rock on top of the throng of people, what would remain of the bodies? Who would find the limbs or the bones? The crushed body would utterly disappear, like the soul.

Now consider the various and diverse dangers at night: how high it is to the lofty roofs (from which roof tiles fall and hit you on the head), how often cracked and broken pots fall from windows, with what weight they mark and damage the pavement when they strike it. You could be considered thoughtless and careless about sudden accidents if you were to go out for dinner without first making a will. For indeed there are as many potential disasters as there are open windows where you are passing by at night. You should therefore pray and carry with you this pitiable wish: that people may be content to empty over you, from their windows, only an open basin.

The violent drunk who has had the misfortune to mug no one feels unsatisfied; he tosses and turns, unable to sleep. For some men, a good mugging induces sleep. Yet, though young and heated with wine, he avoids the man whom a scarlet cloak, a very long line of attendants, and many torches and oil lamps warn should be avoided. Me, however, whom the moon usually escorts or, at best, the thin light of a candle whose wick I carefully nurture—me he fears not. Now imagine the preliminaries to this street fight, if indeed you can call it a fight when he does the beating and I am only beaten. He stands in front of me and orders me to halt. You have to obey. What else can you do when a maniac, and one stronger than you, coerces you? "Where are you coming from'?" he shouts. "At whose house did you have your dinner of vinegar and beans? What shoemaker shared with you his leeks and lips of a boiled sheep? You won't answer? Speak or I'll kick you. Tell me where you hang out. In what Jews' prayer-house can I find you?" Whether you try to speak, or shrink back in silence, it's all the same. In either ease they mug you, and then in a violent rage make you pay for permission to escape. This is the poor man's freedom: having been mugged and battered with fists, he begs and entreats his assailant to allow him to go away with a few teeth left. Yet these things are not all you have to fear. For there is always someone who will rob you even when your house is securely bolted and after all the shops everywhere are locked and quiet with their shutters closed. Sometimes the burglars even carry weapons! And whenever armed police are sent to the Pomptine marsh and Gallinarian forest to secure the area, all the thieves and criminals run from there to Rome, as if to a game preserve. What forge, what anvil is not now producing heavy chains? So much iron is used to make chains that we may well fear that there will not be enough for plows and that there will be a shortage of mattocks and hoes. Happy were our ancestors. Happy were those generations long ago who lived under kings and tribunes and saw Rome content with one jail.

6.6 Bread and Circuses

Besides their control of the army and maintaining the subservience of the Senate, the Emperors also had to keep peace in the city of Rome by controlling the urban mob. Like some of his predecessors, Domitian (81–96 C.E.), a poor and tyrannical Caesar, tried to win popularity by providing the idle masses of the capital with their favorite games and arena spectacles.

Source: William Stearns Davis, ed., Readings in Ancient History: Illustrative Extracts from the Sources, Volume II: Rome and the West, (New York: Allyn and Bacon, 1913), 194–195. (Suetonius, "Life of Domitian," chap. IV, Bohn trans.)

He frequently entertained the people with the most magnificent and costly shows, not only in the amphitheater, but in the circus; where, besides the usual chariot races, with two or four horses abreast, he exhibited the imitation of a battle betwixt cavalry and infantry; and in the amphitheater a sea fight. The people, too, were entertained with wild-beast hunts, and gladiator fights even in the nighttime, by torchlight. He constantly attended the games given by the quaestors, which had been disused for some time, but were revived by him; and upon those occasions, he always gave the people the liberty of demanding two pair of gladiators out of his own [private] "school," who appeared last in court uniforms.

He presented the people with naval fights, performed by fleets almost as numerous as those usually employed in real engagements; making a vast lake near the Tiber, and building seats around it. And he witnessed these fights himself during a very heavy rain.

He likewise instituted in honor of Jupiter Capitolinus, a solemn contest in music to be performed every five years; besides horseracing and gymnastic exercises. There was too a public performance in elocution both Greek and Latin, and beside the musicians who sung to the harp, there were others who played concerted pieces or solos without vocal accompaniment.

Thrice he bestowed upon the people a bounty of 300 sesterces per man, and at a public show of gladiators a very plentiful feast. At the "Festival of the Seven Hills"

[held in December], he distributed large hampers of provisions to the Senatorial and Equestrian orders, and small baskets to the commonalty, and encouraged them to eat by setting the example. The day after, he scattered among the people a variety of cakes and other delicacies to be scrambled after; and on the greater part of them falling amidst the seats of the lower classes, he ordered 500 tickets[1] to be thrown into each range of benches belonging to the Senatorial and Equestrian orders.

Questions for Documents 6.4–6.6
1. How familiar do any of Juvenal's complaints about women and the city sound in the context of our times?
2. Written in satires, how seriously can we take Juvenal's descriptions and opinions of life and people?
3. What do these three selections reveal about the tenor of Roman culture and society at the end of the first century C.E.?

---

[1] Probably lottery tickets. The lucky numbers drew articles of value such as vases, slaves, money, or possibly a small villa.

SECTION 3
Losing the Pax Romana

6.7   Cracks at the Frontier

In 98 C.E., Tacitus, a Roman citizen and senator, wrote *Agricola*, a biography of his father-in-law for whom he had great respect, and *Germania* (Chapter 7, Document 1). Agricola, with an army under his command, extended the Roman Empire's hold on Britain between the years 70–84 C.E. Some of his gains were lost when he was recalled to Rome and trouble spots closer to Rome demanded attention.
Source: Tacitus, *Agricola*, trans. H. Mattingly, revised by S.A. Handford, (New York: Penguin Books, 1981, © 1970), pp. 54–56, 93.

[Agricola] served his military apprenticeship in Britain to the satisfaction of Suetonius Paulinus, a hard-working and sensible officer, who chose him for a staff appointment in order to assess his worth. Agricola was no loose young subaltern, to turn his military career into a life of gaiety; and he would not make his staff-captaincy and his inexperience an excuse for idly enjoying himself and continually going on leave. Instead, he got to know his province and made himself known to the troops. He learned from the experts and chose the best models to follow. He never sought a duty for self-advertisement, never shirked one through cowardice. He acted always with energy and a sense of responsibility.

Neither before nor since has Britain ever been in a more disturbed and perilous state. Veterans had been mas-

sacred, colonies burned to the ground, armies cut off. They had to fight for their lives before they could think of victory. The campaign, of course, was conducted under the direction and leadership of another—the commander to whom belonged the decisive success and the credit for recovering Britain. Yet everything combined to give the young Agricola fresh skill, experience, and ambition; and his spirit was possessed by a passion for military glory—a thankless passion in an age in which a sinister construction was put upon distinction and a great reputation was as dangerous as a bad one.

From Britain Agricola returned to Rome to enter on his career of office, and married Domitia Decidiana, the child of an illustrious house. It was a union that brought him social distinction and aid to his ambition for advancement. They lived in rare accord, maintained by mutual affection and unselfishness; in such a partnership, however, a good wife deserves more than half the praise, just as a bad one deserves more than half the blame. On being elected quaestor, the ballot assigned him Asia as his province and Salvius Titianus as his proconsul. Neither the one nor the other corrupted him, though the province with its wealth invited abuses, and the proconsul, an abject slave to greed, was prepared to indulge his subordinate to any extent: 'You wink at my offences and I will wink at yours.' While he was in Asia a daughter was born to him, which both strengthened his position and consoled him for the loss, shortly afterwards, of a son born previously. He passed the interval between his quaestorship and his tribunate of the people, and also his year of office as tribune, in quiet retirement; for he understood the age of Nero, in which inactivity was tantamount to wisdom. His practorship ran the same quiet course, since no judicial duties had fallen to his lot. In ordering the public games and the other vanities associated with his office, he compromised between economy and excess, steering clear of extravagance but not failing to win popular approval. He was afterwards chosen by Galba to check over the gifts in the temples; and by diligently tracing stolen objects he repaired the losses inflicted on the State by all the temple-robbers except Nero.

•   •   •   •

... And indeed the fortunes of Rome in those ensuing years were such as would not allow Agricola's name to be forgotten. One after another, armies were lost in Moesia and Dacia, in Germany and Pannonia, through the rash follow or cowardice of their generals; one after another, experienced officers were defeated in fortified positions and captured with all their troops. It was no longer the frontier and the Danube line that were threatened, but the permanent quarters of the legions and the maintenance of the empire. So, as one loss followed another and year after year was signalized by death and disaster, public opinion began to clamour for Agricola to take command. His energy and resolution, and his proven courage in war, were universally contrasted with the general slackness and cowardice. It is known that Domitian's own ears were stung by the lash of such talk. The best of his freedmen spoke out of their loyal affection, the worst out of malice and spleen; but all alike goaded on an emperor who was always inclined to pursue evil courses. And so Agricola, by his own virtues and by the faults of others, was carried straight along the perilous path that led to glory.

Questions:
1. By the way Tacitus frames his comments on Agricola, what behaviors may have been common among army officers of this era?
2. By portraying Agricola as atypical of his day, what portrait does Tacitus provide of the Roman Empire (Britain, Asia, and Rome)?
3. What vision and role does Tacitus provide of family life in Agricola's life and more generally? What role might family life have played in political life?

6.8   Loss of Meaning in Roman Life

Augustine, born in 354 c.e. to a father who was a Roman citizen and a Christian mother, grew up in much the traditional way Roman citizens had for centuries. By Augustine's time, however, the Roman Empire was beginning to crumble. It was in this context that Augustine sought meaning for his life in new sources, which he eventually found in Christianity.

Source: Saint Augustine, *Confessions*, trans. R.S. Pine-Coffin, (New York: Penguin Books, 1980, © 1961), pp. 36–37, 44–45, 118–23.

BOOK I

But we are carried away by custom to our own undoing and it is hard to struggle against the stream. Will this torrent never dry up? How much longer will it sweep the sons of Adam down to that vast and terrible sea which cannot easily be passed, even by those who climb upon the ark of the Cross?

This traditional education taught me that Jupiter punishes the wicked with his thunderbolts and yet commits adultery himself. The two roles are quite incompatible. All the same he is represented in this way, and the result is that those who follow his example in adultery can put a bold face on it by making false pretences of thunder. But can any schoolmaster in his gown listen unperturbed to a man who challenges him on his own ground and says 'Homer invented these stories and attributed human sins to the gods. He would have done better to provide men with examples of divine goodness'? It would be nearer the truth to say that Homer certainly invented the tales but peopled them with wicked human characters in the guise of gods. In this way their wickedness would not be reckoned a crime, and all who did as they did could be shown to follow the example of the heavenly gods, not that of sinful mortals.

And yet human children are pitched into this hellish torrent, together with the fees which are paid to have them taught lessons like these. Much business is at stake, too, when these matters are publicly debated, because the law decrees that teachers should be paid a salary in addition to the fees paid by their pupils. And the roar of the torrent beating upon its boulders seems to say 'This is the school where men are made masters of words. This is where they learn the art of persuasion, so necessary in business and debate.'

•   •   •   •

Terence brings on to the stage a dissolute youth who excuses his own fornication by pointing to the example of Jupiter. He looks at a picture painted on the wall, which 'shows how Jupiter is said to have deceived the girl Danae by raining a golden shower into her lap'. These are the words with which he incites himself to lechery, as though he had heavenly authority for it: 'What a god he is! His mighty thunder rocks the sky from end to end. You may say that I am only a man, and thundering is beyond my power. But I played the rest of the part well enough, and willingly too'!

The words are certainly not learnt any the more easily by reason of the filthy moral, but filth is committed with greater confidence as a resulting of learning the words. I have nothing against the words themselves. They are like choice and costly glasses, but they contain the wine of error which had already gone to the heads of the teachers who poured it out for us to drink. If we refused to drink, we were beaten for it, without the right to appeal to a sober judge.

With your eyes upon me, my God, my memory can safely recall those days. But it is true that I learned all these things gladly and took a sinful pleasure in them. And for this very reason I was called a promising boy.

BOOK 2

Was there no one to lull my distress, to turn the fleeting beauty of these new-found attractions to good purpose and set up a goal for their charms, so that the high tide of my youth might have rolled in upon the shore of marriage? The surge might have been calmed and contented by the procreation of children, which is the purpose of marriage, as your law prescribes.

. . . .

But, instead, I was in a ferment of wickedness. I deserted you and allowed myself to be carried away by the sweep of the tide. I broke all your lawful bounds and did not escape your lash. For what man can escape it? You were always present, angry and merciful at once, strewing the pangs of bitterness over all my lawless pleasures to lead me on to look for others unallied with pain. You meant me to find them nowhere but in yourself, O Lord, for you teach us by inflicting pain, you smite so that you may heal, and you kill us so that we may not die away from you. Where was I then and how far was I banished from the bliss of your house in that sixteenth year of my life? This was the age at which the frenzy gripped me and I surrendered myself entirely to lust, which your law forbids but human hearts are not ashamed to sanction. My family made no effort to save me from my fall by marriage. Their only concern was that I should learn how to make a good speech and how to persuade others by my words.

. . . .

No one had anything but praise for my father who, despite his slender resources, was ready to provide his son with all that was needed to enable him to travel so far for the purpose of study. Many of our townsmen, far richer than my father, went to no such trouble for their children's sake. Yet this same father of mine took no trouble at all to see how I was growing in your sight or whether I was chaste or not. He cared only that I should have a fertile tongue, leaving my heart to bear none of your fruits, my God, though you are the only Master, true and good, of its husbandry.

In the meanwhile, during my sixteenth year, the narrow means of my family obliged me to leave school and live idly at home with my parents. The brambles of lust grew high above my head and there was no one to root them out, certainly not my father. One day at the public baths he saw the sign of active virility coming to life in me and this was enough to make him relish the thought of having grandchildren. He was happy to tell my mother about it, for his happiness was due to the intoxication which causes the world to forget you, its Creator, and to love the things you have created instead of loving you, because the world is drunk with the invisible wine of its own perverted, earthbound will. But in my mother's heart you had already begun to build your temple and laid the foundations of your holy dwelling, while my father was still a catechumen and a new one at that. So, in her piety, she became alarmed and apprehensive, and although I had not yet been baptized, she began to dread that I might follow in the crooked path of those who do not keep their eyes on you but turn their backs instead.

BOOK 6 [YEARS LATER]

I was eager for fame and wealth and marriage, but you only decided these ambitions. They caused me to suffer the most galling difficulties, but the less you allowed me to find pleasure in anything that was not yourself, the greater, I know, was your goodness to me. Look into my heart, O Lord, for it was your will that I should remember these things and confess them to you. I pray now that my soul may cling to you, for it was you who released it from the deadly snare in which it was so firmly caught. It was in a state of misery and you probed its wound to the quick, pricking it on to leave all else and turn to you to be healed, to turn to you who are above all things and without whom nothing could exist.

My misery was complete and I remember how, one day, you made me realize how utterly wretched I was. I was preparing a speech in praise of the Emperor, intending that it should include a great many lies which would certainly be applauded by an audience who knew well enough how far from the truth they were.

. . . .

For by all my laborious contriving and intricate manoeuvres I was hoping to win the joy of worldly happiness, the very thing which this man* had already secured at the cost of the few pence which he had begged.

. . . .

[A boy, once freed from the "futile pastimes" of the arena, became a student of Augustine's and embraced the Manichers.] But he did not abandon his career in the world, for his parents would not allow him to forget it. He went to Rome ahead of me to study law and there, strange to relate, he became obsessed with an extra-ordinary craving for gladiatorial shows. At first he detested these displays and refused to attend them. But one day during the season for this cruel and bloodthirsty sport he happened to meet some friends and fellow-students returning from their dinner. In a friendly way they brushed aside his resistance and his stubborn protests and carried him off to the arena.

'You may drag me there bodily,' he protested, 'but do you imagine that you can make me watch the show and give my mind to it? I shall be there, but it will be just as if I were not present, and I shall prove myself stronger than you or the games.'

---

* this man: a beggar Augustine had met in the streets

He did not manage to deter them by what he said, and perhaps the very reason why they took him with them was to discover whether he would be as good as his word. When they arrived at the arena, the place was seething with the lust for cruelty. They found seats as best they could and Alypius shut his eyes tightly, determined to have nothing to do with these atrocities. If only he had closed his ears as well! For an incident in the fight drew a great roar from the crowd, and this thrilled him so deeply that he could not contain his curiosity. Whatever had caused the uproar, he was confident that, if he saw it, he would find it repulsive and remain master of himself. So he opened his eyes, and his soul was stabbed with a wound more deadly than any which the gladiator, whom he was so anxious to see, had received in his body. He fell, and fell more pitifully than the man whose fall had drawn that roar of excitement from the crowd. The din had pierced his ears and forced him to open his eyes, laying his soul open to receive the wound which struck it down. This was presumption, not courage. The weakness of his soul was in relying upon itself instead of trusting in you.

When he saw the blood, it was as though he had drunk a deep draught of savage passion. Instead of turning away, he fixed his eyes upon the scene and drank in all its frenzy, unaware of what he was doing. He revelled in the wickedness of the fighting and was drunk with the fascination of bloodshed. He was no longer the man who had come to the arena, but simply one of the crowd which he had joined, a fit companion for the friends who had brought him.

Need I say more? He watched and cheered and grew hot with excitement, and when he left the arena, he carried away with him a diseased mind which would leave him no peace until he came back again, no longer simply together with the friends who had first dragged him there, but at their head, leading new sheep to the slaughter. Yet you stretched out your almighty, ever merciful hand, O God, and rescued him from this madness. You taught him to trust in you, not in himself. But this was much later.

Questions:
1. What, according to Augustine, are the traditional pursuits (both serious and pleasurable) of a Roman citizen/student?
2. How does he characterize those pursuits?
3. How do his perspectives differ from the traditional Roman view of these pursuits? Use Augustine's own words to help answer this question.

CHAPTER 7
Pagans, Jews, Christians
Religions of the Mediterranean World

(500 B.C.E.–50 C.E.)

SECTION 1
Religious Traditions in the Roman Empire

7.1 Traditional Roman Religious Practices

Roman religion was a religion of ritual and form, rather than of ideas and beliefs, and did not teach ethics or demand good works. Morality and ethical behavior were a family and civic responsibility, rather than a religious one. The first several selections illustrate common religious practices. By the fourth century C.E., however, Christianity began to win the support of the emperors, and in 392 the emperor Theodosius I banned all non-Christian rites. Christianity thus became the one official state religion. The last selection is an appeal to the Roman Emperor by Symmachus (ca. 340–402 C.E.), who had not converted from the old religion to Christianity. He requested that the altar of Victory erected by Augustus that had been removed from the Senate by the previous Christian Emperor be returned. He was unsuccessful.

Source: *As the Romans Did: A Sourcebook in Roman Social History*, ed. Jo-Ann Shelton, (New York: Oxford University Press, 1998), pp. 366, 371–74, 379–80, 390–91.

A HYMN TO DIANA, BY CATULLUS, *POEMS*

Diana, we are in your care, we chaste girls and boys. Come, chaste boys and girls, let us sing in praise of Diana.

O daughter of Leto, mighty offspring of mightiest Jupiter, you who were born beside the Delian olive tree, queen of the mountains and the green forests and the trackless glens and the murmuring streams.

You are called Juno Lucina by women in the agony of childbirth. You are called powerful Trivia. You are called Luna, with your borrowed light.

You, goddess, measuring out the year's progress by your monthly phases, do fill the farmer's humble storerooms with fine produce.

Hallowed be thy name, whatever name it is that you prefer. And, as in years past you have been accustomed to do, so now, too, protect and preserve the race of Romulus with your kindly favor.

PLINY THE ELDER, *NATURAL HISTORY*

It apparently does no good to offer a sacrifice or to consult the gods with due ceremony unless you also speak words of prayer. In addition, some words are appropriate for seeking favorable omens, others for warding off evil, and still others for securing help. We notice, for example, that our highest magistrates make appeals to the gods with specific and set prayers. And in order that no word be omitted or spoken out of turn, one attendant reads the prayer from a book, another is assigned to check it closely, a third is appointed to enforce silence. In addition, a flutist plays to block out any extraneous sounds. There are recorded remarkable cases where either ill-omened noises have interrupted and ruined the ritual or an error has been made in the strict wording of the prayer.

CATO THE ELDER, *ON AGRICULTURE*

Before you harvest your crops, you should offer a sow as a preliminary sacrifice in the following manner. Offer a sow to Ceres before you store up the following crops: spelt, wheat, barley, beans, and rape seed. Before you slaughter the sow, invoke Janus,[1] Jupiter, and Juno, offering incense and wine.

Offer sacrificial crackers to Janus with the following words: "Father Janus, in offering to you these sacrificial crackers I humbly pray that you may be benevolent and well disposed toward me and my children and my home and my family."

Offer an oblation cracker to Jupiter and honor him with the following words: "Jupiter, in offering to you this oblation cracker I humbly pray that you may be benevolent and well disposed toward me and my children and my home and my family, being honored by this oblation cracker."

Afterward offer wine to Janus with the following words: "Father Janus, just as I humbly prayed when I offered to you the sacrificial crackers, so now for the same purpose be honored with sacrificial wine,"

---

[1] Janus was the god of all beginnings (January) and thus appropriately invoked at the beginning of the harvest. He was also the god of doorways and was frequently represented as having two faces, each looking in the opposite direction, even as a door has two faces.

And afterward offer wine to Jupiter with the following words: "Jupiter, be honored by the oblation cracker, be honored by the sacrificial wine."

And then slaughter the sow as a preliminary sacrifice. When the internal organs have been cut out,[2] offer sacrificial crackers to Janus and honor him in the same terms as when you earlier offered him crackers. Offer an oblation cracker to Jupiter and honor him in the same terms as before. Likewise, offer wine to Janus and offer wine to Jupiter in the same terms as it was offered when you earlier offered the sacrificial crackers and the oblation crackers. Afterward offer the internal organs and wine to Ceres.

CATO THE ELDER, *ON AGRICULTURE* 141

It is necessary to purify your farmland in the following way. Have a pig-sheep-bull procession led around the land, while the following words are spoken: "With the benevolence of the gods, and hoping that everything may turn out well, I entrust to you the responsibility of having the pig-sheep-bull procession led around my farm, field, and land, wherever you decide the animals ought to be led or carried."

Invoke Janus and Jupiter with an offering of wine; then speak these words: 'Father Mars, I pray and entreat you to be benevolent and well disposed toward me and my home and my family. And for this reason I have ordered a pig-sheep-bull procession to be led around my field, land, and farm, so that you will hinder, ward off, and turn away diseases seen and unseen, barrenness and crop losses, disasters and storms; and so that you will allow the vegetable crops, the grain crops, the vineyards, and the orchards to grow and achieve a productive maturity; and so that you will protect the shepherds and the flocks and bestow safety and good health upon me and my home and my family. For these reasons, therefore, and because of the purifying of my farm, land, and field, and the offering of a sacrifice for purification, even as I have prayed, be honored by the sacrifice of the suckling pig-sheep-bull. For this reason, therefore, Father Mars, be honored by this suckling pig-sheep-bull sacrifice."

Slaughter the sacrificial animals with a knife. Bring forward sacrificial crackers, and an oblation cracker, and offer them. When you slaughter the pig, lamb, and calf, you must use these words:

"For this reason, therefore, be honored by the sacrifice of the pig-sheep-bull." ... If all the sacrificial victims are not perfect, speak these words: "Father Mars, if somehow the suckling pig-sheep-bull sacrifice was not satisfactory to you, I offer this new pig-sheep-bull sacrifice as atonement." If there is doubt about only one or two of the animals, speak these words: "Father Mars, since that pig was not satisfactory to you, I offer this pig as atonement."

SYMMACHUS, *DISPATCHES TO THE EMPEROR*

Every man has his own customs and his own religious practices. Similarly, the divine mind has given to different cities different religious rites which protect them. And, just as each man receives at birth his own soul, so, too, does each nation receive a *genius*[3] which guides its destiny. We should also take into account the bestowal of favors, which, more than anything else, proves to man the existence of gods. For, since no human reasoning can illuminate this matter, from where else can knowledge of the gods come, and come more correctly, than from the recollection and evidences of prosperity? If the long passage of time gives validity to religious rites, we must keep faith with so many centuries and we must follow our fathers, who followed their fathers and therefore prospered.

Let us imagine that Rome herself is standing before us now and addressing these words to you:

"Best of emperors, fathers of the fatherland, respect my age! The dutiful performance of religious rites has carried me through many years. Let me enjoy the ancient ceremonies, for I do not regret them. Let me live in my own way, for I am free. This is the religion which made the whole world obedient to my laws. These are the rites which drove back Hannibal from my walls and the Senones from my Capitol. Have I been preserved only for this—to be rebuked in my old age? I will consider the changes which people think must be instituted, but modification, in old age, is humiliating and too late."

And so we are asking for amnesty for the gods of our fathers, the gods of our homeland. It is reasonable to assume that whatever each of us worships can be considered one and the same. We look up at the same stars, the same sky is above us all, the same universe encompasses us. What difference does it make which system each of us uses to find the truth? It is not by just one route that man can arrive at so great a mystery.

Questions:

1. What were the basic elements of Roman prayers and rituals?
2. How do the prayers and rituals illustrate the nature and characteristics of traditional Roman religion?
3. What argument does Symmachus use to support his request for the return of the altar of Victory? Why do you think the fourth-century Christians did not find this argument persuasive?

7.2   Revolt Against the Roman Empire: The Jewish Wars

Josephus wrote two major histories of the Jewish people, *Jewish Antiquities*, a history of the Jewish people to his own day, and *The Jewish War*, an

---

[2] The internal organs were first inspected carefully to ascertain the will of the gods [taking an augury] and then burned on the altar. The rest of the pig was eaten by the people who witnessed the sacrifice.

[3] Guardian Spirit.

explanation of the revolt of the Jews against the Roman Empire, 66–70 C.E. Josephus himself was actively involved in the war against the Romans, but survived and later worked for the Emperor Vespasian and Titus who had been in charge of putting down the revolt. This selection explains how the war began.

Source: Paul L. Maier, trans. and ed., *Josephus: The Essential Works*, (Grand Rapids, MI: Kregel Publications, 1994), pp. 288–92.

When Cestius Gallus, governor of Syria, visited Jerusalem at the Passover, a huge throng surrounded him, denouncing Florus as having ruined the country. Florus, who was at his side, scoffed at the protests, but Cestius promised the people greater moderation from Florus in the future and returned to Antioch. Florus accompanied him as far as Caesarea, scheming all the while to drive the Jews into open revolt. For he was afraid that if peace continued, they would accuse him before Caesar, whereas war would conceal his atrocities.

An incident at Caesarea touched off the war. The Jews had a synagogue there, but the adjoining land was owned by a Greek. The Jews had often offered a much higher price for his lot than it was worth, but he refused to sell. Now to insult them, he started to erect some workshops on the site, leaving the Jews only a narrow approach to their place of worship. Some hotheaded youths interrupted the builders, but Florus stopped their violence. The Jews then bribed Florus with eight silver talents to stop the builders, and he promised to do so. But, money in hand, he set out for Sebaste, leaving the riot to take care of itself.

On the following Sabbath; when the Jews came to the synagogue, they encountered a local troublemaker who had placed a pot beside the entrance, bottom-side-up, on which he was sacrificing birds. A certain passionate youth, furious at this outrage, attacked the Caesareans, who were expecting a clash and had arranged the mock sacrifice. Jucundus, master of horse under Florus, removed the pot and tried to quell the tumult. The Jews snatched a copy of their Law and fled to Narbata, about seven miles away. There they sent a delegation to Florus in Sebaste, imploring his assistance and reminding him of the eight talents. But Florus threw them into prison for having taken a copy of the Law from Caesarea!

This news outraged Jerusalem, although the people restrained their feelings. But Florus, determined to drive them to revolt, extracted seventeen talents from the temple treasury, claiming government necessity. The infuriated people rushed to the temple, shouting their contempt for the procurator. Some passed around a basket, begging coppers for the "poor beggar Florus."

Florus marched on Jerusalem, thinking this a good chance to pillage the city, but he should have gone to Caesarea instead, to extinguish the flames of war there. The citizens of Jerusalem, in order to shame him from his purpose, came out to applaud his army. Florus, however, sent a centurion ahead with 50 horsemen to order the people to return

and not to mock with pretended courtesy one whom they had reviled. Dismayed at this message, the crowd went home and spent the night in anxiety and dejection.

FLORUS RAVAGES THE PEOPLE

Florus stayed at the palace, and in the morning summoned the chief priests and leaders before him. He demanded that they hand over those who had insulted him, or face his vengeance. They asked his pardon for any who had spoken disrespectfully, blaming a few indiscreet youths who were impossible to identify. If he wanted to preserve the city and the peace of the nation, they said, he should forgive the few offenders on behalf of the many who were innocent.

Florus became all the more incensed, and shouted to his soldiers to plunder the upper market and kill any they met. The troops not only sacked the market, but broke into the houses and massacred the occupants. The city ran with blood, and 3,600 men, women, and children were cruelly slaughtered or crucified.

King Agrippa was away in Egypt, but Bernice, his sister, was in Jerusalem fulfilling a religious vow. Horrified at the awful sights around her, she continually sent messengers to Florus, imploring him to stop the carnage. She finally came before him herself, barefoot in supplication. But he was deaf to her requests, and the queen had to retreat quickly into the palace to save her own life.

The next day, the multitude gathered in the upper market to lament their dead and shout curses against Florus. But the chief priests and leaders begged them to keep quiet and not to provoke Florus again. Out of respect for those exhorting them, the crowd complied.

Florus was disappointed that the disturbance stopped, and to relight the flames, he sent for the chief priests and leaders. He told them that the one way to prove their peaceful intentions was for the people to go out and welcome two cohorts of troops that were advancing from Caesarea. Florus then sent word to those cohorts not to return the greetings of the Jews, and if they ridiculed him, to attack them.

The priests found it difficult to make the outraged people obey this command, but they warned them that otherwise their country would be pillaged and their temple profaned. The people finally agreed and were led out to meet the troops, whom they saluted. When no response came from the cohorts, some of the Jewish rebels started shouting against Florus. The troops surrounded them and beat them with clubs, while the cavalry pursued and trampled those that fled. Many fell under the blows of the Romans, but many more were crushed to death in the stampede at the city gates when they all tried to get back inside. The troops rushed in with the people, trying to seize the temple and the Antonia fortress. Florus and his men burst out of the palace and also tried to reach the fortress. But they were prevented by the people who so blocked the streets that they could not cut their way through, while others assaulted the Romans from the roofs.

Florus retreated to the palace, but the Jewish rebels, fearing that he might return and use Antonia to capture the temple, cut off the porticoes that connected the two structures. Now unable to plunder the temple's treasures, Florus told the city leaders that he would be leaving. On the promise that they would keep the peace, he left one cohort with them and returned with the rest of his forces to Caesarea.

. . . .

The people now pressured Agrippa and the chief priests to send ambassadors to accuse Florus before Nero. Agrippa did not encourage this mission, since he wanted to discourage the people from war. He assembled them at Xystus, and, placing his sister Bernice conspicuously on the roof of the Hasmonean palace, he delivered a long and eloquent speech. Granting that some of the procurators were brutal, he said, "It does not follow that all Romans are unjust to you. They do not intentionally send us oppressive governors, and cannot in the west see their officers in the east." After due complaint, he continued, moderate successors should follow. But their hopes of gaining independence were too late. If they could not resist part of the Roman forces under Pompey, how could they expect to be successful now when the Romans ruled the world? When so many great nations had been conquered, how could the Jews hope to be victorious? Finally, he described the horrors of war, and the destruction that would surely fall on Jews throughout the empire as well as on themselves, their city, and the temple.

He burst into tears at the end, as did his sister, and the people were touched. Yet many cried out that they had not taken up arms against the Romans, only against Florus. Agrippa replied, "By your actions you are already at war with Rome: you have not paid the tribute to Caesar, and you have destroyed the galleries communicating with the Antonia. If you wish to clear yourselves on the charge of insurrection, repair the porticoes and pay the tribute."

Accepting this advice, the people went with the king and Bernice to the temple and started rebuilding the galleries. The magistrates went out through the villages to levy the taxes, and in a short time, 40 talents were collected. The danger of war seemed past. But when Agrippa tried to persuade the people to obey Florus until Caesar sent a successor, they grew exasperated and abusive at the king, and banished him from the city. Some of the rioters even threw stones at him, and the infuriated Agrippa withdrew to his own dominions.

A party of the most rebellious spirits now attacked the fortress Masada, and killed the Roman guards after capturing it. At the temple, meanwhile, Eleazar, son of Ananias the high priest, persuaded those who conducted the worship to accept no gift or sacrifice from a foreigner. This was the basis of war with Rome, since sacrifices offered in behalf of the emperor and Rome were now suspended. The chief priests and leading Pharisees pleaded with them not to abandon the customary offerings, since it was impious to prevent strangers from offering worship to God. They then presented the priests who were experts on tradition, and they stated that all their ancestors had received the sacrifices of foreigners.

But the revolutionary party would not listen to anything, nor would the temple priests. The leading citizens, then, saw that they could not check the rebellion and that they would be the first to suffer Rome's vengeance. In order to exonerate themselves, they sent a deputation to Florus and another to Agrippa, requesting both to bring an army to the city and crush the rebellion. Florus rejoiced at the news, but dismissed the delegation without a reply. Agrippa, anxious to save the city and the temple, immediately sent 2,000 cavalry to help those opposed to insurrection.

Questions:
1. What problems and incident set off the hostilities?
2. On whom does Josephus place the responsibility for the outbreak of the war?
3. What means and arguments were attempted to avoid the war?

SECTION 2
Defining Christianity

7.3 The Teachings of Jesus; Their Interpretation by Paul

Christianity is based on the teachings and life of Jesus of Nazareth, a Jew who claimed to be the Messiah promised by the Jewish prophets. Emphasizing ethics and denouncing legalism, Jesus attacked the Jewish leadership and religious institutions. After Jesus' crucifixion, his followers proclaimed that he had risen from the dead and a new religion was launched that eventually separated from Judaism and spread throughout the Roman Empire and beyond.

The first selections from the Gospels describe the teachings and life of Jesus. Soon afterwards, the apostle Paul became the chief interpreter of those teachings, his life, death, and resurrection for believers.

Source: The Bible, RSV and New International Version, © 1973, 1978, 1984, International Bible Society.

THE SERMON ON THE MOUNT FROM MATTHEW 5 AND 6 (NIV)

1 Now when he saw the crowds, he went up on a mountainside and sat down. His disciples came to him,

2 and he began to teach them, saying:

3 "Blessed are the poor in spirit, for theirs is the kingdom of heaven.

4 Blessed are those who mourn, for they will be comforted.

5 Blessed are the meek, for they will inherit the earth.

6 Blessed are those who hunger and thirst for righteousness, for they will be filled.

7 Blessed are the merciful, for they will be shown mercy.

8 Blessed are the pure in heart, for they will see God.

9 Blessed are the peacemakers, for they will be called sons of God.

10 Blessed are those who are persecuted because of righteousness, for theirs is the kingdom of heaven.

11 "Blessed are you when people insult you, persecute you and falsely say all kinds of evil against you because of me.

12 Rejoice and be glad, because great is your reward in heaven, for in the same way they persecuted the prophets who were before you.

13 "You are the salt of the earth. But if the salt loses its saltiness, how can it be made salty again? It is no longer good for anything, except to be thrown out and trampled by men.

14 "You are the light of the world. A city on a hill cannot be hidden.

15 Neither do people light a lamp and put it under a bowl. Instead they put it on its stand, and it gives light to everyone in the house.

16 In the same way, let your light shine before men, that they may see your good deeds and praise your Father in heaven.

17 "Do not think that I have come to abolish the Law or the Prophets; I have not come to abolish them but to fulfill them.

27 "You have heard that it was said, 'Do not commit adultery.'

28 But I tell you that anyone who looks at a woman lustfully has already committed adultery with her in his heart.

29–30 If your right eye causes you to sin, gouge it out and throw it away. It is better for you to lose one part of your body than for your whole body to be thrown into hell. And if your right hand causes you to sin, cut it off and throw it away. It is better for you to lose one part of your body than for your whole body to go into hell.

31 "It has been said, 'Anyone who divorces his wife must give her a certificate of divorce.'

32 But I tell you that anyone who divorces his wife, except for marital unfaithfulness, causes her to become an adulteress, and anyone who marries the divorced woman commits adultery.

38 "You have heard that it was said, 'Eye for eye, and tooth for tooth.'

39 But I tell you, Do not resist an evil person. If someone strikes you on the right cheek, turn to him the other also.

40 And if someone wants to sue you and take your tunic, let him have your cloak as well.

41 If someone forces you to go one mile, go with him two miles.

42 Give to the one who asks you, and do not turn away from the one who wants to borrow from you.

43 "You have heard that it was said, 'Love your neighbor and hate your enemy.'

44–45 But I tell you: Love your enemies and pray for those who persecute you, that you may be sons of your Father in heaven. He causes his sun to rise on the evil and the good, and sends rain on the righteous and the unrighteous.

46 If you love those who love you, what reward will you get? Are not even the tax collectors doing that?

47 And if you greet only your brothers, what are you doing more than others? Do not even pagans do that?

48 Be perfect, therefore, as your heavenly Father is perfect.

JOHN 6 (NIV)

1 "Be careful not to do your 'acts of righteousness' before men, to be seen by them. If you do, you will have no reward from your Father in heaven.

2 "So when you give to the needy, do not announce it with trumpets, as the hypocrites do in the synagogues and on the streets, to be honored by men. I tell you the truth, they have received their reward in full.

3–4 But when you give to the needy, do not let your left hand know what your right hand is doing, so that your giving may be in secret. Then your Father, who sees what is done in secret, will reward you.

5 "And when you pray, do not be like the hypocrites, for they love to pray standing in the synagogues and on the street corners to be seen by men. I tell you the truth, they have received their reward in full.

6 But when you pray, go into your room, close the door and pray to your Father, who is unseen. Then your Father, who sees what is done in secret, will reward you.

7 And when you pray, do not keep on babbling like pagans, for they think they will be heard because of their many words.

8 Do not be like them, for your Father knows what you need before you ask him.

9 "This, then, is how you should pray: "'Our Father in heaven, hallowed be your name,

10 your kingdom come, your will be done on earth as it is in heaven.

11 Give us today our daily bread.

12 Forgive us our debts, as we also have forgiven our debtors.

13 And lead us not into temptation, but deliver us from the evil one.'

14 For if you forgive men when they sin against you, your heavenly Father will also forgive you.

15 But if you do not forgive men their sins, your Father will not forgive your sins.

19 "Do not store up for yourselves treasures on earth, where moth and rust destroy, and where thieves break in and steal.

20–21 But store up for yourselves treasures in heaven, where moth and rust do not destroy, and where thieves do not break in and steal. For where your treasure is, there your heart will be also.

24 "No one can serve two masters. Either he will hate the one and love the other, or he will be devoted to the one and despise the other. You cannot serve both God and Money.

25 "Therefore I tell you, do not worry about your life, what you will eat or drink; or about your body, what you will wear. Is not life more important than food, and the body more important than clothes?

26 Look at the birds of the air; they do not sow or reap or store away in barns, and yet your heavenly Father feeds them. Are you not much more valuable than they?

27 Who of you by worrying can add a single hour to his life?

28–29 "And why do you worry about clothes? See how the lilies of the field grow. They do not labor or spin. Yet I tell you that not even Solomon in all his splendor was dressed like one of these.

30 If that is how God clothes the grass of the field, which is here today and tomorrow is thrown into the fire, will he not much more clothe you, 0 you of little faith?

31 So do not worry, saying, 'What shall we eat?' or 'What shall we drink?' or 'What shall we wear?'

32 For the pagans run after all these things, and your heavenly Father knows that you need them.

33 But seek first his kingdom and his righteousness, and all these things will be given to you as well.

34 Therefore do not worry about tomorrow, for tomorrow will worry about itself. Each day has enough trouble of its own.

FROM JOHN 11 (RSV)

1–2 Now a certain man was ill, Lazarus of Bethany, in the village of Mary and her sister Martha. It was Mary who anointed the Lord with ointment and wiped his feet with her hair, whose brother Lazarus was ill.

5 Now Jesus loved Martha and her sister and Lazarus.

17 Now when Jesus came, he found that Lazarus had already been in the tomb four days.

18 Bethany was near Jerusalem, about two miles off, and many of the Jews had come to Martha and Mary to console them concerning their brother.

20 When Martha heard that Jesus was coming, she went and met him, while Mary sat in the house.

21–22 Martha said to Jesus, "Lord, if you had been here, my brother would not have died. And even now I know that whatever you ask from God, God will give you."

23 Jesus said to her, "Your brother will rise again."

24 Martha said to him, "I know that he will rise again in the resurrection at the last day."

25 Jesus said to her, "I am the resurrection and the life; he who believes in me, though he die, yet shall he live, and whoever lives and believes in me shall never die. Do you believe this?"

27 She said to him, "Yes, Lord; I believe that you are the Christ, the Son of God, he who is coming into the world."

32 Then Mary, when she came where Jesus was and saw him, fell at his feet, saying to him, "Lord, if you had been here, my brother would not have died."

33–34 When Jesus saw her weeping, and the Jews who came with her also weeping, he was deeply moved in spirit and troubled; and he said, "Where have you laid him?" They said to him, "Lord, come and see."

35–37 Jesus wept. So the Jews said, "See how he loved him!" But some of them said, "Could not he who opened the eyes of the blind man have kept this man from dying?"

38 Then Jesus, deeply moved again, came to the tomb; it was a cave, and a stone lay upon it.

39 Jesus said, "Take away the stone." Martha, the sister of the dead man, said to him, "Lord, by this time there will be an odor, for he has been dead four days."

40 Jesus said to her, "Did I not tell you that if you would believe you would see the glory of God?"

41–43 So they took away the stone. And Jesus lifted up his eyes and said, "Father, I thank thee that thou hast heard me. I knew that thou hearest me always, but I have said this on account of the people standing by, that they may believe that thou didst send me." When he had said this, he cried with a loud voice, "Lazarus, come out."

44 The dead man came out, his hands and feet bound with bandages, and his face wrapped with a cloth. Jesus said to them, "Unbind him, and let him go."

45 Many of the Jews therefore, who had come with Mary and had seen what he did, believed in him.

46 But some of them went to the Pharisees and told them what Jesus had done.

47–48 Then the chief priests and the Pharisees called a meeting of the Sanhedrin. "What are we accomplishing?" they asked. "Here is this man performing many miraculous signs. If we let him go on like this, everyone will believe in him, and then the Romans will come and take away both our place and our nation."

49–50 Then one of them, named Caiaphas, who was high priest that year, spoke up, "You know nothing at all! You do not realize that it is better for you that one man die for the people than that the whole nation perish."

THE INTERPRETATION OF PAUL

Both Jews and Gentiles will be saved through Faith, not the Law, not Wisdom Romans 3 (NIV)

21–24 But now a righteousness from God, apart from law, has been made known, to which the Law and the Prophets testify. This righteousness from God comes through faith in Jesus Christ to all who believe. There is no difference, for all have sinned and fall short of the glory of God, and are justified freely by his grace through the redemption that came by Christ Jesus.

27–28 Where, then, is boasting? It is excluded. On what principle? On that of observing the law? No, but on that of faith. For we maintain that a man is justified by faith apart from observing the law.

29 Is God the God of Jews only? Is he not the God of Gentiles too? Yes, of Gentiles too, since there is only one God, who will justify the circumcised by faith and the uncircumcised through that same faith.

1 Corinthians 1 (NIV)

17–19 For Christ did not send me to baptize, but to preach the gospel—not with words of human wisdom, lest the cross of Christ be emptied of its power. For the message of the cross is foolishness to those who are perishing, but to us who are being saved it is the power of God. For it is written: "I will destroy the wisdom of the wise; the intelligence of the intelligent I will frustrate."

20 Where is the wise man? Where is the scholar? Where is the philosopher of this age? Has not God made foolish the wisdom of the world?

21 For since in the wisdom of God the world through its wisdom did not know him, God was pleased through the foolishness of what was preached to save those who believe.

22–25 Jews demand miraculous signs and Greeks look for wisdom, but we preach Christ crucified: a stumbling block to Jews and foolishness to Gentiles, but to those whom God has called, both Jews and Greeks, Christ the power of God and the wisdom of God. For the foolishness of God is wiser than man's wisdom, and the weakness of God is stronger than man's strength.

26–29 Brothers, think of what you were when you were called. Not many of you were wise by human standards; not many were influential; not many were of noble birth. But God chose the foolish things of the world to shame the wise; God chose the weak things of the world to shame the strong. He chose the lowly things of this world and the despised things—and the things that are not—to nullify the things that are, so that no one may boast before him.

From Galatians 3

26–27 You are all sons of God through faith in Christ Jesus, for all of you who were baptized into Christ have clothed yourselves with Christ.

28 There is neither Jew nor Greek, slave nor free, male nor female, for you are all one in Christ Jesus.

Paul considers the role of women in the Church 1 Timothy 2 (NIV)

8–10 I desire then that in every place the men should pray, lifting holy hands without anger or quarreling; also that women should adorn themselves modestly and sensibly in seemly apparel, not with braided hair or gold or pearls or costly attire, but by good deeds, as befits women who profess religion.

11–12 Let a woman learn in silence with all submissiveness. I permit no woman to teach or to have authority over men; she is to keep silent.

13–14 For Adam was formed first, then Eve; and Adam was not deceived, but the woman was deceived and became a transgressor.

15 Yet woman will be saved through bearing children, if she continues in faith and love and holiness, with modesty.

On Marriage and Celibacy 1 Corinthians 7 (NIV)

1 Now for the matters you wrote about: It is good for a man not to marry.

2–5 But since there is so much immorality, each man should have his own wife, and each woman her own husband. The husband should fulfill his marital duty to his wife, and likewise the wife to her husband. The wife's body does not belong to her alone but also to her husband. In the same way, the husband's body does not belong to him alone but also to his wife. Do not deprive each other except by mutual consent and for a time, so that you may devote yourselves to prayer. Then come together again so that Satan will not tempt you because of your lack of self-control.

6–7 I say this as a concession, not as a command. I wish that all men were as I am. But each man has his own gift from God; one has this gift, another has that.

8–9 Now to the unmarried and the widows I say: It is good for them to stay unmarried, as I am. But if they cannot control themselves, they should marry, for it is better to marry than to burn with passion.

17 Nevertheless, each one should retain the place in life that the Lord assigned to him and to which God has called him. This is the rule I lay down in all the churches.

Questions:
1. How does Jesus' teaching differ from the law codes of the ancient Near East that you have read (Chapter 1, Documents 7 and 8)?
2. How did the preaching of Paul help Christianity to spread beyond the Jews?
3. To whom did Christianity appeal and why?
4. How did the teachings of Christianity both enlarge and circumscribe women's role in society?

7.4 The Nicene Creed

Long after Jesus, his disciples, and St. Paul were gone, Christianity continued to flourish under the leadership of priests and bishops. Disputes inevitably arose over articles of faith and doctrine. To solve a dispute over the nature of the Trinity, the first ecumenical church council of all the bishops was called at Nicea in 325 C.E. under the auspices of the Emperor Constantine and produced this basic creed of Christian beliefs.[1]

> **Source:** *Readings in the History of Christian Theology, Volume I: From Its Beginnings to the Eve of the Reformation*, ed. William C. Placher, (Philadelphia: The Westminster Press, 1988), p. 53; from *Nicene and Post-Nicene Fathers*, 2nd Series, ed. Philip Schaff and Henry Wace, trans. Henry R. Percival, (New York: Christian Literature Company, 1890–1900), Volume 14, p. 3.

We believe in one God, the Father Almighty, maker of all things, visible and invisible;

And in one Lord Jesus Christ, the Son of God, the only-begotten of his Father, of the substance of the Father, God of God, Light of Light, very God of very God, begotten, not made, being of one substance with the Father. By whom all things were made, both which be in heaven and in earth. Who for us men and for our salvation came down [from heaven] and was incarnate and was made man. He suffered and the third day he rose again, and ascended into heaven. And he shall come again to judge both the quick and the dead.

And [we believe] in the Holy Ghost.

And whosoever shall say that there was a time when the Son of God was not, or that before he was begotten he was not, or that he was made of things that were not,

or that he is of a different substance or essence [from the Father] or that he is a creature, or subject to change or conversion—all that so say, the Catholic and Apostolic Church anathematizes them.

Questions:
1. What was at issue in the dispute over the nature of God?
2. Which doctrinal position does the creed express? (In other words, which side won?)

7.5 Defining the Christian Woman

Women had figured prominently in Jesus' ministry and life. Paul's instructions had circumscribed women's role in the Christian Church, and subsequent male church leaders tended to subordinate and reduce their role even further. Nevertheless, women continued to play an important role in spreading and nurturing the young Christian faith. Augustine, the greatest of all Christian writers (354–430 C.E.), discusses his relationship with his mother Monica and the role she filled in his conversion to the Christian faith.

> **Source:** Saint Augustine, *Confessions*, trans. R.S. Pine-Coffin, (New York: Penguin Books, 1980, © 1961), pp. 67–69.

BOOK III–11

. . . You sent down your help from above[1] and rescued my soul from the depths of this darkness because my mother, your faithful servant, wept to you for me, shedding more tears for my spiritual death than other mothers shed for the bodily death of a son. For in her faith and in the spirit which she had from you she looked on me as dead. You heard her and did not despise the tears which streamed down and watered the earth in every place where she bowed her head in prayer. You heard her, for how else can I explain the dream with which you consoled her, so that she agreed to live with me and eat at the same table in our home? Lately she had refused to do this, because she loathed and shunned the blasphemy of my false beliefs.

She dreamed that she was standing on a wooden rule, and coming towards her in a halo of splendour she saw a young man who smiled at her in joy, although she herself was sad and quite consumed with grief. He asked her the reason for her sorrow and her daily tears, not because he did not know, but because he had something to tell her, for this is what happens in visions. When she replied that her tears were for the soul I had lost, he told her to take heart for, if she looked carefully, she would see that where she was, there also was I. And when she looked, she saw me standing beside her on the same rule.

Where could this dream have come from, unless it

---

[1] Many Christian Churches use an adaptation of the Nicene Creed as it was accepted at the Second Council of Constantinople in 381 C.E.

[1] Psalm 143:7 (144:7)

was that you listened to the prayer of her heart? For your goodness is almighty; you take good care of each of us as if you had no others in your care, and you look after all as you look after each. And surely it was for the same reason that, when she told me of the dream and I tried to interpret it as a message that she need not despair of being one day such as I was then, she said at once and without hesitation 'No! He did not say, "Where he is, you are," but "Where you are, he is." '

I have often said before and, to the best of my memory, I now declare to you, Lord, that I was much moved by this answer, which you gave me through my mother. She was not disturbed by my interpretation of her dream, plausible though it was, but quickly saw the true meaning, which I had not seen until she spoke. I was more deeply moved by this than by the dream itself, in which the joy for which this devout woman had still so long to wait was foretold so long before to comfort her in the time of her distress. For nearly nine years were yet to come during which I wallowed deep in the mire and the darkness of delusion. Often I tried to lift myself, only to plunge the deeper. Yet all the time this chaste, devout, and prudent woman, a widow such as is close to your heart, never ceased to pray at all hours and to offer you the tears she shed for me. The dream had given new spirit to her hope, but she gave no rest to her sighs and her tears. Her prayers reached your presence' and yet you still left me to twist and turn in the dark.

BOOK VI–1

O God, Hope of my youth,[2] where were you all this time? Where were you hiding from me? Were you not my Creator and was it not you who made me different from the beasts that walk on the earth and wiser than the birds that fly in the air? Yet I was walking on a treacherous path, in darkness. I was looking for you outside myself and I did not find the God of my own heart. I had reached the depths of the ocean. I had lost all faith and was in despair of finding the truth.

By now my mother had come to me, for her piety had given her strength to follow me over land and sea, facing all perils in the sure faith she had in you. When the ship was in danger, it was she who put heart into the crew, the very men to whom passengers unused to the sea turn for reassurance when they are alarmed. She promised them that they would make the land in safety, because you had given her this promise in a vision. And she found that I too was in grave danger because of my despair of discovering the truth. I told her that I was not a Catholic Christian, but at least I was no longer a Manichee.[3] Yet she did not leap for joy as

though this news were unexpected. In fact, to this extent, her anxiety for me had already been allayed. For in her prayers to you she wept for me as though I were dead, but she also knew that you would recall me to life. In her heart she offered me to you as though I were laid out on a bier, waiting for you to say to the widow's son, 'Young man, I say to you, stand up.' And he would get up and begin to speak, and you would give him back to his mother.[4] So she felt no great surge of joy and her heart beat none the faster when she heard that the tears and the prayers which she had offered you day after day had at last, in great part, been rewarded. For I had been rescued from falsehood, even if I had not yet grasped the truth. Instead, because she was sure that if you had promised her all, you would also give her what remained to be given, she told me quite serenely, with her heart full of faith, that in Christ she believed that before she left this life she would see me a faithful Catholic. This was what she said to me. But to you, from whom all mercies spring, she poured out her tears and her prayers all the more fervently, begging you to speed your help and give me light in my darkness. She hurried all the more eagerly to church, where she listened with rapt attention to all that Ambrose said. For her his words were like a spring of water within her, that flows continually to bring her everlasting life.[5] She loved him as God's angel,[6] because she had learnt that it was through him that I had been led, for the time being, into a state of wavering uncertainty. She had no doubt that I must pass through this condition, which would lead me from sickness to health. . . .

My heart lies open before you, 0 Lord my God, and this is what I believe. Because he could show me the way of salvation she was greatly devoted to Ambrose, and his heart too had warmed to her for her truly pious way of life, her zeal in good works, and her regular churchgoing. Often, when he saw me, he would break out in praise of her, congratulating me on having such a mother.

Questions:

1. What role did Monica play in the conversion of Augustine to Christianity?
2. From Augustine's description, what sort of person was Monica?
3. How does your impression of Monica compare with Paul's injunctions for Christian women in Document 3?

---

[2] Psalm 70:5 (71:5)

[3] A Manichee was considered a heretic by Catholic Christians. Manichees explained evil in the world by believing in an evil god who had created the world, and that there was a good god who would save one's soul if one rejected the evil material world including the desires of the flesh.
[4] Luke 7:14, 15.
[5] John 4:14
[6] Galatians 4:14.

SECTION 3
Neither Jew nor Greek

7.6   The Roman Policy on Christians

Pliny the Younger was governor of Bithynia from 111–113 C.E. He left a whole set of his correspondence with the emperor Trajan on a variety of administrative political matters. These two letters are the most famous, in which Pliny encounters and deals with Christianity in an administrative and judicial capacity.

Source: *Readings in Ancient History: Illustrative Extracts from the Sources, Vol. II, Rome and the West*, ed. William Stearns Davis, (New York: Allyn and Bacon, 1913), pp. 219–22. (Pliny the Younger, *Letters*, from book X, Firth's trans.)

PLINY'S LETTER TO TRAJAN:

It is my custom, Sire, to refer to you in all cases where I am in doubt, for who can better clear up difficulties and inform me? I have never been present at any legal examination of the Christians, and I do not know, therefore, what are the usual penalties passed upon them, or the limits of those penalties, or how searching an inquiry should he made. I have hesitated a great deal in considering whether any distinctions should be drawn according to the ages of the accused; whether the weak should be punished as severely as the more robust, or whether the man who has once been a Christian gained anything by recanting? [Again] whether the *name* [of being a Christian], even though otherwise innocent of crime, should be punished, or only the crimes that gather around it?

In the meantime, this is the plan which I have adopted in the case of those Christians who have been brought before me. I ask them whether they are Christians, if they say "Yes," then I repeat the question the second time, and also a third—warning them of the penalties involved; and if they persist, I order them away to prison. For I do not doubt that—be their admitted crime what it may—their pertinacity and inflexible obstinacy surely ought to be punished.

There were others who showed similar mad folly, whom I reserved to be sent to Rome, as they were Roman citizens. Later, as is commonly the case, the mere fact of my entertaining the question led to a multiplying of accusations and a variety of cases were brought before me. An anonymous pamphlet was issued, containing a number of names [of alleged Christians]. Those who denied that they were or had been Christians and called upon the gods with the usual formula, reciting the words after me, and those who offered incense and wine before your image—which I had ordered to be brought forward for this purpose, along with the [regular] statues of the gods,—all such I considered acquitted,—especially as they cursed the name of Christ, which it is said *bona fide* Christians cannot be induced to do.

Still others there were, whose names were supplied by an informer. These first said they were Christians, then denied it, insisting they had been, "but were so no longer"; some of them having "recanted many years ago," and more than one "full twenty years back." These all worshiped your image and the god's statues and cursed the name of Christ.

But they declared their guilt or error was simply this—on a fixed day they used to meet before dawn and recite a hymn among themselves to Christ, as though he were a god. So far from binding themselves by oath to commit any crime, they swore to keep from theft, robbery, adultery, breach of faith, and not to deny any trust money deposited with them when called upon to deliver it. This ceremony over, they used to depart and meet again to take food—but it was of no special character, and entirely harmless. They [also] had ceased from this practice after the edict [I issued]—by which, in accord with your orders, I forbade all secret societies.

I then thought it the more needful to get at the facts behind their statements. Therefore I placed two women, called "deaconesses," under torture, but I found only a debased superstition carried to great lengths, so I postponed my examination, and immediately consulted you. This seems a matter worthy of your [prompt] consideration, especially as so many people are endangered. Many of all ages and both sexes are put in peril of their lives by their accusers; and the process will go on, for the contagion of this superstition has spread not merely through the free towns, but into the villages and farms. Still I think it can be halted and things set right. Beyond any doubt, the temples—which were nigh deserted—are beginning again to be thronged with worshipers; the sacred rites, which long have lapsed, are now being renewed, and the food for the sacrificial victims is again finding a sale—though up to recently it had almost no market. So one can safely infer how vast numbers could be reclaimed, if only there were a chance given for repentance.

TRAJAN'S REPLY TO PLINY:

You have adopted the right course, my dear Pliny, in examining the cases of those cited before you as Christians; for no hard and fast rule can be laid down covering such a wide question. The Christians are not to be hunted out. If brought before you, and the offense is proved, they are to be punished, but with this reservation—if any one denies he is a Christian, and makes it clear he is not, by offering prayer to our gods, then he is to be pardoned on his recantation, no matter how suspicious his past. As for anonymous pamphlets, they are to be discarded absolutely, whatever crime they may charge, for they are not only a precedent of a very bad type, but they do not accord with the spirit of our age.

Questions:
1. For what reason were the Christians being punished in Bithynia? Why were they perceived as dangerous?
2. What does Pliny's letter reveal about how the Romans perceived the Christians and their beliefs?
3. How does the legal procedure Pliny and Trajan decide upon in dealing with Christians fit into traditional Roman legal principles? (See the Twelve Tables, Chapter 5, Document 5)

Documents 7.7 and 7.8

These selections show the division between Christian leaders over the topic of Greco-Roman philosophy, which, owing its origins to pagan cultures, was viewed with cynicism by some for the threat it presented to the Christian faith and morality, but wholeheartedly accepted by others who saw in it divine inspiration.

7.7 "What Has Jerusalem to do with Athens?"

Tertullian (ca. 160 –ca. 240 C.E.), a native of Carthage, became a strong defender of Christian morals and wrote a series of attacks on heretics. In his *Prescriptions Against Heretics*, he vehemently warns that heresy arises out of a dependence on Greco-Roman philosophy.

> **Source:** *Sources of the Western Tradition: Volume I: From Ancient Times to the Enlightenment*, ed. Marvin Perry, Joseph R. Peden, and Theodore H. Von Laue, (Boston: Houghton Mifflin Co., 1995), p. 182. Reprinted from *Early Latin Theology*, translated and edited by S.I. Greenslade, Vol. V: The Library of Christian Classics, (Philadelphia: Westminster Press).

. . . Worldly wisdom culminates in philosophy with its rash interpretation of God's nature and purpose. It is philosophy that supplies the heresies[1] with their equipment. . . . The idea of a mortal soul was picked up from the Epicureans, and the denial of the restitution of the flesh was taken from the common tradition of the philosophical schools. . . . Heretics and philosophers [ponder] the same themes and are caught up in the same discussions. What is the origin of evil and why? The origin of man, and how? . . . A plague on Aristotle, who taught them dialectic [logical argumentation], the art which destroys as much as it builds, which changes its

---

[1] A heresy is any belief that differs from official or standard doctrines.

opinions like a coat, forces its conjectures, is stubborn in argument, works hard at being contentious and is a burden even to itself. For it reconsiders every point to make sure it never finishes a discussion.

From philosophy come those fables and . . . fruitless questionings, those "words that creep like as doth a canker." To hold us back from such things, the Apostle [Paul] testifies expressly in his letter to the Colossians [Colossians 2:8] that we should beware of philosophy. "Take heed lest any man [beguile] you through philosophy or vain deceit, after the tradition of men," against the providence of the Holy Ghost. He had been at Athens where he had come to grips with the human wisdom which attacks and perverts truth, being itself divided up into its own swarm of heresies by the variety of its mutually antagonistic sects. What has Jerusalem to do with Athens, the Church with [Plato's] Academy, the Christian with the heretic? Our principles come from the Porch of Solomon,[2] who had himself taught that the Lord is to be sought in simplicity of heart. I have no use for Stoic or a Platonic or a dialectic Christianity. After Jesus Christ we have no need of speculation, after the Gospel no need of research. When we come to believe, we have no desire to believe anything else; for we begin by believing that there is nothing else which we have to believe.

7.8 "Philosophy is a Clear Image of Truth"

Not all Christian leaders believed that philosophy was so dangerous to Christian faith. Here, Clement of Alexandria (ca. 150 –ca. 220 C.E.) expresses admiration for Greek learning and believed it was a gift of God. A Greek Christian theologian, Clement consciously used Platonic thought in explaining Christian doctrine.

> **Source:** Clement of Alexandria, *Stromata (Miscellanies)*, trans. William Wilson in A. Roberts and James Donaldson, Anti-Nicene Christian Library in *The Writings of Clement of Alexandria*, (Edinburgh: T. & T. Clark, 1867–1872), Vol. 4, pp. 303–305, 307–310, 318.

The Greeks should not be condemned by those who have merely glanced at their writings, for comprehension of these works requires careful investigation. Philosophy is not the originator of false practices and base deeds as some have calumniated it; nor does it beguile us and lead us away from faith.

Rather philosophy is a clear image of truth, a divine gift to the Greeks. Before the advent of the Lord, phi-

---

[2] The Stoic philosophers took their name from the Greek word *stoa*, porch, the place where Zeno, their founder, used to teach. *Porch of Solomon* is used to designate the teachings of King Solomon, who built the great Temple in Jerusalem. Tertullian makes it clear he follows Solomon's wisdom.

losophy helped the Greeks to attain righteousness, and it is now conducive to piety; it supplies a preparatory teaching for those who will later embrace the faith. God is the cause of all good things: some given primarily in the form of the Old and the New Testament; others are the consequence of philosophy. Perchance too philosophy was given to the Greeks primarily till the Lord should call the Greeks to serve him. Thus philosophy acted as a school-master to the Greeks, preparing them for Christ, as the laws of the Jews prepared them for Christ.

The way of truth is one. But into it, as into a perennial river, streams flow from all sides. We assert that philosophy, which is characterized by investigation into the form and nature of things, is the truth of which the Lord Himself said, "I am the truth." Thus Greek preparatory culture, including philosophy itself, is shown to have come down from God to men.

Some do not wish to touch either philosophy or logic or to learn natural science. They demand bare faith alone, as if they wished, without bestowing any care on the vine, straightway to gather clusters from the first. I call him truly learned who brings everything to bear on the truth; so that from geometry, music, grammar and philosophy itself, he culls what is useful and guards the faith against assault.

And he who brings everything to bear on a right life, learning from Greeks and non-Greeks, this man is an experienced searcher after truth. And how necessary it is for him who desires to be partaker of the power of God to treat of intellectual subjects by philosophing.

According to some, Greek philosophy apprehended the truth accidentally, dimly, partially. Others will have it that Greek philosophy was instituted by the devil. Several hold that certain powers descending from heaven inspired the whole of philosophy. But if Greek philosophy does not comprehend the whole of truth and does not encompass God's commandments, yet it prepares the way for God's teachings; training in some way or other, molding character, and fitting him who believes in Providence for the reception of truth.

Questions for Documents 7.7 and 7.8
1. Why did Tertullian condemn the study of pagan literature and philosophy as dangerous for Christians?
2. What arguments did Clement use to support his position that Greek philosophy was a gift of God?
3. What might have happened had the Christian Church followed Tertullian's advice rather than Clement's?

CHAPTER 8
After Antiquity
New Peoples of Europe
and Other Peoples of the World
(300–1300 C.E.)

SECTION 1
Europe

8.1 Tacitus Describes the Germanic Tribes

Tacitus describes what he has researched about the nomadic German tribes of Northern Europe in the second century C.E. Since the Germans had no written language and built no cities, his work is our best source for Germanic culture.

> **Source:** Tacitus, *Agricola*, trans. H. Mattingly, revised by S.A. Handford, (New York: Penguin Books, 1981, © 1970), pp. 107–23, passim.

7. They choose their kings for their noble birth, their commanders for their valour. The power even of the kings is not absolute or arbitrary. The commanders rely on example rather than on the authority of their rank—on the admiration they win by showing conspicuous energy and courage and by pressing forward in front of their own troops. Capital punishment, imprisonment, even flogging, are allowed to none but the priests, and are not inflicted merely as punishments or on the commanders' orders, but as it were in obedience to the god whom the Germans believe to be present on the field of battle. . . . A specially powerful incitement to valour is that the squadrons and divisions are not made up at random by the mustering of chance-comers, but are each composed of men of one family or clan. Close by them, too, are their nearest and dearest, so that they can hear the shrieks of their womenfolk and the wailing of their children. These are the witnesses whom each man reverences most highly, whose praise he most desires. It is to their mothers and wives that they go to have their wounds treated, and the women are not afraid to count and compare the gashes. They also carry supplies of food to the combatants and encourage them.

8. It stands on record that armies already wavering and on the point of collapse have been rallied by the women, pleading heroically with their men, thrusting forward their bared bosoms, and making them realize the imminent prospect of enslavement—a fate which the Germans fear more desperately for their women than for themselves. . . .

10. For omens and the casting of lots they have the highest regard. Their procedure in casting lots is always the same. They cut off a branch of a nut–bearing tree and slice it into strips; these they mark with different signs and throw them completely at random onto a white cloth. Then the priest of the state, if the consultation is a public one, or the father of the family if it is private, offers a prayer to the gods, and looking up at the sky picks up three strips, one at a time, and reads their meaning from the signs previously scored on them. If the lots forbid an enterprise, there is no deliberation that day on the matter in question; if they allow it, confirmation by the taking of auspices is required. Although the familiar method of seeking information from the cries and the flight of birds is known to the Germans, they have also a special method of their own—to try to obtain omens and warnings from horses. . . .

11. On matters of minor importance only the chiefs debate; on major affairs, the whole community. But even where the commons have the decision, the subject is considered in advance by the chiefs. Except in case of accident or emergency, they assemble on certain particular days, either shortly after the new moon or shortly before the full moon. These, they hold, are the most auspicious times for embarking on any enterprise. . . . When the assembled crowd thinks fit, they take their seats fully armed. Silence is then commanded by the priests, who on such occasions have power to enforce obedience. Then such hearing is given to the king or state-chief as his age, rank, military distinction, or eloquence can secure—more because his advice carries weight than because he has the power to command. If a proposal displeases them, the people shout their dissent; if they approve, they clash their spears. To express approbation with their weapons is their most complimentary way of showing agreement.

12. The Assembly is competent also to hear criminal charges, especially those uninvolving the risk of capital punishment. The mode of execution varies according to the offense. Traitors and deserters are hanged on trees; cowards, shirkers, and sodomites are pressed down under a wicker hurdle into the slimy mud of a bog. This distinction in the punishments is based on the idea that offenders against the state should be made a public example of, whereas deeds of shame should be buried out of men's sight.

13. They transact no business, public or private, without being armed. But it is a rule that no one shall carry arms until the state authorities are satisfied that he will be competent to use them. Then, in the presence of the Assembly, either one of the chiefs or the young man's father or some other relative presents him with a shield and a spear. These, among the Germans, are the equivalent of the man's toga with us—the first distinction publicly conferred upon a youth, who now ceases to rank merely as a member of a household and becomes a citizen. . . .

14. On the field of battle it is a disgrace to a chief to be surpassed in courage by his followers, and to the followers not to equal the courage of their chief. And to leave a battle alive after their chief has fallen means lifelong infamy and shame. To defend and protect him, and to let him get the credit for their own acts of heroism, are the most solemn obligations of their allegiance. The chiefs fight for victory, the followers for their chief. Many noble youths, if the land of their birth is stagnating in a long period of peace and inactivity, deliberately seek out other tribes which have some war in hand. For the Germans have no taste for peace; . . . Their meals, for which plentiful if homely fare is provided, count in lieu of pay. The wherewithal for this openhandedness comes from war and plunder. A German is not so easily prevailed upon to plough the land and wait patiently for harvest as to challenge a foe and earn wounds for his reward. He thinks it tame and spiritless to accumulate slowly by the sweat of his brow what can be got quickly by the loss of a little blood.

15. When not engaged in warfare they spend a certain amount of time in hunting, but much more in idleness, thinking of nothing else but sleeping and eating. For the boldest and most warlike men have no regular employment, the care of house, home, and fields being left to the women, old men, and weaklings of the family. In thus dawdling away their time they show a strange inconsistency—at one and the same time loving indolence and hating peace. . . .

16. It is a well–known fact that the peoples of Germany never live in cities and will not even have their houses adjoin one another. They dwell apart, dotted about here and there, wherever a spring, plain, or grove takes their fancy. Their villages are not laid out in the Roman style, with buildings adjacent and connected. Every man leaves an open space round his house, perhaps as a precaution against the risk of fire, perhaps because they are inexpert builders. They do not even make use of stones or wall–tiles; for all purposes they employ rough-hewn timber, ugly and unattractive-looking. . . .

18. Their marriage code, however, is strict, and no feature of their morality deserves higher praise. They are almost unique among barbarians in being content with one wife apiece—all of them, that is, except a very few who take more than one wife not to satisfy their desires but because their exalted rank brings them many pressing offers of matrimonial alliances. The dowry is brought by husband to wife, not by wife to husband. Parents and kinsmen attend and approve the gifts—not gifts chosen to please a woman's fancy or gaily deck a young bride, but oxen, a horse with its bridle, or a shield, spear, and sword. In consideration of such gifts a man gets his wife, and she in her turn brings a present of arms to her husband. This interchange of gifts typifies for them the most sacred bond of union, sanctified by mystic rites under the favour of the presiding deities of wedlock. The woman must not think that she is excluded from aspirations to manly virtues or exempt from the hazards of warfare. That is why she is reminded, in the very ceremonies which bless her marriage at its outset, that she enters her husband's home to be the partner of his toils and perils, that both in peace and in war she is to share his sufferings and adventures. That is the meaning of the team of oxen, the horse ready for its rider, and the gift of arms. On these terms she must live her life and bear her children. She is receiving something that she must hand over intact and undepreciated to her children, something for her sons' wives to receive in their turn and pass on to her grandchildren.

19. By such means is the virtue of their women protected, and they live uncorrupted by the temptations of public shows or the excitements of banquets. Clandestine love-letters are unknown to men amid women alike. Adultery is extremely rare, considering the size of the population. A guilty wife is summarily punished by her husband. He cuts off her hair, strips her naked, and in the presence of kinsmen turns her out of his house and flogs her all through the village. They have in fact no mercy on a wife who prostitutes her chastity. Neither beauty, youth, nor wealth can find her another husband. To restrict the number of children, or to kill any of those born after the heir, is considered wicked. Good morality is more effective in Germany than good laws are elsewhere.

20. In every home the children go naked and dirty, and develop that strength of limb and tall stature which excite our admiration. Every mother feeds her child at the breast and does not depute the task to maids or nurses. The young master is not distinguished from the slave by any pampering in his upbringing. They live together among the same flocks and on the same earthen floor, until maturity sets apart the free and the spirit of valour claims them as her own. The young men are slow to mate, and thus they reach manhood with vigour unimpaired. The girls, too, are not hurried into marriage. As old and full-grown as the men, they match their mates in age and strength, and the children inherit the robustness of their parents. The sons of sisters are as highly honoured by their uncles as by their own fathers. The more relatives and connections by marriage a man has, the greater authority he commands in old age. There is nothing to be gained by childlessness in Germany.

21. Heirs are under an obligation to take up both the feuds and the friendships of a father or kinsman. But feuds do not continue for ever unreconciled. Even homicide can be atoned for by a fixed number of cattle or sheep, the compensation being received by the whole family. This is to the advantage of the community: for private feuds are particularly dangerous where there is such complete liberty.

22. Drinking-bouts lasting all day and all night are not considered in any way disgraceful. The quarrels that inevitably arise over the cups are seldom settled merely by hard words, but often by killing amid wounding. Nevertheless, they often make a feast an occasion for discussing such affairs as time ending of feuds, the arrangement of marriage alliances, the adoption of chiefs, and even questions of peace or war. At no other time, they think, is the heart so open to sincere feelings or so quick to warm to noble sentiments. The Germans are not cunning or sophisticated enough to refrain from blurting out their inmost thoughts in the freedom of festive surroundings, so that every man's soul is laid completely bare. On the following day the subject is reconsidered, and thus due account is taken of both occasions. They debate when they are incapable of pretence but reserve their decision for a time when they cannot well make a mistake.

25. Slaves in general do not have particular duties about the house and estate allotted to them, as our slaves do. Each has control of a holding and home of his own. The master demands from him a stated quantity of grain, livestock, or cloth, as he would from a tenant. To this extent the slave is under an obligation of service; but all other duties, including household work, are carried out by the housewife and her children.

26. The employment of capital in order to increase it by usury is unknown in Germany; amid ignorance is here a surer defence than any prohibition. Lands proportioned to their own number are appropriated in turn for tillage by the whole body of tillers. They then divide them among themselves according to rank; the division is made easy by the wide tracts of cultivable ground available. These ploughlands are changed yearly, amid still there is enough and to spare. The fact is that although their land is fertile and extensive, they fail to take full advantage of it because they do not work sufficiently hard. They do not plant orchards, fence off meadows, or irrigate gardens; the only demand they make upon the soil is to produce a corn crop.[1]

27. There is no ostentation about their funerals. The only special observance is that the bodies of famous men are burned with particular kinds of wood. When they have heaped up the pyre they do not throw garments or spices on it; only the dead man's arms, and sometimes his horse too, are cast into the flames. The tomb is a raised mound of turf. They disdain to show honour by laboriously rearing high monuments of stone, which they think would only lie heavy on the dead.

Questions:
1. What role do women play in this society? How does it compare to the role of women in Roman society?
2. How are German methods of rule and decision-making different from Roman

institutions of government?
3. How favorably or unfavorably does Tacitus view Germanic culture?
4. How does the fact that Tacitus views them from a Roman perspective affect his evaluation of the Germanic people?

8.2 Celts: The Bog People

Like the Germans, the Celts had no written language or cities, so most of our information about these people on the fringes of the Roman Empire also originated from the Romans. Archaeology, however, has recently added to our knowledge of these people through the study of their dead.

Source: *The Global Past*, eds. Lanny B. Fields, Russell J. Parker, Cheryl A. Riggs, (Boston: Bedford Press, 1998), p. 15.

For centuries, Europeans have been cutting peat, a spongy mat of decayed plant fibers forming in bogs, and have used it for fuel. Occasionally, bog bodies have been found embedded in the peat. Remarkably preserved by the acidic bog water, these human bodies usually have intact skin, hair, organs, and clothing—materials that rarely are preserved in the archaeological record. These rare, archaeologically valuable bog bodies illustrate how archaeologists use physical remains to reconstruct the past.

Most bog bodies date to the Iron Age (about 1000 B.C.–A.D. 100), their age determined primarily through the use of radiocarbon dating. . . . In northern Europe, almost seven hundred bog bodies have been reported, although many were found before modern techniques of preservation or analysis were available, so the information about them is often scant. Much of the information that follows comes from the analysis of a recent find, the Lindow Man of England.

The mode of death of a bog person can be determined by searching for signs of disease or violence. The bog bodies are distinctive in the high degree of violence evident. Lindow Man is fairly typical, showing a chest wound (probably from a sword), a fractured skull, facial damage, and strangulation with a thong still around the neck. Other bog bodies also have slit throats. The number of violent acts committed against bog people has been called "murderous overkill," because any of the wounds would have been sufficient to cause death.

The bog people are anonymous, of course, but certain deductions can be made about them. Both men and women became bog people, and they were usually in their twenties or thirties at the times of their deaths. The bodies usually were naked or nearly so with no artifacts that could give an indication of a person's status in life. The fingernails, however, provide telltale clues. Modern laborers' fingernails have distinctive scratches and tiny splits in the ends; modern bank clerks, on the other hand, have smooth nails with few blemishes. Bog body fingernails have their closest

---

[1] Cereal grain. What we know as corn originated in the Western Hemisphere.

parallels among bank clerks, suggesting that the bog people were individuals whose station placed them above the necessity of providing manual labor.

Of the bog bodies that have been fully analyzed, most seem to have died in the late spring. This is indicated by the species of pollen in the intestines. This pollen would have been in the air and consumed with food; its hard silica casings resisted digestion and remained intact in the body.

The last meal of the deceased also can be determined by analyzing remains in the intestine. In the case of Lindow Man, several types of grain were present. Electron spin resonance, a technique pioneered by physicists, revealed that the grains were heated to the temperature required for baking bread. Fragments of the grains indicate that part of the bread was burnt.

Taken together, these facts lead to an interpretation of what happened to these bog people. The number and nature of the violent acts committed against many of the bog people suggest that they were human sacrifices—ritually killed, then disposed of in the approved manner in a bog, perhaps in an attempt to ensure the springtime renewal. Those sacrificed were not commoners but rather members of the elite, perhaps nobility. Even the charring of the bread may be significant. During the Beltain festivals of seventeenth-century England, bread was distributed and the person who received a burnt piece by chance was referred to as being given to the gods as a sacrifice and was called "dead" during the rest of the ceremony. The Beltain festival probably was a bloodless carryover of an ancient Iron Age ritual that extended through much of northern Europe.

Questions:
1. How useful is the study of the Bog People in learning about the Celts?
2. Differentiate between the facts about the Bog People in this article and the interpretations archaeologists have made about them. What can we conclude is "truth?"

8.3   St. Patrick's Confession

St. Patrick (ca. 389–461 C.E.) was the son of a Christian Briton family who was seized in a raid by the Irish and taken back to their island as a slave. Escaping, he entered a monastery on the Continent and was ordained a missionary to Ireland in 432. Although there were some Irish Christians in the south before Patrick's mission, it is largely through his thirty years of missionary activity in Ireland that Christianity became established and systemized there. He left a Confession that includes a brief account of his life, of personal spiritual struggles, and of missionary activity.

Source: *The Book of Letters of Saint Patrick the Bishop*, ed. and trans. D.R. Howlett, (Dublin: Four Courts Press, 1994), pp. 53, 57–65, 67–69, 93.

PART I

I, Patrick, a sinner, very rustic, and the least of all the faithful, and very contemptible in the estimation of most men, had as father a certain man called Calpornius, a deacon, son of Potitus, a presbyter, who was in the town Bannaventa Berniae, for he had a little villa nearby, where I conceded capture. In years I was then almost sixteen. For I was ignorant of the true God, and I was led to Ireland in captivity with so many thousands of men according to our deserts, because we withdrew from God, and we did not keep watch over His precepts, and we were not obedient to our priests, who kept admonishing our salvation, and the Lord led down over us the wrath of His anger and dispersed us among many gentiles even as far as the furthest part of land, where now my insignificance is seen to be among members of a strange race. And there the Lord opened the consciousness of my unbelief so that, perhaps, late, I might remember my delicts, and that I might turn with a whole heart to the Lord my God, Who turned His gaze round on my lowliness and took pity on my adolescence and ignorance and kept watch over me before I knew Him and before I was wise or distinguished between good and bad, and He fortified me and consoled me as a father [consoles] a son.

• • • •

As an adolescent, more precisely, as an almost wordless boy, I conceded capture before I knew what I ought to seek or what to avoid. Whence therefore today I blush for shame and vehemently thoroughly fear to strip naked my unlearnedness, because I cannot unfold in speech to those learned in conciseness as, however, my spirit and mind longs, and the emotion of my consciousness suggests. But if, consequently, it had been given to me just as also to others, even so I would not be silent on account of what should be handed back [from me to God]. And if by chance it seems to certain men that I put myself forward in this, with my lack of knowledge and my rather slow tongue, but even so it is, however, written, "Stammering tongues will swiftly learn to speak peace." How much more ought we to seek, we who are, he affirms, The letter of Christ for salvation as far as the furthest part of land, and if not learned, yet valid and very vigorous, written in your hearts not with ink but by the Spirit of the living God, and again the Spirit testifies even rustic work created by the Most High. Whence I, the extreme rustic, a refugee, untaught, doubtless, who do not know how to look forward into the future, but that I do know most certainly, that indeed before I was humbled. I was like a stone that lies in deep mud, and He Who is powerful came and in His pity He raised me up and assuredly to be sure lifted me upward and placed me on the highest wall and therefore I ought forcefully to shout out for something that should be handed back to the Lord also for His benefits so great here and for eternity, which [benefits] the mind of men cannot estimate. Whence, moreover, be astonished, consequently, you great and small who fear God, and you, sirs [lords], clever rhetoricians hear therefore and examine who roused me up, a fool, from the midst of those who seem to be wise and learned by experience in law and powerful in speech and in everything and inspired me, assuredly, beyond the others of this execrable world. . . , in order even after my death to leave behind a legacy to my brothers and Sons whom I have baptized in the Lord, so many thousands of men. . . .

PART II

But after I had come to Ireland, I was consequently pasturing domestic animals daily, and often in the day I was praying. More and more the love of God and fear of Him was approaching, and faith was being increased, and the Spirit was being stirred up, so that in a single day up to a hundred prayers, and in a night nearly the same, even as I was staying in forests and on the mountain, and before dawn I was roused up to prayer, through snow, through frost, through rain, and I was feeling nothing bad, nor was there any sloth in me, as I see now, because the Spirit was being fervent in me then, and there, to be sure, on a certain night in a dream I heard a voice saying to me, "It is well that you are fasting, bound soon to go to your fatherland." And again after a very little time I heard the answer saying to me, "Look, your ship is ready." And it was not near, but perhaps two hundred miles and I had never been there, nor did I have any single acquaintance among men there, and then later I turned to flight, and I abandoned the man with whom I had been for six years, and I came in the power of God, Who was directing my way toward the good, and I was fearing nothing until I came through to that ship, and on that day on which I came through the ship set out from its own place, and I spoke as I had the wherewithal to ship with them, and the captain, it displeased him, and he responded sharply with indignation, "By no means will you seek to go with us."

And when I heard these things I separated myself from them, so that I would come to the little hut where I was staying, and on the journey I began to pray, and before I could bring the prayer to the highest perfection I heard one of them, and he was shouting out vigorously after me, "Come soon, because these men are calling you", and immediately I returned to them, and they began to say to me, "Come, because we are receiving you on faith, make friendship with us in whatever way you will have wished" and on that day, to be sure, I refused to suck their nipples on account of the fear of God, but nevertheless I hoped to come by them to the faith of Jesus Christ, as they were gentiles, and because of this I got my way with them, and we shipped at once.

And after a three-day period we reached land, and for twenty-eight days we made a journey through the desert, and food was not forthcoming for them, and hunger prevailed over them, and on the next day the captain began to say to me, "What is it, Christian? You say your God is great and all-powerful. Why therefore can you not pray for us, because we are imperilled by hunger, for it is not likely that we may ever see any man."

But I said confidently to them, "Be turned in faith with a whole heart to the Lord my God, because nothing is impossible to Him, so that today He may dispatch food to you until you should be satisfied on your way, as there was abundance everywhere for Him." And with God helping it was made so.

Look, a flock of pigs appeared in the way before our eyes, and they killed many of them, and there they remained two nights and were well fed, and they were refilled with their flesh, because many of them fainted away, and were left behind half-alive along the way, and after this they gave the highest thanks to God, and I was made honourable in their eyes, and from this day they had food abundantly; they even discovered [lit. 'came upon'] forest honey, and they offered a part to me, and one of them said, "It is a [pagan] sacrifice." Thanks be to God, I tasted nothing from it.

• • • •

And again after a few years in the Britains I was with my parents, who received me as a son, and in faith requested me whether now I, after such great tribulations which I bore, I should not ever depart from them. And there to be sure I saw in a vision of the night a man coming as if from Ireland, whose name [was] Victoricius, with innumerable epistles, and he gave me one of them, and I read the beginning of the epistle containing 'the Voice of the Irish', and while I was reciting the beginning of the epistle I kept imagining hearing at that very moment the voice of those very men who were beside the Forest of Foclut, which is near the Western Sea [lit. 'the sea of the setting (*sc.* of the sun)'], and thus they shouted out as if from one mouth, "We request you, holy boy, that you come and walk farther among us." And I was especially stabbed at heart, and I could not read further. And thus I have learned by experience, thanks be to God, that after very many years the Lord has supplied them according to their clamour.

• • • •

PART V

Look, again and again briefly I will set out the words of my Confession.

I bear testimony in truth and in exultation of heart before God and His holy angels that I have never had any occasion besides the Gospel and His promises that I should ever go back to that gentile people whence earlier I had barely escaped.

But I beseech those believing and fearing God, whoever will have deigned to look on or receive this writing, which Patrick, a sinner, untaught, to be sure, wrote down in Ireland, that no man should ever say that by my ignorance, if I have accomplished or demonstrated any small thing according to the acceptable purpose of God, but that you judge and it must be most truly believed that it was the gift of God, and this is my Confession before I die.

Questions:
1. What were Patrick's first experiences in Ireland and how did he escape?

2. What problems did Patrick have to overcome to become a Christian missionary?
3. What is his own evaluation of his life and work?

Documents 8.4 and 8.5

These two selections, although both written from a Christian perspective, reveal a great deal about the political nature of the Visigoths and the Saxons.

8.4 Portrait of a Visigothic King

Theodoric II reigned over the Visigoths in South Gaul from 453 to 466 C.E. This portrait of him is by a courtly Gallo-Roman bishop who had every reason to flatter this leader of the recent conquerors.

> **Source:** "A Letter of Sidonius Apollinaris," found abridged in William Stearns Davis, ed., *Readings in Ancient History: Illustrative Extracts from the Sources, Volume II: Rome and the West*, (New York: Allyn and Bacon, 1913), pp. 319–21.

He is a prince well worthy of being known even by those not admitted to his intimate acquaintance, to such a degree have Nature and God, the sovereign Arbiter of all things, accumulated in his person gifts of varied excellence. His character is such that even envy itself, that universal accompaniment of all royalty, could not defraud him of his due praise.

You ask me to describe his daily outdoor life. Accompanied by a very small suite he attends before daybreak the services of the Church in his own household; he is careful in his devotions, but although his tone is suppressed, you may perceive that this is more a matter of habit with him than of religious principle. The business of administration occupies the rest of the morning. An armed aide-de-camp stands beside his throne; his band of fur-clad bodyguards is admitted to the Palace in order that they may be near to the royal presence; while in order that there may not be too much noise, they are kept out of the room; and so they talk in murmurs, inside a railing and outside the hangings [of the hall of audience].

Envoys from foreign powers are then introduced. The King listens much and says little. If their business calls for discussion, he puts it off, if for prompt action, he presses it forward. At eight o'clock he rises, and proceeds to examine either his treasures, or his stables. When he goes to hunt, he does not deem it suitable to the royal dignity to carry his bow upon his own person; when, however, any one points out to him a wild animal or bird, he puts out his hand, and receives his bow unstrung from a page: for, just as he regards it as an undignified thing to carry the weapon in its case, so does he deem it unmanly it should be prepared by another for his use. He selects an arrow and lets fly, first asking what you wish him to strike. You make your choice and invariably he hits the mark; indeed if there is ever any mistake, it is oftener in the sight of him who points out the object than in the aim of him who shoots at it.

His banquets do not differ from those of a private gentleman. You never see the vulgarity of a vast mass of tarnished plate, heaped upon a groaning table by a puffing and perspiring slave. The only thing that is weighty is the conversation: for either serious subjects are discussed, or none at all. Sometimes purple, and sometimes fine silk are employed in adorning the furniture of the dining room. The dinner is recommended by the skill of the cookery, not by the costliness of the provisions—the plate by its brightness, not by its massive weight. The guests are much more frequently called upon to complain of thirst, from finding the goblet too seldom pressed, than to shun inebriety by refusing it. In brief, one sees there the elegance of Greece and promptness of Italy, the splendor of a public along with the personal attention of a private entertainment, likewise the regular order of a royal household. After dinner Theodoric either takes no siesta at all or a very short one. When he feels like it, he picks up the dice quickly, looks at them carefully, shakes them scientifically, throws them at once, jocularly addresses them, and awaits the result with patience. When the cast is a good one he says nothing: when bad, he laughs; good or bad he is never angry, and takes both philosophically.

About three in the afternoon again come the cares of government, back come the suitors, and back those whose duty it is to keep them at a distance. On all sides is heard a wrangling and intriguing crowd, which, prolonged to the royal dinner hour, then only begins to diminish; after that it disperses, every man to seek his own patron. Occasionally, though not often, jesters are admitted to the royal banquet, without, however, being permitted to vent their malicious raillery upon any persons present. When he has risen from table, the guard of the treasury commences its nightly vigil: armed men take their station at all approaches to the palace, whose duty it will be to watch there during the first hours of the night."

[Despite this eulogy, Theodoric II had climbed to power by the foul murder of his brother, the rightful king.]

8.5 The Saxons Convert to Christianity

In the years after St. Patrick, Irish monasteries became famous across Europe for their learning and missionary vigor. This zeal was transported back to England as Irish monks established monasteries and schools, converting to Christianity the Saxons who had conquered Britain. Bede, generally called the "Venerable," was the outstanding product of this northern intellectual movement. He embraced all available learning, combining the Irish-Saxon-Roman-Christian heritage, to become the great teacher of his age. Above all, he is remembered for his Ecclesiastical History of the English People, a work of acknowledged intellectual merit. (ca. 672 –735 C.E.)

> **Source:** Bede, *A History of the English Church and People*, trans. Leo Sherley-Price, revised by

R.E. Latham (New York: Penguin Books, 1979, © 1968), pp. 176–81.

About this time the Middle Angles, ruled by their king Peada, son of Penda, accepted the true Faith and its sacraments. Peada, who was a noble young man, well deserving the title and dignity of a king, whom his father had appointed to the kingship of this people, went to Oswy king of the Northumbrians and requested the hand of his daughter Alchfled in marriage. Oswy, however, would not agree to this unless the king and his people accepted the Christian Faith and were baptized. So when Peada had received instruction in the true Faith, and had learned of the promises of the kingdom of heaven and of man's hope of resurrection and eternal life to come, he said that he would gladly become a Christian, even if he were refused the princess. He was chiefly influenced to accept the Faith by King Oswy's son Alchfrid, who was his kinsman and friend, and had married his sister Cyniburg, daughter of King Penda.

Accordingly, Peada was baptized by Bishop Finan, together with his companions and thanes and all their servants, at a well-known village belonging to the king known as At-Wall. Then, taking with him four priests, chosen for their learning and holy life, to instruct and baptize his people, he returned home.

About this time also, the East Saxons, who had once rejected the Faith and driven out Bishop Mellitus, again accepted it under the influence of King Oswy. For Sigbert, their king, successor to Sigbert the Small, was a friend of Oswy and often used to visit him in the province of the Northumbrians. Oswy used to reason with him how gods made by man's handiwork could not be gods, and how god could not be made from a log or block of stone, the rest of which might be burned or made into articles of everyday use or possibly thrown away as rubbish to be trampled underfoot and reduced to dust. He showed him how God is rather to be understood as a being of boundless majesty, invisible to human eyes, almighty, everlasting, Creator of heaven and earth and of the human race. He told him that he rules and will judge the world in justice, abiding in eternity, not in base and perishable metal; and that it should be rightly understood that all who know and do the will of their Creator will receive an eternal reward from him. King Oswy advanced these and other arguments during friendly and brotherly talks with Sigbert, who, encouraged by the agreement of his friends, was at length convinced. So he talked it over with his advisers, and with one accord they accepted the Faith and were baptized with him by Bishop Finan in the king's village of At-Wall, so named because it stands close to the wall which the Romans once built to protect Britain, about twelve miles from the eastern coast.

Having now become a citizen of the kingdom of heaven, Sigbert returned to the capital of his earthly kingdom after asking Oswy to send him teachers to convert his people to the Faith of Christ and baptize them. Accordingly Oswy sent to the province of the Middle Angles and summoned the man of God, Cedd, whom he dispatched with another priest as companion to evangelize the East Saxons. When these priests had visited the entire province and established a strong Christian community, Cedd returned home to Lindisfarne for consultations with Bishop Finan. When the latter learned the great success of his preaching, he invited two other bishops to assist him, and consecrated Cedd Bishop of the East Saxons. And when Cedd had been raised to the dignity of bishop, he returned to his province and used his increased authority to promote the work already begun. He built churches in several places and ordained priests and deacons to assist in teaching the Faith and baptizing the people, especially in the city which the Saxons call Ythancaestir and that called Tilaburg. The former place stands on the bank of the River Pant, the latter on the River Thames. Here Cedd established communities of the servants of Christ and taught them to maintain the discipline of the regular life so far as these untutored folk were then capable of doing.

To the great joy of the king and all his people, the Gospel of eternal life made daily headway throughout the province for a considerable time until, at the instigation of the Enemy of all good men, the king was murdered by his own kinsmen. This horrid crime was committed by two brothers who, on being asked their motive, had no answer to make except that they hated the king because he was too lenient towards his enemies and too readily forgave injuries when offenders asked pardon. This then was the fault for which the king was killed, that he sincerely observed the teachings of the Gospel. Yet in this undeserved fate he was overtaken by punishment for his real fault, as the man of God had once foretold. For one of the nobles who murdered him had contracted an illicit marriage, and the bishop, being unable to prevent or correct this, had therefore excommunicated him, forbidding anyone to enter his house or eat at his table. But the king had disregarded this ban and had accepted the noble's invitation to a feast. As he was leaving the house, the bishop met him, and the king immediately dismounted form his horse and fell trembling at his feet, begging pardon for his fault. The bishop, for he too had been on horseback, also dismounted in great anger and, touching the prostrate king with the staff in his hand, exercised his pontifical authority and said: 'I tell you that, since you have refused to avoid the house of a man who is lost and damned, this very house will be the place of your death.' However, since the death of this religious king was due to his loyal obedience to Christ's commandments, we may believe that it atoned for his earlier offence and increased his merits.

Questions for Documents 8.4 and 8.5:
1. What do these documents tell us about the nature of Germanic kingship among the Visigoths and Saxons?
2. How did Christianity affect that kingship?
3. How do the authors' Christian point of view affect their interpretation of these kings and political events?
4. What does Bede's account reveal about how different nations of people converted to Christianity?

SECTION 2
The Byzantine Empire

8.6 Justinian Suppresses the Nika Revolt

As the Roman Empire fell into the hands of conquering Germanic kings in western Europe and North Africa, the Roman Empire continued to flourish in the east. Cut off from Rome and its Latin heritage, and its capital moved to Constantinople (Byzantium), the empire increasingly became more Greek-oriented in its culture. Justinian (527–565 C.E.) was the last "Roman" Emperor who spoke Latin. From this point on, the Roman Empire that remained is known as the Byzantine Empire.

At the beginning of his reign, Justinian successfully fought the Persians on his eastern borders. Just when he had established a firm frontier, however, the Nika revolt erupted in Constantinople (Byzantium), nearly running him out of town. This document is from the History of the Wars, by Procopius of Caesarea (in Palestine), the most important source for information about the reign of the emperor Justinian and his wife Theodora (d. 547/8 C.E.).

Source: Procopius, *History of the Wars, I,* xxiv, H.B. Dewing trans. (New York: Macmillan, 1914), pp. 219–230, abridged and reprinted in Leon Barnard and Theodore B. Hodges, *Readings in European History* (New York: Macmillan, 1958), 52–55.

At this time [January 1, 532] an insurrection broke out unexpectedly in Byzantium among the populace, and, contrary to expectation, it proved to be a very serious affair, and ended in great harm to the people and to the senate, as the following account will show.

In every city the population has been divided for a long time past into the Blue and the Green factions; but within comparatively recent times it has come about that, for the sake of these names and the seats which the rival factions occupy in watching the games, they spend their money and abandon their bodies to the most cruel tortures, and even do not think it unworthy to die a most shameful death. And they fight against their opponents knowing not for what end they imperil themselves, but knowing well that, even if they overcome their enemy in the fight, the conclusion of the matter for them will be to be carried off straight away to the prison, and finally, after suffering extreme torture, to be destroyed. So there grows up in them against their fellow men a hostility which has no cause, and at no time does it cease or disappear, for it gives place neither to the ties of marriage nor of relationship nor of friendship, and the case is the same even though those who differ with respect to these colours be

brothers or any other kin. . . . I, for my part, am unable to call this anything except a disease of the soul. . . .

At this time the officers of the city administration in Byzantium were leading away to death some of the rioters. But the members of the two factions conspiring together and declaring a truce with each other, seized the prisoners and then straightway entered the prison and released all those who were in confinement there. . . . Fire was applied to the city as if it had fallen under the hand of an enemy. . . . The emperor and his consort, with a few members of the senate shut themselves up in the palace and remained quietly there. Now the watch-word which the populace passed to one another was Nika [i.e., "Conquer"]. . . .

On the fifth day of the insurrection in the late afternoon the Emperor Justinian gave orders to Hypatius and Pompeius, nephews of the late emperor, Anastasius, to go home as quickly as possible, either because he suspected that some plot was being matured by them against his own person, or, it may be, because destiny brought them to this. But they feared that the people would force them to the throne (as in fact fell out), and they said that they would be doing wrong if they should abandon their sovereign when he found himself in such danger. When the Emperor Justinian heard this, he inclined still more to his suspicion, and he bade them quit the palace instantly. . . .

On the following day at sunrise it became known to the people that both men had quit the palace where they had been staying. So the whole population ran to them, and they declared Hypatius emperor and prepared to lead him to the market place to assume the power. But the wife of Hypatius, Mary, a discreet woman, who had the greatest reputation for prudence, laid hold of her husband and would not let go, but cried out with loud lamentation and with entreaties to all her kinsmen that the people were leading him on the road to death. But since the throng overpowered her, she unwillingly released her husband, and he by no will of his own came to the Forum of Constantine, where they summoned him to the throne; . . .

The emperor and his court were deliberating as to whether it would be better for them if they remained or if they took to flight in the ships. And many opinions were expressed favouring either course. And the Empress Theodora also spoke to the following effect: "My opinion then is that the present time, above all others, is inopportune for flight, even though it bring safety. . . . For one who has been emperor it is unendurable to be a fugitive. May I never be separated from this purple, and may I not live that day on which those who meet me shall not address me as mistress. If, now, it is your wish to save yourself, O Emperor, there is no difficulty. For we have much money, and there is the sea, here the boats. However consider whether it will not come about after you have been saved that you would gladly exchange that safety for death. For as for myself, I approve a certain ancient saying that royalty is a good burial-shroud." When the queen had spoken thus, all were filled with boldness, and, turning their thoughts towards resistance, they began to consider how they might be able to defend themselves if any hostile force should come against them. . . . All the hopes of the emperor were centered upon Belisarius and Mundus, of whom the former, Belisarius, had recently returned from the Persian war bringing with him a following which was both powerful and imposing, and in particular he had a great number of spearmen and guards who had received their training in battles and the perils of warfare. . . .

When Hypatius reached the hippodrome, he went up immediately to where the emperor is accustomed to take his place and seated himself on the royal throne from which the emperor was always accustomed to view the equestrian and athletic contests. And from the palace Mundus went out through the gate which, from the circling descent, has been given the name of the Snail. . . . Belisarius, with difficulty and not without danger and great exertion, made his way over ground covered by ruins and half-burned buildings, and ascended to the stadium. . . . Concluding that he must go against the populace who had taken their stand in the hippodrome—a vast multitude crowding each other in great disorder—he drew his sword from its sheath and, commanding the others to do likewise, with a shout he advanced upon them at a run. But the populace, who were standing in a mass and not in order, at the sight of armoured soldiers who had a great reputation for bravery and experience in war, and seeing that they struck out with their swords unsparingly, beat a hasty retreat. . . . [Mundus] straightway made a sally into the hippodrome through the entrance which they call the Gate of Death. Then indeed from both sides the partisans of Hypatius were assailed with might and main and destroyed. . . . There perished among the populace on that day more than thirty thousand. . . . The soldiers killed both [Hypatius and Pompeius] on the following day and threw bodies into the sea. . . . This was the end of the insurrection in Byzantium.

Questions:
1. What were the causes of the Nika Rebellion?
2. What seems to be Procopius' evaluation of Justinian's handling of the crisis?

8.7 Justinian and Theodora: A Negative View

Procopius also left the unpublished manuscript *Secret History*. This was a vitriolic attack on the character of Justinian and his notorious wife Theodora. Procopius claims that *Secret History* supplies information that he could not include in his published work for fear of retribution from the two rulers.

Source: Procopius, *Secret History*, translated by Richard Atwater, (Chicago: P. Covici, 1927; New York: Covici Friede, 1927), reprinted, Ann Arbor, MI: University of Michigan Press, 1961.

8. CHARACTER AND APPEARANCE OF JUSTINIAN

. . . As soon as [the Emperor Justinian] took over the rule from his uncle [Justin], his measure was to spend the public money without restraint, now that he had control of it. He gave much of it to the Huns who, from time to time, entered the state; and in consequence the Roman provinces were subject to constant incursions, for these barbarians, having once tasted Roman wealth, never forgot the road that led to it. And he threw much money into the sea in the form of moles, as if to master the eternal roaring of the breakers. For he jealously hurled stone breakwaters far out from the mainland against the onset of the sea, as if by the power of wealth he could outmatch the might of ocean.

He gathered to himself the private estates of Roman citizens from all over the Empire: some by accusing their possessors of crimes of which they were innocent, others by juggling their owners' words into the semblance of a gift to him of their property. And many, caught in the act of murder and other crimes, turned their possessions over to him and thus escaped the penalty for their sins.

. . . I think this is as good a time as any to describe the personal appearance of the man. Now in physique he was neither tall nor short, but of average height; not thin, but moderately plump; his face was round, and not bad looking, for he had good color, even when he fasted for two days. To make a long description short, he much resembled Domitian, Vespasian's son. He was the one whom the Romans so hated that even tearing him into pieces did not satisfy their wrath against him, but a decree was passed by the Senate that the name of this Emperor should never be written, and that no statue of him should be preserved.

. . . Now such was Justinian in appearance; but his character was something I could not fully describe. For he was at once villainous and amenable; as people say colloquially, a moron. He was never truthful with anyone, but always guileful in what he said and did, yet easily hoodwinked by any who wanted to deceive him. His nature was an unnatural mixture of folly and wickedness. What in olden times a peripatetic philosopher said was also true of him, that opposite qualities combine in a man as in the mixing of colors. I will try to portray him, however, insofar as I can fathom his complexity.

This Emperor, then, was deceitful, devious, false, hypocritical, two-faced, cruel, skilled in dissembling his thought, never moved to tears by either joy or pain, though he could summon them artfully at will when the occasion demanded, a liar always, not only offhand, but in writing, and when he swore sacred oaths to his subjects in their very hearing. Then he would immediately break his agreements and pledges, like the vilest of slaves, whom indeed only the fear of torture drives to confess their perjury. A faithless friend, he was a treacherous enemy, insane for murder and plunder, quarrelsome and revolutionary, easily led to anything evil, but never willing to listen to good counsel, quick to plan mischief and carry it out, but finding even the hearing of anything good distasteful to his ears.

How could anyone put Justinian's ways into words? These and many even worse vices were disclosed in him as in no other mortal nature seemed to have taken the wickedness of all other men combined and planted it in this man's soul. And besides this, he was too prone to listen to accusations; and too quick to punish. For he decided such cases without full examination, naming the punishment when he had heard only the accuser's side of the matter. Without hesitation he wrote decrees for the plundering of countries, sacking of cities, and slavery of whole nations, for no cause whatever. So that if one wished to take all the calamities which had befallen the Romans before this time and weigh them against his crimes, I think it would be found that more men had been murdered by this single man than in all previous history.

He had no scruples about appropriating other people's property, and did not even think any excuse necessary, legal or illegal, for confiscating what did not belong to him. And when it was his, he was more than ready to squander it in insane display, or give it as an unnecessary bribe to the barbarians. In short, he neither held on to any money himself nor let anyone else keep any: as if his reason were not avarice, but jealousy of those who had riches. Driving all wealth from the country of the Romans in this manner, he became the cause of universal poverty.

Now this was the character of Justinian, so far as I can portray it.

9. HOW THEODORA, MOST DEPRAVED OF ALL COURTESANS, WON HIS LOVE

He took a wife: and in what manner she was born and bred, and, wedded to this man, tore up the Roman Empire by the very roots, I shall now relate.

. . . As soon as [Theodora] arrived at the age of youth, and was now ready for the world, her mother put her on the stage. Forthwith, she became a courtesan, and such as the ancient Greeks used to call a common one, at that: for she was not a flute or harp player, nor was she even trained to dance, but only gave her youth to anyone she met, in utter abandonment. Her general favors included, of course, the actors in the theater; and in their productions she took part in the low comedy scenes. For she was very funny and a good mimic, and immediately became popular in this art. There was no shame in the girl, and no one ever saw her dismayed: no role was too scandalous for her to accept without a blush.

She was the kind of comedienne who delights the audience by letting herself be cuffed and slapped on the cheeks, and makes them guffaw by raising her skirts to reveal to the spectators those feminine secrets here and there which custom veils from the eyes of the opposite sex. With pretended laziness she mocked her lovers, and coquettishly adopting ever new ways of embracing, was able to keep in a constant turmoil the hearts of the sophisticated. And she did not wait to be asked by anyone she met, but on the contrary, with inviting jests and a comic flaunting of her skirts herself tempted all men who passed by, especially those who were adolescent.

On the field of pleasure she was never defeated. Often she would go picnicking with ten young men or more, in the flower of their strength and virility, and dallied with them all, the whole night through. When they wearied of the sport, she would approach their servants, perhaps thirty in number, and fight a duel with each of these; and even thus found no allayment of her craving. . . .

Frequently, she conceived but as she employed every artifice immediately, a miscarriage was straightway effected. Often, even in the theater, in the sight of all the people, she removed her costume and stood nude in their midst, except for a girdle about the groin: not that she was abashed at revealing that, too, to the audience, but because there was a law against appearing altogether naked on the stage, without at least this much of a fig-leaf. . .

So perverse was her wantonness that she should have hid not only the customary part of her person, as other women do, but her face as well. Thus those who were intimate with her were straightway recognized from that very fact to be perverts, and any more respectable man who chanced upon her in the Forum avoided her and withdrew in haste, lest the hem of his mantle, touching such a creature, might be thought to share in her pollution. For to those who saw her, especially at dawn, she was a bird of ill omen. And toward her fellow actresses she was as savage as a scorpion: for she was very malicious.

Later, she followed Hecebolus, a Tyrian who had been made governor of Pentapolis, serving him in the basest of ways; but finally she quarreled with him and was sent summarily away. Consequently, she found herself destitute of the means of life, which she proceeded to earn by prostitution, as she had done before this adventure. She came thus to Alexandria, and then traversing all the East, worked her way to Constantinople; in every city plying a trade (which it is safer, I fancy, in the sight of God not to name too clearly) as if the Devil were determined there be no land on earth that should not know the sins of Theodora.

Thus was this woman born and bred, and her name was a byword beyond that of other common wenches on the tongues of all men.

But when she came back to Constantinople, Justinian fell violently in love with her. At first he kept her only as a mistress, though he raised her to patrician rank. Through him Theodora was able immediately to acquire an unholy power and exceedingly great riches. She seemed to him the sweetest thing in the world, and like all lovers, he desired to please his charmer with every possible favor and requite her with all his wealth. The extravagance added fuel to the flames of passion. With her now to help spend his money he plundered the people more than ever, not only in the capital, but throughout the Roman Empire. As both of them had for a long time been of the Blue party, they gave this faction almost complete control of the affairs of state. It was long afterward that the worst of this evil was checked. . . .

Questions:
1. According to Procopius, how good a ruler was Justinian?
2. Why do you think he was so hostile toward Theodora?
3. How reliable do you think Procopius is as an historian?

8.8   *Corpus Juris Civilis:* **Prologue**

Roman law grew from abstract principles of justice on which the actual rules of law were legislated. The Emperor Justinian ordered a codification of all these laws that had accumulated from the time of the Republic to his own decrees. He issued the Corpus Juris Civilis (Body of Civil Law) in Latin consisting of three parts, the Digest, the Institutes, and a textbook that eventually transmitted Roman legal principles to Western Europe during the twelfth century, influencing church and continental law.

> **Source:** From *The Digest of Justinian*, C. H. Monro, ed. (Cambridge, MA: Cambridge University Press, 1904).

THE DIGEST: PROLOGUE

The Emperor Caesar, Flavius, Justinianus, Pious, Fortunate, Renowned, Conqueror, and Triumpher, Ever Augustus, to Tribonianus His Quaestor.,

Greeting:
With the aid of God governing Our Empire which was delivered to Us by His Celestial Majesty, We carry on war successfully. We adorn peace and maintain the Constitution of the State, and have such confidence in the protection of Almighty God that We do not depend upon Our arms, or upon Our soldiers, or upon those who conduct Our Wars, or upon Our own genius, but We solely, place Our reliance upon the providence of the Holy Trinity, from which are derived the elements of the entire world and their disposition throughout the globe.

Therefore, since there is nothing to be found in all things as worthy of attention as the authority of the law, which properly regulates all affairs both divine and human,

and expels all injustice; We have found the entire arrangement of the law which has come down to us from the foundation of the City of Rome and the times of Romulus, to be so confused that it is extended to an infinite length and is not within the grasp of human capacity; and hence We were first induced to begin by examining what had been enacted by former most venerated princes, to correct their constitutions, and make them more easily understood; to the end that being included in a single Code, and having had removed all that is superfluous in resemblance and all iniquitous discord, they may afford to all men the ready assistance of true meaning.

After having concluded this work and collected it all in a single volume under Our illustrious name, raising Ourself above small and comparatively insignificant matters, We have hastened to attempt the most complete and thorough amendment of the entire law, to collect and revise the whole body of Roman jurisprudence, and to assemble in one book the scattered treatises of so many authors which no one else has heretofore ventured to hope for or to expect and it has indeed been considered by Ourselves a most difficult undertaking, nay, one that was almost impossible; but with Our hands raised to heaven and having invoked the Divine aid, We have kept this object in Our mind, confiding in God who can grant the accomplishment of things which are almost desperate, and can Himself carry them into effect by virtue of the greatness of His power.

• • • •

We desire you to be careful with regard to the following: if you find in the old books anything that is not suitably arranged, superfluous, or incomplete, you must remove all superfluities, supply what is lacking, and present the entire work in regular form, and with as excellent an appearance as possible.

You must also observe the following, namely: if you find anything which the ancients have inserted in their old laws or constitutions that is incorrectly worded, you must correct this, and place it in its proper order, so that it may appear to be true, expressed in the best language, and written in this way in the first place; so that by comparing it with the original text, no one can venture to call in question as defective what you have selected and arranged.

Since by an ancient law, which is styled the Lex Regia, all the rights and power of the Roman people were transferred to the Emperor, We do not derive Our authority from that of other different compilations, but wish that it shall all be entirely Ours, for how can antiquity abrogate our laws?

Questions:
1. How can you tell that the Roman Empire is now Christian?
2. Why was the compilation of law undertaken?
3. What were the instructions given to the scholars who codified the Law?

SECTION 3
Their Neighbors: Muslims and Mongols

8.9 The *Koran*

The *Koran* (Qur 'an) means "the recital" and is, according to Islamic belief, the direct words of God as told to his prophet Muhammad through the angel Gabriel. It is the sacred text for Muslims. Excerpts from one of the books, entitled "The Cow," are reproduced below.

Source: *The Koran*, trans. N.J. Dawood, (New York: Penguin Books, 1990), pp. 11–42 passim.

THE COW

In the Name of God, the Compassionate, the Merciful

Alif *lām mīm*. This Book is not to be doubted. It is a guide for the righteous, who have faith in the unseen and are steadfast in prayer; who bestow in charity a part of what We have given them; who trust what has been revealed to you[1] and to others before you, and firmly believe in the life to come. These are rightly guided by their Lord; these shall surely triumph.

As for the unbelievers, it is the same whether or not you forewarn them; they will not have faith. God has set a seal upon their hearts and ears; their sight is dimmed and grievous punishment awaits them.

There are some who declare: 'We believe in God and the Last Day,' yet they are no true believers. They seek to deceive God and those who believe in Him: but they deceive none save themselves, though they may not perceive it. There is a sickness in their hearts which God has aggravated: they shall be sternly punished for the lies they told.

. . . .

Proclaim good tidings to those who have faith and do good works. They shall dwell in gardens watered by running streams: whenever they are given fruit to eat they will say: 'This is what we used to eat before,' for they shall be given the like. Wedded to chaste virgins, they shall abide therein for ever.

. . . .

To Adam We said: 'Dwell with your wife in Paradise and eat of its fruits to your hearts' content wherever you will. But never approach this tree or you shall both become transgressors.'

But Satan removed them thence and brought about their banishment. 'Go hence,' We said, 'and be enemies to each other. The earth will for a while provide your dwelling and sustenance.'

Then Adam received commandments from his Lord, and his Lord relented towards him. He is the Forgiving One, the Merciful.

'Go down hence, all,' We said. 'When our guidance is revealed those that accept it shall have nothing to fear or to regret; but those that deny and reject Our revelations shall be the heirs of Hell, and there they shall abide for ever.'

Children of Israel, remember the blessing I have bestowed on you, and that I have exalted you above the nations. Guard yourselves against the day on which no soul shall avail another: when neither intercession nor ransom shall be accepted from it, nor any help be given it.

. . . .

To Moses We gave the Scriptures and after him We sent other apostles. We gave Jesus the son of Mary veritable signs and strengthened him with the Holy Spirit. Will you then scorn each apostle whose message does not suit your fancies, charging some with imposture and slaying others?

. . . .

And now that a Book confirming their own has come to them from God, they deny it, although they know it to be the truth and have long prayed for help against the unbelievers. God's curse be upon the infidels! Evil is that for which they have bartered away their souls. To deny God's own revelation, grudging that He should reveal His bounty to whom He chooses from among His servants! They have incurred God's most inexorable wrath. An ignominious punishment awaits the unbelievers.

. . . .

Say: 'Whoever is an enemy of Gabriel' (who has by God's grace revealed to you[2] the Koran as a guide and joyful tidings for the faithful, confirming previous scriptures) 'whoever is an enemy of God, His angels, or His apostles, or of Gabriel or Michael, will surely find that God is the enemy of the unbelievers.'

. . . .

When his Lord put Abraham to the proof by enjoining on him certain commandments and Abraham fulfilled them, He said: 'I have appointed you a leader of mankind.'

'And what of my descendants?' asked Abraham.

'My covenant,' said He, 'does not apply to the evildoers.'

We made the House[3] a resort and a sanctuary for mankind, saying: 'Make the place where Abraham stood a house of worship.' We enjoined Abraham and Ishmael to cleanse Our House for those who walk round it, who meditate in it, and who kneel and prostrate themselves.

---

[1] Muhammad

[2] Muhammad
[3] The Ka'bah at Mecca.

. . . .

Who but a foolish man would renounce the faith of Abraham? We chose him in this world, and in the world to come he shall abide among the righteous. When his Lord said to him: 'Submit,' he answered: 'I have submitted to the Lord of the Universe.'

. . . .

They say: 'Accept the Jewish or the Christian faith and you shall be rightly guided.'

Say: 'By no means! We believe in the faith of Abraham, the upright one. He was no idolater.'

Say: 'We believe in God and that which is revealed to us; in what was revealed to Abraham, Ishmael, Isaac, Jacob, and the tribes; to Moses and Jesus and the other prophets by their Lord. We make no distinction among any of them, and to God we have surrendered ourselves.'

. . . .

Righteousness does not consist in whether you face towards the East or the West. The righteous man is he who believes in God and the Last Day, in the angels and the Book and the prophets; who, though he loves it dearly, gives away his wealth to kinsfolk, to orphans, to the helpless, to the traveller in need and to beggars, and for the redemption of captives; who attends to his prayers and renders the alms levy; who is true to his promises and steadfast in trial and adversity and in times of war. Such are the true believers; such are the God-fearing.

Believers, retaliation is decreed for you in bloodshed: a free man for a free man, a slave for a slave, and a female for a female. He who is pardoned by his aggrieved brother shall be prosecuted according to usage and shall pay him a liberal fine. This is a merciful dispensation from your Lord. He that transgresses thereafter shall be sternly punished.

. . . .

Believers, fasting is decreed for you as it was decreed for those before you; perchance you will guard yourselves against evil. Fast a certain number of days, but if any one among you is ill or on a journey, let him fast a similar number of days later; and for those that cannot endure it there is a ransom: the feeding of a poor man. He that does good of his own accord shall be well rewarded; but to fast is better for you, if you but knew it.

In the month of Ramadān the Koran was revealed, a book of guidance with proofs of guidance distinguishing right from wrong. Therefore whoever of you is present in that month let him fast. But he who is ill or on a journey shall fast a similar number of days later on.

God desires your well-being, not your discomfort. He desires you to fast the whole month so that you may magnify Him and render thanks to Him for giving you His guidance.

. . . .

It is now lawful for you to lie with your wives on the night of the fast; they are a comfort to you as you are to them. God knew that you were deceiving yourselves. He has relented towards you and pardoned you. Therefore you may now lie with them and seek what God has ordained for you.

Eat and drink until you can tell a white thread from a black one in the light of the coming dawn. Then resume the fast till nightfall and do not approach them, but stay at your prayers in the mosques.

. . . .

Do not devour one another's property by unjust means, nor bribe with it the judges in order that you may wrongfully and knowingly usurp the possessions of other men.

. . . .

Fight for the sake of God those that fight against you, but do not attack them first. God does not love the aggressors.

Slay them wherever you find them. Drive them out of the places from which they drove you. Idolatry is worse than carnage. But do not fight them within the precincts of the Holy Mosque unless they attack you there; if they attack you put them to the sword. Thus shall the unbelievers be rewarded: but if they mend their ways, know that God is forgiving and merciful.

. . . .

Make the pilgrimage and visit the Sacred House for His sake. If you cannot, send such offerings as you can afford and do not shave your heads until the offerings have reached their destination. But if any of you is ill or suffers from an ailment of the head, he must pay a ransom either by fasting or by almsgiving or by offering a sacrifice.

. . . .

Make the pilgrimage in the appointed months. He that intends to perform it in those months must abstain from sexual intercourse, obscene language, and acrimonious disputes while on pilgrimage. God is aware of whatever good you do. Provide well for yourselves: the best provision is piety. Fear Me, then, you that are endowed with understanding.

It shall be no offence for you to seek the bounty of your Lord.

. . . .

There are some who say: 'Lord, give us abundance in this world.' These shall have no share in the world to come. But there are others who say: 'Lord, give us what is good both in this world and in the hereafter and keep us from the torment of the Fire.' These shall have a share, according to what they did. Swift is God's reckoning.

. . . .

They ask you about drinking and gambling. Say: 'There is great harm in both, although they have some benefit for men; but their harm is far greater than their benefit.'

They ask you what they should give in alms. Say: 'What you can spare.' Thus God makes plain to you His revelations so that you may reflect upon this world and the hereafter.

They question you concerning orphans. Say: 'To deal justly with them is best. If you mix their affairs with yours, remember they are your brothers. God knows the just from the unjust. If God pleased, He could afflict you. He is mighty and wise.'

. . . .

You shall not wed pagan women, unless they embrace the Faith. A believing slave-girl is better than an idolatress, although she may please you. Nor shall you wed idolaters, unless they embrace the Faith. A believing slave is better than an idolater, although he may please you. These call you to Hell-fire; but God calls you, by His will, to Paradise and to forgiveness. He makes plain His revelations to mankind, so that they may take heed.

They ask you about menstruation. Say: 'It is an indisposition. Keep aloof from women during their menstrual periods and do not touch them until they are clean again. Then have intercourse with them in the way God enjoined you. God loves those that turn to Him in repentance and strive to keep themselves clean.'

Women are your fields: go, then, into your fields whence you please. Do good works and fear God. Bear in mind that you shall meet Him. Give good tidings to the believers.

⋅ ⋅ ⋅ ⋅

Those that renounce their wives on oath must wait four months. If they change their minds, God is forgiving and merciful; but if they decide to divorce them, know that God hears all and knows all.

Divorced women must wait, keeping themselves from men, three menstrual courses. It is unlawful for them, if they believe in God and the Last Day, to hide what God has created in their wombs: in which case their husbands would do well to take them back, should they desire reconciliation.

Women shall with justice have rights similar to those exercised against them, although men have a status above women. God is almight and wise.

Divorce[4] may be pronounced twice, and then a woman must be retained in honour or allowed to go with kindness. It is unlawful for husbands to take from them anything they have given them, unless both fear that they may not be able to keep within the bounds set by God; in which case it shall be no offence for either of them if the wife ransom herself.

⋅ ⋅ ⋅ ⋅

Mothers shall give such to their children for two whole years if the father wishes the sucking to be completed. They must be maintained and clothed in a reasonable manner by the child's father. None should be charged with more than one can bear. A mother should not be allowed to suffer on account of her child, nor should a father on account of his child. The same duties devolve upon the father's heir. But if, after consultation, they choose by mutual consent to wean the child, they shall incur no guilt. Nor shall it be any offence for you if you prefer to have a nurse for your children, provided that you pay her what you promise, according to usage. Have fear of God and know that God is cognizant of all your actions.

Widows shall wait, keeping themselves apart from men for four months and ten days after their husbands' death. When they have reached the end of their waiting period, it shall be no offence for you to let them do whatever they choose for themselves, provided that it is decent. God is cognizant of all your actions.

⋅ ⋅ ⋅ ⋅

You shall bequeath your widows a year's maintenance without causing them to leave their homes; but if they leave of their own accord, no blame shall be attached to you for any course they may deem fit to pursue. God is mighty and wise. Reasonable provision shall also be made for divorced women. That is incumbent on righteous men.

⋅ ⋅ ⋅ ⋅

There shall be no compulsion in religion. True guidance is now distinct from error. He that renounces idol-worship and puts his faith in God shall grasp a firm handle that will never break. God hears all and knows all.

God is the Patron of the faithful. He leads them from darkness to the light. As for the unbelievers, their patrons are false gods, who lead them from light to darkness. They are the heirs of Hell and shall abide in it for ever.

⋅ ⋅ ⋅ ⋅

Satan threatens you with poverty and orders you to commit what is indecent. But God promises you His forgiveness and His bounty. God is munificent and all-knowing.

He gives wisdom to whom He will; and he that receives the gift of wisdom is rich indeed. Yet none except men of sense bear this in mind.

Whatever alms you give and whatever vows you make are known to God. The evil-doers shall have none to help them.

To be charitable in public is good, but to give alms to the poor in private is better and will atone for some of your sins. God has knowledge of all your actions.

It is not for you to guide them. God gives guidance to whom He will.

Whatever alms you give shall rebound to your own advantage, provided that you give them for the love of God. And whatever alms you give shall be paid back to you in full: you shall not be wronged.

⋅ ⋅ ⋅ ⋅

Those that live on usury shall rise up before God like men whom Satan has demented by his touch; for they claim that trading is no different from usury. But God has permitted trading and made usury unlawful. He that has received an admonition from his Lord and mended his ways may keep his previous gains; God will be his judge. Those that turn back shall be the inmates of the Fire, wherein they shall abide for ever.

God has laid His curse on usury and blessed alms-giving with increase. God bears no love for the impious and the sinful.

⋅ ⋅ ⋅ ⋅

Believers, when you contract a debt for a fixed period, put it in writing. Let a scribe write it down for you with fairness; no scribe should refuse to write as God has taught him.

⋅ ⋅ ⋅ ⋅

Call in two male witnesses from among you, but if two men cannot be found, then one man and two women whom you judge fit to act as witnesses; so that if either of them commit an error, the other will remember. Witnesses must not refuse to give evidence if called upon to do so . . .

⋅ ⋅ ⋅ ⋅

---

4 Revocable divorce, or the renunciation of one's wife on oath.

'This is more just in the sight of God; it ensures accuracy in testifying and is the best way to remove all doubt. But if the transaction in hand be a bargain concluded on the spot, it is no offence for you if you do not commit it to writing.

See that witnesses are present when you barter with one another, and let no harm be done to either scribe or witness.

Questions:
1. According to the *Koran*, what are the relations between Muslims and the Jews and Christians?
2. What are the requirements of the believers? What if one does not follow them? Are there exceptions?
3. In what ways does the *Koran* provide guidelines in the realm of society, economics, and politics?
4. What does the *Koran* say about fighting against unbelievers, often called *Jihad* (holy wars)?
5. How are women and relations between men and women treated in the *Koran*?

8.10   Baghdad: City of Wonders

This description of Baghdad is by an unknown Persian nobleman (perhaps a student at the university in Baghdad) in a letter to his father, written during the reign of Haroun al-Rashid (786–809). The nobleman is describing the city only fifty years after it was built to be the capital of the Abbasid Caliphate. The city was built as a walled fortress town with the caliphate's residence in the center of town behind its own ninety foot wall and moat. As can be seen by this description, it quickly became a prosperous town at the center of Islamic trade, with a population close to one million (this is less than the number cited in the document, but numbers tend to be exaggerated in such documents).

> **Source:** *Primary Source Document Workbook to Accompany World Civilizations*, by Philip J. Adler; prepared by Robert Welborn, (New York: West Publishing Company, 1996), pp. 29–30. (Introduction based on Welborn's introduction to the Document.)

THE BAGHDAD OF HAROUN AL-RASHID

When I wandered about in the city after a long absence, I found it in an expansion of prosperity that I had not observed before this time. The resplendent buildings that rose in the city . . . were not sufficient for its wealthy people until they extended to the houses in this eastern quarter known as Rusafa. They built high castles and ornamented houses in this quarter, and set up markets, mosques, and public baths. The attention of al-Rashid . . . was directed toward adorning

it with public buildings, until the old Baghdad became like an ancient town whose beauties were assembled in a section of the city which was created near by it.

I admired the arrival of buildings in Baghdad because of the over crowdedness of the people I had seen in its sections. Their billowing is like the sea in its expanses; their number is said to exceed 1,500,000, and no other city in the world has such a sum or even half its amount. . . .

It is difficult for me, with this pen which is of limited substance, to describe the glorious qualities of the city which are but a small part of the honor it achieves, such that it prides itself in the splendor of power. . . . The people of wealth walk with slave boys and and retinue whose number the listener will fancy to be far from the truth. I witnessed at Attabiyya station a prince who was riding with a hundred horsemen and was surrounded by slave boys, even filling the road and blocking the path of the people until they passed. . . . Nor was any Caliph ever known to be more generous than he (Haroun al-Rashid) in the handing out of wealth. It is said that he spends ten thousand dirhams (a silver coin) every day for his food, and perhaps the cooks would prepare for him thirty kinds of food. Abu Yusuf informed me that when the Caliph consummated his marriage to Zubaida, the daughter of Ja'far the Barmakid, he gave a banquet unprecedented in Islam. He gave away unlimited presents at this banquet, even giving containers of gold filled with silver, containers of silver filled with gold, bags of musk, and pieces of ambergris. The total expenditure on this banquet reached 55,000,000 dirhams. The Caliph commanded that Zubaida be presented in a gown of pearls whose price no one was able to appraise. He adorned her with pieces of jewelry, so much so that she was not able to walk because of the great number of jewels which were upon her. This example of extravagance had no precedent among the kings of Persia, the emperors of Byzantium, or the princes of the Umayyads, despite the great amounts of money which they had at their disposal. . . .

Affluence is abundant among the upper rank of those who are masters of the state. It then diminishes little by little among those of lesser rank, until only a small amount remains for the general public. As for those who do not enjoy the exalted power and breadth of bounty of the kings, they begin to equip themselves with all the good things after they have gone on journeys which gain them experience, show them wondrous things, and give them profits. The people in the provinces come to them with the grandest of all types of their wares, until markets have become plentiful in Baghdad. They have advanced from requesting necessities to the acquisition of things for beautification and decoration. This may be seen in the case of their purchase of arms inlaid with gold, their competing in costly jewels, ornamented vessels, and splendid furniture, and their acquisition of a large number of slave boys, female singers, and those things which they send out their retainers to seek in the provinces. When every expensive and rare thing in the country was brought to them, I realized that the beauties of the world had been assembled in Baghdad. . . .

Questions:
1. How would you characterize Baghdad based on this description? Consider wealth, social classes/occupations, kinds of goods available.
2. Why do you think the city is so prosperous only fifty years after its creation?
3. What does the description of the caliph reveal about the time, the city, the religion, social practices, etc?

8.11 *The Arabian Nights*

The Arabian Nights is a collection of tales, some of which may go back to the eighth century C.E., others may have been written as late as the sixteenth century. They come from Persia at a time when the dominant religion was Islam, and thus represent a combination of Islamic religion with Persian culture. The introduction tells of King Shahryar and his brother who discover that their wives have been engaging in sex with a black slave each time the husband leaves home. In addition, in the queen's party were ten of the King's concubines paired off with ten white slaves. "Cuckolded," both kill their wives and the others involved, and then they each take a new woman to bed each night only to kill her the next morning. Shahrazad is one of these women; in order to escape her fate, she tells the king a story that ends with a lead into another story (. . . . to be continued). In this way, night after night, she comes to tell 1001 stories. In this excerpt is provided one of her stories (one that takes place in eighth-century Baghdad during the reign of Haroun al-Rashid—see Document 10) and portions of the conclusion.

> **Source:** *The Arabian Nights' Entertainments or The Book of A Thousand Nights and A Night*, trans. Richard F. Burton, (New York: The Modern Library-Random House, 1932), pp. 367–69, 815–16.

SINBAD THE SEAMAN AND SINBAD THE LANDSMAN

There lived in the city of Baghdad, during the reign of the Commander of the Faithful, Harun al-Rashid, a man named Sinbad the Hammal, one in poor case who bore burdens on his head for hire. It happened to him one day of great heat that whilst he was carrying a heavy load, he became exceeding weary and sweated profusely, the heat and the weight alike oppressing him. Presently, as he was passing the gate of a merchant's house, before which the ground was swept and watered, and there the air was temperate, he sighted a broad bench beside the door; so he set his load thereon, to take rest and smell the air. He sat down on the edge of the bench, and at once heard from within the melodious sound of lutes and other stringed instruments, and mirth-exciting voices singing and reciting, together with the song of bird

warbling and glorifying Almighty Allah in various tunes and tongues; turtles, mocking-birds, merles, nightingales, cushats and stone-curlews, whereat he marvelled in himself and was moved to mighty joy and solace. Then he went up to the gate and saw within a great flower-garden wherein were pages and black slaves and such a train of servants and attendants and so forth as is found only with Kings and Sultans; and his nostrils were greeted with the savoury odours of all manner meats rich and delicate, and delicious and generous wines. So he raised his eyes heavenwards and said, "Glory to Thee, O Lord, O Creator and Provider, who providest whomso Thou wilt without count or stint! O mine Holy One, I cry Thee pardon for all sins and turn to Thee repenting of all offences

> How many by my labours, that evermore endure,
> All goods of life enjoy and in cooly shade recline?
> Each morn that dawns I wake in travail and in woe,
>   And strange is my condition
>   and my burden gars me pine:
> Many others are in luck and from miseries are free,
>   And Fortune never load them with loads
>   the like o' mine:
> They live their happy days in all solace and delight;
> Eat, drink and dwell in honour 'mid the noble and the
>   digne:
> All living things were made of a little drop of sperm,
>   Thine origin is mine and my provenance is thine;
>   Yet the difference and distance 'twixt
>   the twain of us are far
> As the difference of savour 'twixt vinegar and wine:
> But at Thee, O God All-wise! I venture not to rail
>   Whose ordinance is just and whose justice
>   cannot fail.

When Sinbad the Porter had made an end of reciting his verses, he bore up his burden and was about to fare on, when there came forth to him from the gate a little footpage, fair of face and shapely of shape and dainty of dress who caught him by the hand saying, "Come in and speak with my lord, for he calleth for thee." The Porter would have excused himself to the page but the lad would take no refusal; so he left his load with the doorkeeper in the vestibule and followed the boy into the house, which he found to be a goodly mansion, radiant and full of majesty, till he brought him to a grand sitting-room wherein he saw a company of nobles and great lords, seated at tables garnished with all manner of flowers and sweet-scented herbs, besides great plenty of dainty viands and fruits dried and fresh and confections and wines of the choicest vintages. There also were instruments of music and mirth and lovely slave-girls playing and singing. All the company was ranged according to rank; and in the highest place sat a man of worshipful and noble aspect whose beardsides hoariness had stricken; and he was stately of stature and fair of favour, agreeable of aspect and full of gravity and dignity and majesty. So Sinbad the Porter was confounded at that which he beheld and said in himself, "By Allah, this must be either a piece of Paradise or some King's palace!" Then he saluted the company with much respect praying for their prosperity, and kissing the ground before them, stood with his head bowed down in humble attitude. The master of the house bade him draw near and be seated and bespoke him kindly, bidding him welcome. Then he set before him various kinds of viands, rich and delicate and delicious, and the Porter, after saying his Bismillah, fell to and ate his fill, after which he exclaimed, "Praised be Allah whatso be our case!" and, washing his hands, returned thanks to the company for his entertainment. Quoth the host, "Thou art welcome and thy day is a blessed. But what is thy name and calling?" Quoth the other, "O my lord, my name is Sinbad the Hammal, and I carry folk's goods on my head for hire." The house-master smiled and rejoined, "Know, O Porter, that thy name is even as mine, for I am Sindbad the Seaman; and now, O Porter, I would have thee let me hear the couplets thou recitedst at the gate anon." The Porter was abashed and replied, "Allah upon thee! Excuse me, for toil and travail and lack of luck when the hand is empty, teach a man ill manners and boorish ways." Said the host, "Be not ashamed; thou art become my brother; but repeat to me the verses, for they pleased me whenas I heard thee recite them at the gate." Hereupon the Porter repeated the couplets and they delighted the merchant, who said to him:—Know, O Hammal, that my story is a wonderful one, and thou shalt hear all that befel me and all I underwent ere I rose to this state of prosperity and became the lord of this place wherein thou seest me; for I came not to this high estate save after travail sore and perils galore, and how much toil and trouble have I not suffered in days of yore! I have made seven voyages, by each of which hangeth a marvellous tale, such as confoundeth the reason, and all this came to pass by doom of fortune and fate; for from what destiny both write there is neither refute nor flight. Know, then, good my lords (continued he), that I am about to relate the. . . .

CONCLUSION

Now, during this time, Shahrazad had borne the King three boy children: so, when she had made an end of the story of Ma'aruf, she rose to her feet and kissing ground before him, said, "O King of the time and unique one of the age and the tide, I am thine handmaid and these thousand nights and a night have I entertained thee with stories of folk gone before and admonitory instances of the men of yore. May I then make bold to crave a boon of Thy Highness?" He replied, "Ask, O Shahrazad, and it shall be granted to thee." Whereupon she cried out to the nurses and the eunuchs, saying, "Bring me my children." So they brought them to her in haste, and they were three boy children, one walking, one crawling and one suckling. She took them and setting them before the King, again kissed the ground and said, "O King of the age, these are they children and I crave that thou release me from the doom of death, as a dole to these

infants; for, an thou kill me, they will become motherless and will find none among women to rear them as they should be reared." When the King heard this, he wept and straining the boys to his bosom, said, "By Allah, O Shahrazad, I pardoned thee before the coming of these children, for that I found thee chaste, pure, ingenuous and pious! Allah bless thee and thy father and thy mother and thy root and thy branch! I take the Almighty to witness against me that I exempt thee from aught that can harm thee." So she kissed his hands and feet and rejoiced with exceeding joy, saying, "The Lord make thy life long and increase thee in dignity and majesty!"; presently adding, "Thou marvelledst at that which befel thee on the part of women; yet there betided the Kings of the Chosroes before thee greater mishaps more grievous than that which hath befallen thee, and indeed I have set forth unto thee that which happened to Caliphs and Kings and others with their women, but the relation is longsome and hearkening groweth tedious, and in this is all-sufficient warning for the man of wits and admonishment for the wise." Then she ceased to speak, and when King Shahriyar heard her speech and profited by that which she said, he summoned up his reasoning powers and cleansed his heart and caused his understanding revert and turned to Allah Almighty and said to himself, "Since there befel the Kings of the Chosroes more than that which hath befallen me, never, whilst I live, shall I cease to blame myself for the past. As for this Shahrazad, her like is not found in the lands; so praise be to Him who appointed her a means for delivering His creatures from oppression and slaughter!" Then he arose from his seance and kissed her head, whereat she rejoiced, she and her sister Dunvazad, with exceeding joy. When the morning morrowed, the King went forth and sitting down on the throne of the Kingship, summoned the Lords of his land; whereupon the Chamberlains and Nabobs and Captains of the host went in to him and kissed ground before him. He distinguished the Wazir, Shahrazad's sire, with special favour and bestowed on him a costly and splendid robe of honour and entreated him with the utmost kindness, and said to him "Allah protect thee for that thou gavest me to wife thy noble daughter, who hath been the means of my repentance from slaying the daughters of folk. Indeed I have found her pure and pious, chaste and ingenuous, and Allah hath vouchsafed me by her three boy children; wherefore praised be He for his passing favour." Then he bestowed robes of honour upon his Wazirs, and Emirs and Chief Officers and he set forth to them briefly that which had betided him with Shahrazad and how he had turned from his former ways and repented him of what he had done and purposed to take the Wazir's daughter, Shahrazad, to wife and let draw up the marriage-contract with her.

Questions:

1. In what ways does Islam feature in these stories?
2. In what ways are women viewed? What are the consequences of these perspectives?

8.12 A Christian's Description of the Mongols

The Europeans came in contact with the Mongols while they were fighting the Muslims in the Crusades in the thirteenth century. In 1245, Pope Innocent IV sent a Christian missionary to the Mongols to try to convince them not to attack Europe and to convert to Christianity (See Chapter 10, Document 1 for the Pope's bull and the Mongol leader's response). The Missionary provided the following description of the Mongols.

> **Source**: John of Piano Carpini, *History of the Mongols*, IV, in *The Mongol Mission. Narratives and Letters of the Franciscan Missionairies (sic) in Mongolia and China in the Thirteenth and Fourteenth Centuries*, trans. A nun of Stanbrook Abbey, ed. C. Dawson, (New York: Sheed and Ward, *1955*, pp. 32–38); reprinted in *The Crusades: A Documentary Survey*, ed. James A. Brundage, (Milwaukee, WI: The Marquette University Press, 1976, c. 1962), pp. 254–57.

These men, that is to say the Tartars, are more obedient to their masters than any other men in the world, be they religious or seculars; they show great respect to them nor do they lightly lie to them. They rarely or never contend with each other in word, and in action never. Fights, brawls, wounding, murder are never met with among them. Nor are robbers and thieves who steal on a large scale found there; consequently their dwellings and the carts in which they keep their valuables are not secured by bolts and bars. If any animals are lost, whoever comes across them either leaves them alone or takes them to men appointed for this purpose; the owners of the animals apply for them to these men and they get them back without any difficulty. They show considerable respect to each other and are very friendly together, and they willingly share their food with each other, although there is little enough of it. They are also long-suffering. When they are without food, eating nothing at all for one or two days, they do not easily show impatience, but they sing and make merry as if they had eaten well. On horseback they endure great cold and they also put up with excessive heat. Nor are they men fond of luxury; they are not envious of each other; there is practically no litigation among them. No one scorns another but helps him and promotes his good as far as circumstances permit.

Their women are chaste, nor does one hear any mention among them of any shameful behavior on their part; some of them, however, in jest make use of vile and disgusting language. Discord among them seems to arise rarely or never, and although they may get very drunk, yet in their intoxication they never come to words or blows.

Now that the good characteristics of the Tartars have been described, it is time for something to be said about their bad. They are most arrogant to other people and look down on all, indeed they consider them as nought, be they of high rank or low born. . . .

They are quickly roused to anger with other people and are of an impatient nature; they also tell lies to others and practically no truth is to be found among them. At first indeed they are smooth-tongued, but in the end they sting like a scorpion. They are full of slyness and deceit, and if they can, they get round everyone by their cunning. They are men who are dirty in the way they take food and drink and do other things. Any evil they intend to do to others they conceal in a wonderful way so that the latter can take no precautions nor devise anything to offset their cunning. Drunkenness is considered an honorable thing by them and when anyone drinks too much, he is sick there and then, nor does this prevent him from drinking again. They are exceedingly grasping and avaricious; they are extremely exacting in their demands, most tenacious in holding on to what they have and most niggardly in giving. They consider the slaughter of other people as nothing. In short, it is impossible to put down in writing all their evil characteristics on account of the very great number of them.

Their food consists of everything that can be eaten, for they eat dogs, wolves, foxes, and horses and, when driven by necessity, they feed on human flesh. For instance, when they were fighting against a city of the Kitayans, where the emperor was residing, they besieged it for so long that they themselves completely ran out of supplies and, since they had nothing at all to eat, they thereupon took out one of every ten men for food. They eat the filth which comes from mares when they bring forth foals. Nay, I have even seen them eating lice. They would say, "Why should I not eat them since they eat the flesh of my son and drink his blood?" I have also seen them eat mice.

They do not use tablecloths or napkins. They have neither bread nor herbs nor vegetables nor anything else, nothing but meat, of which, however, they eat so little that other people would scarcely be able to exist on it. They make their hands very dirty with the grease of the meat, but when they eat they wipe them on their leggings or the grass or some other such thing. It is the custom for the more respectable among them to have small bits of cloth with which to wipe their hands at the end when they eat meat. One of them cuts the morsels and another takes them on the point of a knife and offers them to each, to some more, to some less, according to whether they wish to show them greater or less honor. They do not wash their dishes, and, if occasionally they rinse them with the meat broth, they put it back with the meat into the pot. Pots also or spoons or other articles intended for this use, if they are cleaned at all, are washed in the same manner. They consider it a great sin if any food or drink is allowed to be wasted in any way; consequently they do not allow bones to be given to dogs until the marrow has been extracted. They do not wash their clothes nor allow them to be washed, especially from the time when thunderstorms begin until the weather changes. They drink mare's milk in very great quantities if they have it; they also drink the milk of ewes, cows, goats and even camels. They do not have wine, ale, or mead unless it is sent or given to them by other nations. In the winter, moreover, unless they are wealthy, they do not have mare's milk. They boil millet in water and make it so thin that they cannot eat it but have to drink it. Each one of them drinks one or two cups in the morning and they eat nothing more during the day; in the evening, however, they are all given a little meat, and they drink the meat broth. But in the summer, seeing they have plenty of mare's milk, they seldom eat meat, unless it happens to be given to them or they catch some animal or bird when hunting.

They also have a law or custom of putting to death any man and woman they find openly committing adultery; similarly if a virgin commits fornication with anyone, they kill both the man and the woman. If any is found in the act of plundering or stealing in the territory under their power, he is put to death without any mercy. Again, if anyone reveals their plans, especially when they intend going to war, he is given a hundred stripes on his back, as heavy as a peasant can give with a big stick. If any of the lower class offend in any way, they are not spared by their superiors, but are soundly beaten. There is no distinction between the son of a concubine and the son of a wife, but the father gives to each what he will; and if they are of a family of princes, then the son of a concubine is a prince just the same as the son of a legitimate wife. When a Tartar has many wives, each one has her own dwelling and her household, and the husband eats and drinks and sleeps one day with one, and the next with another. One, however, is chief among the others and with her he stays more often than with the others. In spite of their numbers, they never easily quarrel among themselves.

The men do not make anything at all, with the exception of arrows, and they also sometimes tend the flocks, but they hunt and practice archery, for they are all, big and little, excellent archers, and their children begin as soon as they are two or three years old to ride and manage horses and to gallop on them, and they are given bows to suit their stature and are taught to shoot; they are extremely agile and also intrepid.

Young girls and women ride and gallop on horseback with agility like the men. We even saw them carrying bows and arrows. Both the men and the women are able to endure long stretches of riding. They have very short stirrups; they look after their horses very well, indeed they take the very greatest care of all their possessions. Their women make everything, leather garments, tunics, shoes, leggings, and everything made of leather; they also drive the carts and repair them, they load the camels, and in all their tasks they are very swift and energetic. All the women wear breeches and some of them shoot like the men.

Questions:

1. What characteristics does the European missionary use to describe the Mongols?
2. Given the way he describes the Mongols, how might he perceive the Europeans to be?
3. Based on this description, what do we learn about the culture of the Mongols? Is there room for misunderstanding or misrepresentation on the part of the missionary? Note that cannibalism was a common attribute Europeans gave to non-Europeans.

Part THREE
THE WEST TAKES FORM
Medieval Society, Politics, Economy, and Culture (500–1500)

CHAPTER 9
Workers, Warriors, and Kings
Politics and Society in the Middle Ages (800–1500)

SECTION 1
Workers

9.1 Manorial Court Records

The lord of the manor held a court for his tenants, both free and unfree, regulating rights in land and settling disputes according to local custom. For the unfree serfs, this was their only court for legal redress. In England, the manorial courts sometimes absorbed the local "hundred courts" over which the county sheriff theoretically ought to have presided. As a result, the jurisdiction of the manorial court was quite varied. Below are some thirteenth-century records of manorial courts held by the Abbey of Bec in England.

> **Source:** Maitland, F. W., ed. *Select Pleas in Manorial and Other Seignorial Courts* (Publications of the Selden Society: London, 1889), pp. 6–9, 11–13.

PLEAS OF THE MANORS IN ENGLAND OF THE ABBEY OF BEC FOR THE HOKEDAY TERM, 1246

Bledlow [Buckinghamshire]. Saturday before Ascension Day.

1 The court has presented that Simon Combe has set up a fence on the lord's land. Therefore let it be abated.[1]

2 Simone Combe gives 18 d[2]. for leave to compromise with Simon Besmere. Pledges, John Sperling and John Harding.

3 A day is given to Alice of Standen at the next court to produce her charter and her heir.

4 John Sperling complains that Richard of Newmere on the Sunday next before S. Bartholomew's day last past with his cattle, horses and pigs wrongfully destroyed the corn on his [John's] land to his damage to the extent of one thrave of wheat, and to his dishonour to the extent of two shillings; and of this he produces suit. And Richard comes and defends all of it. Therefore let him go to the law six-handed.[3] His pledges, Simon Combe and Hugh Frith.

Swincombe [Oxfordshire]. Sunday before Ascension Day.

5 Richard Rastold [essoins himself][4] of the general summons by William Henry's son.

---

[1] Removed.

[2] The abbreviations for coins were: d. = pence, s. = shilling, and l = pound. Twelve pence = 1 shilling and 20 shillings = 1 pound. The amount 6s.8d. was equal to 1 mark which was not a coin, but an amount of money. (For example: The old expression "2 bits" equals a quarter coin, but there was never coin minted that equaled one "bit") Three marks = 1 pound.

[3] To "make his law" or "go to the law six-handed" means that he must bring five men of lawful reputation to swear with him that they believe he is a man who is telling the truth.

[4] Presents a legal excuse for himself for not appearing in court when summoned to do so.

6 Hugh Pike and Robert his son are in mercy for wood of the lord thievishly carried away. The fine for each, 6 s. 8 d. Pledges, Richard Mile and William Shepherd.

7 Peter Alexander's son in mercy for the same. Fine, 2 s. Pledge, Alexander his father.

8 Henry Mile in mercy for waste of the lord's corn. Pledges, Richard Mile and William Shepherd.

9 John Smith in mercy for not producing what he was pledge to produce. Pledges, Richard Etys and Hugh Wood. Fine, 12 d.

10 Roger Abovewood and William Shepherd in mercy for not producing what they were pledges to produce. . . . Fine, half a sextary of wine.

Tooting [Surrey]. Sunday after Ascension Day.

11 The court presented that the following had encroached on the lord's land, to wit,[5] William Cobbler, Maud Robin's widow (fined 12 d.), John Shepherd (fined 12 d.), Walter Reeve (fined 2 s.), William of Moreville (fined 12 d.), Hamo of Hageldon (fined 12 d.), Mabel Spendlove's widow (fined 6 d.). Therefore they are in mercy.

12 . . . Roger Rede in mercy for detention of rent. Pledge, John of Stratham. Fine, 6 d.

13 William of Streatham is in mercy for not producing what he was pledge to produce. Fine, 12d.

Ruislip [Middlesex]. Tuesday after Ascension Day.

14 The court presents that Nicholas Brakespeare is not in a tithing[6] and holds land. Therefore let him be distrained.[7]

15 Breakers of the assize[8]: Alice Salvage's widow (fined 12 d.), Agnotta the Shepherd's mistress, Roger Canon (fined 6 d.), the wife of Richard Chayham, the widow of Peter Beyondgrove, the wife of Ralph Coke (fined 6 d.), Ailwin (fined 6 d.), John Shepherd (fined 6 d.), Geoffrey Carpenter, Roise the Miller's wife (fined 6 d.), William White, John Carpenter, John Bradif.

16 Roger Hamo's son gives 20 s. to have seisin[9] of the land which was his father's and to have an inquest of twelve as to a certain croft which Gilbert Bisuthe holds. Pledges, Gilbert Lamb, William John's son and Robert King.

17 Isabella Peter's widow is in mercy for a trespass which her son John had committed in the lord's wood. Fine, 18 d. Pledges, Gilbert Bisuthe and Richard Robin.

18 Richard Maleville is at his law against the lord [to prove] that he did not take from the lord's servants goods taken in distress to the damage and dishonour of his lord [to the extent of] 20 s. Pledges, Gilbert Bisuthe and Richard Hubert.

19 Hugh Tree in mercy for his beasts caught in the lord's garden. Pledges, Walter Hill and William Slipper. Fine, 6 d.

20 [The] twelve jurors say that Hugh Cross has right in the bank and hedge about which there was a dispute between him and William White. Therefore let him hold in peace and let William be distrained for his many trespasses. (Afterwards he made fine[10] for 12 s.) They say also that the hedge which is between the Widow Druet and William Slipper so far as the bank extends should be divided along the middle of the bank, so that the crest of the bank should be the boundary between them, for the crest was thrown up along the ancient boundary.

21 [The roll is torn in places for the next two entries] . . . son of Roger Clerk gives 20 s. to have seisin of the land which was his father's. Pledges, Gilbert . . .and Hugh Cross.

22 [Name missing] gives 13 s. 4d. to have seisin of the land which was his mother's beyond the wood. Pledges, William . . . and Robert Mareleward.

PLEAS OF THE MANORS OF THE ABBEY OF BEC FOR THE MARTINMAS TERM A.D. 1247.

Weedon Beck [Northamptonshire]. Vigil of St. Michael.

23 Richard le Boys of Aldeston has sworn fealty for the land which was his father's and has found pledges for 4 s. as his relief, to wit, William Clerk of the same place, Godfrey Elder and Roger Smith.

24 Elias Deynte in full court resigned his land and William Deynte his son was put in seisin of it and swore fealty and found the same pledges for 5 s. as his relief. Afterwards he paid.

25 The township presents that they suspect Robert Dochy and William Tale because they made fine with the knights, [who formed the jury] before the justices [in eyre][11] when they were accused of larceny.

26 Breakers of the assize: William Paris, Richard Cappe, Maud widow of Robert Carter, Walter Carter, Roger Smith, Richard Guy's son, William Green, Gilbert Vicar's son, Guy Lawman.

---

[5] Namely.

[6] All adult free males in England became a member of a "tithing" about the age 14. A tithing was a group of about ten men who were legally responsible for one another's actions. At the "Hundred" court, the local court like a township court, the sheriff would question the members of a tithing to report crimes and problems as well as locate people when they were needed in court.

[7] "Distrained" means that some part of Nicholas' property will be taken into the custody of the court to motivate him to join a tithing like any law abiding landholder ought to.

[8] "Breakers of the assize" sold ale or bread that did not meet the established standards of quality and price.

[9] Lawful possession.

[10] Made Payment.

[11] The Justices in eyre were the king's justices that went from county to county in England on a regular circuit.

27 William Green and Guy Lawman have gallons which are too small.

28 John Mercer will give three chickens yearly at Martinmas for having the lord's patronage and he is received into a tithing.

Wretham [Norfolk]. Friday after the feast of S. Michael.

30 Gilbert Richard's son gives 5 s. for license to marry a wife. Pledge, Seaman. Term [for payment,] the Purification.

Tooting [Surrey]. Tuesday after the feast of S. Denis.

31 William Jordan in mercy for bad ploughing on the lord's land. Pledge, Arthur. Fine, 6 d.

32 John Shepherd in mercy for encroaching beyond the boundary of his land. Pledge, Walter Reeve. Fine, 6 d.

33 . . . Elias of Streatham in mercy for default of service in the autumn. Fine, 6 d.

34 Bartholomew Chaloner who was at his law against Reginald Swain's son has made default in his law. Therefore he is in mercy and let him make satisfaction to Reginald for his damage and dishonour with 6 s. Pledges, William Cobbler and William Spendlove. Fine, 6 gallons.

35 Ralph of Morville gives a half-mark on the security of Jordan of Streatham and William Spendlove to have a jury to inquire whether he be the next heir to the land which William of Morville holds. And [the] twelve jurors come and say that he has no right in the said land but that William Scot has greater right in the said land than any one else. And the said William [Scot] gives 1 mark on the security of Hamo of Hageldon, William of Morville, Reginald Swain and Richard Leaware that he may have seisin of the said land after the death of William of Morville in case he [William Scot] shall survive him [William of Morville].

36 Afterwards came the said William Scot and by the lord's leave quit-claimed[12] all the right that he had in the said land with its appurtenances to a certain William son of William of Morville, who gives 20 s. to have seisin of the said land and is put in seisin of it and has sworn fealty. Walter the serjeant is to receive the pledges.

Deverill [Wiltshire]. Saturday after the feast of S. Leonard.

37 . . . Arnold Smith is in mercy for not producing the said William Scut whose pledge he was.

38 The parson of the church is in mercy for his cow caught in the lord's meadow. Pledges, Thomas Guner and William Coke.

---

[12] Gave up his claim to the land.

39 From William Cobbe, William Coke and Walter Dogskin 2 s. for the ward of seven pigs belonging to Robert Gentil and for the damage that they did in the lord's corn. [Maitland believes that they were amerced for not guarding the lord's crops]

40 From Martin Shepherd 6 d. for the wound that he gave Pekin.

Questions:
1. What range of cases and business was heard at these manorial courts?
2. What do you think a "pledge" did? What does "in mercy" mean?
3. How did the court determine the facts in disputes?
4. What sort of penalties did the court lay on the guilty?
5. What happened when a juvenile did something wrong?

9.2 The *Domesday Book*

William, Duke of Normandy and King of England, commissioned a census known as the *Domesday Book* of 1086. This census undertook to assess the extent of the resources in land and people that the king had available, recording the various customs affecting the king's control over them as well. It ended up as one of the most extensive land surveys of the Middle Ages. This is the account for the town of Hereford.

> **Source:** *Sources of English Constitutional History, Volume I: A selection of Documents from A.D. 600 to the Interregnum*, ed. and trans. Carl Stephenson and F. G. Marcham, (New York: Harper and Row, 1972), pp. 41–42.

In this city Earl Harold[1] had 27 burgesses enjoying the same customs as the other burgesses. From this city the reeve rendered £12 to King Edward and £6 to Earl Harold, and he had in his farm all the aforesaid customs.[2] The king, however, had in his demesne three forfeitures: namely, breach of his peace, house-breaking, and assault by ambush. Whoever committed one of these [offenses] paid the king 100s. fine, whosesoever man he was.[3] Now the king has the city of Hereford in demesne,[4] and the English burgesses who dwell

---

[1] The Normans refused to recognize Harold's title to the throne.
[2] The borough including the revenues described above, was farmed by the portreeve for £18 a year, two-thirds to the king and one-third to the earl.
[3] The list of crown pleas varied from region to region; cf. the customs of Worcestershire and Nottinghamshire below, and Canute, II, 12
[4] Earlier there had been three great border earls who enjoyed all regalian rights within their respective territories: Roger de Montgomery, earl of Shrewsbury; Hugh d'Avranches, earl of Chester; and William Fitz-Osbern, earl of Hereford. Before 1086, however, the third of these earldoms had been forfeited as the consequence of a rebellion.

there have their previous customs. The French burgesses, however, are quit, through [payment of] 12*d*., of all forfeitures except the three aforesaid. This city renders to the king £60 by tale in assayed money. Between the city and the eighteen manors that render their farms in Hereford £335. 18*s*. are accounted for, besides the pleas of the hundred and county [courts].[5]

In Archenfield the king has three churches. The priests of these churches undertake the king's embassies into Wales, and each of them sings for the king two masses every week. When any one of them dies, the king customarily has 20*s*. from him. If any Welshman steals a man or a woman, a horse, an ox, or a cow, on being convicted, he first returns what has been stolen and [then] pays 20*s*. as a fine. For theft of a sheep, however, or of a bundle of sheaves, he pays 2*s*. fine. If any one kills a man of the king or commits house-breaking, he pays the king 20*s*. compensation for the man and 100*s*. as fine. If he kills any thegn's man, he gives 10*s*. to the lord of the slain man. But if a Welshman kills a Welshman, the relatives of the slain man come together and plunder the slayer and his kin and burn their houses until, toward noon on the following day, the body of the slain man is buried. Of this plunder the king has the third part, but they enjoy all the rest of it in peace. He, however, who burns a house in another fashion, on being accused of doing so, defends himself by [the oath of] forty men. But if he cannot [clear himself], he has to pay 20*s*. fine to the king. If any one conceals a sester of honey out of a customary payment, and is convicted of it, he renders five sesters for one, should he hold enough land to warrant the payment. If the sheriff calls them to the shire court, six or seven of the better men among them go with him [as escort]. He who is summoned [to the court] and does not go gives the king 2*s*. or an ox; and whoever stays away from the hundred [court] pays the same amount. He who is commanded by the sheriff to go with him into Wales, and does not do so, pays a similar fine. But if the sheriff does not go, none of them has to go. When the army advances against the enemy, they customarily form the advance guard, and on return [they form] the rear guard. These were the customs of the Welshmen in Archenfield during the time of King Edward.

Here are set down those holding lands in Herefordshire and in Archenfield and in Wales. . . .[6]

The land of the king. . . . The king holds Leominster. Queen Edith held it. . . . In this manor . . . there were 80 hides, and in demesne 30 ploughs.[7] In it were 8 reeves, 8 beadles, 8 ridingmen, 238 villeins, 75 bordars, and 82 serfs and bondwomen.[8] These together had 230 ploughs. The villeins ploughed 140 acres of the lord's land and sowed it with their own seed grain, and by custom they paid £11. 52*d*. The ridingmen paid 14*s*. 4*d*. and 3 sesters of honey; and there were eight mills [with an income] of 73*s*. and 30 sticks of eels.[9] The wood rendered 24*s*. besides pannage.[10] Now in this manor the king has in demesne 60 hides and 29 ploughs; and 6 priests, 6 ridingmen, 7 reeves, 7 beadles, 224 villeins, 81 bordars. and 25 serfs and bondwomen. Among them all they have 201 ploughs. They plough and sow with their own grains 125 acres, and by custom they pay £7. 14*s*. 8 1/2*d*.; also 17*s* [worth] of fish, 8*s*. of salt, and 65*s*. of honey. In it are eight mills [with an income] of 108*s*. and 100 sticks of eels less 10. A wood 6 leagues[11] long and 3 leagues wide renders 22*s*. Of these shillings 5 are paid for buying wood at Droitwich, and thence are obtained 30 mitts of salt.[12] Each villein possessing ten pigs gives one pig for pannage. From woodland brought under cultivation come 17*s*. 4*d*. An eyrie of hawks is there. . . . Altogether this revenue, except the eels, is computed at £23. 2*s*. This manor is at farm for £60 in addition to the maintenance of the nuns. The county[13] says that, if it were freed [of that obligation], this manor would be worth six score, that is to say, £120. . . .

Questions:

1. What can historians (like you) learn from the Domesday Book about life in twelfth-century Hereford?
2. What responsibilities and duties did the men have to fulfill for the governing of the community?

---

[5] These manors had earlier belonged to Earl William, and so had been brought into a financial organization centering in Hereford.

[6] According to the regular plan, the king heads the list of landholders and is followed by his barons, first the ecclesiastics and after them the laymen. The lands held by each person in the list are then described in turn, manor by manor.

[7] By *caruca* is meant, not merely the plough proper, but also the team of eight oxen. The hide in Domesday is a unit of assessment for geld and other royal services. It was divided into 4 virgates or yardlands, 8 bovates, and 120 acres.

[8] The beadle appears in Domesday as the subordinate of a manorial reeve. The *radcniht* or ridingman seems to have been much the same as a *geneat*; see above, p. 8, n. 8. The *villani* of Domesday, being distinguished from *servi*, were legally free; for it was only later that serfdom and villeinage came to be arbitrarily identified. According to Domesday, the normal villein holding was thirty acres of arable. The bordar or cotter, on the other hand, held only a hut and a garden plot. See especially Maitland, *Domesday Book and Beyond*, pp. 26 f.; Vinogradoff, *Villeinage in England*.

[9] About two dozen eels were counted as a stick. Most of them, obviously, were taken from mill-pounds.

[10] Swine were commonly allowed to run wild in woodland. Rent paid for the privilege was called pannage; see immediately below.

[11] The Domesday league is a mile and a half, but these measurements are only rough approximations.

[12] Salt-wiches are a prominent feature of this region; see Tait, *The Domesday Survey of Cheshire*, pp. 39 f. The wood bought at Droitwich was for the furnaces used in connection with salt-pans. The mitt included two ambers of four bushels each.

[13] I.e., the jury that spoke for it.

SECTION 2
Warriors

9.3 Contracts between Lords and Vassals

Every vassal in medieval society concluded a contract of mutual obligations with his lord who granted him possession of a fief, an estate in land. Vassals often held many fiefs, with conflicting obligations to various lords. Such overlapping jurisdictions, created by the custom of vassals making their own grants of fiefs to others (a process called subinfeudation), could and did cause conflict and warfare in Europe during the Middle Ages. Here are three records of such contractual agreements: the grant of a fief by King Louis VII of France to the Bishop of Beauvais in 1167, a grant by the Count of Troyes to Jocelyn d'Avalon in 1200, and a contract of 1221 between the Countess of Nevers and her lord, Philip II, King of France.

Source: *Translations and Reprints from the Original Sources of European History*, Edward P. Cheyney, ed., (Philadelphia: University of Pennsylvania, 1897), vol. IV, no. 3, pp. 15–16, 18–20, 24–25.

GRANT OF A FIEF, 1167 C.E.

In the name of the Holy and Undivided Trinity, Amen. I, Louis, by the grace of God, king of the French, make known to all present as well as to come, that at Mante in our presence, Count Henry of Champagne conceded the fief of Savigny to Bartholomew, bishop of Beauvais, and his successors. And for that fief the said bishop has made promise and engagement for one knight and justice and service to Count Henry; and he has also agreed that the bishops who shall come after him will do likewise. In order that this may be understood and known to posterity we have caused the present charter to be corroborated by our seal; done at Mante, in the year of the Incarnate Word 1167; present in our palace those whose names and seals are appended: seal of count Thiebault, our steward; seal of Guy, the butler; seal of Matthew, the chamberlain; seal of Ralph, the constable. Given by the hand of Hugh, the chancellor.

GRANT OF A FIEF, 1200 C.E.

I, Thiebault, count palantine of Troyes, make known to those present and to come that I have given in fee to Jocelyn d'Avalon and his heirs the manor which is called Gillencourt, which is of the castellanerie of La Ferte sur Aube; and whatever the same Jocelyn shall be able to acquire in the same manor I have granted to him arid his heirs in augmentation of that fief. I have granted, moreover, to him that in no free manor of mine will I retain men who are of this gift. The same Jocelyn, moreover, on account of this has become my liege man, saving, however, his allegiance to Gerard d'Arcy, and to the lord duke of Burgundy, and to Peter, count of Auxerre. Done at Chouaude, by my own witness, in the year of the Incarnation of our Lord 1200, in the month of January. Given by the hand of Walter, my chancellor.

AUTHORITY OF A LORD OVER TITLE MARRIAGE OF VASSALS, 1221 C.E.

Eventually women were allowed to hold and inherit fiefs. Because military service was a major obligation of the vassal, a lord would be concerned about whom the heiress married.

I, Matilda, countess of Nevers make known to all who see this present letter, that I have sworn upon the sacred gospels to my dearest lord, Philip, by the grace of God, the illustrious king of France, that I will do to him good and faithful service against all living men and women, and that I will not marry except by his will and grace. For keeping these agreements firmly I have given pledges to the same lord king from my men whom I had with me, on their oaths, in this wise, that if I should fail to keep the said agreements with the lord king, (though this shall not be), these are held to come to the lord king with all their lands and fiefs which are held from me, and shall take their oaths to him against me until it shall have been made good to him to his satisfaction. And whenever the lord king shall ask me I will cause him to have similar oaths from my men who were not present with me before the lord king, that is to say from all whom I may have, in good faith, and without evil intention, and similarly the fealty of my town. And in order that this may remain firm and stable, I have written the present letters supported by my seal. Given at Melun, in the year of the Lord 1221, in the month of February.

Questions:
1. What are the obligations that each document requires of the parties involved?
2. In what ways did granting a fief to a member of the ecclesiastical hierarchy involve that spiritual vassal in secular politics and create the possibility of a conflict of loyalties?
3. When a man held fiefs from different lords, how did the feudal system resolve questions of divided loyalty and service?
4. Why would or could a lord reasonably demand the right to consent to the marriage of heiresses to the fief?

9.4 *The Song of Roland*

In 778 Charlemagne (768–814) was returning from an expedition in Spain when his rear guard was attacked and slaughtered by marauding Christian Basques in the Pyrenees Mountains. According to the contemporary chronicles, one of the fallen knights was Roland, duke of the Marches of Brittany. By the time the epic poem was written in the eleventh century, popular legend had altered the story from a disastrous but minor skirmish, to a major battle between Muslim and Christian culminating in the confrontation of two titans, the great Muslim emir and the Emperor Charlemagne. In the process, the fallen Roland had become Charlemagne's favorite nephew.

Source: *The Song of Roland*, trans. Dorothy Sayers, (New York: Penguin Books, 1973, c. 1957), pp. 187–89.

259

Charles of fair France is a great man of might,
And the Emir knows naught of fear or flight.
Their naked swords they brandish now on high,
Lay on the shields stiff strokes from either side,
Shearing the leather and wood of double ply;
The rivets fall, in shreds the buckles fly.
In their bare byrnies now breast to breast they fight,
The glittering sparks flash from the helmets bright.
Nothing at all can ever end their strife
Till one confess he's wrong, the other right.

260

Quoth the Emir: "Bethink thee, Charles, and see
That thou repent what thou hast done to me.
My son is slain; I know it was by thee;
And on my lands thou wrongfully hast seized.
Become my man, and I will by thy liege;
Then come and serve me from here unto the East."
Quoth Carlon: "Nay, I'd hold it treachery;
Never to Paynims may I show love or peace.
Do thou confess the Faith by God revealed,
Take Christendom, and they fast friend I'll be.
The King Almighty then serve thou and believe."
Quoth Baligant: "Thy sermon's but ill preached."
Once more with swords they battle, each to each.
AOI

261

The great Emir is full of power and skill;
On Carlon's helm he lays a mighty hit,
That on his head the steel is rent and split;
Downward the blade through hair and scalp he brings
And of the flesh shears off a whole palm's width,
So that the bone shows bare beneath the skin.
King Carlon reels and well-nigh falls with it.
But God wills not he be o'ercome or killed;
Saint Gabriel comes hastening down to him:
"And what," saith he, "art thou about, great King?"

262

When Charles thus hears the blessed Angel say,
He fears not death, he's free from all dismay,
His strength returns, he is himself again.
At the Emir he drives his good French blade,
He carves the helm with jewel-stones ablaze,
He splits the skull, he dashes out the brains,
Down to the beard he cleaves him through the face,
And, past all healing, he flings him down, clean slain.
His rallying-cry, "Mountjoy!", he shouts straightway.
At this, Duke Naimon comes, leading by the rein
Good Tenecendur, and up mounts Charlemayn.
The Paynims fly, God will not have them stay.
All's done, all's won; the French have gained the day.

263

The Paynims fly, for God has willed it so.
Hard in pursuit see Franks and Emperor go!
Then saith the King: "My lords, avenge your woes;
Work all your will, lift up your hearts and souls,
For, but this morning, I saw your eyes o'erflow."
"Sir," say the Franks, "indeed it so behoves."
With all their might they deal tremendous blows;
Of those who're there few will escape their strokes.

264

Fierce is the heat, the dust goes up in clouds.
The Paynims flee, the French behind them scour,
The chase endures to Saragossa town.
Queen Bramimonda mounts up into her tower;
Beside her stand her clerks and canons vowed
To that false faith which God has disallowed—
Priests without orders, no tonsures on their crowns.
Seeing the Arabs thus beaten all about,
In a shrill voice she cries: "To help, Mahound!
Ah, noble King! our men are put to rout!
The great Emir is killed! O shameful hour!"
When this he hears, Marsilion turns him round
Face to the wall; he weeps, he droops his brow,
He dies of grief, by direful doom struck down,
And yields his soul to the infernal powers.

265

The Paynims all are dead or fled in terror,
And Carlon's war is gloriously ended.
He lays the gate of Saragossa level;
Right well he knows it will not be defended.
He takes the city and with his army enters;
That night they lie there, as victors in possession;
Proudly he goes, the silver-bearded Emperor.
All of her towers Queen Bramimond surrenders—
Her ten tall towers and fifty that are lesser.
Well speeds that man which hath God for his helper.

266

The day is past, the dark draws on to night,
Clear is the moon, the stars are shining bright;
All Saragossa lies in the Emperor's might.
Some thousand French search the whole town, to spy
Synagogues out and mosques and heathen shrines.
With heavy hammers and with mallets of iron
They smash the idols, the images they smite,
Make a clean sweep of mummeries and lies,
For Charles fears God and still to serve Him strives.
The Bishops next the water sanctify;
Then to the font the Paynim folk they drive.
Should Carlon's orders by any be defied
The man is hanged or slain or burned with fire.
An hundred thousand or more are thus baptized
And christened,—only the Queen fares otherwise:
She's to go captive to fair France by and by,
Her would the King convert by love to Christ.

Questions:
1. How do these verses illustrate the qualities of the ideal Christian knight?
2. According to the poem, why did the French fight and why were they victorious?
3. For what sort of audience was this epic composed?

Documents 9.5 and 9.6

These selections are accounts of two battles that took place during the Crusades, about fifty years apart. The first details the capture of Jerusalem from Muslim Turks by the Christian Crusaders, while the second describes the seige of the Portuguese city of Lisbon—under the control of the Muslim Moors—by Crusaders from Northern Europe.

9.5 The Capture of Jerusalem

The Crusades had been launched in 1095 for the purpose of freeing the Holy Land, particularly Jerusalem, from the hands of the Muslims. The Crusaders captured Jerusalem in 1099 and held it until 1187.

> **Source:** *The Crusades: A Documentary Chronicle*, James A. Brundage, ed., (Milwaukee, WI: The Marquette University Press, 1976, © 1962), pp. 63–65.

The final attack began on the evening of July 13. It lasted through the night and the whole next day. Late in the morning on July 15 the final breakthrough occurred.

We attacked the city from all sides, Day and night, on Wednesday and Thursday. But. before we attacked the city, the bishops and priests, by preaching and exhortation, ordered everyone to hold a procession in honor of God all around the city and arranged for prayers, almsgiving, and fasting.

At dawn on Friday we attacked the city from all sides without being able to make any headway. We were all trembling and stunned. At the approach of the hour at which our Lord Jesus Christ deigned to suffer on the cross for us our knights in the tower, namely Duke Godfrey and his brother, Count Eustace, made a fierce attack. Then one of our knights, named Lethold, climbed over the city wall. As soon as he ascended, all the city's defenders fled from the wall. Our men followed, killing and beheading them all the way to the Temple of Solomon. There was such slaughter there that our men waded in blood up to their ankles. . . .

The emir who was in the Tower of David surrendered to the Count and opened to him the gate where pilgrims used to pay the tribute. Our pilgrims, on entering the city, pursued and slaughtered the Saracens all the way to the Temple of Solomon, where the Turks were gathered. The enemy fought most vigorously for a whole day amid their blood flowed through the temple. Finally the pagans were overcome. Our men captured a number of men and women in the Temple. The captives were either killed or allowed to live, as our men saw fit. On the roof of Solomon's Temple there was a very large gathering of pagans of both sexes. To these people Tancred and Gaston of Beam had given their banners.[1] Soon our men were running all around the city, seizing gold and silver, horses and mules, amid houses filled with all kinds of goods.

Rejoicing and weeping for joy, our people came to the sepulcher of Jesus our Savior to worship and pay their debt.[2] At dawn our men cautiously went up to the roof of the Temple and attacked the Saracen men and women, beheading them with naked swords. Some of the Saracens, however, leaped from the Temple roof. Tancred, seeing this, was greatly angered.

Our men then took counsel and decided that everyone should pray and give alms so that God might choose for them whomever he pleased to rule over the others and govern the city. They ordered that all the dead Saracens should be cast out of the city because of the great stench, since the city was filled with their corpses. The living Saracens dragged the dead outside the gates made heaps of them, as large as houses. No one ever saw or heard of such a slaughter of pagan peoples, for funeral pyres were formed of them like pyramids and no one knows their number save God alone.

9.6 The Siege of Lisbon

On the way to join the Second Crusade in 1147, Crusading knights from England, Germany, Flanders, and Normandy interrupted their voyage to assist King Alfonso of Castile besiege Lisbon, held by Muslim rulers since the eighth century. In return

---
[1] As a sign that they were Tancred's and Gaston's prizes and thus as a safeguard against assault by the other Crusaders.
[2] That is, to fulfill their Crusading vows by worshiping at the Holy Sepulcher.

for their help, the king promised that they could plunder and pillage the city when it fell.

> **Source:** *Medieval Iberia: Readings from Christian, Muslim and Jewish Sources*, ed. Olivia Remie Constable, (Philadelphia: University of Pennsylvania Press, 1997), pp. 135–36.

Then our men, attending more strictly to the siege, began to dig a subterranean mine between the tower and the Porta do Ferro in order that they might bring down the wall. When this had been discovered, for it was quite accessible to the enemy, it proved greatly to our detriment after the investment of the city, for many days were consumed in its vain defense. Besides, two Balearic mangonels were set up by our forces—one on the river bank which was operated by seamen, the other in front of the Porta do Ferro, which was operated by the knights and their table companions. All these men having been divided into groups of one hundred, on a given signal the first hundred retired and another took their places, so that within the space of ten hours five thousand stones were hurled. And the enemy were greatly harassed by this action. Again the Normans and the English and those who were with them began the erection of a movable tower eighty-three feet in height. Once more, with a view to bringing down the wall, the men of Cologne and the Flemings began to dig a mine beneath the wall of the stronghold higher up—a mine which, marvelous to relate, had five entrances and extended inside to a depth of forty cubits from the front; and they completed it within a month.

Meanwhile, hunger and the stench of corpses greatly tormented the enemy, for there was no burial space within the city. And for food they collected the refuse which was thrown out from our ships and borne up by the waves beneath their walls. A ridiculous incident occurred as a result of their hunger when some of the Flemings, while keeping guard among the ruins of houses, were eating figs and, having had enough, left some lying about unconsumed. When this was discovered by four of the Moors, they came up stealthily and cautiously like birds approaching food. And when the Flemings observed this, they frequently scattered refuse of this sort about in order that they might lure them on with bait. And, finally, having set snares in the accustomed places, they caught three of the Moors in them and thereby caused enormous merriment among us.

When the wall had been undermined and inflammable material had been placed within the mine and lighted, the same night at cockcrow about thirty cubits of the wall crumbled to the ground. Then the Moors who were guarding the wall were heard to cry out in their anguish that they might now make an end of their long labors and that this very day would be their last and that it would have to be divided with death, and that this would be their greatest consolation for death, if, without fearing it, they might exchange their lives for ours. For it was necessary to go yonder whence there was no need of returning; and, if a life were well ended, it would nowhere be said to have been cut short. For what mattered was not how long but how well a life had been lived; and a life would have lasted as long as it should, even though not as long as it naturally could, provided it closed in a fitting end. And so the Moors gathered from all sides for the defense of the breach in the wall, placing against it a barrier of beams. Accordingly, when the men of Cologne and the Flemings went out to attempt an entrance, they were repulsed. For, although the wall had collapsed, the nature of the situation [on the steep hillside] prevented an entry merely by the heap [of ruins]. But when they failed to overcome the defenders in a hand-to-hand encounter, they attacked them furiously from a distance with arrows, so that they looked like hedgehogs as, bristling with bolts, they stood immovably at the defense and endured as if unharmed. Thus the defense was maintained against the onslaught of the attackers until the first hour of the day, when the latter retired to camp. The Normans and the English came under arms to take up the struggle in place of their associates, supposing that an entrance would be easy now that the enemy were wounded and exhausted. But they were prevented by the leaders of the Flemings and the men of Cologne, who assailed them with insults and demanded that we attempt an entrance in any way it might be accomplished with our own engines; for they said that they had prepared the breach which now stood open for themselves, not for us. And so for several days they were altogether repulsed from the breach.

Questions for Documents 9.5 and 9.6

1. How did the Crusaders prepare before battle?
2. What machines and techniques did they use in besieging and taking the cities?
3. How were the city's inhabitants and defenders treated by the Christian knights?
4. What sort of cooperation was there between different nationalities of Crusaders?

SECTION 3
Kings

9.7 Charlemagne: An Official Biography

Charlemagne (768–814) forged the concept of a united Christian Europe, reaching beyond the eastern frontiers of the old Roman empire, and reestablished a semblance of stability in government. Einhard, the contemporary biographer of Charlemagne, left a vivid portrait of this legendary figure.

Source: Einhard, *Life of Charlemagne*, (Ann Arbor, MI: The University of Michigan Press, 1979), pp. 45–60, passim.

xviii. Thus did Charles defend and increase as well as beautify his kingdom, as is well known; and here let me express my admiration of his great qualities and his extraordinary constancy alike in good and evil fortune. I will now forthwith proceed to give the details of his private and family life.

After his father's death, while sharing the kingdom with his brother, he bore his unfriendliness and jealousy most patiently, and, to the wonder of all, could not be provoked to be angry with him. Later he married a daughter of Desiderius, King of the Lombards, at the [insistence] of his mother; but he repudiated her at the end of a year for some reason unknown, and married Hildegard, a woman of high birth, of Suabian origin. He had three sons by her—Charles, Pepin and Louis—and as many daughters—Hruodrud, Bertha, and Gisela. He had three other daughters besides these—Theoderada, Hiltrud, and Ruodhaid—two by his third wife, Fastrada, a woman of East Frankish (that is to say, of German) origin, and the third by a concubine, whose name for the moment escapes me. At the death of Fastrada, he married Liutgard, an Alemannic woman, who bore him no children. After her death he had three concubines Gersuinda, a Saxon, by whom he had Adaltrud; Regina, who was the mother of Drogo and Hugh; and Ethelind, by whom he had Theodoric. Charles' mother, Berthrada, passed her old age with him in great honor; he entertained the greatest veneration for her; and there was never any disagreement between them except when he divorced the daughter of King Desiderius, whom he had married to please her. She died soon after Hildegard, after living to see three grandsons and as many granddaughters in her son's house, and he buried her with great pomp in the Basilica of St. Denis, where his father lay. He had an only sister, Gisela, who had consecrated herself to a religious life from girlhood, and he cherished as much affection for her as for his mother. She also died a few years before him in the nunnery where she had passed her life.

xix. The plan that he adopted for his children's education was, first of all, to have both boys and girls instructed in the liberal arts, to which he also turned his own attention. As soon as their years admitted, in accordance with the custom of the Franks, the boys had to learn horsemanship, and to practice war and the chase, and the girls to familiarize themselves with cloth-making, and to handle distaff and spindle, that they might not grow indolent through idleness, and he fostered in them every virtuous sentiment. . . .

The King gave a striking proof of his fatherly affection at the time of Pepin's death: he appointed the grandson to succeed Pepin, and had the granddaughters brought up with his own daughters. When his sons and his daughter died, he was not so calm as might have been expected from his remarkably strong mind, for his affections were no less strong, and moved him to tears. . . .

xxiv. Charles was temperate in eating, and particularly so in drinking, for he abominated drunkenness in anybody, much more in himself and those of his household; but he could not easily abstain from food, and often complained that fasts injured his health. He very rarely gave entertainments, only on great feastdays, and then to large numbers of people. His meals ordinarily consisted of four courses, not counting the roast, which his huntsmen used to bring in on the spit; he was more fond of this than of any other dish. While at table, he listened to reading or music. The subjects of the readings were the stories and deeds of olden time: he was fond, too, of St. Augustine's books, and especially of the one entitled *The City of God*. He was so moderate in the use of wine and all sorts of drink that he rarely allowed himself more than three cups in the course of a meal. In summer, after the midday meal, he would eat some fruit, drain a single cup, put off his clothes and shoes, just as he did for the night, and rest for two or three hours. He was in the habit of awaking and rising from bed four or five times during the night. While he was dressing and putting on his shoes, he not only gave audience to his friends, but if the Count of the Palace told him of any suit in which his judgment was necessary, he had the parties brought before him forthwith, took cognizance of the case and gave his decision, just as if he were sitting on the judgment seat. This was not the only business that he transacted at this time, but he performed any duty of the day whatever, whether he had to attend to the matter himself, or to give commands concerning it to his officers.

xxv. Charles had the gift of ready and fluent speech, and could express whatever he had to say with the utmost clearness. He was not satisfied with command of his native language merely, but gave attention to the study of foreign ones, and in particular was such a master of Latin that he could speak it as well as his native tongue; but he could understand Greek better than he could speak it. He was so eloquent, indeed, that he might have passed for a teacher of eloquence. He most zealously cultivated the liberal arts, held those who taught them in great esteem, and conferred great honors upon them. He took lessons in grammar of the deacon Peter of Pisa, at that time an aged man. Another deacon, Albin of Britain surnamed Alcuin, a man of Saxon extraction, who was the greatest scholar of the day, was his teacher in other branches of learning. The King spent much time and labor with him studying rhetoric, dialectics, and especially astronomy; he learned to reckon, and used to investigate the motions of the heavenly bodies most curiously, with an intelligent scrutiny. He also tried to write, and used to keep tablets and blanks in bed under his pillow, that at leisure hours he might accustom his hand to form the letters; however, as he did not begin his efforts in due season, but late in life, they met with ill success.

xxvi. He cherished with the greatest fervor and devotion the principles of the Christian religion, which had been instilled into him from infancy. Hence it was that he built the beautiful basilica at Aix-la-Chapelle, which he adorned with gold and silver and lamps, and with rails and doors of solid brass. He had the columns and marbles for this structure brought from Rome and Ravenna for he could not find such as were suitable elsewhere. He was a constant worshipper at this church as long as his health permitted, going morning and evening, even after nightfall, besides attending mass; and he took care that all the services there conducted should be administered with the utmost possible propriety, very often warning the sextons not to let any improper or unclean thing be brought into the building or remain in it. He provided it with a great number of sacred vessels of gold and silver and with such a quantity of clerical robes that not even the doorkeepers who fill the humblest office in the church were obliged to wear their everyday clothes when in the exercise of their duties. He was at great pains to improve the church reading and psalmody, for he was well skilled in both, although he neither read in public nor sang, except in a low tone and with others.

xxviii. . . . The Romans had inflicted many injuries upon the Pope Leo, tearing out his eyes and cutting out his tongue, so that he had been compelled to call upon the King for help. Charles accordingly went to Rome, to set in order the affairs of the Church, which were in great confusion, and passed the whole winter there. It was then that he received the titles of Emperor and Augustus, to which he at first had such an aversion that he declared that he would not have set foot in the Church the day that they were conferred, although it was a great feast-day, if he could have foreseen the design of the Pope. He bore very patiently with the jealousy which the Roman [Byzantine] emperors showed upon his assuming these titles, for they took this step very ill; and by dint of frequent embassies and letters, in which he addressed them as brothers, he made their haughtiness yield to his magnanimity, a quality in which he was unquestionably much their superior.

xxix. It was after he had received the imperial name that, finding the laws of his people very defective (the Franks have two sets of laws, very different in many particulars), he determined to add what was wanting, to reconcile the discrepancies, and to correct what was vicious and wrongly cited in them. However, he went no further in this matter than to supplement the laws by a few capitularies, and those imperfect ones; but he caused the unwritten laws of all the tribes that came under his rule to be compiled and reduced to writing. He also had the old rude songs that celebrate the deeds and wars of the ancient kings written out for transmission to posterity. He began a grammar of his native language.

xxx. Toward the close of his life, when he was broken by ill-health and old age, he summoned Louis, King of Aquitania, his only surviving son by Hildegard, and gathered together all the chief men of the whole kingdom of the Franks in a solemn assembly. He appointed Louis, with their unanimous consent, to rule with himself over the whole kingdom, and constituted him heir to the imperial name; then, placing the diadem upon his son's head, he bade him be proclaimed Emperor and Augustus. This step was hailed by all present with great favor, for it really seemed as if God had prompted him to it for the kingdom's good; it increased the King's dignity, and struck no little terror into foreign nations. . . . He died January twenty-eighth, the seventh day from the time that he took to his bed, at nine o'clock in the morning, after partaking of the holy communion, in the seventy-second year of his age and the forty-seventh of his reign. [Jan. 28, 814]. . .

Questions:
1. What does *Einhard* appear to regard as Charlemagne's greatest accomplishments and worthy qualities?
2. How does this description reveal his Germanic heritage?
3. How historically reliable do you *think* this biography is?

9.8 *Magna Carta*

Few English kings have as black a historical reputation as King John. Although he was no more evil or cruel than many other medieval kings, he was temperamental and injudicious. Not a great warrior like his predecessor and brother Richard the Lionheart (1189–1199), his disastrous wars lost the English crown most of its continental possessions. In 1215 Magna Carta was imposed upon King John by a group of Anglo-Norman barons and bishops who insisted that John fulfill the duties of good lordship toward his vassals. The charter was a solemn agreement—extracted from the king by force—that both king and barons would respect their mutual obligations, as defined in homage, fealty, and investiture. Although John soon repudiated the charter, later kings reissued and confirmed many of its articles, making it the basis of good government in England.

Source: G.R.C. Davis, *Magna Carta*, Revised Edition, British Library, 1989. Copyright © 1997, The British Library Board. From Portico The British Library's Online Information Server, <gopher://portico.bl.uk/00/portico/services/publish/publishl.txt>

JOHN, by the grace of God King of England, Lord of Ireland, Duke of Normandy and Aquitaine, and Count of Anjou, to his archbishops, bishops, abbots, earls, barons, justices, foresters, sheriffs, stewards, servants, and to all his officials and loyal subjects, Greeting. . . .

(1) First, that we have granted to God, and by this present charter have confirmed for us and our heirs forever, that the English Church shall be free, and shall have its rights undiminished, and its liberties unimpaired. That we wish this so to be observed, appears from the fact that of our own free will, before the outbreak of the present dispute between us and our barons, we granted and confirmed by charter the freedom of the Church's elections—a right reckoned to be of the greatest necessity and importance to it—and caused this to be confirmed by Pope Innocent III. This freedom we shall observe ourselves, and desire to be observed in good faith by our heirs forever.

To all free men of our kingdom we have also granted, for us and our heirs forever, all the liberties written out below, to have and to keep for them and their heirs, of us and our heirs:

(2) If any earl, baron, or other person that holds lands directly of the Crown by military service, shall die, and at his death his heir shall be of full age and owe a relief, the heir shall have his inheritance on payment of the ancient scale of relief. That is to say, the heir or heirs of an earl shall pay £100 for the entire earl's barony, the heir or heirs of a knight 100s. at most for the entire knight's fee[1], and any man that owes less shall pay less, in accordance with the ancient usage of fees.

(5) For so long as a guardian has guardianship of such land, he shall maintain the houses, parks, fish preserves, ponds, mills, and everything else pertaining to it, from the revenues of the land itself. When the heir comes of age, he shall restore the whole land to him, stocked with plough teams and such implements of husbandry as the season demands and the revenues from the land can reasonably bear.

(6) Heirs may be given in marriage, but not to someone of lower social standing. Before a marriage takes place, it shall be made known to the heir's next-of-kin.

(7) At her husband's death, a widow may have her marriage portion and inheritance at once and without trouble. She shall pay nothing for her dower, marriage portion, or any inheritance that she and her husband held jointly on the day of his death. She may remain in her husband's house for forty days after his death, and within this period her dower shall be assigned to her.

(8) No widow shall be compelled to marry, so long as she wishes to remain without a husband. But she must give security that she will not marry without royal consent, if she holds her lands of the Crown, or without the consent of whatever other lord she may hold them of.

(12) No scutage[2] or aid may be levied in our kingdom without its general consent, unless it is for the ransom of our person, to make our eldest son a knight, and (once) to marry our eldest daughter. For these purposes only a reasonable aid may be levied. Aids from the city of London are to be treated similarly.

(13) The city of London shall enjoy all its ancient liberties and free customs, both by land and by water. We also will and grant that all other cities, boroughs, towns, and ports shall enjoy all their liberties and free customs.

(14) To obtain the general consent of the realm for the assessment of an aid - except in the three cases specified above—or a scutage, we will cause the archbishops, bishops, abbots, earls, and greater barons to be summoned individually by letter. To those who hold lands directly of us we will cause a general summons to be issued, through the sheriffs and other officials, to come together on a fixed day (of which at least forty days notice shall be given) and at a fixed place. In all letters of summons, the cause of the summons will be stated. When a summons has been issued, the business appointed for the day shall go forward in accordance with the resolution of those present, even if not all those who were summoned have appeared.

(17) Ordinary lawsuits shall not follow the royal court around, but shall be held in a fixed place.

(18) Inquests of novel disseisin, mort d'ancestor, and darrein presentment[3] shall be taken only in their proper county court. We ourselves, or in our absence abroad our chief justice, will send two justices to each county four times a year, and these justices, with four knights of the county elected by the county itself, shall hold the assizes in the county court, on the day and in the place where the court meets.

---

[1] A fee is a fief.

[2] Scutage is a money payment a vassal owned his lord in place of personal military service. The king could then more easily employ and pay mercenaries, hire ships, etc:

[3] the legal actions determining the possession of land that used a twelve-man jury

(20) For a trivial offence, a free man shall be fined only in proportion to the degree of his offence, and for a serious offence correspondingly, but not so heavily as to deprive him of his livelihood. In the same way, a merchant shall be spared his merchandise, and a husbandman the implements of his husbandry, if they fall upon the mercy of a royal court. None of these fines shall be imposed except by the assessment on oath of reputable men of the neighbourhood.

(21) Earls and barons shall be fined only by their peers, and in proportion to the gravity of their offence.

(28) No constable or other royal official shall take corn or other movable goods from any man without immediate payment, unless the seller voluntarily offers postponement of this.

(35) There shall be standard measures of wine, ale, and corn (the London quarter), throughout the kingdom. There shall also be a standard width of dyed cloth, russett, and haberject, namely two ells within the selvedges. Weights are to be standardised similarly.

(38) In future no official shall place a man on trial upon his own unsupported statement, without producing credible witnesses to the truth of it.

(39) No free man shall be seized or imprisoned, or stripped of his rights or possessions, or outlawed or exiled, or deprived of his standing in any other way, nor will we proceed with force against him, or send others to do so, except by the lawful judgement of his equals or by the law of the land.

(40) To no one will we sell, to no one deny or delay right or justice.

(41) All merchants may enter or leave England unharmed and without fear, and may stay or travel within it, by land or water, for purposes of trade, free from all illegal exactions, in accordance with ancient and lawful customs. This, however, does not apply in time of war to merchants from a country that is at war with us. Any such merchants found in our country at the outbreak of war shall be detained without injury to their persons or property, until we or our chief justice have discovered how our own merchants are being treated in the country at war with us. If our own merchants are safe they shall be safe too.

(45) We will appoint as justices, constables, sheriffs, or other officials, only men that know the law of the realm and are minded to keep it well.

(54) No one shall be arrested or imprisoned on the appeal of a woman for the death of any person except her husband.

(60) All these customs and liberties that we have granted shall be observed in our kingdom in so far as concerns our own relations with our subjects. Let all men of our kingdom, whether clergy or laymen, observe them similarly in their relations with their own men.

(61) SINCE WE HAVE GRANTED ALL THESE THINGS for God, for the better ordering of our kingdom, and to allay the discord that has arisen between us and our barons, and since we desire that they shall be enjoyed in their entirety, with lasting strength, for ever, we give and grant to the barons the following security:

The barons shall elect twenty-five of their number to keep, and cause to be observed with all their might, the peace and liberties granted and confirmed to them by this charter. . . .

(63) IT IS ACCORDINGLY OUR WISH AND COMMAND that the English Church shall be free, and that men in our kingdom shall have and keep all these liberties, rights, and concessions, well and peaceably in their fullness and entirety for them and their heirs, of us and our heirs, in all things and all places for ever.

Both we and the barons have sworn that all this shall be observed in good faith and without deceit. Witness. . . .

Given by our hand in the meadow that is called Runnymede, between Windsor and Staines, on the fifteenth day of June in the seventeenth year of our reign (1215).

Questions:
1. What particular grievances does this charter address?
2. How can you tell that this is a document concerned about obligations between lord and vassal?
3. What glimpse do we get of the feudal origin of later English government institutions?
4. What basic rights conceded to disgruntled barons in Magna Carta later became the basis of Anglo-American Bills of Rights?

CHAPTER 10
The Spiritual Sword
Religion and Culture in the Middle Ages
(500–1500)

SECTION 1
Brandishing the Sword

Documents 10.1–10.4

In the following documents, we explore the Church's claim to authority, often in the face of significant resistance between the 1200s and the 1500s. Two questions follow each document, and two questions pertaining to all four documents follow Document 4.

10.1   God Is on My Side: Two Views (The Pope's Bull and the Khan's Reply)

In 1245, nearing the end of the Crusades against the Muslims, the Christians (and Muslims) faced a new threat from further east. The Mongols, united in 1206, went on throughout the century to conquer lands across Asia. Pope Innocent IV sent the following bull (or papal proclamation) with an ambassador, John of Piano Carpini (Chapter 8, Document 12), to the Mongols. The Mongol leader's reply is also reproduced below.

> **Source:** "A Bull of Pope Innocent IV to the Emperor of the Tartars" and Guyuk Khan's Reply to Pope Innocent IV," in *The Mongol Mission. Narratives and Letters of the Franciscan Missionairies (sic) in Mongolia and China in the Thirteenth and Fourteenth Centuries*, trans. A nun of Stanbrook Abbey, ed. C. Dawson, (New York: Sheed and Ward, 1955, pp. 75–76, 85–86); reprinted in *The Crusades: A Documentary Survey*, ed. James A. Brundage, (Milwaukee, WI: The Marquette University Press, 1976, © 1962), pp. 258–60.

A BULL OF POPE INNOCENT IV TO THE EMPEROR OF THE TARTARS

Seeing that not only men but even irrational animals, nay, the very elements which go to make up the world machine, are united by a certain innate law after the manner of the celestial spirits, all of which God the Creator had divided into choirs in the enduring stability of the peaceful order, it is not without cause that we are driven to express in strong terms our amazement that you, as we have heard, have invaded many countries belonging both to Christians and to others and are laying them waste in a horrible desolation, and with a fury still unabated you do not cease from stretching out your destroying hand to more distant lands, but, breaking the bond of natural ties, sparing neither sex nor age, you rage against all indiscriminately with the sword of chastisement. We, therefore, following the example of the King of Peace, and desiring that all men should live united in concord in the fear of God, do admonish, beg, and earnestly beseech all of you that for the future you desist entirely from assaults of this kind and especially from the persecution of Christians, and that after so many and such grievous offenses you conciliate by a fitting penance the wrath of Divine Majesty, which without doubt you have seriously aroused by such provocation; nor should you be emboldened to commit further savagery by the fact that when the sword of your might has raged against other men Almighty God has up to the present allowed various nations to fall before your face; for sometimes he refrains from chastising the proud in this world for the moment, for this reason, that if they neglect to humble themselves of their own accord he may not only no longer put off the punishment of their wickedness in this life but may also take greater vengeance in the world to come. On this account, we have thought fit to send to you our beloved son [John of Plano Carpini] and his companions, the bearers of this letter, men remarkable for their religious spirit, comedy in their virtue, and gifted with a knowledge of Holy Scripture; receive them kindly and treat them with honor out of reverence for God, indeed as if receiving us in their persons, and deal honestly with them in those matters of which they will speak to you on our behalf, and when you have had profitable discussions with them concerning the aforesaid affairs, especially those pertaining to peace, make fully known to us through these same friars what moved you to destroy other nations and what your intentions are for the future, furnishing them with a safe conduct and other necessities on both their outward and return journey, so that they can safely make their way back to our presence when they wish.

Lyons, March 13, 1245

GUYUK KHAN'S REPLY TO POPE INNOCENT IV

We, by the power of the eternal heaven,
Khan of the great Ulus
Our command:

This is a version sent to the great Pope, that he may know and understand in the [Moslim] tongue, what has been written. The petition of the assembly held in the lands of the emperor [for our support] has been heard from your emissaries.

If he reaches [you] with his own report, thou who art the great Pope, together with all the princes, come in person to serve us. At that time I shall make known all the commands of the *Yasa*.

You have also said that supplication and prayer have been offered by you, that I might find a good entry into baptism. This prayer of thine I have not understood. Other words which thou hast sent me: "I am surprised that thou has seized all the lands of the Magyar and the Christians. Tell us what their fault is." These words of thine I have also not understood. The eternal God has slain and annihilated these lands and peoples, because they have neither adhered to Jenghiz Khan, nor the Khagan, nor to the command of God. Like thy words, they also were impudent, they were proud and they slew our messenger-emissaries. How could anybody seize or kill by his own power contrary to the command of God?

Though thou likewise sayest that I should become a trembling Nestorian Christian, worship God, and be an ascetic, how knowest thou whom God absolves, in truth to whom He shows mercy? How dost thou know that such words as thou speakest are with God's sanction? From the rising of the sun to its setting, all the lands have been made subject to me. Who could do this contrary to the command of God?

Now thou should say with a sincere heart: "I will submit and serve you." Thou thyself, at the head of all the princes, come at once to serve and wait upon us! At that time I shall recognize your submission.

If you do not observe God's command, and if you ignore my command, I shall know you as my enemy. Likewise, I shall make you understand. If you do otherwise, God knows what I know.

At the end of Jumada the second in the year 644.

The Seal

We, by the power of the eternal Tengri, universal Khan of the great Mongol Ulus—our command. If this reaches peoples who have made their submission, let them respect and stand in awe of it.

Questions:

1. How does each leader understand and interpret his opponent?
2. What do we learn about each group and the controversies between them from these two documents?

10.2 *Unam Sanctam:* Two Swords

Pope Boniface VIII had tried to limit the fighting within Europe, particularly between the English and the French, by issuing a bull in 1296, that prohibited monarchs from taxing the clergy without papal authorization. King Philip the Fair of France and Edward I of England rejected this bull; they needed those taxes to fund their war efforts. When they retaliated in ways that sharply diminished the papacy's finances, the Pope retreated. After continued dispute, the Pope issued another bull, the Unam Sanctam, excerpted below. Philip responded to this bull by having the Pope captured in order to put him on trial. Instead, he quickly released him, but not before the Pope had suffered both physically and in terms of his pride. When he died a few weeks later, he was replaced by a French pope, Clement V (1305–1314), who soon moved the papacy to Avignon, France.

Source: "The Bull *Unam Sanctam* of Boniface VIII," in *Translations and Reprints from the Original Sources of European History*, vol. III, no. 6, (Philadelphia: The Department of History of the University of Pennsylvania, 1912), pp. 20–23; reprinted in ed. John L. Beatty and Oliver A. Johnson, *Heritage of Western Civilization*, vol. 1, 7th edition, (Englewood Cliffs, NJ: Prentice Hall, 1991), pp. 319–21.

That there is one Holy Catholic and Apostolic Church we are impelled by our faith to believe and to hold—this we do firmly believe and openly confess—and outside of this there is neither salvation or remission of sins, as the bridegroom proclaims in Canticles, "My dove, my undefiled is but one; she is the only one of her mother; she is the choice one of her that bare her." The Church represents one mystic body and of this body Christ is the head; of Christ, indeed. God is the head. In it is one Lord, and one faith, and one baptism. In the time of the flood, there was one ark of Noah, prefiguring the one Church, finished in one cubit, having one Noah as steersman and commander. Outside of this, all things upon the face of the earth were, as we read, destroyed. This Church we venerate and this alone, the Lord saying through his prophets, "Deliver my soul, O God, from the sword; my darling from the power of the dog." He prays thus for his soul, that is for Himself, as head, and also for the body, which He calls one, namely, the Church on account of the unity of the bridegroom, of the faith, of the sacraments, and of the charity of the Church. It is that seamless coat of the Lord, which was not rent, but fell by lot. Therefore, in this one and only Church, there is one body and one head—not two heads as if it were a monster—namely, Christ and Christ's Vicar. Peter and Peter's successor, for the Lord said to Peter himself, "Feed my sheep": *my* sheep, he said, using a general term and not designating these or those sheep, so that we must believe that all the sheep were committed to him. If, then, the Greeks or others, shall say that they were not entrusted to Peter and his successors, they must perforce admit that they are not of Christ's sheep, as the Lord says in John, "there is one fold, and one shepherd."

In this Church and in its power are two swords, to wit, a spiritual and a temporal, and this we are taught by the words of the Gospel, for when the Apostles said, "Behold, here are two swords" (in the Church, namely, since the Apostles were speaking), the Lord did not reply that it was too many, but enough. And surely he who claims that the temporal sword is not in the power of Peter has but ill understood the word of our Lord when he said, "Put up the sword in its scabbard." Both, therefore, the spiritual and material swords, are in the power of the Church, the latter indeed to be used for the Church, the former by the Church, the one by the priest, the other by the hand of kings and soldiers, but by the will and sufferance of the priest. It is fitting, moreover, that one sword should be under the other, and the temporal authority subject to the spiritual power. For when the Apostle said "there is no power but of God and the powers that are of God are ordained," they would not be ordained unless one sword were under the other, and one, as inferior, was brought back by the other to the highest place. For, according to the Holy Dionysius, the law of divinity is to lead the lowest through the intermediate to the highest. Therefore, according to the law of the universe, things are not reduced to order directly, and upon the same footing, but the lowest through the intermediate and the inferior through the superior. It behooves us, therefore, the more freely to confess that the spiritual power excels in dignity and nobility any form whatsoever of earthly power, as spiritual interests exceed the temporal in importance. All this we see fairly from the giving of tithes, from the benediction and sanctification, from the recognition of this power and the control of the same things. For the truth bearing witness, it is for the spiritual power to establish the earthly power and judge it, if it be not good. Thus, in the case of the Church and the power of the Church, the prophecy of Jeremiah is fulfilled: "See, I have this day set thee over the nations and over the kingdoms"—and so forth. Therefore, if the earthly power shall err, it shall be judged by the spiritual power: if the lesser spiritual power err, it shall be judged by the higher. But if the supreme power err, it can be judged by God alone and not by man, the apostles bearing witness saying, the spiritual man judges all things but he himself is judged by no one. Hence this power, although given to man and exercised by man, is not human, but rather divine power, given by the divine lips to Peter, and founded on a rock for Him and his successors in Him whom he confessed, the Lord saying to Peter himself, "Whatsoever thou shalt bind," etc. Whoever, therefore, shall resist this power, ordained by God, resists the ordination of God, unless there should be two beginnings, as the Manichaean imagines. But this we judge to be false and heretical, since, by the testimony of Moses, not in the *beginnings*, but in the *beginning*,

God created the heaven and the earth. We, moreover, proclaim, declare, and pronounce that it is altogether necessary to salvation for every human being to be subject to the Roman Pontiff.

Given at the Lateran the twelfth day before the Kalends of December, in our eighth year, as a perpetual memorial of this matter.

Questions:
1. What are the two swords?
2. What does Boniface claim is the relationship between the two swords? Based on what justification or principles?

10.3 The Expulsion of the Jews from Spain

In 1492, Ferdinand and Isabella, king and queen of Spain, issued a "Charter of Expulsion of the Jews." Later that same year, they also expelled all Muslims. The challenge for the king and queen as they consolidated power in Spain was to create and maintain a single religion among its populace, which they deemed essential to the imposition and maintenance of order. The king and queen feared that many who had converted to Christianity (often by force) were returning to their original faith (apostatized). The issue of the Charter was delayed one month, perhaps because of attempts to have the order rescinded. These efforts failed, and the Jews had only three months to leave their homes. This expulsion was not the first expulsion of Jews from European land, e.g. Philip IV "the Fair" (1285–1314) expelled the Jews and Italian moneylenders as one of many means he used to increase the state's revenues in order to carry on war.

> **Source:** "Charter of Expulsion of the Jews" (1492), trans. Edward Peters, in Edward Peters, "Jewish History and Gentile Memory: The Expulsion of 1492," *Jewish History 9 (1995):* 9–34, at 23–28; reprinted in *Medieval Iberia: Readings from Christian, Muslim, and Jewish Sources*, ed. Olivia Remie Constable, (Philadelphia: University of Pennsylvania Press, 1997), pp. 353–56.

31 March 1492. Granada

[1] Lord Ferdinand and Lady Isabella, by the grace of God king and queen of Castile, León, Aragon, Sicily, Granada, Toledo, Valencia, Galicia, the Balearic Islands, Seville, Sardinia, Córdoba, Corsica, Murcia, Jaén, of the Algarve, Algeciras, Gibraltar, and of the Canary Islands, count and countess of Barcelona and lords of Biscay and Molina, dukes of Athens and Neopatria, counts of Rousillon and Cerdana, marquises of Oristan and of Gociano, to the prince Lord Juan, our very dear and much

loved son, and to the [other] royal children, prelates, dukes, marquises, counts, masters of [military] orders, priors, grandees, knight commanders, governors of castles and fortified places of our kingdoms and lordships, and to councils, magistrates, mayors, constables, district judges, knights, official squires, and all good men of the noble and loyal city of Burgos and other cities, towns, and villages of its bishopric and of other archbishoprics, bishoprics, dioceses of our kingdoms and lordships, and to the residential quarters of the Jews of the said city of Burgos and of all the aforesaid cities, towns, and villages of its bishopric and of the other cities, towns, and villages of our aforementioned kingdoms and lordships, and to all Jews and to all individual Jews of those places, and to barons and women of whatever age they may be, and to all other persons of whatever law, estate, dignity, preeminence, and condition they may be, and to all to whom the matter contained in this charter pertains or may pertain. Salutations and grace.

[2] You know well, or ought to know, that whereas we have been informed that in these our kingdoms there were some wicked Christians who Judaized and apostatized from our holy Catholic faith, the great cause of which was interaction between the Jews and these Christians, in the cortes which we held in the city of Toledo in the past year of one thousand, four hundred and eighty, we ordered the separation of the said Jews in all the cities, towns, and villages of our kingdoms and lordships and [commanded] that they be given Jewish quarters and separated places where they should live, hoping that by their separation the situation would remedy itself. Furthermore, we procured and gave orders that inquisition should be made in our aforementioned kingdoms and lordships, which as you know has for twelve years been made and is being made, and by it many guilty persons have been discovered, as is very well known, and accordingly we are informed by the inquisitors and by other devout persons, ecclesiastical and secular, that great injury has resulted and still results, since the Christians have engaged in and continue to engage in social interaction and communication they have had and continue to have with Jews, who, it seems, seek always and by whatever means and ways they can to subvert and to steal faithful Christians from our holy Catholic faith and to separate them from it, and to draw them to themselves and subvert them to their own wicked belief and conviction, instructing them in the ceremonies and observances of their law, holding meetings at which they read and teach that which people must hold and believe according to their law, achieving that the Christians and their children be circumcised, and giving them books from which they may read their prayers and declaring to them the fasts that they must keep, and joining with them to read and teach them the history of their law, indicating to them the festivals before they occur, advising them of what in them they are to hold and observe, carrying to them and giving to them from their houses unleavened bread and meats ritually slaughtered, instructing them about the things from which they must refrain, as much in eating as in other things in order to observe their law, and persuading them as much as they can to hold and observe the law of Moses, convincing them that there is no other law or truth except for that one. This proved by many statements and confessions, both from these same Jews and from those who have been perverted and enticed by them, which has redounded to the great injury, detriment, and opprobrium of our holy Catholic faith.

[3] Notwithstanding that we were informed of the great part of this before now and we knew that the true remedy for all these injuries and inconveniences was to prohibit all interaction between the said Jews and Christians and banish them from all our kingdoms, we desired to content ourselves by commanding them to leave all cities, towns, and villages of Andalusia where it appears that they have done the greatest injury, believing that that would be sufficient so that those of other cities, towns, and villages of our kingdoms and lordships would cease to do and commit the aforesaid acts. And since we are informed that neither that step nor the passing of sentence [of condemnation] against the said Jews who have been most guilty of the said crimes and delicts against our holy Catholic faith have been sufficient as a complete remedy to obviate and correct so great an opprobrium and offense to the faith and the Christian religion, because every day it is found and appears that the said Jews increase in continuing their evil and wicked purpose wherever they live and congregate, and so that there will not be any place where they further offend our holy faith, and corrupt those whom God has until now most desired to preserve, as well as those who had fallen but amended and returned to Holy Mother Church, which according to the weakness of our humanity and by diabolical astuteness and suggestion that continually wages war against us may easily occur unless the principal cause of it be removed, which is to banish the said Jews from our kingdoms. Because whenever any grave and detestable crime is committed by members of any organization or corporation, it is reasonable that such an organization or corporation should be dissolved and annihilated and that the lesser members as well as the greater and everyone for the others be punished, and that those who perturb the good and honest life of cities and towns and by contagion can injure others should be expelled from those places and even if for lighter causes that may be injurious to the Republic, how much more for those greater and most dangerous and most contagious crimes such as this.

[4] Therefore, we, with the counsel and advice of prelates, great noblemen of our kingdoms, and other persons of learning and wisdom of our council, having taken deliberation about this matter, resolve to order the said Jews and Jewesses of our kingdoms to depart and never to return or come back to them or to any of them. And concerning this we command this our charter to be given, by which we order all Jews and Jewesses of whatever age they may be, who live, reside, and exist in our said kingdoms and lordships, as much those who are natives as those who are not, who by whatever manner or whatever cause have come to live and reside therein, that by the end of the month of July

next of the present year, they depart from all of these our said realms and lordships, along with their sons and daughters, manservants and maidservants, Jewish familiars, those who are great as well as the lesser folk, of whatever age they may be, and they shall not dare to return to those places, nor to reside in them, nor to live in any part of them, neither temporarily on the way to somewhere else nor in any other manner, under pain that if they do not perform and comply with this command and should be found in our said kingdom and lordships and should in any manner live in them, they incur the penalty of death and the confiscation of all their possessions by our Chamber of Finance, incurring these penalties by the act itself, without further trial, sentence, or declaration. And we command and forbid that any person or persons of the said kingdoms, of whatever estate, condition, or dignity that they may be, shall dare to receive, protect, defend, nor hold publicly or secretly any Jews or Jewess beyond the date of the end of July and from henceforth forever, in their lands, houses, or in other parts of any of our said kingdoms and lordships, under pain of losing all their possessions, vassals, fortified places, and other inheritances, and beyond this of losing whatever financial grants they hold from us by our Chamber of Finance.

[5] And so that the said Jews and Jewesses during the stated period of time until the end of the said month of July may be better able to dispose of themselves, and their possessions, and their estates, for the present we take and receive them under our security, protection, and royal safeguard, and we secure to them and to their possessions that for the duration of the said time until the said last day of the said month of July they may travel and be safe, they may enter, sell, trade, and alienate all their movable and rooted possessions and dispose of them freely and at their will, and that during the said time, no one shall harm them, nor injure them, no wrong shall be done to them against justice, in their persons or in their possessions, under the penalty which falls on and is incurred by those who violate the royal safeguard. And we likewise give license and faculty to those said Jews and Jewesses that they be able to export their goods and estates out of these our said kingdoms and lordships by sea or land as long as they do not export gold or silver or coined money or other things prohibited by the laws of our kingdoms, excepting merchandise and things that are not prohibited.

[6] And we command all councils, justices, magistrates, knights, squires, officials, and all good men of the said city of Burgos and of the other cities, towns, and villages of our said kingdoms and lordships and all our new vassals, subjects, and natives that they preserve and comply with and cause to be preserved and compiled with this our charter and all that is contained in it, and to give and to cause to be given all assistance and favor in its application under penalty of [being at] our mercy and the confiscation of all their possessions and offices by our Chamber of Finance. And because this must be brought to the notice of all, so that no one may pretend ignorance, we command that this our charter be posted in the customary plazas and places of the said city and of the principal cities, towns, and villages of its bishopric as an announcement and as a public document. And no one shall do any damage to it in any manner under penalty of being at our mercy and the deprivation of their offices and the confiscation of their possessions, which will happen to each one who might do this. Moreover, we command the [man] who shows them this our charter that he summon [those who act against the charter] to appear before us at our court wherever we may be, on the day that they are summoned during the fifteen days following the crime under the said penalty, under which we command whichever public scribe who would be called for the purpose of reading this our charter that the signed charter with its seal should be shown to you all so that we may know that our command is carried out.

[7] Given in our city of Granada, the XXXI day of the month of March, the year of the birth of our lord Jesus Christ one thousand four hundred and ninety-two years. I, the king, I, the queen, I, Juan de Coloma, secretary of the king and queen our lords, have caused this to be written at their command. Registered by Cabrera, Almacan chancellor.

Questions:

1. What arguments are used to justify the expulsions?
2. What basis did they claim for these arguments?

10.4 Penitentials

Penitentials were issued to help priests learn and understand their duties as confessors. Confession with penance had been imposed on parishioners at least once a year in the Fourth Lateran Council in 1215. The following penitential was issued by Cardinal St. Charles Borromeo (1538–84), who pushed for Church reform and discipline during the Counter-Reformation. The excerpt includes the introduction which outlines the purpose of the penitential and a selection of penances required for various sins listed under each commandment.

Source: "The Milan Penitential of Cardinal Borromeo (ca. 1565–82)"; reprinted in *Medieval Handbooks of Penance: A Translation of the principal libri poenitentiales* and selections from related documents, ed. John T. McNeill and Helena M. Gamer, (New York: Octagon Books, Inc., 1965) pp. 364–68.

Penitential Canons, Knowledge of Which Is Necessary for Parish Priests and Confessors, Set Forth according to the Plan and Order of the Decalog

The fathers taught how very necessary for priests who are engaged in hearing the confessions of penitents is a knowledge of the penitential canons. And indeed if all things that pertain to the method of penance are to be administered not only with prudence and piety but also with justice, assuredly the pattern of this ought to be taken from the penitential canons. For there are, so to speak, two rules by which priests and confessors are so directed as both to discern the gravity of an offense committed and in relation to this to impose a true penance: that they severally accurately investigate both the things that pertain to the greatness of the sin and those that pertain to the status, condition, and age of the penitent and the inmost sorrow of the contrite heart—and then, that they temper the penance with their own justice and prudence. And indeed the method explained by the fathers so disposed these things and everything else that is complicated of this necessary knowledge, that, as was said above in its proper place, the penitential canons set forth according to the plan of the Decalog are held over to the last part of the book, whence some knowledge of them can be drawn by the confessor-priests themselves. . . .

The chief penitential canons collected according to the order of the Decalog from various councils and penitentiary books in the Instruction of St. Charles B[orromeo]

On the First Commandment of the Decalog

1. He who falls away from the faith shall do penance for ten years.

2. He who observes auguries and divinations [and] he who makes diabolical incantations, seven years. One who beholds things to come in an astrolabe, two years.

3. If anyone makes knots or enchantments, two years.

4. He who consults magicians, five years.

On the Second Commandment

1. Whoever knowingly commits perjury, shall do penance for forty days on bread and water, and seven succeeding years; and he shall never be without penance. And he shall never be accepted as a witness; and after these things he shall take communion.

2. He who commits perjury in a church, ten years.

3. If anyone publicly blasphemes God or the Blessed Virgin or any saint, he shall stand in the open in front of the doors of the church on seven Sundays, while the solemnities of the masses are performed, and on the last of these days, without robe and shoes, with a cord tied about his neck; and on the seven preceding Fridays he shall fast on bread and water; and he shall then by no means enter the church. Moreover, on each of these seven Sundays he shall feed three or two or one, if he is able. Otherwise he shall do another penance; if he refuses, he shall be forbidden to enter the church; in [case of] his death he shall be denied ecclesiastical burial.

4. He who violates a simple vow shall do penance for three years.

On the Third Commandment

1. He who does any servile work on the Lord's day or on a feast day shall do penance for seven days on bread and water.

2. If anyone violates fasts set by Holy Church, he shall do penance for forty days on bread and water.

3. He who violates the fast in Lent shall do a seven-day penance for one day.

4. He who without unavoidable necessity eats flesh in Lent shall not take communion at Easter and shall thereafter abstain from flesh.

On the Fourth Commandment

1. He who reviles his parents shall be a penitent for forty days on bread and water.

2. He who does an injury to his parents, three years.

3. He who beats [them], seven years.

4. If anyone rises up against his bishop, his pastor and father, he shall do penance in a monastery all the days of his life.

5. If anyone despises or derides the command of his bishop, or of the bishop's servants, or of his parish priest, he shall do penance for forty days on bread and water.

On the Fifth Commandment

1. He who kills a presbyter shall do penance for twelve years.

2. If anyone kills his mother, father, or sister, he shall not take the Lord's body throughout his whole life, except at his departure; he shall abstain from flesh and wine, while he lives; he shall fast on Monday, Wednesday, and Friday.

3. If anyone kills a man he shall always be at the door of the church, and at death he shall receive communion. [Sections 4–10 omitted.]

On the Sixth Commandment

[Sections 1–6 omitted.]

7. If any woman paints herself with ceruse or other pigment in order to please men, she shall do penance for three years.

8. If a priest is intimate with his own spiritual daughter, that is, one whom he has baptized or who has confessed to him, he ought to do penance for twelve years; and if the offense is publicly known, he ought to be deposed and do penance for twelve years on pilgrimage, and thereafter enter a monastery to remain there throughout his life. For adultery penances of seven, and of ten, years, are imposed; for unchaste kissing or embracing a penance of thirty days is commanded.

On the Seventh Commandment

1. If anyone commits a theft of a thing of small value he shall do penance for a year.

2. He who steals anything from the furniture of a church or from the treasury, or ecclesiastical property, or

offerings made to the church shall be a penitent for seven years.

3. He who retains to himself his tithe or neglects to pay it, shall restore fourfold and do penance for twenty days on bread and water.

4. He who takes usury commits robbery; he shall do penance for three years on bread and water.

On the Eighth Commandment

1. He who conspires in falsification of evidence shall be a penitent for five years.

2. A forger shall do penance on bread and water as long as he lives.

3. If anyone slanders his neighbor, he shall be a penitent for seven days on bread and water.

On the Ninth and Tenth Commandments

1. He who basely covets another's goods and is avaricious shall be a penitent for three years.

2. If anyone desires to commit fornication, if a bishop, he shall be a penitent for seven years; if a presbyter, five; if a deacon or monk three; if a cleric or layman, two years.

Questions:
1. What role did the priest have in applying the penitentials?
2. With what kind of sins were the penitentials concerned, and which were considered the worst?

Questions for Documents 10.1–10.4:
1. What threats to their authority did the leaders of the Church (or state, in the case of Spain) face, and what means did they use to confront these threats? What were the effects of those actions?
2. Thinking broadly: given that each of these statements of authority was asserted at points of threat to the Church, what can be learned about the Church, power, and resistance? Can any analogies be made to more recent history or to the present day?

SECTION 2
Victims of the Sword

10.5 Letters from Heloise

Peter Abelard (1079–1142), a brilliant theologian and philosopher, was the most popular and controversial teacher of his era. While teaching in Paris, he lodged with Fulbert, who engaged him to tutor his intelligent eighteen-year-old niece, Heloise. Their relationship turned passionate and Heloise became pregnant.[1] Enraged, Fulbert not only forced the couple to marry over Heloise's objections, but hired thugs to castrate Abelard. Unwillingly, Heloise entered a convent while Abelard took monastic vows at St. Denis. He eventually became an abbot, and continued his writings in theology, managing in his egotistical way to antagonize both St. Bernard, the foremost monastic leader of his century, as well as the pope. Some of his writings were burned as heretical. Heloise, meanwhile, became abbess of a convent that Abelard founded. This is the first of a series of letters between Heloise and Abelard in which she discusses her experiences and motivations.

Source: *The Letters of Abelard and Heloise,* trans. Betty Radice, (New York: Penguin Books, 1974), pp. 109–18.

To her master, or rather her father, husband, or rather brother; his handmaid, or rather his daughter, wife, or rather sister; to Abelard, Heloise.

Not long ago, my beloved, by chance someone brought me the letter of consolation you had sent to a friend. I saw at once from the superscription that it was yours, and was all the more eager to read it since the writer is so dear to my heart. I hoped for renewal of strength, at least from the writer's words which would picture for me the reality I have lost. But nearly every line of this letter was filled, I remember, with gall and wormwood, as it told the pitiful story of our entry into religion and the cross of unending suffering which you, my only love, continue to bear.

In that letter you did indeed carry out the promise you made your friend at the beginning, that he would think his own troubles insignificant or nothing, in comparison with your own. First you revealed the persecution you suffered from your teachers, then the supreme treachery of the mutilation of your person, and then described the abominable jealousy and violent attacks of your fellow-students, Alberic of Rheims and Lotulf of Lombardy. You did not gloss over what at their instigation was done to your distinguished theological work or what amounted to a prison sentence passed on yourself. Then you went on to the plotting

against you by your abbot and false brethren, the serious slanders from those two pseudo-apostles, spread against you by the same rivals, and the scandal stirred up among many people because you had acted contrary to custom in naming your oratory after the Paraclete. You went on to the incessant, intolerable persecutions which you still endure at the hands of that cruel tyrant and the evil monks you call your sons, and so brought your sad story to an end.

No one, I think, could read or hear it dry-eyed; my own sorrows are renewed by the detail in which you have told it, and redoubled because you say your perils are still increasing. All of us here are driven to despair of your life, and every day we await in fear and trembling the final word of your death. And so in the name of Christ, who is still giving you some protection for his service, we beseech you to write as often as you think fit to us who are his handmaids and yours, with news of the perils in which you are still storm-tossed. We are all that are left you, so at least you should let us share your sorrow or your joy.

It is always some consolation in sorrow to feel that it is shared, and any burden laid on several is carried more lightly or removed. And if this storm has quietened down for a while, you must be all the more prompt to send us a letter which will be the more gladly received. But whatever you write about will bring us no small relief in the mere proof that you have us in mind. Letters from absent friends are welcome indeed, as Seneca himself shows us by his own example when he writes these words in a passage of a letter to his friend Lucilius:

> Thank you for writing to me often, the one way in which you can make your presence felt, for I never have a letter from you without the immediate feeling that we are together. If pictures of absent friends give us pleasure, renewing our memories and relieving the pain of separation even if they cheat us with empty comfort, how much more welcome is a letter which comes to us in the very handwriting of an absent friend.

Thank God that here at least is a way of restoring your presence to us which no malice can prevent, nor any obstacle hinder; then do not, I beseech you, allow any negligence to hold you back.

. . . For you after God are the sole founder of this place, the sole builder of this oratory, the sole creator of this community. You have built nothing here upon another man's foundation. Everything here is your own creation. This was a wilderness open to wild beasts and brigands, a place which had known no home nor habitation of men. In the very lairs of wild beasts and lurking-places of robbers, where the name of God was never heard, you built a sanc-

---

[1] Their child, a boy, was raised by Peter Abelard's sister.

tuary to God and dedicated a shrine in the name of the Holy Spirit. To build it you drew nothing from the riches of kings and princes, though their wealth was great and could have been yours for the asking: whatever was done, the credit was to be yours alone. Clerks and scholars came flocking here, eager for your teaching, and ministered to all your needs; and even those who had lived on the benefices of the Church and knew only how to receive offerings, not to make them, whose hands were held out to take but not to give, became pressing in their lavish offers of assistance.

And so it is yours, truly your own, this new plantation for God's purpose, but it is sown with plants which are still very tender and need watering if they are to thrive. Through its feminine nature this plantation would be weak and frail even if it were not new; and so it needs a more careful and regular cultivation. . . .

You know, beloved, as the whole world knows, how much I have lost in you, how at one wretched stroke of fortune that supreme act of flagrant treachery robbed me of my very self in robbing me of you; and how my sorrow for my loss is nothing compared with what I feel for the manner in which I lost you. Surely the greater the cause for grief the greater the need for the help of consolation, and this no one can bring but you; you are the sole cause of my sorrow, and you alone can grant me the grace of consolation. You alone have the power to make me sad, to bring me happiness or comfort; you alone have so great a debate to repay me, particularly now when I have carried out all your orders so implicitly that when I was powerless to oppose you in anything, I found strength at your command to destroy myself. I did more, strange to say—my love rose to such heights of madness that it robbed itself of what it most desired beyond hope of recovery, when immediately at your bidding I changed my clothing along with my mind, in order to prove you the sole possessor of my body and my will alike. God knows I never sought anything in you except yourself; I wanted simply you, nothing of yours. I looked for no marriage-bond, no marriage portion, and it was not my own pleasures and wishes I sought to gratify, as you well know, but yours. The name of wife may seem more sacred or more binding, but sweeter for me will always be the word mistress, or, if you will permit me, that of concubine or whore. I believed that the more I humbled myself on your account, the more gratitude I should win from you, and also the less damage I should do to the brightness of your reputation.

You yourself on your own account did not altogether forget this in the letter of consolation I have spoken of which you wrote to a friend; there you thought fit to set out some of the reasons I gave in trying to dissuade you from binding us together in an ill-starred marriage. But you kept silent about most of my arguments for preferring love to wedlock and freedom to chains. God is my witness that if Augustus, Emperor of the whole world, thought fit to honour me with marriage and conferred all the earth on me to possess for ever, it would be dearer and more honourable to me to be called not his Empress but your whore.

For a man's worth does not rest on his wealth or power; these depend on fortune, but worth on his merits. And a woman should realize that if she marries a rich man more readily than a poor one, and desires her husband more for his possessions than for himself, she is offering herself for sale. Certainly any woman who comes to marry through desires of this kind deserves wages, not gratitude, for clearly her mind is on the man's property, not himself, and she would be ready to prostitute herself to a richer man, if she could. . . .

. . . What king or philosopher could match your fame? What district, town or village did not long to see you? When you appeared in public, who did not hurry to catch a glimpse of you, or crane his neck and strain his eyes to follow your departure? Every wife, every young girl desired you in absence and was on fire in your presence; queens and great ladies envied me my joys and my bed.

You had besides, I admit, two special gifts whereby to win at once the heart of any woman—your gifts for composing verse and song, in which we know other philosophers have rarely been successful. This was for you no more than a diversion, a recreation from the labours of your philosophic work, but you left many love-songs and verses which won wide popularity for the charm of their words and tunes and kept your name continually on everyone's lips. The beauty of the airs ensured that even the unlettered did not forget you; more than anything this made women sigh for love of you. And as most of these songs told of our love, they soon made me widely known and roused the envy of many women against me. For your manhood was adorned by every grace of mind and body, and among the women who envied me then, could there be one now who does not feel compelled by my misfortune to sympathize with my loss of such joys? . . .

Tell me one thing, if you can. Why, after our entry into religion, which was your decision alone, have I been so neglected and forgotten by you that I have neither a word from you when you are here to give me strength nor the consolation of a letter in absence? Tell me, I say, if you can—or I will tell you what I think and indeed the world suspects. It was desire, not affection which bound you to me, the flame of lust rather than love. So when the end came to what you desired, any show of feeling you used to make went with it. This is not merely my own opinion, beloved, it is everyone's. There is nothing personal or private about it; it is the general view which is widely held. I only wish that it *were* mine alone, and that the love you professed could find someone to defend it and so comfort me in my grief for a while. I wish I could think of some explanation which would excuse you and somehow cover up the way you hold me cheap.

I beg you then to listen to what I ask—you will see that it is a small favour which you can easily grant. While I am denied your presence, give me at least through your words—of which you have enough and to spare—some sweet semblance of yourself. It is no use my hoping for generosity in deeds if you are grudging in words. Up to now I had thought I deserved much of you, seeing that I carried out everything for your sake and continue up to the present moment in complete obedience to you. It was not any sense of vocation which brought me as a young girl to accept the austerities of the cloister, but your bidding alone, and if I deserve no gratitude from you, you may judge for yourself how my labours are in vain. I can expect no reward for this from God, for it is certain that I have done nothing as yet for love of him. When you hurried towards God I followed you, indeed, I went first to take the veil—perhaps you were thinking how Lot's wife turned back when you made me put on the religious habit and take my vows before you gave yourself to God. Your lack of trust in me over this one thing, I confess, overwhelmed me with grief and shame. I would have had no hesitation, God knows, in following you or going ahead at your bidding to the flames of Hell.

Remember, I implore you, what I have done, and think how much you owe me. While I enjoyed with you the pleasures of the flesh, many were uncertain whether I was prompted by love or lust; but now the end is proof of the beginning. I have finally denied myself every pleasure in obedience to your will, kept nothing for myself except to prove that now, even more, I am yours. Consider then your injustice, if when I deserve more you give me less, or rather, nothing at all, especially when it is a small thing I ask of you and one you could so easily grant. And so, in the name of God to whom you have dedicated yourself, I beg you to restore your presence to me in the way you can—by writing me some word of comfort, so that in this at least I may find increased strength and readiness to serve God. When in the past you sought me out for sinful pleasures your letters came to me thick and fast, and your many songs put your Heloise on everyone's lips, so that every street and house echoed with my name. Is it not far better now to summon me to God than it was then to satisfy our lust? I beg you, think what you owe me, give ear to my pleas, and I will finish a long letter with a brief ending: farewell, my only love.

Questions:

1. Why does Heloise attempt to reestablish contact with Abelard?
2. What attracted Heloise to Abelard?
3. How does Heloise feel about marriage in general and to Abelard in particular?
4. In what way is Heloise extraordinary for her age? In what way is she typical?

10.6   Massacre of the Jews

By the end of the eleventh century, communities of Jews were living in the thriving European towns despite being surrounded by a sometimes hostile Christian population. The First Crusade (1096), however, unleashed a wave of religious fanaticism that resulted in the massacre of thousands of Jews and the destruction of their homes and communities.

Source: *Sources of the Western Tradition: Volume I: From Ancient Times to the Enlightenment*, ed. Marvin Perry, Joseph R. Peden, and Theodore H. Von Laue, (Boston: Houghton Muffin Co., 1995), pp. 251.

At the beginning of summer in the same year in which Peter [the Hermit] and Gottschalk,[1] after collecting an army, had set out, there assembled in like fashion a large and innumerable host of Christians from diverse kingdoms and lands; namely, from the realms of France, England, Flanders, and Lorraine. . . . I know not whether by a judgment of the Lord, or by some error of mind, they rose in a spirit of cruelty against the Jewish people scattered throughout these cities and slaughtered them without mercy, especially in the Kingdom of Lorraine,[2] asserting it to be the beginning of their expedition and their duty against the enemies of the Christian faith. This slaughter of Jews was done first by citizens of Cologne.[3] These suddenly fell upon a small band of Jews and severely wounded and killed many; they destroyed the houses and synagogues of the Jews and divided among themselves a very large amount of money. When the Jews saw this cruelty, about two hundred in the silence of the night began flight by boat to Neuss. The pilgrims and crusaders discovered them, and after taking away all their possessions, inflicted on them similar slaughter, leaving not even one alive.

Not long after this, they started upon their journey, as they had vowed, and arrived in a great multitude at the city of Mainz. There Count Emico, a nobleman, a very might man in this region, was awaiting, with a large band of Teutons [German soldiers], the arrival of the pilgrims who were coming thither from diverse lands by the King's highway.

The Jews of this city, knowing of the slaughter of their brethren, and that they themselves could not escape the hands of so many, fled in hope of safety to Bishop Rothard. They put an infinite treasure in his guard and trust, having much faith in his protection, because he was Bishop of the city. Then that excellent Bishop of the city cautiously set aside the incredible amount of money received from them. He placed the Jews in the very spacious hall of his own house, away from the sight of Count Emico and his follow-

---

[1] A brilliant propagandist, Peter the Hermit raised a large army of poor and sparsely armed Frenchmen, who marched to Cologne to begin a Crusade to the Holy Land. Most of them were killed by Turkish forces after crossing into Asia Minor. Gottschalk was a German priest who gathered a band of undisciplined soldiers to join the First Crusade. His forces were killed by Hungarians defending their families and property from these Crusaders.

[2] Lorraine, a duchy in the western part of the Holy Roman Empire, is now part of France.

[3] Cologne (Köln), founded by the Romans in the first century A.D., was the largest city in the Rhine Valley, a center of commerce, industry, and learning. Its politically powerful archbishop was a prince of the Holy Roman Empire.

ers, that they might remain safe and sound in a very secure and strong place.

But Emico and the rest of his band held a council and, after sunrise, attacked the Jews in the hall with arrows and lances. Breaking the bolts and doors, they killed the Jews, about seven hundred in number, who in vain resisted the force and attack of so many thousands. They killed the women, also, and with their swords pierced tender children of whatever age and sex. The Jews, seeing that their Christian enemies were attacking them and their children, and that they were sparing no age, likewise fell upon one another, brother, children, wives, and sisters, and thus they perished at each other's hands. Horrible to say, mothers cut the throats of nursing children with knives and stabbed others, preferring them to perish thus by their own hands rather than to be killed by the weapons of the uncircumcised.

From this cruel slaughter of the Jews a few escaped; and a few because of fear, rather than because of love of the Christian faith, were baptized. With very great spoils taken from these people, Count Emico, Clarebold, Thomas, and all that intolerable company of men and women then continued on their way to Jerusalem.

Questions:
1. Who were the attackers of the Jews and what was their rationale for doing so?
2. What was the role of Church leaders in these events?
3. How did the Jews react to these attacks?

10.7 A Heretic Sect: The Albigensians

Often we know about heretical beliefs only through the writings of opponents or inquisitors. Such is the case of the Albigensians, a somewhat organized sect that was popular in southern France with beliefs similar to the Manichees of St. Augustine's. Not only did Pope Innocent III declare a crusade against them and the nobles who protected them, but he also instituted the papal inquisition to root out their unorthodox beliefs.

Source: Samuel R. Maitland, *Facts and Documents illustrative of the History, Doctrine and Rites of the Ancient Albigenses and Waldenses*, (London: Rivington, 1832), pp. 392–94.

First it is to be known that the heretics held that there are two Creators; viz. one of invisible things, whom they called the benevolent God, and another of visible things, whom they named the malevolent God. The New Testament they attributed to the benevolent God; but the Old Testament to the malevolent God, and rejected it altogether, except certain authorities which are inserted in the New Testament from the Old; which, out of reverence to the New Testament, they

esteemed worthy of reception. They charged the author of the Old Testament with falsehood, because the Creator said, "In the day that ye eat of the tree of the knowledge of good and evil ye shall die;" nor (as they say) after eating did they die; when, in fact, after eating the forbidden fruit they were subjected to the misery of death. They also call him a homicide, as well because he burned up Sodom and Gomorrah, and destroyed the world by the waters of the deluge, as because he overwhelmed Pharaoh, and the Egyptians, in the sea. They affirmed also, that all the fathers of the Old Testament were damned; that John the Baptist was one of the greater demons. They said also, in their secret doctrine, . . . that that Christ who was born in the visible, and terrestrial Bethlehem, and crucified in Jerusalem, was a bad man, and that Mary Magdalene was his concubine; and that she was the woman taken in adultery, of whom we read in the gospel. For the good Christ, as they said, never ate, nor drank, nor took upon him true flesh, nor ever was in this world, except spiritually in the body of Paul. . . .

They said that almost all the Church of Rome was a den of thieves; and that it was the harlot of which we read in the Apocalypse. They so far annulled the sacraments of the Church, as publicly to teach that the water of holy Baptism was just the same as river water, and that the Host of the most holy body of Christ did not differ from common bread; instilling into the ears of the simple this blasphemy, that the body of Christ, even though it had been as great as the Alps, would have been long ago consumed, and annihilated by those who had eaten of it. Confirmation and Confession, they considered as altogether vain and frivolous. They preached that Holy Matrimony was [false and spurious], and that none could be saved in it, if they should beget children. Denying also the Resurrection of the flesh, they invented some unheard of notions, saying, that our souls are those of angelic spirits who, being cast down from heaven by the apostacy of pride, left their glorified bodies in the air; and that these souls themselves, after successively inhabiting seven terrene bodies, of one sort or another, having at length fulfilled their penance, return to those deserted bodies.

It is also to be known that some among the heretics were called "perfect" or "good men;" others "believers" of the heretics. Those who were called perfect, wore a black dress, falsely pretended to chastity, abhorred the eating of flesh, eggs and cheese, wished to appear not liars, when they were continually telling lies, chiefly respecting God. They said also that they ought not on any account to swear.

Those were called "believers" of the heretics, who lived after the manner of the world, and who, though they did not attain so far as to imitate the life of the perfect, nevertheless hoped to be saved in their faith; and though they differed as to their mode of life, they were one with them in belief and unbelief. Those who were called believers of the heretics were given to usury, rapine, homicide, lust, perjury and every vice; and they, in fact, sinned with more security, and less restraint, because they believed that without restitution, without confession and penance, they should be saved, if only, when on the point of death, they could say a *Pater noster*, and received imposition of hands from their [Deacons and Bishops]. . . . [whereupon they] immediately took wing to heaven.

Questions:
1. What doctrines did the author ascribe to the Albigensians?
2. What was their attitude toward the Catholic Church?
3. Why do you think that they believed that having children was wrong?

10.8   Individual Heretics: Saints and Witches

In the later middle ages (from the fourteenth century on) many changes rocked society, including the devastating mortality of the Black Death, rural migration to cities, disruption in the Church, new technology, discoveries, and ideas. Increasing uncertainty placed marginal people at further risk and made everyone more suspicious of others who threatened the accepted order and authority. The following two accounts reveal how some people were condemned in Florence for such dubious behavior or beliefs.

Source: *The Society of Renaissance Florence: A Documentary Study*, ed.Gene Brucker, (Harper and Row, Inc., 1972), pp. 253–57, 270–73.

THE EXECUTION OF FRA MICHELE OF CALCI, 1389

[April 30, 1389] This is the condemnation of Giovanni, called Fra Michele di Berti of Calci, in the territory of Pisa, a man of low condition, evil conversation, life, and reputation, and a heretic against the Catholic faith, against whom we have proceeded by means of inquisition. . . . It has come to our attention that this Giovanni . . . with the spirit and intent of being a heretic, had relations with the Fraticelli, called the Little Brothers of Poverty, heretics and schismatics and denounced by the Holy Roman Church, and that he joined that depraved sect in a place called the grotto of the *Dieci Yoffensi*, in which place they congregated and stayed. . . . With the intention of proclaiming this heresy and of contaminating faithful Christians, the accused came to the city of Florence and in public places he did maintain, affirm, and preach the heretical teachings hereby stated:

Item, that Christ, our Redeemer, possessed no property either individually or in common but divested himself of all things, as the Holy Scripture testifies.

Item, that Christ and his Apostles, according to the Scriptures, denounced the taking, holding, or exchanging of goods as against divine law.

Item, that Pope John XXII [d. 1334] of blessed memory was a heretic and lost all power and ecclesiastical authority as pope and as a heretic had no authority to appoint bishops or prelates, and that all prelates so appointed by him do not legally hold their office and that they sin by pretending to do so.

Item, that all cardinals, prelates, and clerics who accepted the teaching of John XXII on apostolic poverty, and who should resist these teachings and who do not resist, are also heretics and have lost all authority as priests of Christ.

Item, that this Giovanni, a heretic and schismatic, not content with all this mentioned above, but desiring also the damnation of others, in the months of March and April sought to persuade many men and women of the city of Florence, to induce them to believe inland to enter the above-mentioned sect of the Fraticelli. He told them about the above-mentioned sect; with false words and with erroneous reasons he claimed that this sect was the true religion and the true observance of the rule and life of the blessed Francis; and that all those who observe this doctrine and life are in a state of grace, and that all other friars and priests are heretics and schismatics and are damned.

And since this Giovanni appeared before us and our court and confessed to the above-mentioned charges . . . and refused to recant or to reject these teachings, we hereby decree that unless this Giovanni gives up his false teaching and beliefs, that as an example to others, he be taken to the place of justice and there he is to be burned with fire and the flames of fire so that he shall die and his spirit be separated from his body.

Now everything which I here describe, I who write both saw or heard. Fra Michele, having come into the courtyard, waited attentively to hear the condemnation. And the vicar [general of the bishop] spoke: "The bishop and the Inquisitor have sent me here to tell you that if you wish to return to the Holy Church and renounce your errors, then do so, in order that the people may see that the church is merciful." And Fra Michele replied, "I believe in the poor crucified Christ, and I believe that Christ, showing the way to perfection, possessed nothing. . . ." Having read his confession, the judge turned his back upon Fra Michele . . . and the guards seized him and with great force pushed him outside of the gate of the judge's palace. He remained there alone, surrounded by scoundrels, appearing in truth as one of the martyrs. And there was such a great crowd that one could scarcely see. And the throng increased in size, shouting: "You don't want to die!" And Fra Michele replied, "I will die for Christ." And the crowd answered: "Oh! You aren't dying for Christ! You don't believe in God!" And Fra Michele replied: "I believe in God, in the Virgin Mary, and in the Holy Church!" And someone said to him, "You wretch! The devil is pushing you from behind!"

And when he arrived in the district of the Proconsolo, there was a great press of people who came to watch. And one of the faithful cried: "Fra Michele! Pray to God for us. . . ." When he arrived at S. Giovanni, they shouted to him: "Repent, repent! You don't want to die." And he said:

"I have repented of my sins. . . ." And at the Mercato Vecchio, they shouted even louder: "Save yourself! Save yourself!" And he replied, "Save yourselves from damnation." And at the Mercato Nuovo, the shouts grew louder:

"Repent, repent!" And he replied, "Repent of your sins; repent of your usury and your false merchandising. . . .And at the Piazza del Grano, there were many women in the windows of the houses who cried to him: "Repent, repent!" And he replied, "Repent of your sins, your usury, your gambling, your fornication. . . ." When he arrived at S. Croce, near the gate of the friars, the image of St. Francis was shown to him and he raised his eyes to heaven and said, "St. Francis, my father, pray to Christ for me."

And then moving toward the gate of Justice, the crowd cried in unison: "Recant, recant! You don't want to die!" And he replied, "Christ died for us." And some said to him, mocking: "Ho, you're not Christ and you don't have to die for us." And he replied, "I wish to die for Him." And then another shouted, "Ho, you're not among pagans," and he answered, "I wish to die for the truth. . . .

And when he arrived at the gate near the place of execution, one of the faithful began to cry, "Remain firm, martyr of Christ, for soon you will receive the crown. . . ." And arriving at the place of execution, there was a great turmoil and the crowd urged him to repent and save himself and he refused. . . . And the guards pushed the crowd back and formed a circle of horsemen around the pyre so that no one could enter. I myself did not enter but climbed upon the river bank to see, but I was unable to hear. . . . And he was bound to the stake . . . and the crowd begged him to recant, except one of the faithful, who comforted him. And they set fire to the wood . . . and Fra Michele began to recite the Te Deum. . . . And when he had said, "In your hands, O Lord, I commend my spirit," the fire burned the cords which bound him and he fell dead . . . to the earth.

And many of the onlookers said, "He seems to be a saint." Even his enemies whispered it . . . and then they slowly began to return to their homes. They talked about Michele and the majority said that he was wrong and that no one should speak such evil of the priests. And some said, "He is a martyr," and others said, "He is a saint," and still others denied it. And there was a greater tumult and disturbance in Florence than there had ever been.

CONDEMNATION OF A WITCH (JUNE 7, 1427)

. . .We condemn . . . Giovanna called Caterina, daughter of Francesco called El Toso, a resident of the parish of S. Ambrogio of Florence . . . who is a magician, witch, and sorceress, and a practitioner of the black arts.

It happened that Giovanni Ceresani of the parish of S. Jacopo tra le Fosse was passing by her door and stared

at her fixedly. She thought that she would draw the chaste spirit of Giovanni to her for carnal purposes by means of the black arts. . . . She went to the shop of Monna Gilia, the druggist, and purchased from her a small amount of lead . . . and then she took a bowl and placed the lead in it and put it on the fire so that the lead would melt. With this melted lead she made a small chain and spoke certain words which have significance for this magical and diabolical art (and which, lest the people learn about them, shall not be recorded). . . . All this which was done and spoken against Giovanni's safety by Giovanna was so powerful that his chaste spirit was deflected to lust after her, so that willynilly he went several times to her house and there he fulfilled her perfidious desire.

With the desire of doing further harm to Giovanni's health through the black arts, and so persisting in what she had begun, she acquired a little gold, frankincense, and myrrh, and then took a little bowl with some glowing charcoal inside, and having prepared these ingredients and having lit the candle which she held in her left hand, she genuflected before the image and placed the bowl at the foot of the figure. Calling out the name of Giovanni, she threw the gold, frankincense, and myrrh upon the charcoal. And when the smoke from the charcoal covered the whole image, Giovanna spoke certain words, the tenor of which is vile and detestable, and which should be buried in silence lest the people be given information for committing sin.

When she realized that what she had done against Giovanni's health was not sufficient to satisfy completely her insatiable lust, she learned from a certain priest that . . . if water from the skulls of dead men was distilled and given with a little wine to any man, that it was a most valid test. . . . Night and day, that woman thought of nothing but how she could give that water to Giovanni to drink. . . . She visited the priest and bought from him a small amount of that water . . . and that accursed woman gave Giovanni that water mixed with wine to drink. After he drank it, Giovanni could think of nothing but satisfying his lust with Giovanna. And his health has been somewhat damaged, in the opinion of good and worthy [men].

In the time when Giovanna was menstruating, she took a little of her menses, that quantity which is required by the diabolical ceremonies, and placed it in a small beaker, and then poured it into another flask filled with wine and gave it to Giovanni to drink. And on account of this and the other things described above, Giovanni no longer has time for his affairs as he did in the past, and he has left his home and his wife and son . . . and does only what pleases Giovanna. . . .

On several occasions, Giovanna had intercourse with a certain Jacopo di Andrea, a doublet-maker, of the parish of S. Niccolo. Desiring to possess his chaste spirit totally for her lust and against his health, Giovanna . . . thought to give Jacopo some of her menses, since she knew that it was very efficacious. . . . Having observed several diabolical rites, she took the beaker with the menses . . . and gave it to Jacopo to drink. After he had drunk, she uttered these words among others: "I will catch you in my net if you don't flee." . . . When they were engaged in the act of intercourse, she placed her hand on her private parts . . . and after uttering certain diabolical words, she put a finger on Jacopo's lips. . . . Thereafter, in the opinion of everyone, Jacopo's health deteriorated and he was forced by necessity to obey her in everything.

Several years ago, Giovanna was the concubine of Niccolo di Ser Casciotto of the parish of S. Giorgio, and she had three children by him. Having a great affection for Niccolo, who was then in Hungary, she wanted him to return to her in Florence. . . . So she planned a diabolical experiment by invoking a demon, to the detriment of Niccolo's health. . . . She went to someone who shall not be identified . . . and asked him to go to another diabolical woman, a sorceress (whose name shall not be publicized, for the public good), and asked her to make for Giovanna a wax image in the form of a woman, and also some pins and other items required by this diabolical experiment. . . . Giovanna took that image and placed it in a chest in her house. When, a few days later, she had to leave that house and move to another, she left the image in the chest. Later it was discovered by the residents of that house, who burned it.

She collected nine beans, a piece of cloth, some charcoal, several olive leaves which had been blessed and which stood before the image of the Virgin Mary, a coin with a cross, and a grain of salt. With these in her hand she gen-uflected . . . [before the image] and recited three times the Pater Noster and the Ave Maria, spurning the divine prayers composed for the worship of God and his mother the Virgin Mary. Having done this, she placed these items on a piece of linen cloth and slept over them for three nights. And after-wards, she took them in her hand and thrice repeated the Pater Noster and the Ave Maria. . . . And thus Giovanna knew that her future husband would not love her. And so it happened, for after the celebration and the consummation of the marriage, her husband Giovanni stayed with her for a few days, and then left her and has not yet returned. [Giovanna confessed to these crimes and was beheaded.]

Questions:
1. Why would both church and civil authorities consider Fra Michele's teachings dangerous while others hailed him as a saint?
2. What role do you think gender played in the accusation and conviction of Giovanna?
3. How could her alleged behavior be considered threatening to the social order?
4. Do you think Giovanna and Giovanni were victims or guilty mischief-makers in Florence?

Documents 10.9 and 10.10

The following two selections deal with two promi-nent Christian mystics of the late 14th and early 15th centuries—who happened to be women. Catherine of Siena, who ultimately achieved saint-hood, sought to restore the papacy to Rome, while

Margery Kempe—viewed by many of her contem-poraries as a heretic—remained in obscurity until approximately 500 years after her death with the discovery of her writings in a country house in Yorkshire in 1934.

10.9 Christian Women: Catherine of Siena

Catherine of Siena (1347–1380) is an excellent example of a medieval mystic, a Christian who sought direct communion with God through prayer. She was a social worker, an able theolo-gian, and an emissary for the pope. Yet mystics such as Catherine, St. Francis of Assisi, and St. Bernard, however revered by the Church, repre-sented a subtle threat to the institutional church. Mysticism, after all, provided a way to reach God that did not necessarily require the intervention of priest or sacrament.

Source: *Heritage of Western Civilization*, Sev-enth Edition, ed. John L. Beatty and Oliver A. Johnson, (Prentice Hall, 1991). pp. 347–48.

FROM CATHERINE OF SIENA'S DIALOGUE WITH GOD

Prologue: In the Name of Christ Crucified and of Gentle Mary

A soul rises up, restless with tremendous desire for God's honor and the salvation of souls. She has for some time exercised herself in virtue and has become accustomed to dwelling in the cell of self-knowledge in order to know better God's goodness toward her, since upon knowledge follows love. And loving, she seeks to pursue truth and clothe herself in it.

But there is no way she can so savor and be enlight-ened by this truth as in continual humble prayer, grounded in the knowledge of herself and of God. For by such prayer the soul is united with God, following in the footsteps of Christ crucified, and through desire and affection and the union of love he makes of her another himself. So Christ seems to have meant when he said, 'If you will love me and keep my word, I will show myself to you, and you will be one thing with me and I with you." And we find similar words in other places from which we can see it is the truth that by love's affection the soul becomes another himself.

To make this clearer still, I remember having heard from a certain servant of God that, when she was at prayer, lifted high in spirit, God would not hide from her mind's eye his love for his servants. No, he would reveal it, saying among other things, "Open your mind's eye and look within me, and you will see the dignity and beauty of my reason-ing creature. But beyond the beauty I have given the soul by creating her in my image and likeness, look at those who are clothed in the wedding garment of charity, adorned with many true virtues: They are united with me through love. So I say, if you should ask me who they are, I would answer," said the gentle loving Word, "that they are another me; for they have lost and drowned their own will and have clothed themselves and united themselves and conformed themselves with mine."

It is true, then, that the soul is united to God through love's affection.

Now this soul's will was to know and follow truth more courageously. So she addressed four petitions to the most high and eternal Father, holding up her desire for herself first of all—for she knew that she could be of no service to her neighbors in teaching or example or prayer without first doing herself the service of attaining and possessing virtue.

Her first petition, therefore, was for herself. The second was for the reform of holy Church. The third was for the whole world in general, and in particular for the peace of Christians who are rebelling against holy Church with great disrespect and persecution. In her forth petition she asked divine providence to supply in general and in particular for a certain case which had arisen.

This desire of hers was great and continuous. But it grew even more when First Truth [God—Ed.] showed her the world's need and how storm-tossed and offensive to God it is. And she had on her mind, besides, a letter she had received from her spiritual father, a letter in which he expressed pain and unbearable sadness over the offense against God, the damnation of souls, and persecutions against holy Church. All of this stirred up the flame of her holy desire with grief for the offense but with gladness in the hope by which she waited for God to provide against such great evils.

She found herself eager for the next day's Mass—it would be Mary's day[1]—because in communion the soul seems more sweetly bound to God and better knows his truth. For then the soul is in God and God in the soul just as the fish is in the sea and the sea in the fish. So when it was morning and time for Mass she took her place with eager desire. From her deep knowledge of herself, a holy justice gave birth to hatred and displeasure against herself, ashamed as she was of her imperfection which seemed to her to be the cause of all the evils in the world. In this knowledge and hatred and justice she washed away the stains of guilt, which it seemed to her were, and which indeed were, in her own soul, saying, 'O eternal Father, I accuse myself before you, asking that you punish my sins in this life. And since I by my sins am the cause of the sufferings my neighbors must endure, I beg you in mercy to punish me for them."

10.10 Christian Women: Margery Kempe

The second excerpt is from the autobiography of Margery Kempe (ca. 1373–ca. 1438) and reveals

---

[1] Saturday, the day traditionally dedicated to Mary

how a woman who embraced mysticism had to cope with the accusation of heresy. Lollards were followers of John Wyclif, who had been declared a heretic in the years following his death in 1384. Many of his teachings were reaffirmed in the Protestant Reformation in the fifteenth century.

Source: *Medieval England as Viewed by Contemporaries*, ed. W.O. Hassall, (New York: Harper Torchbooks, 1965, c. 1957), pp. 195–97.

FROM THE BOOK OF MARGERY KEMPE

Afterwards, set she forth to Leicester, and a good man also—Thomas Marchale—of whom is written before; and there she came into a fair church where she beheld a crucifix that was piteously portrayed and lamentable to behold, through beholding which, the Passion of Our Lord entered her mind, so that she began to melt and to relent by tears of pity and compassion. Then the fire of love kindled so eagerly in her heart that she could not keep it secret, for, whether she would or not, it caused her to break out with a loud voice and cry marvelously, and weep and sob so hideously that many a man and woman wondered on her therefore.

When it was overcome and she was going out of the church door, a man took her by the sleeve and said:

'Damsel, why weepest thou so sore?'

'Sir,' she said, 'it is not you to tell.'

So she and the good man, Thomas Marchale, went forth, and took her hostel and there ate their meat. When they had eaten, she prayed Thomas Marchale to write a letter and send it to her husband, that he might fetch her home. And while the letter was in writing, the hosteler came up to her chamber in great haste, and took her scrip and bade her come quickly and speak with the Mayor. And so she did.

Then the Mayor asked her of what country she was, and whose daughter she was.

'Sir,' she said, 'I am of Lynne in Norfolk, a good man's daughter of the same Lynne, who hath been mayor five times of that worshipful borough, and alderman also many years; and I have a good man, also a burgess of the said town of Lynne, for my husband'

'Ah!' said the Mayor, 'Saint Katherine told what kindred she came of, and yet ye are not like her, for thou art a false strumpet, a false Lollard, and a false deceiver of the people, and I shall have thee in prison.'

And she answered: 'I am as ready, sir, to go to prison for God's love, as ye are ready to go to church.'

When the Mayor had long chidden her and said many evil and horrible words to her, and she, by the grace of Jesus, had reasonably answered to all that he could say, he commanded the jailer's man to lead her to prison.

The jailer's man, having compassion on her with weeping tears, said to the Mayor:—''Sir, I have no house to put her in, unless I put her amongst men.'

Then she was moved with compassion for the man who had compassion on her. Praying for grace and mercy to that man, as for her own soul, she said to the Mayor:—I pray you, sir, put me not among men.'

Then said the jailer his own self to the Mayor:—'Sir, I will be under bond to keep this woman in safe ward till ye will have her back.'

Then was there a man of Boston, who said to the good wife, where she was at hostel:—'Forsooth,' he said, 'in Boston this woman is held to be a holy woman and a blessed woman.' Then the jailer took her into his ward, and led her home into his own house, and put her in a fair chamber, shutting the door with a key, and commending his wife the key to keep.

Nevertheless, he let her go to church when she would, and let her eat at his own table and made her right good cheer for Our Lord's sake, thanked be Almighty God thereof.

Questions:
1. What was Catherine's desire as expressed in her prayer?
2. Why was Margery's behavior interpreted as heretical or a threat to the established order?
3. Why do you think medieval women might be particularly attracted to mysticism?

CHAPTER 11
In the Name of Profit
Cities, Merchants, and
Trade in the Middle Ages
(1000–1500)

SECTION 1
The Environment for Profit

11.1 Town Charters: Jaca and Lorris

The reason and the purpose of town charters were to create an environment that fostered trade for with trade came wealth. Kings, counts, bishops and other lords granted charters to lure people to settle in towns by ensuring their personal freedom, providing protection for their businesses, and safety for their persons. From the eleventh century, as the number and population of towns increased, a distinctive urban culture emerged. The first town charter is for Jaca, granted by the King of Aragon in 1077. The French king granted the second charter in 1155 to the town of Lorris.

> **Sources:** Medieval Iberia: Readings from Christian, Muslim and Jewish Sources, ed. Olivia Remie Constable, (Philadelphia: University of Pennsylvania Press, 1997), pp.123–25. Heritage of Western Civilization, Seventh Edition, ed. John L. Beatty and Oliver A. Johnson, (Prentice Hall, 1991). pp. 304–306.

CHARTER OF JACA[1]

[Emblem of Christ] In the name of our Lord Jesus Christ and of the undivided Trinity, Father and Son and Holy Spirit, amen. This is a charter of authority and confirmation which I Sancho, by the grace of God king of the Aragonese and Pamplonese, make to you.

Notice to all men who are even in the east and west and north and south that I wish to establish a city in my village which is called "Jaca"

1 First, I remit to you all bad *fueros*[2] which you had until this day that I established Jaca to be a city; and so, because I wish it to be well settled, I concede and confirm to you and to all who settle in my city Jaca all the good *fueros* which you have asked of me in order that my city be well settled.

2 And each one may enclose his part[3] as he can.

3 And if it happen that anyone of you comes to dispute and will strike anyone before me or in my palace when I am standing there, let him fine for 1000 s. or lose the fight.

4 And if anyone, whether knight or burgher or peasant, should strike another, and not in my presence nor in my palace although I be in Jaca, let him not pay the fine except according to the *fuero* you have when I am not in

5 And if it happen that someone be found killed in a robbery in Jaca or its district, you are not obligated to pay homicide.[4]

6 I give and concede to you and your successors with good will that you not go in the army unless with bread for three days. And this should be in the name of battle in the field or where I or my successors are surrounded by our enemies. And if the lord of the house does not wish to go there, let him substitute one armed footman.

7 And wherever you can buy anything in Jaca or outside of Jaca, or acquire any man's inheritance, you may have it free and unencumbered without any bad cut.[5]

8 And after you hold it undisturbed for a year and a day, anyone wishing to disturb them or take it away from you shall give me 60 s., and shall confirm your inheritance.

9 And as far as you can go and return in a day, everywhere, you may have pastures and woods, observing the boundaries of the men living there.

10 And that you should not have duel-war between you, unless agreeable to both; nor with men from elsewhere, unless with consent of the men of Jaca.

11 And that none of you should sit captive giving pledges of your foot.[6]

12 And if any of you commits fornication with any willing woman, except a married one, you shall not pay calumny.[7] And if it happen that he forces her, let him give

---
[1] Translated from Latin by Thomas N. Bisson
[2] Customary privilege.

[3] Here "part" means property within the town.
[4] That is, the murder fine sometimes imposed by lords on communities.
[5] The "cut' like tallage elsewhere, was an arbitrary tax.
[6] Meaning unclear.
[7] Calumny was a payment exacted for slander.

her a husband or receive her as his wife. And if the raped woman appeals on the first or second day, let her prove by truthful witnesses of Jaca. If she wishes to appeal after three days, it shall avail her nothing.

13 And if any of you goes against his neighbor in anger and armed with lance, sword, club, or knife, let him fine for it 1000 s. or lose the fight.

14 And if anyone kills another let him pay 500 s.

15 And if one strikes another in conflict or grabs him by the hair, let him pay 25 s. for it.

16 And if he falls to the ground, let him pay 250 s.

17 And if anyone enters his neighbor's house in anger, or makes seizures there, let him pay 25 s. to the lord of the house.

18 And that my agent not receive calumny from any man of Jaca save with the approval of six better men of Jaca.

19 And none of all the men of Jaca should go to judgment anywhere but in Jaca.

20 And if anyone has false measure or weight, let him pay 60 s.

21 And that all men should go to mill in mills where they wish, except Jews and those who make bread for sale.

22 And you should not give or sell your honors to the church or to *infanzones*.[8]

23 And if any man is imprisoned for debt, let him who wishes to capture him do so with my agent; and let him put [him] in my palace, and let my jailer guard him; and after three days, he who took him should give him farthing's worth; and if he refuse to do [this], my jailer may release him.

24 And if any man seize as pledge the Saracen man or Saracen woman of his neighbor, let him put him in my palace; and the lord of the male and female Saracen shall give him bread and water, because he is a human being and should not starve like a beast.

And whoever wishes to disrupt this charter which I make to the settlers of Jaca, let him be excommunicated and anathematized for his cruelty and wholly separated from all God's faithful, whether he be of. my stock or of another.

Amen, amen, amen.

Let it be done, let it be done, let it be done.

The charter made in the [1077] year from the Incarnation of our Lord Jesus Christ

I Sancho, by God's grace king of the Aragonese and Pamplonese, have ordered these aforesaid things and I have made this sign [sign of cross] of Sancho with my hand.

I Pedro, son of King Sancho of the Aragonese, son of King Ramiro, wished these aforesaid things to be written and I have made this sign [sign of Pedro I, in Arabic] with my hand.[9]

---

[8] The *infanzones* were the lesser aristocracy of knights in Aragon
[9] The charter has the form of a confirmation by King Pedro I (r.1094–1104).

CHARTER OF THE LIBERTIES OF LORRIS

1. Let whoever shall have a house in the parish of Lorris pay a quit-rent[10] of six deniers[11] only for his house, and each acre of land which he shall have in this parish; and if he make such an acquisition, let that be the quit-rent of his house.

2. Let no inhabitant of the parish of Lorris pay a duty of entry nor any tax for his food, and let him not pay any duty of measurement for the corn which his labor, or that of the animals which he may have shall procure him, and let him pay no duty for the wine which he shall get from his vines.

3. Let none of them go on a [military] expedition on foot or horseback, whence he cannot return home the same day if he desire to do so.

4. Let none of them pay toll to Étampes or Orleans, or to Milly, which is in Gatinais, or to Melun.

5. Let no one who has property in the parish of Lorris lose any of it for any misdeed whatsoever, unless the said misdeed be committed against us or any of our guests.

6. Let no one going to the fairs or markets of Lorris, or in returning, be stopped or inconvenienced unless he shall have committed some misdeed that same day; and let no one on a fair or market day at Lorris, seize the bail given by his security; unless the bail be given the same day.

7. Let forfeitures of sixty sous[12] be reduced to five, that of five sous to twelve deniers, and the provost's fee in cases of plaint, to four deniers.

8. Let no man of Lorris be forced to go out of it to plead before the lord king.

9. Let no one, neither us nor any other, take any tax, offering, or exaction from the men of Lorris.

10. Let no one sell wine at Lorris with public notice, except the king, who shall sell his wine in his cellar with that notice.

11. We will have at Lorris, for our service and that of the queen, a credit of a full fortnight, in the articles of provisions; and if any inhabitant have received a gage from the lord king, he shall not be bound to keep it more than eight days, unless he please.

12. If any have had a quarrel with another, but without breaking a closed house, and if it be accommodated without plaint brought before the provost, no fine shall be due, on this account, to us or to our provost; and if there has been a plaint they can still come to an agreement when they shall have paid the fine. And if any one bear plaint against another, and there has been no fine awarded against either one to the other, they shall not, on that account, owe anything to us or our provost.

13. If any one owe an oath to another, let the latter have permission to remit it.

---

[10] The only rent the tenant is obligated to pay to his lord.
[11] The French coin comparable to the English penny.
[12] The French coin comparable to the English shilling.

14. If any men of Lorris have rashly given their pledge of a duel, and if with the consent of the provost they accommodate it before the pledges have been given, let each pay two sous and a half; and if the pledges have been given, let each pay seven sous and a half; and if the duel has been between men having the right of fighting in the list, then let the hostages of the conquered pay one hundred and twelve sous.

15. Let no man of Lorris do forced work for us, unless it be twice a year to take our wine to Orleans, and nowhere else; and those only shall do this work who shall have horses and carts, and they shall be informed of it beforehand; and they shall receive no lodging from us. The laborers also shall bring wood for our kitchen.

16. No one shall be detained in prison if he can furnish bail for his appearance in court.

17. Whoever desires to sell his property may do so; and having received the price, he may leave the town, free and unmolested, if he please so to do, unless he has committed any misdeed in the town.

18. Whoever shall have remained a year and a day in the parish of Lorris without any claim having pursued him thither, and without the right having been interdicted him, whether by us or our provost, he shall remain there free and tranquil.

19. No one shall plead against another unless it be to recover, and ensure the observance of, what is his due.

20. When the men of Lorris shall go to Orleans with merchandise, they shall pay, upon leaving the town, one denier [for their cart, when they go not for the sake of the fair; and when they go for the sake of the fair and the market, they shall pay, upon leaving Orleans, four deniers for each cart, and on entering, two deniers.

21. At marriages in Lorris, the public crier shall have no fee, nor he who keeps watch.

22. No cultivator of the parish of Lorris, cultivating his land with the plow, shall give, in the time of harvest more than one hermine [six bushels] of rye to all the serjeants of Lorris.

23. [omitted].

24. There shall be at Lorris no duty paid for using the oven.

25. There shall be at Lorris no watch rate.

26. All men of Lorris who shall take salt or wine to Orleans, shall pay only one denier for each cart.

27. No men of Lorris shall owe any fine to the provost of Étampes, nor to the provost of Pirhiviers nor to any in Gâtinais.

28. None among them shall pay the entry dues in Ferrières, nor in Château-Landon, nor in Puiseaux, nor in Nibelle.

29. Let the men of Lorris take the dead wood in the forest for their own use.

30. Whosoever, in the market of Lorris, shall have bought or sold anything, and shall have forgotten to pay the duty, may pay it within eight days without being troubled, if he can swear that he did not withhold the right wittingly.

31. No man of Lorris having a house or a vineyard, or a meadow, or a field, or any buildings in the domain of St. Benedict, shall be under the jurisdiction of the abbot of St. Benedict or his serjeant, unless it be with regard to the quit-rent in kind, to which he is bound; and, in that case. he shall not go out of Lorris to be judged.

32. If any of the men of Lorris be accused of anything. and the accuser cannot prove it by witness, he shall clear himself by a single oath from the assertion of his accuser.

33. No man of this parish shall pay any duty because of what he shall buy or sell for his use on the territory of the precincts, nor for what he shall buy on Wednesday at the market.

34. These customs are granted to the men of Lorris, and they are common to the men who inhabit Courpalais, Chanteloup, and the bailiwick of Harpard.

35. We order that whenever the provost shall be changed in the town, he shall swear faithfully to observe these customs; and the same shall be done by new serjeants when they shall be instituted.

Given at Orleans in the year of our Lord 1155.

Questions:
1. How does the location of these two towns affect the provisions in the charters?
2. What rights and privileges does the lord retain in each of the towns? Are they similar?
3. What privileges and liberties does he grant to the townspeople?
4. How do either of the charters illustrate the old adage, "Town air is free air?"

11.2 To Trade and Protect: The Hanseatic League

During the thirteenth century certain coastal towns of northern and eastern Europe concluded treaties with one another to cooperate in matters of trade and protection. These interlocking treaties eventually created a network of German cities known as the Hanseatic League.

Source: *The Western World To 1700*, Wallace E. Adams, Richard B. Barlow, Gerald R. Kleinfeld, Ronald D. Smith, William W. Wootton, (New York: Dodd, Mead & Co., 1969), pp. 317–18.

AGREEMENT BETWEEN LÜBECK AND HAMBURG, 1241

The advocate, council and commune of Lübeck. . . . We have made the following agreement with our dear friends, the citizens of Hamburg.

1. If robbers or other depredators attack citizens of either city anywhere from the mouth of the Trave river to

Hamburg, or anywhere on the Elbe river, the two cities shall bear the expenses equally in destroying and extirpating them.

    2. If anyone who lives outside the city, kills, wounds, beats, or mishandles, without cause, a citizen of either city, the two cities shall bear the expenses equally in punishing the offender. We furthermore agree to share the expenses equally in punishing those who injure their citizens in the neighborhood of their city and those who injure our citizens in the neighborhood of our city.

    3. If any of their citizens are injured near our city [Lübeck], they shall ask our officials to punish the offender, and if any of our citizens are injured near their city [Hamburg], they shall ask their officials to punish the offender.

DECREES OF THE HANSEATIC LEAGUE, 1260–64

We wish to inform you of the action taken in support of all merchants who are governed by the law of Lübeck.

    (1) Each city shall, to the best of her ability, keep the sea clear of pirates, so that merchants may freely carry on their business by sea.

    (2) Whoever is expelled from one city because of a crime shall not be received in another.

    (3) If a citizen is seized [by pirates, robbers, or bandits] he shall not be ransomed, but his sword-belt and knife shall be sent to him [as a threat to his captors].

    (4) Any merchant ransoming him shall lose all his possessions in all the cities which have the law of Lübeck.

    (5) Whoever is proscribed in one city for robbery or theft shall be proscribed in all.

    (6) If a lord besieges a city, no one shall aid him in any way to the detriment of the besieged city, unless the besieger is his lord.

    (7) If there is a war in the country, no city shall on that account injure a citizen from the other cities, either in his person or goods, but shall give him protection.

    (8) If any man marries a woman in one city, and another woman from some other city comes and proves that he is her lawful husband, he shall be beheaded.

    (9) If a citizen gives his daughter or niece in marriage to a man [from another city], and another man comes and says that she is his lawful wife, but cannot prove it, he shall be beheaded.

    This law shall be binding for a year, and after that the cities shall inform each other by letter of what decisions they make.

Questions:
1. What benefits did cities gain from pacts like the one between Lübeck and Hamburg?
2. Why do you think the decrees for the Hanseatic League forbade people to ransom those kidnapped by pirates?
3. Why were bigamous marriages an important enough concern to be included in the articles of the League?

11.3 *Fabliaux:* Ribald Tales of the French City

Versions of many of these tales popular in the growing urban culture may originally be found in Greek and Roman literature. Most were bawdy and concluded with a less than moral lesson. The author of the second story is Marie de France who wrote in the second half of the twelfth century, the first woman known to have written in the French language.

    Source: *Fabliaux: Ribald Tales from the Old French*, trans. Robert Heliman and Robert O'Gorman, (New York: Crowell, 1965), pp. 67–70, 95–96.

THE PETTICOAT, BY JEAN DE CONDÉ

There are those who take more delight in hearing jests and sly mockeries than they do in sermons. Therefore I am often asked to write of light matters, and I should like now to tell a true tale about a remarkable and quick-witted piece of deception. But had someone discovered this fine deceit and the way it was devised, the lady of our tale would surely have been in a fine mess.

    There was once a lady, the wife of a merchant, who, without her husband's knowing it, took a lover, a young and handsome squire. One night as he lay in bed with her (for her husband was not at home) the merchant returned quietly and softly lit a candle, with so little stir that nobody knew he was there. The wife, who lay side by side with her lover and held him in her arms, was not expecting such a guest. And the merchant, who knew nothing of this and suspected nothing, came straight into the chamber with the candle in his hand.

    The wife was astonished when she saw the candle and sat up in terror, for she thought she had been betrayed. The squire, cheated of his pleasure, did not know what to say or do but duck under the covers and lie there trembling with fear and rage.

    "Alas!" cried the wife. "Who is there? God and the sweet Virgin help me! Who can it be? My husband! Oh, how this terrible man has frightened me! I've almost lost my wits! Nice people don't come home like this, to spy on their wives. You've frightened me to death!"

    "Be quiet," said the merchant. "Don't be afraid. Calm yourself, sweet sister, for never has it been in my heart to come home to spy on you, nor have I ever had any idea that I could catch you in some wickedness. So be easy, don't let this upset you." And he sat down at the foot of the bed. The heart of the squire under the covers began to pound, and he shook and trembled like an omelet over the fire. The merchant comforted his wife, who was so deathly pale that he didn't know what to do for her or how to reassure her.

    "Sister," he said, "I have done wrong in this, but forgive me my fault, for I have never suspected you of anything." And his wife replied: "Then tell me, if you had found a man here by my side, and no mistake about it, what would you have done? Would you have allowed such a thing to pass?"

The merchant answered: "With this sword I would have cut off his head, and I would have killed you beside him."

Then the wife, who was a very clever woman and quick–witted when the occasion required it, laughed aloud and said to her husband: "You don't know what I would have done or how I would have defended myself. Why, I would have scarcely been afraid." She took her petticoat off the bed and threw it over her husband's head and held it there about his neck and face and so blinded the fool. Then she kicked her lover, who was trembling with anguish, all naked out of the bed, and he with a naked blade in his hand with which he had meant to defend himself and, if he could, to sell his life dearly. The lady held the merchant tight and laughed aloud and fooled with him, while the squire ran out of the room naked as he was. He would not be caught today.

"So I would have held you tight," said the lady, waiting for her chance to let him go, "until I had sent him on his way." And when she saw that her husband had no intention of doing her harm or injury, she took away the petticoat and left off her game. "Now he has escaped," she said. "He will not be caught today. Run after him! He is getting away!"

Have you ever heard of a neater trick? It was a beautiful one and a graceful one, full of cunning and sly malice. And she used it to great advantage, for through that trick she prevented a great misfortune.

When she had worked her purpose, the wife's heart was easy and at rest. She was joyous and happy. And her husband too, who took it all as a joke, was happy. The two of them had a great deal of fun together. And so it ended without more ado.

I do not know what else to say of this matter: one needn't worry about her hiding the squire's clothes, for if she could carry out such a trick, the clothes would not present her with much difficulty. Truly I know no more about it, and so I end my tale here.

THE WOMAN WHO HANGED HER HUSBAND'S BODY, BY MARIE DE FRANCE

The tale is written of a man who died and was buried. His wife mourned with great sorrow night and day on his grave. Nearby there was a thief who had been hanged for his misdeeds. A certain knight took him down (he was a relative of his) and buried him. And it was announced throughout the country that whoever had removed the thief's body would suffer the same fate: if he were caught, he would be hanged.

The knight did not know where to turn for deliverance, for many people knew that the thief was his relation. He went straight to the cemetery where the good woman was mourning so hard for her husband. He spoke to her fondly, told her to take heart, and said that he would be very happy if she would love him. The good woman looked at him and grew joyful. She promised to grant his desire.

Then the knight told her of the misfortune that had befallen him because of the thief he had taken down from the gallows. If she could not help him, he would have to leave the country. The good woman replied: "Let us dig up my husband who is buried here and hang him in the other's place. No one will know the difference. The living, to whom one looks for joy, must be saved by the dead."

From this lesson we can learn how much trust the dead may place in the living. So false and frivolous is the world.

Questions:
1. In these versions of the tales, how can you tell they were recorded in a medieval context?
2. How does the story told by Marie de France differ in its attitude toward woman when compared to the other?

SECTION 2
Instruments of Trade

11.4   How to Succeed in Business

Merchant entrepreneurs on the geographical fringes of Europe became increasingly adventurous in pursuit of profit. Here an anonymous writer explains the skills and characteristics necessary for a successful businessman in the thirteenth century.

Source: *Sources of the Western Tradition: Volume I: From Ancient Times to the Enlightenment,* ed. Marvin Perry, Joseph R. Peden, and Theodore H. Von Laue, (Boston: Houghton Mifflin Co., 1995), p.223–24. Reprinted with permission from *The King's Mirror,* ed. Larson, (The Scandinavian Foundation, 1917).

The man who is to be a trader will have to brave many perils, sometimes at sea and sometimes in heathen lands, but nearly always among alien peoples; and it must be his constant purpose to act discreetly wherever he happens to be. On the sea he must be alert and fearless.

When you are in a market town, or wherever you are, be polite and agreeable; then you will secure the friendship of all good men. Make it a habit to rise early in the morning, and go first and immediately to church. . . .

. . . When the services are over, go out to look after your business affairs. If you are unacquainted with the traffic of the town, observe carefully how those who are reputed the best and most prominent merchants conduct their business. You must also be careful to examine the wares that you buy before the purchase is finally made to make sure that they are sound and flawless. And whenever you make a purchase, call in a few trusty men to serve as witnesses as to how the bargain was made.

You should keep occupied with your business till breakfast or, if necessity demands it, till midday; after that you should eat your meal. Keep your table well provided and set with a white cloth, clean victuals, and good drinks. Serve enjoyable meals, if you can afford it. After the meal you may either take a nap or stroll about a little while for pastime and to see what other good merchants are employed with, or whether any new wares have come to the borough which you ought to buy. On returning to your lodgings examine your wares, lest they suffer damage after coming into your hands. If they are found to be injured and you are about to dispose of them, do not conceal the flaws from the purchaser: show him what the defects are and make such a bargain as you can; then you cannot be called a deceiver. Also put a good price on your wares, though not too high, and yet very near what you see can be obtained; then you cannot be called a foister [trickster].

Finally, remember this, that whenever you have an hour to spare you should give thought to your studies, espe-cially to the law books; for it is clear that those who gain knowledge from books have keener wits than others, since those who are the most learned have the best proofs for their knowledge. Make a study of all the laws. . . . If you are acquainted with the law, you will not be annoyed by quibbles when you have suits to bring against men of your own class, but will be able to plead according to law in every case.

But although I have most to say about laws, I regard no man perfect in knowledge unless he has thoroughly learned and mastered the customs of the place where he is sojourning. And if you wish to become perfect in knowledge, you must learn all the languages, first of all Latin and French, for these idioms are most widely used; and yet, do not neglect your native tongue or speech.

. . . Train yourself to be as active as possible, though not so as to injure your health. Strive never to be downcast, for a downcast mind is always morbid; try rather to be friendly and genial at all times, of an even temper and never moody. Be upright and teach the right to every man who wishes to learn from you; and always associate with the best men. Guard your tongue carefully; this is good counsel, for your tongue may honor you, but it may also condemn you. Though you be angry speak few words and never in passion; for unless one is careful, he may utter words in wrath that he would later give gold to have unspoken. On the whole, I know of no revenge, though many employ it, that profits a man less than to bandy heated words with another, even though he has a quarrel to settle with him. You shall know of a truth that no virtue is higher or stronger than the power to keep one's tongue from foul or profane speech, tattling, or slanderous talk in any form. If children be given to you, let them not grow up without learning a trade; for we may expect a man to keep closer to knowledge and business when he comes of age, if he is trained in youth while under control.

And further, there are certain things which you must beware of and shun like the devil himself; these are drinking, chess, harlots, quarreling, and throwing dice for stakes. For upon such foundations the greatest calamities are built; and unless they strive to avoid these things, few only are able to live long without blame or sin.

Observe carefully how the sky is lighted, the course of the heavenly bodies, the grouping of the hours, and the points of the horizon. Learn also how to mark the movements of the ocean and to discern how its turmoil ebbs and swells; for that is knowledge which all must possess who wish to trade abroad. Learn arithmetic thoroughly, for merchants have great need of that.

If you come to a place where the king or some other chief who is in authority has his officials, seek to win their friendship; and if they demand any necessary fees on the ruler's behalf, be prompt to render all such payments, lest by holding too tightly to little things you lose the greater.... If you can dispose of your wares at suitable prices, do not hold them long; for it is the wont of merchants to buy constantly and to sell rapidly....

... If you attend carefully to all these things, with God's mercy you may hope for success. This, too, you must keep constantly in mind, if you wish to be counted a wise man, that you ought never to let a day pass without learning something that will profit you. Be not like those who think it beneath their dignity to hear or learn from others such things even as might avail them much if they knew them. For a man must regard it as great an honor to learn as to teach, if he wishes to be considered thoroughly informed....

... Always buy good clothes and eat good fare if your means permit; and never keep unruly or quarrelsome men as attendants or messmates. Keep your temper calm though not to the point of suffering abuse or bringing upon yourself the reproach of cowardice. Though necessity may force you into strife, be not in a hurry to take revenge; first make sure that your effort will succeed and strike where it ought. Never display a heated temper when you see that you are likely to fail, but be sure to maintain your honor at some later time, unless your opponent should offer a satisfactory atonement.

If your wealth takes on rapid growth, divide it and invest it in a partnership trade in fields where you do not yourself travel; but be cautious in selecting partners. Always let Almighty God, the holy Virgin Mary, and the saint whom you have most frequently called upon to intercede for you be counted among your partners. Watch with care over the property which the saints are to share with you and always bring it faithfully to the place to which it was originally promised.

Questions:
1. What are the personal characteristics and acquired skills of a successful merchant?
2. What appears to be the goal for the successful businessman in this essay?
3. What part of this advice would no longer be included in a best-selling "How to Succeed in Business if you Try Real Hard" book for the twenty-first century?

Documents 11.5 and 11.6
The next two groups of documents focus on the burgeoning growth of commerce in Europe in the Middle Ages, its maintenance, as well as the increasing social and fiscal responsibility that came with this growth, indicated by the creation of guilds.

11.5   Guilds: Regulating the Craft

Tradesmen, craftsmen, and merchants organized themselves into guilds, associations that maintained a monopoly, guar-

anteed quality, and regulated prices and standards of production. The following articles regulated the Spurriers (1345) in London and illustrate the guild principle as it applied to the industrial trade of making spurs.

Source: Articles of the Spurriers" in Henry Thomas Riley, ed., *Memorials of London and London Life*, A.D. 1276–1419 (London: Longmans, Green, and Co., 1868), pp. 226–28, 239–40.

ARTICLES OF THE LONDON SPURRIERS, 1347

Be it remembered, that on Tuesday, the morrow of St. Peter's Chains [1 August], in the 19th year of the reign of King Edward the Third etc., the Articles underwritten were read before John Hamond, Mayor, Roger de Depham, Recorder, and the other Aldermen; and seeing that the same were deemed befitting, they were accepted and enrolled, in these words:

"In the first place,—that no one of the trade of Spurriers shall work longer than from the beginning of the day until curfew rung out at the Church of St. Sepulchre, without Neugate; by reason that no man can work so neatly by night as by day.

And many persons of the said trade, who compass how to practise deception in their work, desire to work by night rather than by day: and then they introduce false iron, and iron that has been cracked, for tin, and also, they put gilt on false copper, and cracked.

And further, many of the said trade are wandering about all day, without working at all at their trade; and then, when they have become drunk and frantic, they take to their work, to the annoyance of the sick and of all their neighbourhood, as well as by reason of the broils that arise between them and the strange folks who are dwelling among them.

And then they blow up their fires so vigorously, that their forges begin all at once to blaze; to the great peril of themselves and of all the neighbourhood around. And then too, all the neighbours are much in dread of the sparks, which so vigorously issue forth in all directions from the mouths of the chimneys in their forges.

By reason whereof, it seems unto them that working by night [should be put an end to,] in order such false work and such perils to avoid; and therefore, the Mayor and Aldermen do will, by assent of the good folks of the said trade, and for the common profit, that from henceforth such time for working, and such false work made in the trade, shall be forbidden.

And if any person shall be found in the said trade to do to the contrary hereof, let him be amerced[1], the first time in 40 *d* [pence]., one half thereof to go to the use of the Chamber of the Guildhall of London, and the other half to the use of the said trade; the second time, in half a mark, and the third time, in 10 *s*. [shillings], to the use of the same

---
[1] Fined.

Chamber and trade; and the fourth time, let him forswear the trade for ever.

"Also,—that no one of the said trade shall hang his spurs out on Sunday, or on other days that are Double Feasts; but only a sign indicating his business: and such spurs as they shall so sell, they are to show and sell within their shops, without exposing them without, or opening the doors or windows of their shops, on the pain aforesaid.

"Also,—that no one of the said trade shall keep a house or shop to carry on his business, unless he is free of the City;[2] and that no one shall cause to be sold, or exposed for sale, any manner of old spurs for new ones; or shall garnish them, or change them for new ones.

"Also,—that no one of the said trade shall take an apprentice for a less term than seven years; and such apprentice shall be enrolled, according to the usages of the said city.

"Also,—that if any one of the said trade, who is not a freeman, shall take an apprentice for a term of years, he shall be amerced, as aforesaid.

"Also,—that no one of the said trade shall receive the apprentice, serving-man, or journeyman, of another in the same trade, during the term agreed upon between his master and him; on the pain aforesaid.

"Also,—that no alien of another country, or foreigner of this country, shall follow or use the said trade, unless he is enfranchised before the Mayor, Aldermen, and Chamberlain; and that, by witness and surety of the good folks of the said trade, who will undertake for him as to his loyalty and his good behaviour.

"Also,—that no one of the said trade shall work on Saturdays, after None has been rung out in the City; and not from that hour until the Monday morning following."

11.6 "For the Honor of the Guild," Social Responsibility

These documents each pertain to one of the various guilds in Florence. The first are the articles regulating the wine merchants; the second is a petition from the silk guild to the government of Florence; and the last is a decree passed by the Lana (Wool) guild. Each of these three sources reveals another dimension of the guilds that extended beyond simple regulation of their trade.

Source: *The Society of Renaissance Florence: A Documentary Study*, ed. Gene Brucker, (Harper and Row, Inc., 1972), pp. 90–94.

THE CORPORATION OF WINE MERCHANTS

[Chapter 18] It is also decreed and ordained that the consuls [of the guild] are required, by their oath, to force all of the

winesellers . . . who sell at retail in the city and *contado* of Florence to swear allegiance to this guild and for this guild. And for this purpose they must make a monthly search through the city and the suburbs of Florence, and if they find anyone who is not matriculated in the guild, they must require him to swear allegiance. . . . And whoever, as has been said, is engaged in this trade, even though he is not . . . matriculated in the guild . . . is considered to be a member of the guild. . . . And each newly matriculated wineseller . . . must pay . . . 5 lire to the guild treasurer . . . as his matriculation fee. . . . If, however, he is a father or son of a guild member, then he is not required to pay anything.

[Chapter 20] The consuls, treasurer, and notary of the guild are required to assemble together wherever they wish . . . to render justice to whoever demands it of the men of this guild, against any and all those . . . who sell wine at retail . . . in the city, *contado*, and district of Florence.

. . . [They must] hear, take cognizance of, make decisions, and act on everything which pertains to their office, and accept every appeal which is brought before them by whosoever has any claim upon any member of the guild. . . . They must record [these acts] in their protocols and render justice with good faith and without fraud on one day of each week.

With respect to these disputes, the consuls are required to proceed in the following manner. If any dispute or quarrel is brought against any member of the guild . . . and it involves a sum of 3 Florentine lire di piccolo or less, this dispute is to be decided summarily by the consuls, after the parties have sworn an oath, in favor of whoever appears to be more honest and of better reputation. . . . If the dispute involves 60 soldi or more, the consuls, after receiving the complaint, are required to demand that . . . the defendant appear to reply to the complaint. . . . [Witnesses are to be called and interrogated in such major disputes, and the consuls must announce their judgment within one month.]

[Chapter 21] It is decreed and ordained that each wine-seller shall come to the assembly of the guild as often as he is summoned by the consuls. . . . The consuls are required to levy a fine of 10 soldi . . . against whoever violates this [rule], and the same penalty is to be incurred by anyone who fails to respond to the consuls' order to come to the guild's offering in a church. . . . And if necessity requires that the members of the guild assemble under their banner to stand guard, or to go on a march, by day or night, in the city and *contado* of Florence or elsewhere, every member of the guild is required to appear in person, with or without arms as ordered, with their standard-bearer and under their banner, or pay a fine of 10 lire.

[Chapter 35] For the honor of the guild and of the members of the guild, it is decreed and ordained that whenever any member of the guild dies, all guild members in the city and suburbs who are summoned by the messenger of the guild . . . are required to go to the service for the dead man, and to stay there until he is buried. . . . And the consuls are required to send the guild messenger, requesting and

---

[2] He must have earned the right to carry on business in the City.

inviting the members of the guild to participate in the obsequies for the dead.

A CHARITABLE ENTERPRISE, 1421

. . . This petition is presented with all due reverence to you, lord priors, on behalf of your devoted sons of the guild of Por Santa Maria [the silk guild] and the merchants and guildsmen of that association. It is well known to all of the people of Florence that this guild has sought, through pious acts, to conserve . . . and also to promote your republic and this guild. It has begun to construct a most beautiful edifice in the city of Florence and in the parish of S. Michele Visdomini, next to the piazza called the "Frati de' Servi." [This building is] a hospital called S.Maria degli Innocenti, in which shall be received those who, against natural law, have been deserted by their fathers or their mothers, that is, infants, who in the vernacular are called *gittatelli* [literally, castaways; foundlings]. Without the help and favor of your benign lordships, it will not be possible to transform this laudable objective into reality nor after it has been achieved, to preserve and conserve it.

And since [we] realized that your lordships and all of the people are, in the highest degree, committed to works of charity, [we have] decided to have recourse to your clemency, and to request, most devotedly, all of the things which are described below. So on behalf of the above-mentioned guild, you are humbly petitioned . . . to enact a law that this guild of Por Santa Maria and its members and guildsmen—as founders, originators, and principals of this hospital—are understood in perpetuity to be . . . the sole patrons, defenders, protectors, and supporters of this hospital as representatives of, and in the name of, the *popolo* and Commune of Florence.

Item, the consuls of the guild . . . have authority to choose supervisors and governors of the hospital and of the children and servants.

GUILD RIVALRY, 1425

The above-mentioned consuls, assembled together in the palace of the [Lana][1] guild in sufficient numbers and in the accustomed manner for the exercise of their office . . . have diligently considered the law approved by the captains of the society of the blessed Virgin Mary of Orsanmichele. This law decreed, in effect, that for the ornamentation of that oratory, each of the twenty-one guilds of the city of Florence . . . in a place assigned to each of them by the captains of the society, should construct . . . a tabernacle, properly and carefully decorated, for the honor of the city and the beautification of the oratory. The consuls have considered that all of the guilds have finished their tabernacles, and that those constructed by the Calimala and Cambio guilds, and by other guilds, surpass in beauty and ornamen-

tation that of the Lana guild. So it may truly be said that this does not redound to the honor of the Lana guild, particularly when one considers the magnificence of that guild which has always sought to be the master and the superior of the other guilds.

For the splendor and honor of the guild, the lord consuls desire to provide a remedy for this. . . . They decree that through the month of August, the existing lord consuls and their successors in office, by authority of the present provision, are to construct, fabricate, and remake a tabernacle and a statue of the blessed Stephen, protomartyr, protector and defender of the renowned Lana guild, in his honor and in reverence to God. They are to do this by whatever ways and means they choose, which will most honorably contribute to the splendor of the guild, so that this tabernacle will exceed, or at least equal, in beauty and decoration the more beautiful ones. In the construction of this tabernacle and statue, the lord consuls . . . may spend . . . up to 1,000 florins. And during this time, the lord consuls may commission that statue and tabernacle to the person or persons, and for that price or prices, and with whatever agreement and time or times which seem to them to be most useful for the guild.

Questions for Documents 11.5 and 11.6:
1. In what ways did their articles guarantee a monopoly to guild members? How did the guilds maintain quality and prevent fraud?
2. Who was eligible for membership in the guilds?
3. With what other activities besides regulation of their trade did the guilds concern themselves?
4. How did rivalry between guilds express itself in Florence?

11.7 Workers Revolt: The Demands of the Ciompi

The demographic disaster of the Black Death (1347–1350) and economic troubles of the fourteenth century deeply disturbed the social stability of Europe. Workers and peasants revolted against the ruling elites across Europe. In 1378 an urban revolt broke out in Florence, Italy. The revolutionaries, the Ciompi issued their demands to the Florentine Republic that was dominated by an oligarchy of wealthy merchants. Although concessions were initially granted, by 1382, the reforms were rescinded.

Source: *The Society of Renaissance Florence: A Documentary Study*, ed.Gene Brucker, (New York: Harper and Row, 1971), pp. 236–39.

[July 21, 1378] When the *popolo* and the guildsmen had seized the palace [of the podestá], they sent a message to the Signoria . . . that they wished to make certain demands by

---
[1] The Wool guild.

means of petitions, which were just and reasonable. . . . They said that, for the peace and repose of the city, they wanted certain things which they had decided among themselves . . . and they begged the priors to have them read, and then to deliberate on them, and to present them to their colleges.

The first chapter [of the petition] stated that the Lana guild[1] would no longer have a [police] official of the guild. Another was that the combers, carders, trimmers, washers, and other cloth workers would have their own [guild] consuls, and would no longer be subject to the Lana guild.

Another chapter [stated that] the Commune's funded debt would no longer pay interest, but the capital would be restored [to the shareholders] within twelve years.

Another chapter was that all outlaws and those who had been condemned by the Commune . . . except rebels and traitors would be pardoned. Moreover, all penalties involving a loss of a limb would be cancelled, and those who were condemned would pay a money fine. . . . Furthermore, for two years none of the poor people could be prosecuted for debts of 50 florins or less. For a period of six months, no forced loans were to be levied. . . . And within that six months' period, a schedule for levying direct taxes [estimo] was to be compiled. . . .

The *popolo* entered the palace and [the podestá] departed, without any harm being done to him. They ascended the bell tower and placed there the emblem of the blacksmiths' guild, that is, the tongs. Then the banners of the other guilds, both great and small, were unfurled from the windows of the [palace of] the podestá, and also the standard of justice, but there was no flag of the Lana guild. Those inside the palace threw out and burned . . . every document which they found. And they remained there, all that day and night, in honor of God. Both rich and poor were there, each one to protect the standard of his guild.

The next morning the *popolo* brought the standard of justice from the palace and they marched, all armed, to the Piazza della Signoria, shouting: "Long live the *popolo minuto!*". . . . Then they began to cry "that the Signoria should leave, and if they didn't wish to depart, they would be taken to their homes." Into the piazza came a certain Michele di Lando, a wool-comber, who was the son of Monna Simona, who sold provisions to the prisoners in the Stinche . . . and he was seized and the standard of justice placed in his hands. . . . Then the *popolo* ordered the priors to abandon the palace. It was well furnished with supplies necessary [for defense] but they were frightened men and they left [the palace], which was the best course. Then the *popolo* entered, taking with them the standard of justice . . . and they entered all the rooms and they found many ropes which [the authorities] had bought to hang the poor

people. . . . Several young men climbed the bell tower and rang the bells to signal the victory which they had won in seizing the palace, in God's honor. Then they decided to do everything necessary to fortify themselves and to liberate the *popolo minuto*. Then they acclaimed the woolcomber, Michele di Lando, as *signore* and standard-bearer of justice, and he was *signore* for two days. . . . Then [the *popolo*] decided to call other priors who would be good comrades and who would fill up the office of those priors who had been expelled. And so by acclamation, they named eight priors and the Twelve and the [Sixteen] standard-bearers.

When they wished to convene a council, these priors called together the colleges and the consuls of the guilds. . . . This council enacted a decree that everyone who had been proscribed as a Ghibelline since 1357 was to be restored to Guelf status[2]. . . . And this was done to give a part to more people, and so that each would be content, and each would have a share of the offices, and so that all of the citizens would be united. Thus poor men would have their due, for they have always borne the expenses [of government], and only the rich have profited.

. . . And they deliberated to expand the lower guilds, and where there had been fourteen, there would now be seventeen, and thus they would be stronger, and this was done. The first new guild comprised those who worked in the woolen industry: factors, brokers in wool and in thread, workers who were employed in the dye shops and the stretching sheds, menders, sorters, shearers, beaters, combers, and weavers. These were all banded together, some nine thousand men. . . . The second new guild was made up of dyers, washers, carders, and makers of combs. . . . In the third guild were menders, trimmers, stretchers, washers, shirtmakers, tailors, stocking-makers, and makers of flags. . . . So all together, the lower guilds increased by some thirteen thousand men.

The lord priors and the colleges decided to burn the old Communal scrutiny lists, and this was done. Then a new scrutiny was held. The Offices were divided as follows: the [seven] greater guilds had three priors; the fourteen [lower] guilds had another three, and the three new guilds had three priors. And so a new scrutiny was completed, which satisfied many who had never before had any share of the offices, and had always borne the expenses.

Questions:
1. Who were the workers who made up the Ciompi?
2. What were their demands for changes in the guilds and the government?

---

[1] The Lana Guild is the Wool Guild dominated by the wool merchants.

[2] These were the two chief political groups fighting for control of the Florentine Republic.

Part FOUR
THE WEST EXPANDS
The Self, the State, the World
(1200–1750)

CHAPTER 12
City Life
Public and Private Life in the
Late Medieval Cities (1200–1500)

SECTION 1
Public Life

12.1 "The Sports of the City"

In the late twelfth century traveler William FitzStephen writes in his description of London, "Furthermore let us consider also the sports of the City, since it is not meet that a city should only be useful and sober, unless it also be pleasant and merry."

Source: William FitzStephen, A Description of London, prefixed to his *Life of Thomas a Becket*, trans. H. E. Butler, (Historical Association, 1934) reprinted in *Everyone a Witness: The Plantagenet Age*, ed. Arthur S. Finlay, (New York: Thomas Y. Crowell, 1976), pp. 112–14.

London in place of shows in the theatre and stage-plays has holier plays, wherein are shown forth the miracles wrought by Holy Confessors or the sufferings which glorified the constancy of Martyrs.

Moreover, each year upon the day called Carnival—to begin with the sports of boys (for we were all boys once)—boys from the schools bring fighting-cocks to their master, and the whole forenoon is given up to boyish sport; for they have a holiday in the schools that they may watch their cocks do battle. After dinner all the youth of the City goes out into the fields in a much-frequented game of ball. The scholars of each school have their own ball, and almost all the workers of each trade have theirs also in their hands. Elder men and fathers and rich citizens come on horseback to watch the contests of their juniors and after their fashion are young again with the young; and it seems that the motion of their natural heat is kindled by the contemplation of such violent motion and by their partaking in the joys of untrammelled youth.

Every Sunday in Lent after dinner a 'fresh swarm of young gentles' goes forth on war-horses, 'steeds skilled in the contest, of which each is 'apt and schooled to wheel in circles round'. From the gates burst forth in throngs the lay sons of citizens, armed with lance and shield, the younger with shafts forked at the end, but with steel point removed. 'They wake war's semblance' and in mimic contest exercise their skill at arms. Many courtiers come too, when the King is in residence; and from the households of Earls and Barons come young men not yet invested with the belt of knighthood, that they may there contend together. Each one of them is on fire with hope of victory. The fierce horses neigh, 'their limbs tremble; they champ the bit; impatient of delay they cannot stand still'. When at length 'the hoof of trampling steeds careers along', the youthful riders divide their hosts; some pursue those that fly before, and cannot overtake them; others unhorse their comrades and speed by.

At the feast of Easter they make sport with naval tourneys, as it were. For a shield being strongly bound to a stout pole in mid-stream, a small vessel, swiftly driven on by many an oar and by the river's flow, carries a youth standing at the prow, who is to strike the shield with his lance. If he break the lance by striking the shield and keep his feet unshaken, he has achieved his purpose and fulfilled his desire. If, however, he strike it strongly without splintering his lance, he is thrown into the rushing river, and the boat of its own speed passes him by. But there are on each side of the shield two vessels moored, and in them are many youths to snatch up the striker who has been sucked down by the stream, as soon as he emerges into sight or 'once more bubbles on the topmost wave'. On the bridge and the galleries above the river are spectators of the sport 'ready to laugh their fill'.

On feast-days throughout the summer the youths exercise themselves in leaping, archery and wrestling, putting the stone, and throwing the thonged javelin beyond a mark, and fighting with sword and buckler. 'Cytherea leads the dance of maidens and the earth is smitten with free foot at moonrise.'

In winter on almost every feast-day before dinner either foaming boars and hogs, armed with 'tusks lightning-swift', themselves soon to be bacon, fight for their lives, or fat bulls with butting horns, or huge bears, do combat to the death against hounds let loose upon them.

When the great marsh that washes the northern walls of the City is frozen, dense throngs of youths go forth to disport themselves upon the ice. Some gathering speed by a run, glide sidelong, with feet set well apart, over a vast space of ice. Others make themselves seats of ice like mill-stones and are dragged along by a number who run before them holding hands. Sometimes they slip owing to the greatness of their speed and fall, every one of them, upon their faces. Others there are, more skilled to sport upon the ice, who fit to their feet the shin-bones of beasts, lashing them beneath their ankles, and with ironshod poles in their hands they strike ever and anon against the ice and are borne along swift as a bird in flight or a bolt shot from a mangonel. But sometimes two by agreement run one against the other from a great distance and, raising their poles, strike one another. One or both fall, not without bodily hurt, since on falling they are borne a long way in opposite directions.

Many of the citizens delight in taking their sport with birds of the air, merlins and falcons and the like, and with dogs that wage warfare in the woods. The citizens have the special privilege of hunting in Middlesex, Hertfordshire and all Chiltern, and in Kent as far as the river Cray.

Questions:
1. What kind of sports were popular in London?
2. Who is missing from this description of public play in London? Why?

12.2   College Life: Between Students and Their Fathers

European universities first emerged in the middle ages and western universities today are descended from them. The administrative structure, system of degrees, and even the robes worn at graduation are vestiges of the twelfth century. The following selections reveal the personal and social aspect of college life.

Source: *Sources of the Western Tradition: Volume I: From Ancient Times to the Enlightenment*, ed. Marvin Perry, Joseph R. Peden, and Theodore H. Von Laue, (Boston: Houghton Mif-

flin Co., 1995), p. 182. Used with permission from G.G. Coulton, *Life in the Middle Ages*, Vol. 3, (Cambridge: Cambridge University Press, 1928/29).

FATHERS TO SONS

I

I have recently discovered that you live dissolutely and slothfully, preferring license to restraint and play to work and strumming a guitar while the others are at their studies, whence it happens that you have read but one volume of law while your more industrious companions have read several. Wherefore I have decided to exhort you herewith to repent utterly of your dissolute and careless ways, that you may no longer be called a waster and your shame may be turned to good repute.

II

I have learned—not from your master, although he ought not to hide such things from me, but from a certain trustworthy source—that you do not study in your room or act in the schools as a good student should, but play and wander about, disobedient to your master and indulging in sport and in certain other dishonorable practices which I do not now care to explain by letter.

SONS TO FATHERS

I

"Well-beloved father, I have not a penny, nor can I get any save through you, for all things at the University are so dear: nor can I study in my Code or my Digest, for they are all tattered. Moreover, I owe ten crowns in dues to the Provost, and can find no man to lend them to me; I send you word of greetings and of money.

The Student hath need of many things if he will profit here; his father and his kin must needs supply him freely, that he be not compelled to pawn his books, but have ready money in his purse, with gowns and furs and decent clothing, or he will be damned for a beggar; wherefore, that men may not take me for a beast, I send you word of greetings and of money.

Wines are dear, and hostels, and other good things; I owe in every street, and am hard bested to free myself from such snares. Dear father, design to help me! I fear to be excommunicated; already have I been cited, and there is not even a dry bone in my larder. If I find not the money before this feast of Easter, the church door will be shut in my face: wherefore grant my supplication, for I send you word of greetings and of money.

L'Envoy

Well-beloved father, to ease my debts contracted at the tavern, at the baker's, with the doctor and the bedells [a minor college official], and to pay my subscriptions to the laundress and the barber, I send you word of greetings and of money."

II

Sing unto the Lord a new song, praise him with stringed instruments and organs, rejoice upon the high-sounding cymbals, for your son has held a glorious disputation, which was attended by a great number of teachers and scholars. He answered all questions without a mistake, and no one could get the better of him or prevail against his arguments. Moreover he celebrated a famous banquet, at which both rich and poor were honoured as never before, and he has duly begun to give lectures which are already so popular that others' classrooms are deserted and his own are filled.

Questions:
1. How do the relationships between these fathers and sons resemble those of the present day?
2. From these letters, can you discern any major differences between college life today and 500 years ago?

12.3   Regulating Behavior in the City

Like many cities in the fourteenth century, Florence had social and economic problems stemming both from the increasing affluence of the merchants and the results of the Black Death. Below are records of Florence's efforts to deal with these problems.

Source: Brucker, Gene, editor. *The Society of Renaissance Florence: A Documentary Study.* New York: Harper and Row, 1971, pp. 180–83, 190–95.

REGULATING PROSTITUTION

The Establishment of Communal Brothels in Florence, 1415

Desiring to eliminate a worse evil by means of a lesser one, the lord priors . . . [and their colleges] have decreed that . . . the priors . . . [and their colleges] may authorize the establishment of two public brothels in the city of Florence, in addition to the one which already exists: one in the quarter of S. Spirito and the other in the quarter of S. Croce. [They are to be located] in suitable places or in places where the exercise of such scandalous activity can best be concealed, for the honor of the city and of those who live in the neighborhood in which these prostitutes must stay to hire their bodies for lucre, as other prostitutes stay in the other brothel. For establishing these places . . . in a proper manner and for their construction, furnishing, and improvement, they may spend up to 1,000 florins.

Prostitutes and the Courts, 1398–1400

This is the inquisition carried out by the excellent and honorable doctor of law, Messer Giovanni of Montepulciano, the appellate judge . . . of the city of Florence against Salvaza, wife of Seze, parish of S. Lucia Ogni Santi. . . .

It has come to the attention of the abovementioned judge and his court . . . that this Salvaza, wife of Seze has publicly committed adultery with several persons and has sold her body for money. . . . With respect to all of these charges, the judge intends to discover the truth; and if she is found guilty of walking without gloves and bells on her head or with high-heeled slippers, to punish her according to the Communal statutes; and if innocent, to absolve her from this accusation.

This inquisition was begun by the judge against Salvaza on November x6, 1400. Sitting in tribunal in the accustomed seat of his office, the judge ordered . . . Bartolo di Bartolo, a public messenger of the Commune of Florence, to go to the home of Salvaza and order her to appear before the judge to clear herself of this accusation and to defend herself.

November 16. The messenger has informed the judge and myself, the notary, that he went to the house of Salvaza and finding her there, informed her of everything herein inscribed and personally left a copy of this inquisition.

November 19, 1400. Salvaza appeared personally at the residence of the judge, and since according to the statutes, no woman is allowed to enter there, the judge . . . ordered me, Jacopo de Silis, his notary, to descend to her near the entrance door . . . to hear and receive her reply, defense, and excuse. Before me, the notary, Salvaza replied to this accusation by stating that it was not true. . . . [She was then informed that she had eight days in which to furnish evidence of her innocence.]

November 24, 1400. Bartolo di Bartolo informed me, Jacopo de Silis, that he had personally informed the witnesses, identified below, from the parish of S. Lucia Ogni Santi, to appear on that same day before him at his accustomed residence to swear to tell the truth . . . concerning the statements in this accusation.

The following witnesses against Salvaza were sworn in and examined by the judge and myself, the notary, on November 24, 1400.

Antonio di Ugo, parish of S. Lucia Ogni Santi . . . stated that everything in the accusation was true. When asked how he knew this, the witness replied that on numerous occasions, he had seen Salvaza enter the houses of many men—both natives and foreigners—by day and night. They played and danced with her, and did many illicit and indecent things with her, touching her and fondling her with their hands, as is done by public prostitutes. Asked whom he had seen touching and fondling her, and in whose houses, he replied that Salvaza went to the house of a certain Mancino, a Florentine citizen, and stayed with him for several days; also a certain pimp named Nanni, Niccolo, a tiler, and many others whose names he did not know. Asked about Salvaza's reputation, he replied that she is commonly regarded as a whore. When asked who voices this opinion, and where he heard it, he replied that it was the general opinion of nearly everyone in the parish. Asked about Salvaza's physical appearance and age, he replied that she is a big woman, about forty-five, quite attractive, with a dark complexion.

Vanni Migliore, parish of S. Lucia, . . . stated that he knew Salvaza, wife of Seze, very well; she lives in the street called the Prato Ogni Santi. He said that the contents of this accusation are true. When asked how he knew, he replied that he had seen many men, both citizens and foreigners, enter her house both day and night, and that she committed adultery with them. He had seen her engaged in indecent acts with them. Asked whom he had seen entering this house and participating in these indecencies, he identified a certain Martino of the parish of S. Paolo, Niccolo, a tiler, and many others whom he did not know. He stated that one night his door was closed and he was told that Niccolo had closed it. Thereupon, the witness encountered Niccolo and quarreled with him and told him that he was doing wrong. And Niccolo replied: "And I will fornicate wherever I please," and he held a key in his hands, and Salvaza was mouthing obscenities at him. Asked about Salvaza's reputation, he replied that among all of the residents of the parish, she had a bad reputation as a prostitute. Asked about her physical appearance and age, he replied that she was a large, dark woman of about forty years of age.

. . . [*Other witnesses corroborate the accusation.*]

Margherita, widow of Ugo . . . stated that the contents of the accusation were true. When asked how she knew this, she replied that she is a near neighbor of Salvaza, and that she had often seen men enter her house. . . . The witness said that she had frequently looked through a window of Salvaza's house and had seen her nude in bed with men, engaging in those indecent acts which are practiced by prostitutes. [Salvaza was declared to be a public prostitute, and was required to wear gloves, bells, and high-heeled slippers.]

SUMPTUARY LEGISLATION IN FLORENCE:

The Social Rationale

[1433] After diligent examination and mature deliberation, the lord priors have seen, heard, and considered certain regulations issued in the current year in the month of August by Francesco di Andrea da Quarata and other officials who are called "the officials to restrain female ornaments and dress." They are aware of the authority granted to the lord priors and the officials responsible for ornaments by a provision passed in July of the current year. . . . They realize the great desire of these officials to restrain the barbarous and irrepressible bestiality of women, who, not considering the fragility of their nature, but rather with that reprobate and diabolical nature, they force their men, with their honeyed poison, to submit to them. But it is not in accordance with nature for women to be burdened by so many expensive ornaments, and on account of these unbearable expenses, men are avoiding matrimony. . . . But women were created to replenish this free city, and to live chastely in matrimony, and not to spend gold and silver on clothing and jewelry. For did not God himself say: "Increase and multiply and replenish the earth"?

Questions:

1. Why did Florence license brothels?
2. Explain the rationale for sumptuary laws.
3. What do these documents have to say about women, dress, and power in this society?

12.4   The Flagellants

Although flagellation (voluntary whipping) had been practiced in monastic communities long before, it does not emerge as a public group activity until the midthirteenth century. When Europe experienced the Black Death (1347–1350), the Brotherhood of Flagellants (it included women also) resorted to even more spectacular public flagellation. The movement probably originated in Eastern Europe and took root most deeply in German areas. As we see from the following report of Robert of Avesbury, however, they also crossed the English Channel.

Sources: *Medieval England as Viewed by Contemporaries*, ed. W. O. Hassall, (New York: Harper Torchbooks, 1965, © 1957), pp. 157–58.

About Michaelmas 1349 over six hundred men came to London from Flanders, mostly of Zeeland and Holland origin. Sometimes at St. Paul's and sometimes at other points in the city they made two daily public appearances wearing cloths from the thighs to the ankles, but otherwise stripped bare. Each wore a cap marked with a red cross in front and behind. Each had in his right hand a scourge with three tails. Each tail had a knot and though the middle of it there were sometimes sharp nails fixed. They marched naked in a file one behind the other and whipped themselves with these scourges on their naked and bleeding bodies. Four of them would chant in their native tongue and another four would chant in response like a litany. Thrice they would all cast themselves on the ground in this sort of procession, stretching out their hands like the arms of a cross. The singing would go on and, the one who was in the rear of those thus prostrate acting first, each of them in turn would step over the others and give one stroke with his scourge to the man lying under him. This went on from the first to the last until each of them had observed the ritual to the full tale of those on the ground. Then each put on his customary garments and always wearing their caps and carrying their whips in their hands they retired to their lodgings. It is said that every night they performed the same penance.

Questions:

1. What was the motivation behind the flagellant movement?
2. Why do you think most church authorities discouraged such activities? Why do you think secular and church authorities allowed them to continue?

SECTION 2
Private Life

12.5 When Medieval Marriages Go Bad

We have few records of the private lives of common people in medieval society. Monastic chronicles focus on the lives of the rich and noble, but Church court records expose the humblest of lives and their problems. Couples that ended up in the Church courts cannot be considered as the norm, but they do pull aside the curtains to reveal that dysfunctional families existed in the fourteenth century also. Both of the following cases are from England, 1347.

Source: *Registrum Hamonis Hethe*, ed. Johnson, p. 974; and Lincoln Dean and Chapter, A/2/24, fo. 72v. Translations by Paul Hyams of Cornell University, cases supplied by Larry Poos, Catholic University. Printed with permission.

Additional source information:

First case source: Charles Johnson ed., *Registrum Hamonis Hethe, Dioceses Roffensis (1319–52),* (Canterbury and York Society xlix, 1948), p. 974. Translated by Paul Hyams, Cornell University.

Second case source: Lincolnshire Archives Office D&C A/2/24 fo 72v, edited by Larry Poos, Catholic University of America, trans. by Paul Hyams, Cornell University.

Henry Cook of Trotteslyve (Kent) and his wife were summoned because each has turned away from the other and they do not live together. Both appear in person. And Henry then alleged that he did not know why his wife left him but she behaved as badly as possible towards him, with contumelious words and other evil deeds, as he asserts. His [unnamed] wife said that her said husband loved several other women and therefore had a malevolent mind towards her, and she could not go on living with Henry on account of his cruelty. Finally both of them swore after touching the gospels that they would live together in future and give each other the usual conjugal services ("suffragia"), and that she [blank left for name] will now be humble and "familiaris" with her husband and not fighting, contumelious or insulting; and that the husband will treat his wife with marital affection from now on.

John Marabel, a married man, is cited of adultery and incest with Alice, daughter of Robert de Wywell, daughter of the said John's wife. The man appears and admits (his sin). The woman is not found. And John is forbidden from coition with either the mother or the daughter in future, unless the mother, who is the wife, seeks the debt and he pays it with sadness. And he will have as penance to make a pilgrimage with bare feet to St. Mary at Lincoln, to St. Thomas [Becket] at Canterbury, and to [St. Thomas Cantilupe] at Hereford and to beatings in penitential fashion round the church and round the marketplace of Grantham. And he will forswear the sin and suspect locations for the said Alice under pain of 40/-. It is later held that the same John on his pilgrimage would take much from his said wife, (so) the penance was changed so that he will fast on bread and water as long as he lives every fourth and sixth day [i.e., of the week], unless work or sickness prevents this. . . . We John warn thee, the aforesaid John, once, twice and a third time that you, having been parted for good from your wife, will eject the said Alice from your company within the next six days under pain of greater excommunication which is now (pronounced) most firmly on your person in these writings if you should disdain to carry out the aforegoing.

Questions:
1. What was the problem in each of these cases?
2. How did the church court deal with each situation?

Documents 12.6 and 12.7

These documents each offer a perspective on the ideal wife—note that the second selection comes from a woman who has lost the two primary male figures in her life.

12.6 The Ideal Wife of a Merchant

Alberti, a Florentine Renaissance humanist, presents a picture of the ideal wife as described by a fictional, rich old Florentine merchant.

Source: *Not in God's Image: Women in History from the Greeks to the Victorian*, eds. Julia O'Faolain, and Lauro Martines, (New York: Harper and Row, 1973), pp. 187–89.

After my wife had been settled in my house a few days, and after her first pangs of longing for her mother and family had begun to fade, I took her by the hand and showed her around the whole house. I explained that the loft was the place for grain and that the stores of wine and wood were kept in the cellar. I showed her where things needed for the table were kept, and so on, through the whole house. At the end there were no household goods of which my wife had not learned both the place and the purpose. Then we returned to my room, and, having locked the door, I showed her my treasures, silver, tapestry, garments, jewels, and where each thing had its place. . . .

Only my books and records and those of my ancestors did I determine to keep well sealed. . . . These my wife not only could not read, she could not even lay hands on them. I kept my records at all times . . . locked up and arranged in order in my study, almost like sacred and religious objects. I never gave my wife permission to enter that place, with me or alone. I also ordered her, if she ever came across any writing of mine, to give it over to my keeping at once. To take away any taste she might have for looking at my notes or prying into my private affairs, I often used to express my disapproval of bold and forward females who try too hard to know about things outside the house and about the concerns of their husband and of men in general. . . .

[Husbands] who take counsel with their wives . . . are madmen if they think true prudence or good counsel lies in the female brain. . . . For this very reason I have always tried carefully not to let any secret of mine be known to a woman. I did not doubt that my wife was most loving, and more discreet and modest in her ways than any, but I still considered it safer to have her unable, and not merely unwilling, to harm me. . . . Furthermore, I made it a rule never to speak with her of anything but household matters or questions of conduct, or of the children. Of these matters I spoke a good deal to her. . . .

When my wife had seen and understood the place of everything in the house, I said to her, 'My dear wife . . . you have seen our treasures now, and thanks be to God they are such that we ought to be contented with them. If we know how to preserve them, these things will serve you and me and our children. It is up to you, therefore, my dear wife, to keep no less careful watch over them than I.'

. . . She said she would be happy to do conscientiously whatever she knew how to do and had the skill to do, hoping it might please me. To this I said, 'Dear wife, listen to me. I shall be most pleased if you do just three things: first, my wife, see that you never want another man to share this bed but me. You understand.' She blushed and cast down her eyes. Still I repeated that she should never receive anyone into that room but myself. That was the first point. The second, I said, was that she should take care of the household, preside over it with modesty, serenity, tranquillity, and peace. That was the second point. The third thing, I said, was that she should see that nothing went wrong in the house.

. . . I could not describe to you how reverently she replied to me. She said her mother had taught her only how to spin and sew, and how to be virtuous and obedient. Now she would gladly learn from me how to rule the family and whatever I might wish to teach her.

Then she and I knelt down and prayed to God to give us the power to make good use of those possessions which he, in his mercy and kindness, had allowed us to enjoy. We also prayed . . . that he might grant us the grace to live together in peace and harmony for many happy years, and with many male children, and that he might grant to me riches, friendship, and honor, and to her, integrity, purity, and the character of a perfect mistress of the household.

Then, when we had stood up, I said to her: 'My dear wife, to have prayed God for these things is not enough. . . . I shall seek with all my powers to gain what we have asked of God. You, too, must set your whole will, all your mind, and all your modesty to work to make yourself a person whom God has heard. . . . You should realize that in this regard nothing is so important for yourself, so acceptable to God, so pleasing to me, and precious in the sight of your children as your chastity. The woman's character is the jewel of her family; the mother's purity has always been a part of the dowry she passes on to her daughters; her purity has always far outweighed her beauty. . . . Shun every sort of dishonor, my dear wife. Use every means to appear to all people as a highly respectable woman. To seem less would be to offend God, me, our children, and yourself.'

. . . . Never, at any moment, did I choose to show in word or action even the least bit of self-surrender in front of my wife. I did not imagine for a moment that I could hope to win obedience from one to whom I had confessed myself a slave. Always, therefore, I showed myself virile and a real man.

12.7   The City of Ladies: Wives of Artisans

Christine de Pisan (c. 1363 c. 1434) was one of the most prolific of French writers in the later Middle Ages. The daughter of a famous professor at Bologna, she received an excellent education. The deaths of both her husband and her father left her alone to raise and support her three small children. She did so by her pen. Always an advocate of the women's role in society, she wrote books on morality, history, religion, love, and advice for women.

Source: Christine de Pisan, *The Treasure of the City of Ladies*, (New York, Penguin Books, 1985), pp. 167–68.

Now it is time for us to speak of the station in life of women married to artisans who live in cities and fine towns, like Paris and elsewhere. They can use all the good things that have been said before, but yet some tradesmen like goldsmiths, embroiderers, armourers, tapestry makers and many others are more respectable than are masons, shoemakers and such like. All wives of artisans should be very painstaking and diligent if they wish to have the necessities of life. They should encourage their husbands or their workmen to get to work early in the morning and work until late, for mark our words, there is no trade so good that if you neglect your work you will not have difficulty putting bread on the table. And besides encouraging the others, the wife herself should be involved in the work to the extent that she know all about it, so that she may know how to oversee his workers if her husband is absent and to reprove them if they do not do well. She ought to oversee them to keep them from idleness; for through careless workers the master is sometimes ruined. And when customers come to her husband and try to drive a hard bargain, she ought to warn him solicitously to take care that he does not make a bad deal. She should advise him to be chary of giving too much credit if he does not know precisely where and to whom it is going; for in this way many come to poverty, although sometimes the greed to earn more or to accept a tempting proposition makes them do it.

In addition, she ought to keep her husbands love as much as she can, to this end: that he will stay at home more willingly and that he may not have any reason to join the foolish crowds of other young men in taverns and indulge in unnecessary and extravagant expense, as many tradesmen do, especially in Paris. By treating him kindly she should protect him as well as she can from this. It is said that three things drive a man from his home: a quarrelsome wife, a smoking fireplace and a leaking roof. She too ought to stay at home gladly and not go every day traipsing hither and yon gossiping with the neighbours and visiting her chums to find out what everyone is doing. That is done by slovenly housewives roaming about the town in groups. Nor should she go off on these pilgrimages got up for no good reason and involving a lot of needless expense. Futhermore, she ought to remind her husband that they should live so frugally that their expenditure does not exceed their income, so that at the end of the year they do not find themselves in debt.

If she has children, she should have them instructed and taught first at school by educated people so that they may know how better to serve God. Afterwards they may be put to some trade by which they may earn a living, for whoever gives a trade or business training to her child gives a great possession. The children should be kept from wantonness and from voluptuousness above all else, for truly it is something that most shames the children of good towns and is a great sin of mothers and fathers who ought to be the cause of the virtue and good behaviour of their children, but they are sometimes the reason (because of bringing them up to be finicky and indulging them too much) for their wickedness and ruin.

Questions for Documents 12.6 and 12.7

1. What does the Florentine merchant expect of his wife?
2. According to Christine de Pisan, what should be the role of the wife of an artisan?
3. How do Christine de Pisan's instructions for the wives of artisans compare to the instructions the Florentine merchant gave his wife?

12.8   How They Died

The following selections are Coroner Reports from the City of London during the fourteenth century. The untimely death of these ordinary townspeople also reveals many details about their everyday lives.

Source: *Calendar of Coroners Rolls of the City of London, 1300–1378.* ed. R. R. Sharpe, (London: Richard Clay and Sons, 1913), pp. 56–57, 63–69, 86–87, 127, 183. Language has been modernized by the editors.

1. ON THE DEATH OF ROBERT, SON OF JOHN DE ST. BOTULPH

Saturday before the Feast of St. Margaret [20 July] in the year [16 Edward II, A.D. 1322], information was given to the . . . Coroner and Sheriffs that a certain Robert, son of John de St. Botulph, a boy seven years old, lay dead of a death other than his rightful death in a certain shop which the said Robert held of Richard de Wirhale in the parish of St. Michael de Paternosterchurch in the Ward of Vintry. Thereupon the Coroner and Sheriffs proceeded there and, having summoned good men of that Ward and of the three nearest Wards, namely Douuegate, Queenhithe and Corde-wanerstreet, they diligently inquired how it happened. The jurors say that when on the Sunday next before the Feast of St. Dunstan [19 May], [Robert son of] John, Richard son of John de Chesthunt, and two other boys, names unknown, were playing on certain pieces of timber in a lane called "Kyrounelane" in the Ward of Vintry, a certain piece fell on [Robert] and broke his right leg. In the course of time Johanna, his mother, arrived, and rolled the timber off him, and carried him to a shop where he lingered until Friday . . . when he died at the hour of Prime of the broken leg and of no other felony, nor do they suspect anyone of the death, but only the accident and the fracture. Being asked who were present when it happened, they say the aforesaid Robert, Richard son of John de Chesthunt and two boys whose names they know not and no others.

Four neighbors attached, namely:
Richard Daske, by Peter Cosyn and Roger le Roper.
Anketin de Gisors, by Robert de Wynton and
    Andrew de Gloucester.
Thomas le Roper, by Richard de Colyngstoke and
    Thomas atte March.
John Amys, by John de Shirbourne and John de
    Lincoln.

2. ON THE DEATH OF NICHOLAS, SERVANT OF SIMON DE KNOTTYNGLEY

On Monday in Pentecost week the year [A.D. 1324], it happened that Nicholas, the servant of Simon de Knottyngley, lay killed before the gate of the house of William de Pomfreit in the high street in the parish of St. Botulph de Bisshopsgate. . . . On hearing this, the . . . Coroner and Sheriffs proceeded there, and having summoned good men of that Ward and of the three nearest Wards . . . , they diligently inquired how it happened. The jurors say that on that Monday, at break of day, William de la March, the late palfrey-man [a type of groom] of Henry de Percy, Thomas the servant of Henry de Percy's cook, John the servant to Henry

Krok, who was Henry's esquire, assaulted, beat and wounded Nicholas in the house held by Alice de Witteney, a courtesan, whose landlord was John de Assheby. . . . William de la March struck Nicholas with a knife called an "Irishknife" under the right breast and penetrating to the belly, inflicting a wound an inch long and in depth half through the body. [Nicholas] thus wounded went from there to the place where he was found dead, where he died at daybreak of the same day. Being asked what became of the said William, Thomas and John, the jurors say that they immediately fled, but where they went or who received them they know not, nor do they suspect any one except those three. Being asked as to their goods and chattels, the jurors say that they had none, so far as could be ascertained. Being asked who first found the corpse, they say it was Thomas, son of John le Marshall, who raised the cry so that the country came. The corpse was viewed on which the wound appeared. [Order] to the Sheriff to attach the said William, Thomas and John as soon as they be found in their bailiwick.

Afterwards the William de la March was captured by Adam de Salisbury, the Sheriff and committed to New-gate [prison]. William has a surcoat which is confiscated [because of] his flight, worth two shillings, for which Adam de Salisbury the Sheriff [is responsible].

Four neighbors attached, namely:
John Assheby, by Thomas Starling and Walter de Stanes.
Walter de Bedefunte, by Walter de Northampton and John le Barber.
William de Pomfreit, by William de Chalke and Roger Swetyng.
Adam le Fuitz Robert, by Eustace le Hattere and Thomas de Borham.

3. ON THE DEATH OF THOMAS LE POUNTAGER

On Saturday the Feast of St. Laurence [10 Aug.] the year [A.D. 1325], it happened that a certain Thomas, son of John le Pountager, lay drowned in the water of the Thames before the wharf of Richard Dorking in the parish of St. Martin, in the Ward of Vintry. On hearing this, the Coroner and Sheriffs proceeded there, and having summoned good men of that Ward and of the three nearest Wards . . . they diligently inquired how it happened. The jurors say that when on the preceding Friday, at dusk, Thomas had placed himself on the quay of Edward le Blount to bathe in the Thames, he was accidentally drowned, no one being present; that he remained in the water until Saturday, when at the third hour John Fleg a boatman discovered his corpse and raised the cry so that the country came. The corpse viewed on which no wound or bruise appeared.

The above John Fleg, the finder of the body, attached by Robert de Lenne and Robert de Taunton.

Four neighbors attached [their names are listed in the report].

4. ON THE DEATH OF JOHANNA, DAUGHTER OF BERNARD OF IRLAUNDE

Friday after the Feast of St. Dunstan [19 May] the year [A.D. 1322], it happened that Johanna daughter of Bernard de Irlaunde, a child one month old, lay dead of a death other than her rightful death, in a shop held by the said Bernard . . . in the parish of St. Michael, in the Ward of Queenhithe. On hearing this, the Coroner and Sheriffs proceeded there, and having summoned good men of that Ward and of the three nearest Wards. . ., they diligently inquired how it happened. The jurors say that when on the preceding Thursday, before the hour of Vespers, Johanna was lying in her cradle alone, the shop door being open there entered a certain sow which mortally bit the right side of the head of Johanna. At length there came Margaret, . . . Johanna's mother, and raised the cry and snatched up Johanna and kept her alive until midnight Friday when she died of the said bite and of no other felony. Being asked who were present, [the jurors] say, "No one except Margaret," nor do they suspect [any other cause] except the bite . the corpse of the said Johanna viewed on which no [other?] hurt appeared [sic]. The sow appraised by the jurors at 13 *d.* for which Richard Costantin, the Sheriff; [is responsible].

The above Margaret who found the body attached by John de Bedford and Andrew de Gloucester.

Four neighbors attached [their names are listed in the report].

5. ON THE DEATH OF MATILDA LA CAMBESTER AND MARGERY HER DAUGHTER

Friday after the Feast of St. Ambrose [4 April, 1337], information given to the Coroner and Sheriffs, that Matilda la Cambester and Margery her daughter aged one mouth, lay dead of a death other than their rightful death in a shop in the rent of the Prior of Tortyton in the parish of St Swythin in the Ward of Walbrok. Thereupon they proceeded there, and having summoned good men of that Ward, they diligently inquired how it happened. The jurors . . . say that on the preceding Thursday, after the hour of curfew when Matilda and Margery lay asleep in the shop a lighted candle which Matilda had negligently left on the wall, fell down among some straw and set fire to the shop so that the said Matilda and Margery were suffocated and burnt before the neighbors knew anything about it. The bodies viewed, &c.

Four neighbors attached [their names are listed in the report].

6. ON THE DEATH OF LUCY FAUKES

On Monday before the Feast of St. Michael [29 Sept., 1322], it happened that a certain Lucy Faukes lay dead of a death other than her rightful death in a certain shop which Richard le Sherman held of John Priour, senior, in the parish of St. Olave in the Ward of Alegate. On hearing this, the

Coroner and Sheriffs proceeded thither, and having summoned good men of that Ward and of the three nearest Wards, . . . they diligently inquired how it happened. The jurors say that on Sunday before the Feast of St. Matthew [2 Sept., 1322], about the hour of curfew, Lucy came to the shop in order to pass the night there with . . . Richard le Sherman and Cristina his wife, as she oftentimes was accustomed, and because Lucy was clad in good clothes, Richard and Cristina began to quarrel with her in order to obtain a reason for killing her for her clothes. At length Robert took up a staff called 'Balstaf;' and with the force and assistance of Cristina, struck her on the top of the head, and mortally broke and crushed the whole of her head, so that she died at once. Richard and Cristina stripped Lucy of her clothes, and immediately fled, but where they went or who received them, [the jurors] do not know. Being asked who were present when this happened, they say, "No one except the said Richard, Cristina and Lucy." Nor do they suspect anyone of the death except Richard and Cristina. Being asked about the goods and chattels of Richard and Cristina, the jurors say that they had nothing except what they took away with them. Being asked who found the dead Lucy's dead body, they say a certain Giles le Portor who raised the cry so that the country came. Order to the Sheriffs to attach the said Richard and Cristina when found in their bailiwick.

. . . Four neighbors attached [their names are listed in the report].

Questions:
1. What role do members of the community have in the event of "a death other than a rightful death?"
2. What do these reports inform us about the living conditions in the city of London?
3 What do they reveal about the roles of male and female among working urban dwellers?

CHAPTER 13
Rebirth in Italy
The Civilization of the Italian Renaissance
(1300–1500)

SECTION 1
The Renaissance Man

Documents 13.1–13.4

Questions on the Renaissance man (Documents 1–4) follow Document 4. Questions concerning both the Renaissance man and woman (Documents 1–6) follow Document 6 (in Section 2).

13.1 Petrarch: Rules for the Ruler

Petrarch (1304–74) was one of the first humanists who made his living as a public writer, receiving patronage from the wealthy political leaders of the Italian city-states. His concerns, more than his medieval predecessors, were secular, though he did not entirely ignore religion, especially later in life. In this excerpt, he duly praises his patron and then speaks more generally about how one ought to rule a state. Like Dante a generation before him, he used the vernacular and helped to make Italian a literary language.

> **Source:** Francesco Petrarca, *How a Ruler Ought to Govern His State*, trans. Benjamin G. Kohl, cited in *The Earthly Republic: Italian Humanists on Government and Society*, ed. Benjamin G. Kohl and Ronald G. Witt, (University of Pennsylvania Press, 1981, © 1978), pp. 35–80, passim.

. . . .

You ruled with such competence and such maturity that no rumor, no hint of rebellion, disturbed the city in that time of great change. Next, after a short time, you transformed into a large surplus the enormous deficit that debts to foreign powers had left in your treasury. And now the years and experience in government have so matured you that you are esteemed as an outstanding lord, not only by your own citizens but also by the lords of many other cities, who hold you up as a model. As a result, I have often heard neighboring peoples express the wish that they could be governed by you and nurture envy for your subjects. You have never devoted yourself to either the arrogance of pompous display or to the idleness of pleasure, but you have devoted yourself to just rule so that everyone acknowledges that you are peaceful without being feckless and dignified without being prideful. As a result, modesty coexists with magnanimity in your character. You are thus full of dignity. Although, because of your incredible humanity, you permit easy access to yourself even to the most humble, still one of your most outstanding acts is to have at the same time contracted for your daughters very advantageous marriages with noble families in distant lands.[1] And you have been, above all other rulers, a lover of public order and peace—a peace that was never thought possible by the citizen-body when Padua was ruled by a communal regime or by any of your family, no matter how long they held the power—you alone constructed many strong fortresses at suitable points along the Paduan frontiers. Thus you acted in every way so that the citizens felt free and secure with you as a ruler, and no innocent blood was spilled. You also have pacified all your neighbors either by fear or by love or by admiration for your excellence, so that for many years now you have ruled a flourishing state with serene tranquility and in continual peace. But at last the adversary of the human race, that enemy of peace [the Devil], suddenly stirred up a dangerous war with that power you never feared. Consequently, although you still loved peace, you fought with Venice bravely and with great determination over a long time, even though you lacked the aid from allies that you had hoped for. And when it seemed most advantageous to do so, you skillfully concluded peace so that at one stroke you won twofold praise both for your bravery and your political wisdom.[2] From these facts and from many others I shall omit, you have been viewed as vastly superior to all other rulers of your state and to all rulers of other cities, not only in the judgment of your own subjects but indeed in the opinion of the whole world as well.

. . . .

The first quality is that a lord should be friendly, never terrifying, to the good citizens, even though it is inevitable that he be terrifying to evil citizens if he is to be a friend to justice. "For he does not carry a sword without good cause,

---

[1] Francesco da Carrara contracted marriages for several of his daughters with the scions of noble houses in Italy and Germany, including the count of Oettingen, the count of Veglie, and the duke of Saxony.

[2] An allusion to the border war fought with Venice in 1372–73, which Francesco da Carrara ended by agreeing to the payment of an indemnity to Venice while he maintained substantially his original frontiers. See Paolo Sambin, "La guerra del 1372–73 tra Venezia e Padova," *Archivio Veneti* ser., 38–41 (1946–47):1–76.

since he is a minister of God," as the Apostle says. Now nothing is more foolish, nothing is more destructive to the stability of the state, than to wish to be dreaded by everyone. Many princes, both in antiquity and in modern times, have wanted nothing more than to be feared and have believed that nothing is more useful than fear and cruelty in maintaining their power. Concerning this belief we have an example in the case of the barbaric emperor named Maximinus. In fact, nothing is farther from the truth than these opinions; rather, it is much more advantageous to be loved than to be feared, unless we are speaking of the way in which a devoted child fears a good father. Any other kind of fear is diametrically opposed to what a ruler should desire. Rulers in general want to reign for a long time and to lead their lives in security, but to be feared is opposed to both of these desires, and to be loved is consistent with both.

. . . .

What I can say is that the nature of public love is the same as private love. Seneca says: "I shall show you a love potion that is made without medicines, without herbs, without the incantations of any poison-maker. If you want to be loved, love." There it is. Although many other things could be said, this saying is the summation of everything. What is the need for magical arts, what for any reward or labor? Love is free; it is sought out by love alone. And who can be found with such a steely heart that he would not want to return an honorable love? "Honorable" I say, for a dishonorable love is not love at all, but rather hatred hidden under the guise of love. Now to return love to someone who loves basely is to do nothing other than to compound one crime with another and to become a part of another person's disgraceful deceit.

. . . .

Indeed, from the discussion of this topic nothing but immense and honorable pleasure ought to come to you since you are so beloved by your subjects that you seem to them to be not a lord over citizens but the "father of your country." In fact this was the title of almost all of the emperors of antiquity; some of them bore the name justly, but others carried it so injustly that nothing more perverse can be conceived. Both Caesar Augustus and Nero were called "father of his country." The first was a true father, the second was an enemy of both his country and of religion. But this title really does belong to you.

. . . .

You should know, moreover, that to merit this kind of esteem you must always render justice and treat your citizens with goodwill. Do you really want to be a father to your citizens? Then you must want for your subjects what you want for your own children.

. . . .

Now I shall speak of justice, the very important and noble function that is to give to each person his due so that no one is punished without good reason. Even when there is a good reason for punishment you should incline to mercy, following the example of Our Heavenly Judge and Eternal King. For no one of us is immune from sin and all of us are weak by our very nature, so there is no one of us who does not need mercy.

. . . .

Indeed, I do not deny, nor am I ignorant of, the fact that the lord of a city ought to take every precaution to avoid useless and superfluous expenditures. In this way he will not exhaust the treasury and have nothing left for necessary expenditures. Therefore, a lord should spend nothing and do nothing whatsoever that does not further the beauty and good order of the city over which he rules. To put it briefly, he ought to act as a careful guardian of the state, not as its lord. Such was the advice that the Philosopher gave at great length in his *Politics*, advice that is found to be very useful and clearly consistent with justice.[3] Rulers who act otherwise are to be judged as thieves rather than as defenders and preservers of the state.

. . . .

From these concerns, however, derives not just the happiness of the people, but the security of the ruling class as well. For no one is more terrifying than a starving commoner of whom it has been said: "the hungry pleb knows no fear." Indeed, there are not just ancient examples but contemporary ones, especially from recent events in the city of Rome, which bear out this saying.[4]

. . . .

Among those honored for their abilities in governing, the first place ought to go to learned men. And among these learned men, a major place should go to those whose knowledge in law is always very useful to the state. If, indeed, love of and devotion to justice is added to their knowledge of law, these citizens are (as Cicero puts it) "learned not just in the law, but in justice."[5] However, there are those who follow the law but do no justice, and these are unworthy to bear the name of the legal profession. For it is not enough simply to have knowledge; you must want to use it. A good lawyer adds good intentions to his legal knowledge. Indeed, there have been many lawyers who have added luster to ancient Rome and other places: Adrianus Julius Celsus, Salvius Julianus, Neratius Priscus, Antonius Scaevola, Severus Papinianus, Alexander Domitius Ulpianus, Fabius Sabinus, Julius Paulus, and many others.[6] And you too (as much as our own times permit) have by the patronage of your university added honor to your country. There are other kinds of learned men, some of whom you can depend on for advice and learned conversation, and (as Alexander used

---

[3] Aristotle *Politica* 5.9, 1314b40ff, which Petrarch knew only in medieval Latin translation.

[4] An allusion to a revolt—caused by famine—by the lower classes of Rome against the senatorial families in 1353, just before the return to the city of the demagogic Cola di Rienzo. See F. Gregorovius, *History of the City of Rome in the Middle Ages*, trans. A. Hamilton, 8 vols. (London, 1898), 6:337ff.

[5] Cicero *Orationes Philippicae* 9.5.10.

[6] Petrarch derived this list of famous legal experts from the time of the Roman Empire mainly from his reading of the *Scriptores historiae Augusta* passim.

to say) invent literary tales.[7] One reads that Julius Caesar, in like fashion, used to confer Roman citizenship on doctors of medicine and on teachers of the liberal arts.[8] Now, among learned men there is no doubt that we ought to give preference to those who teach the knowledge of sacred things (or what we call theology), provided that these men have kept themselves free from any foolish sophistries.

That very wise emperor Augustus used to bestow patronage on learned men to encourage them to remain in Rome, and hope of such a reward stimulated others to study, for at that time Roman citizenship was a highly valued honor. Indeed, when St. Paul claimed that he was a Roman citizen, the tribune judging the case said to him: "I myself have at a high price obtained this status."[9]

• • • •

Even if it were not written in any book, still death is certain, as our common nature tells us. Now I do not know whether it is because of human nature or from some longstanding custom that at the death of our close friends and relatives we can scarcely contain our grief and tears, and that our funeral services are often attended by wailings and lamentations. But I do know that scarcely ever has this propensity for public grief been so deep-rooted in other cities as it is in yours. Someone dies—and I do not care whether he is a noble or a commoner, the grief displayed by the commoners is certainly no less manifest, and perhaps more so, than that of the nobles, for the plebs are more apt to show their emotions and less likely to be moved by what is proper; as soon as he breathes his last, a great howling and torrent of tears begins. Now I am not asking you to forbid expressions of grief. This would be difficult and probably impossible, given human nature. But what Jeremiah says is true: "You should not bemoan the dead, nor bathe the corpse in tears."[10] As the great poet Euripides wrote in Crespontes: "Considering the evil of our present existence, we ought to lament at our birth and rejoice at our death."[11] But these philosophic opinions are not well known, and, in any case, the common people would find them unthinkable and strange.

Therefore, I will tell you what I am asking. Take an example: Some old dowager dies, and they carry her body into the streets and through the public squares accompanied by loud and indecent wailing so that someone who did not know what was happening could easily think that here was a madman on the loose or that the city was under enemy attack. Now, when the funeral cortege finally gets to the church, the horrible keening redoubles, and at the very spot where there ought to be hymns to Christ or devoted prayers for the soul of the deceased in a subdued voice or even silence, the walls resound with the lamentations of the mourners and the holy altars shake with the wailing of women. All this simply because a human being has died. This custom is contrary to any decent and honorable behav-

ior and unworthy of any city under your rule. I wish you would have it changed. In fact, I am not just advising you, I am (if I may) begging you to do so. Order that wailing women should not be permitted to step outside their homes; and if some lamentation is necessary to the grieved, let them do it at home and do not let them disturb the public thoroughfares.

I have said to you perhaps more than I should, but less than I would like to say. And if it seems to you, illustrious sir, that I am mistaken in one place or another, I beg your pardon, and I ask you to consider only the good advice. May you rule your city long and happily. Farewell. Arquà, the 28th of November.

13.2 Machiavelli: Life in Exile

Machiavelli learned much in his fourteen years in Florentine politics, (1498–1512), which included frequent diplomatic missions abroad. In 1512, when the Medicis came to power, however, Machiavelli found himself exiled from his beloved city of Florence and without a post in the government. He retreated to his country home just outside Florence, where he produced the works for which he remains famous. In this letter to the Florentine ambassador to Rome, he describes his typical day in the country. During this time he wrote *The Prince (Deprincipatibus)* as a means to try to get back into the good favor of the Medici family and back into politics.

Source: Letter from Niccolo Machiavelli to Francesco Vettori in Rome, December 10, 1513, cited in *The Portable Machiavelli,* ed. and trans. Peter Bondanella and Mark Musa, (New York: Penguin Books, 1982, ©1979), pp. 66–71.

Magnificent Ambassador.

• • •

now I have found your favor once again in your last letter of the twenty-third of the past month. I am very happy to see how regularly and calmly you carry on your public office, and urge you to continue in this way, since anyone who loses his own interests for those of others sacrifices his own and receives no thanks from the others. And since it is Fortune that does everything, it is she who wishes us to leave her alone, to be quiet and not to give her trouble, and to wait until she allows us to act again; then you will do well to strive harder, to observe things more closely, and it will be time for me to leave my country home and say: "Here I am!" In the meantime, I can only tell you in this letter of mine what my life is like, wishing to match favor with favor, and if you think you would like to exchange yours for mine, I would be very happy to do so.

I live in the country, and since my recent misadventures in Florence I have not spent, in total, twenty days there. Until recently, I have been snaring thrushes with my

---

[7] *Scriptores historiae Augustae* 18.34.6.
[8] Seutonius *Divus Julius* 42.
[9] Acts 22:28.
[10] Jeremiah 22:10.
[11] Cf. Cicero *Tusculane disputationes* 1.48.115, quoting Euripides.

own hands. Rising before daybreak, I prepare the birdlime and go out with such a bundle of bird cages on my back that I look like Geta when he returned from port with the books of Amphitryon,[1] I usually catch at least two, at the most six thrushes. I spent all of September doing this. Then this pastime, vile and foreign to my nature as it is, came to an end, to my displeasure; let me tell you what my life is like now: I rise in the morning with the sun and go into a wood that I am having cut, where I remain two hours in order to check the work done the day before and to pass the time with the woodcutters, who always have some argument at hand among themselves or with their neighbors. And concerning this wood, I could tell you a thousand entertaining things that have happened to me in my affairs with Frosino da Panzano and with others who wanted part of it.

. . .

Leaving the wood, I go to a spring, and from there to my bird-snare. I have a book with me, either Dante or Petrarca or one of the lesser poets like Tibullus, Ovid, and the like: I read about their amorous passions and about their loves, I remember my own, and I revel for a moment in this thought. I then move on up the road to the inn, I speak with those who pass, and I ask them for news of their area; I learn many things and note the different and diverse tastes and ways of thinking of men. Lunchtime comes, when my family and I eat that food which this poor farm and my meager patrimony permit. After eating, I return to the inn: there I usually find the innkeeper, a butcher, a miller, and two bakers. With these men I waste my time playing cards all day and from these games a thousand disagreements and countless offensive words arise, and most of the time our arguments are over a few cents; nevertheless, we can be heard yelling from San Casciano. Caught this way among these lice I wipe the mold from my brain and release my feeling of being ill-treated by Fate; I am happy to be driven along this road by her, as I wait to see if she will be ashamed of doing so.

When evening comes, I return to my home, and I go into my study; and on the threshold, I take off my everyday clothes, which are covered with mud and mire, and I put on regal and curial robes; and dressed in a more appropriate manner I enter into the ancient courts of ancient men and am welcomed by them kindly, and there I taste the food that alone is mine, and for which I was born; and there I am not ashamed to speak to them, to ask them the reasons for their actions; and they, in their humanity, answer me; and for four hours I feel no boredom, I dismiss every affliction, I no longer fear poverty nor do I tremble at the thought of death: I become completely part of them. And as Dante says that knowledge does not exist without the retention of it by memory,[2] I have noted down what I have learned from their conversation, and I composed a little work, *De princi-*

patibus, where I delve as deeply as I can into thoughts on this subject, discussing what a principality is, what kinds there are, how they are acquired, how they are maintained, why they are lost. And if any of my fantasies has ever pleased you, this should not displease you; and to a prince, and especially to a new prince, it should be welcomed; therefore, I am dedicating it to his Magnificence, Giuliano.[3] Filippo Casavecchia has seen it; he can give you some idea both of the work itself and of the discussion we have had concerning it, although I am still enlarging it and polishing it up.

You would like me, Magnificent Ambassador, to leave this life here and to come to enjoy yours with you. I shall do it, come what may, but what keeps me back at present are certain affairs of mine which I shall settle within six weeks. What makes me hesitate is that the Soderini[4] are there, and I would be obliged, coming there, to visit them and speak to them. I would not be surprised if on my return I might have to stay at the Bargello prison rather than at home, since although this state has very strong foundations and great security, it is also new and, because of this, suspicious, and there are plenty of sly men who, to appear like Pagolo Bertini,[5] would put others in debt and leave the worries to me. I beg you to relieve me of this fear, and then, whatever happens, I shall come within the time established to find you.

I talked with Filippo about this little book of mine: whether or not I should present it to him [Giuliano], and whether, giving it to him, I should bring it myself or have it delivered to you. Giving it makes me afraid that Giuliano won't read it and that Ardinghelli[6] will take the credit for this, my latest labor. I am urged to give it by the necessity that drives me: I am wearing myself away, and I cannot remain in this state for long without being despised for my poverty, not to mention my desire that these Medici lords begin to make use of me, even if they start me off by rolling stones. If I could not win their favor with this work, then I should have myself to blame; and in this work, if it were read, they would see that I have been at the study of statecraft for fifteen years and have not slept nor played about; and each one of them should be happy to obtain the services of one who is full of experience at another man's expense. And they should not doubt my loyalty, for always having kept my word, I have not now learned to break it; and anyone who has been faithful and honest for forty-three years, as I have been, cannot change his character; and my poverty is witness to my honesty and goodness.

1 An allusion to a popular novella of the fifteenth century, *Geta and Birria*.
2 *Paradiso*, V, 41–42.
3 Initially *The Prince* was dedicated to Giuliano de' Medici, but after his death in 1516 the work was addressed to his successor, Lorenzo de' Medici, Duke of Urbino.
4 Machiavelli here refers to his former superior, Piero Soderini, and his brother, Cardinal Francesco Soderini, both of whom had received permission from the Medici Pope, Leo X, to reside in Rome. Machiavelli's visit might have aroused Medici suspicion that he was in league with a Soderini-led republican plot.
5 One of the ardent Medici supporters and, therefore, a potential enemy of Machiavelli.
6 Pietro Ardinghelli, a papal secretary at Leo X's court.

I should like you, therefore, to write me what you think about this matter, and I commend myself to you. *Sis felix.* December 10, 1513.

Niccolò Machiavelli in Florence

13.3   Cellini: The Artist

Cellini (1500–1571) was an artist who made his living as a goldsmith in the Italian city-states of Florence and Rome. He was also quite a talented musician. The following excerpt, from his autobiography, written between 1558–1562, describes his life and work as an artist. It was not published until the eighteenth century, when it became quite popular.

Source: Benvenuto Cellini, *The Life of Benvenuto Ceillini*, 4th edition, trans. J. A. Symonds, cited in ed. John L. Beatty and Oliver A. Johnson, *Heritage of Western Civilization*, vol. 1, 7th edition, (Englewood Cliffs, NJ: Prentice Hall, 1991), pp. 397–411, passim.

II

It is true that men who have laboured with some show of excellence, have already given knowledge of themselves to the world; and this alone ought to suffice them; I mean the fact that they have proved their manhood and achieved renown. Yet one must needs live like others; and so in a work like this there will always be found occasion for natural bragging, which is of divers kinds, and the first is that a man should let others know he draws his lineage from persons of worth and most ancient origin.

When I reached the age of fifteen, I put myself, against my father's will, to the goldsmith's trade with a man called Antonio, son of Sandro, known commonly as Marcone the goldsmith. He was a most excellent craftsman and a very good fellow to boot, high-spirited and frank in all his ways. My father would not let him give me wages like the other apprentices; for having taken up the study of this art to please myself, he wished me to indulge by whim for drawing to the full. I did so willingly enough; and that honest master of mine took marvellous delight in my performances. He had an only son, a bastard, to whom he often gave his orders, in order to spare me. My liking for the art was so great, or, I may truly say, my natural bias, both one and the other, that in a few months I caught up the good, nay, the best young craftsmen in our business, and began to reap the fruits of my labours. I did not, however, neglect to gratify my good father from time to time by playing on the flute or cornet. Each time he heard me, I used to make his tears fall accompanied with deep-drawn sighs of satisfaction. My filial piety often made me give him that contentment, and induced me to pretend that I enjoyed the music too.

XIV

[. . . Later, after traveling to Rome, he entered a new workshop]

"Welcome to my workshop; and do as you have promised; let your hands declare what man you are."

He gave me a very fine piece of silver plate to work on for a cardinal. It was a little oblong box, copied from the prophyry sarcophagus before the door of the Rotonda. Beside what I copied, I enriched it with so many elegant masks of my invention, that my master went about showing it through the art, and boasting that so good a piece of work had been turned out from his shop. It was about half a cubit in size, and was so constructed as to serve for a salt-cellar at table. This was the first earning that I touched at Rome, and part of it I sent to assist my good father; the rest I kept for my own use, living upon it while I went about studying the antiquities of Rome, until my money failed, and I had to return to the shop for work.

• • •

After undertaking some new commissions, I took it into my head, as soon as I had finished them, to change my master; I had indeed been worried into doing so by a certain Milanese, called Pagolo Arsago. My first master, Firenzuola, had a great quarrel about this with Arsago, and abused him in my presence; whereupon I took up speech in defence of my new master. I said that I was born free, and free I meant to live, and that there was no reason to complain of him, far less of me, since some few crowns of wages were still due to me; also that I chose to go, like a free journeyman, where it pleased me, knowing I did wrong to no man. My new master then put in with his excuses, saying that he had not asked me to come, and that I should gratify him by returning to Firenzuola. To this I replied that I was not aware of wronging the latter in any way, and as I had completed his commissions, I chose to be my own master and not the man of others, and that he who wanted me must beg me of myself. Firenzuola cried: "I don't intend to beg you of yourself; I have done with you; don't show yourself again upon my premises." I reminded him of the money he owed me. He laughed me in the face; on which I said that if I knew how to use my tools in handicraft as well as he had seen, I could be quite as clever with my sword in claiming the just payment of my labour. While we were exchanging these words, an old man happened to come up, called Maestro Antonio, of San Marino. He was the chief among the Roman goldsmiths, and had been Firenzuola's master. Hearing what I had to say, which I took good care that he should understand, he immediately espoused my cause, and bade Firenzuola pay me. The dispute waxed warm, because Firenzuola was an admirable swordsman, far better than he was a goldsmith. Yet reason made itself heard; and I backed my cause with the same spirit, till I got myself paid. In course of time Firenzuola and I became friends, and at his request I stood godfather to one of his children.

XV

I went on working with Pagolo Arsago, and earned a good deal of money, the greater part of which I always sent to my good father. At the end of two years, upon my father's entreaty, I returned to Florence, and put myself once more under Francesco Salimbene, with whom I earned a great deal, and took continual pains to improve in my arts. I renewed my intimacy with Francesco di Filippo; and though I was too much given to pleasure, owing to that accursed music, I never neglected to devote some hours of the day or night to study.

· · ·

XIX

· · ·

During that time I went to draw sometimes in Michel Agnolo's chapel, and sometimes in the house of Agostino Chigi of Siena, which contained many incomparable paintings by the hand of that great master Raffaello., This I did on feast-days, because the house was then inhabited by Messer Gismondo, Agostino's brother. They plumed themselves exceedingly when they saw young men of my sort coming to study in their palaces. Gismondo's wife, noticing my frequent presence in that house—she was a lady as courteous as could be, and of surpassing beauty—came up to me one day, looked at my drawings, and asked me if I was a sculptor or a painter; to whom I said I was a goldsmith. She remarked that I drew too well for a goldsmith; and having made one of her waiting-maids bring a lily of the finest diamonds set in gold, she showed it to me, and bade me value it. I valued it at 800 crowns. Then she said that I had very nearly hit the mark, and asked me whether I felt capable of setting the stones really well. I said that I should much like to do so, and began before her eyes to make a little sketch for it, working all the better because of the pleasure I took in conversing with so lovely and agreeable a gentlewoman. When the sketch was finished, another Roman lady of great beauty joined us; she had been above, and now descending to the ground-floor, asked Madonna Porzia what she was doing there. She answered with a smile: "I am amusing myself by watching this worthy young man at his drawing; he is as good as he is handsome." I had by this time acquired a trifle of assurance, mixed, however, with some honest bashfulness; so I blushed and said: "Such as I am, lady, I shall ever be most ready to serve you." The gentlewoman, also slightly blushing, said: "You know well that I want you to serve me"; and reaching me the lily, told me to take it away; and gave me besides twenty golden crowns which she had in her bag, and added: "Set me the jewel after the fashion you have sketched, and keep for me the old gold in which it is now set." On this the Roman lady observed: "If I were in that young man's body, I should go off without asking leave." Madonna Porzia replied that virtues rarely are at home with vices, and that if I did such

a thing, I should strongly belie my good looks of an honest man. Then turning round, she took the Roman lady's hand, and with a pleasant smile said: "Farewell, Benvenuto." I stayed on a short while at the drawing I was making, which was a copy of a Jove by Raffaello. When I had finished it and left the house, I set myself to making a little model of wax, in order to show how the jewel would look when it was completed. This I took to Madonna Porzia, whom I found with the same Roman lady. Both of them were highly satisfied with my work, and treated me so kindly that, being somewhat emboldened, I promised the jewel should be twice as good as the model. Accordingly I set hand to it, and in twelve days I finished it in the form of a fleur-de-lys, as I have said above, ornamenting it with little masks, children, and animals, exquisitely enamelled, whereby the diamonds which formed the lily were more than doubled in effect.

XX

While I was working at this piece, Lucagnolo, of whose ability I have before spoken, showed considerable discontent, telling me over and over again that I might acquire far more profit and honour by helping him to execute large plate, as I had done at first. I made him answer that, whenever I chose, I should always be capable of working at great silver pieces; but that things like that on which I was now engaged were not commissioned every day; and beside their bringing no less honour than large silver plate, there was also more profit to be made by them. He laughed me in the face, and said: "Wait and see Benvenuto; for by the time that you have finished that work of yours, I will make haste to have finished this vase, which I took in hand when you did the jewel; and then experience shall teach you what profit I shall get from my vase, and what you will get from your ornament." I answered that I was very glad indeed to enter into such a competition with so good a craftsman as he was, because the end would show which of us was mistaken. Accordingly both the one and the other of us, with a scornful smile upon our lips, bent our heads in grim earnest to the work, which both were now desirous of accomplishing; so that after about ten days, each had finished his undertaking with the great delicacy and artistic skill.

· · ·

So he took his vase and carried it to the Pope, who was very well pleased with it, and ordered at once that he should be paid at the ordinary rate of such large plate. Meanwhile I carried mine to Madonna Porzia, who looked at it with astonishment, and told me I had far surpassed my promise. Then she bade me ask for my reward whatever I liked; for it seemed to her my desert was so great that if I craved a castle she could hardly recompense me; but since that was not in her hands to bestow, she added laughing that I must beg what lay within her power. I answered that the greatest reward I could desire for my labour was to have satisfied her ladyship. Then, smiling in my turn, and bowing to her,

I took my leave, saying I wanted no reward but that. She turned to the Roman lady and said: "You see that the qualities we discerned in him are companied by virtues, and not vices." They both expressed their admiration, and then Madonna Porzio continued: "Friend Benvenuto, have you never heard it said that when the poor give to the rich, the devil laughs?" I replied: "Quite true! and yet, in the midst of all his troubles, I should like this time to see him laugh"; and as I took my leave, she said that this time she had no will to bestow on him that favour.

When I came back to the shop, Lucagnolo had the money for his vase in a paper packet; and on my arrive he cried out: "Come and compare the price of your jewel with the price of my plate." I said that he must leave things as they were till the next day, because I hoped that even as my work in its kind was not less excellent than his, so I should be able to show him quite an equal price for it.

XXI

On the following, Madonna Porzia sent a major-domo of hers to my shop, who called me out, and putting into my hands a paper packet full of money from his lady, told me that she did not choose the devil should have his whole laugh out; by which she hinted that the money sent me was not the entire payment merited by my industry, and other messages were added worthy of so courteous a lady. Lucagnolo, who was burning to compare his packet with mine, burst into the shop, then in the presence of twelve journeymen and some neighbors, eager to behold the result of this competition, he seized his packetd, scornfully exclaiming "Ou! Ou!" three or four times, while he poured his money on the counter with a great noise. They were twenty-five crowns in giulios; and he fancied that mine would be four or five crowns *di moneta*. I for my part, stunned and stifled by his cries, and by the looks and smiles of the bystanders, first peeped into my packet; then, after seeing that it contained nothing but gold, I retired to one end of the counter, and keeping my eyes lowered and making no noise at all, I lifted it with both hands suddenly above my head, and emptied it like a mill hopper. My coin was twice as much as his; which caused the onlookers, who had fixed their eyes on me with some derision, to turn round suddenly to him and say: "Lucagnolo, Benvenuto's pieces, being all of gold and twice as many as yours, make a far finer effect." I thought for certain that, what with jealousy and what with shame, Lucagnolo would have fallen dead upon the spot; and though he took the third part of my gain, since I was a journeymen (for such is the custom of the trade, two-thirds fall to the workman and one-third to the masters of the shop), yet inconsiderate envy had more power in him than avarice: it ought indeed to have worked quite the other way; he being a peasant's son from Iesi. He cursed his art and those who taught it to him, vowing that thenceforth he would never work at large plate, but give his whole attention to those whoreson gewgaws, since they were so well paid. Equally engaged on my side, I answered that

every bird sang its own note; that he talked after the fashion of the hovels he came from; but that I dared swear that I should succeed with ease in making his lubberly lumber, while he would never be successful in my whoreson gewgaws. Thus I flung off in a passion, telling him that I would soon show him that I spoke truth. The bystanders openly declared against him, holding him for a lout, as indeed he was, and me for a man, as I had proved myself.

. . .

XXIII

While I was pushing forward Salamanca's vase, I had only one little boy as help, whom I had taken at the entreaty of friends, and half against my own will, to be my workman. He was about fourteen years of age, bore the name of Paulino, and was son to a Roman burgess, who lived upon the income of his property. Paulino was the best-mannered, the most honest, and the most beautiful boy I ever saw in my whole life. His modest ways and actions, together with his superlative beauty and his devotion to myself, bred in me as great an affection for him as a man's breast can hold. This passionate love led me often-times to delight the lad with music; for I observed that his marvellous features, which by complexion wore a tone of modest melancholy, brightened up, and when I took my cornet, broke into a smile so lovely and sweet, that I do not marvel at the silly stories which the Greeks have written about the deities of heaven. Indeed, if my boy had lived in those times, he would probably have turned their heads still more. He had a sister, named Faustina, more beautiful, I verily believe, than that Faustina about whom the old books gossip so. Sometimes he took me to their vineyard, and, so far as I could judge, it struck me that Paulino's good father would have welcomed me as a son-in-law. This affair led me to play more than I was used to do.

It happened at that time that one Giangiacomo of Cesena, a musician in the Pope's band, and a very excellent performer, sent word through Lorenzo, the trumpeter of Lucca, who is now in our Duke's service, to inquire whether I was inclined to help them at the Pope's Ferragosto, playing soprano with my cornet in some motets of great beauty selected by them for that occasion. Although I had the greatest desire to finish the vase I had begun, yet, since music has a wondrous charm of its own, and also because I wished to please my old father, I consented to join them. During eight days before the festival we practised two hours a day together; then on the first of August we went to the Belvedere, and while Pope Clemente was at table, we played those carefully studied motets so well that his Holiness protested he had never heard music more sweetly executed or with better harmony of parts. He sent for Giangiacomo, and asked him where and how he had procured so excellent a cornet for soprano, and inquired particularly who I was. Giangiacomo told him my name in full. Whereupon the Pope said: "So, then, he is the son of Maestro Giovanni?" On being assured I was, the Pope expressed his wish to have me in his service with the other bandsmen. Giangiacomo replied: "Most blessed Father, I cannot pretend for certain that you will get him, for his profession, to which he devotes himself assiduously, is that of a goldsmith, and he works in it miraculously well, and earns by it far more than he could do by playing." To this the Pope added: "I am the better inclined to him now that I find him possessor of a talent more than I expected. See that he obtains the same salary as the rest of you; and tell him from me to join my service, and that I will find work enough by the day for him to do at his other trade." Then stretching out his hand, he gave him a hundred golden crowns of the Camera in a handkerchief, and said: "Divide these so that he may take his share."

13.4   Rabelais: Mocking the Monks

Rabelais, once a French monk, left the monastery and became a physician in the service of the Cardinal du Belay of Lyons. Being in the service of the cardinal provided some protection for his criticisms of the Church. He wrote not in Latin, but in the vernacular French; each vernacular language was becoming established as the individual nation-states developed. His great satirical work, *Gargantua and Pantagruel*, was published over a twenty-year period, 1532–52.

> **Source:** François Rabelais, *Gargantua and Pantagruel*, in *Tout ce qui existe de ses oeuvres* (Paris: Gamier 'Frères Libraires-Editeurs, 1880), cited in The Western World, vol. 1, ed. Wallace E. Adams, et al., (New York: Dodd, Mead and Company, 1968), pp. 383–86.

They [a marauding group of robbers and thieves] roamed the countryside, and finally came to Seville. There, they robbed everyone, both men and women, and took everything which was not nailed down. The Plague had already reached Seville, but this did not seem to bother the thieves, who plundered the town, and none of them seemed to catch the dread disease. All curates, vicars, preachers, doctors, and apothecaries, those normally appointed to care for the ill, had themselves taken sick and been carried away by the Plague. The devilish robbers escaped in good health. Then, they went on to the Abbey itself. . . . The monks did not know quite what to do, and tried to think which of the saints it would be best to pray to in such an emergency. Having reached no decision, the monks finally decided to ring the bells and to welcome the murderers with a procession, offering lectures, litanies, prayers, and the like.

Fortunately, however, there was in the Abbey at that time, a particular monk called Friar John of the Goblets; he was young, frisky, gallant, lusty, nimble, quick, active, bold, adventurous, resolute, tall and lean, a monk with a large mouth and a long nose, who was a pretty fair despatcher of the morning prayers, a magnificent runner-

through of masses, and a superb expediter of vigils—to conclude, to summarize in a word, a perfect monk, if ever there was any since a monking world first monked a monkery. John, hearing the dreadful clamor that the robbers were making in the monastery vineyard, went out to see what the matter was. He saw the thieves cutting and gathering the grapes—the very foundation of the next year's wine. At great haste, John rushed to the choir of the church, wherein he found the other monks, who were singing and chanting im, im, pe, e, e, e, tum, um, in, i, ni, i, mi, co, o, o, o, o, tum, um. "Well sung," he shouted, "but By the virtue of God, why not sing instead that the vintage is gone? The thieves are in the vineyards, cutting both the vines and the grapes. It will be four years before we will have any wine! By Saint James' belly what will we drink in the meantime? Lord God, da mihi potum?" To which the prior replied: "What should we do with this drunkard who dares to interrupt the divine service?" "Nay," replied John, "the vine service, let us take care that it not be interrupted. You, yourself, lord prior, love to drink the best of the wine, and so does every honest man. No worthy man has ever disliked good wine; Why, it is a monastic proverb. Those hymns you chant are not in season now. Otherwise, how is it that our devotions are short during harvest time, and long in the winter? The late friar, Mace Pellosse, told me this himself. Come on, you who love the wine, follow me, or let Saint Anthony see me burn if I let these murderers taste one drop of our good wine. Let us fight to save the vines—By the belly of Saint Anthony, for the good of the Church! Ho, ho! By the devil, didn't Saint Thomas of England die for the same cause? If I were to do likewise, would I not also be a saint? . . ."

As he spoke these words Friar John took off his monk's habit and grabbed the staff of the cross, which was made of wood from an apple tree and was as long as a lance, covered with the lilies of France (a little faded, to be sure). Thus, he went out, with his frock thrown like a scarf across his chest, and his staff of the cross. Finding his enemies simply gathering the grapes, after they had laid down their trumpets, drums, and the like, he flailed away at them briskly, lustily, and fiercely. The drummers and flag-carriers had laid down their equipment, having even broken open the drums to fill them with grapes. The trumpeters were loaded down with great bunches cut from the vines. The entire mob of thieves was in disarray to begin with. The good friar rushed into the vineyard quickly without a chance for anyone to cry: "Look out!" He threw the robbers about as if they were hogs, striking first on one side and then on the other. Some of them had their brains beaten out, for others the friar simply crushed their arms, battered their legs, or whacked their sides till their ribs cracked. Some of the murderers had their necks broken, or the good friar slashed their faces, unjointed their chins, or swung at them with such ferocity that he mowed them down like blades of grass. Some received a whack in the kidneys, others a smash across the back. Friar John broke the thighbones of some, pushed in the noses of others, gouged out their eyes, crushed their jaws, bashed their teeth down their throats, tore their skin, bruised their shins, dislocated their hipbones, and generally thumped and mauled them so magnificently that it seemed that he were threshing wheat. If any of the thieves tried to hide in the vines, the friar caught him and laid him low. Some thought to flee, all to no avail, for the good monk crushed their skulls. A few tried to scramble up some trees, but they were impaled by the stout lance.

One or two of the friar's old friends among the robbers cried out: "Ho, Friar John, quarter! Quarter! I yield!" But the monk replied: "and would you yield your soul to all the devils in Hell?" Whereupon he gave them a great variety of thumps, bangs, raps, and thwacks to suffice to send them on their way and to warn Pluto of their coming. Those who tried to resist were run through, right through the stomach or the heart, or the intestines. It was the most horrible spectacle that had ever been seen in that part of the country, Some cried out to Saint Barbara, others to Saint George. Some appealed for mercy to Saint Nytouche, others . . . to Our Lady of Loretto, . . . or to Saint Mary. Some vowed a pilgrimage to Saint James, and others to the holy handkerchief at Chamberry. Some pleaded with Saint Cadouin, others sent up their vows to Saint John d'Angly . . . Some invoked Saint Mesmes of Chinon, others Saint Martin of Candes . . . Some died without speaking, others spoke without dying; some died in speaking, others spoke in dying . . . So great was the crying, that the Prior of the Abbey came out with all of the other monks to offer confession to some of the dying. Many of the monks now came to Friar John and asked if they could help him. He told them to slit the throats of those who lay prostrate on the ground. They speedily rushed to their task. . . .

Thus, by the great prowess and valor of Friar John all of the army that had entered the vineyard of the abbey were sent scurrying away or were dispatched, to the number of 13,622, besides the women and children, which is, of course, always to be understood. Never did Maugis the Hermit strike so against the Saracens . . . than this monk thrash his enemies with the staff of the cross.

HOW GARGANTUA WELCOMED FRIAR JOHN

[Some time later, Friar John was invited to a sumptuous dinner by Gargantua]. As the monk arrived, Gargantua greeted him with a thousand embraces: "Ha, Friar John, my friend, Friar John, my brave cousin . . . welcome." ". . . Ho, bring wine for the good friar . . ." One of the guests [later] exclaimed: "By the faith of a Christian, I am so greatly pleased at the honesty and good fellowship of this monk [John], for he makes us all so merry. How is it then, that people generally exclude monks from all good parties, call-

ing them spoilsports, enemies of joviality, and disturbers of civil conversation? . . . To which Gargantua replied: "Ah, yes, there is nothing so true as that their monastic garb draws to them the injuries, the odium, the evils of the world, just as the wind attracts the clouds. The true reason is that they eat the filth and excrement of the world, that is to say, the sins of the people, and are thus cast into the privies of the earth—the convents and the abbeys . . . After all, . . . monks . . . do not labor and work, like the peasant or artisan; they do not keep and defend the country, like the soldier; they do not cure the sick and diseased, like the physician; they do not preach and teach, as the Evangelical doctors and schoolmasters; they do not import goods necessary to the Commonwealth, as the merchants do. For these reasons, they are hooted at, hated, and despised." "But, ho," answered Grangousier, "they pray to God for us." "Nothing less," replied Gargantua, "it is certainly true that with that jingle-jangle jangling of bells they trouble and upset all their neighbors." "Quite right," said the monk, "a mass, a matin, a vesper well rung is half said." "Oh, they mumble out a great store of legends and psalms, which they do not clearly understand themselves. They say hundreds of paternosters interlarded with Ave Marias, without thinking about them or comprehending their meaning . . . which is in reality a mocking of God, and certainly not prayers. . . . But . . . Friar John is a good man to have in company. He is no bigot or hypocrite. He is not torn between reality and appearance. He is no wretch with a miserable disposition. On the contrary, he is honest, jovial, resolute, and a good fellow all around. He travels, he labors, he defends the oppressed, comforts the afflicted, helps the needy, and keeps the vineyard of the Abbey." "Oh, no," replied Friar John, "I do a good deal more than that. While we are dispatching our prayers in the choir, I make strings for cross-bows, polish glass bottles, twist rope, and weave nets and all sorts of things. I am never idle. But, now, come here! Bring something to drink! Some drink here! Bring fruit! . . ."

Questions for Documents 13.1–13.4:
1. What examples and sources are used to support various claims by these authors?
2. What relation do these authors have to the ancient authors of Rome and Greece?
3. What attitudes and aptitudes seem to describe the Renaissance man? How are each of these men Renaissance men?
4. What attitudes are expressed about the world and people about them?
5. What are the relationships between the individual and society, the individual and other individuals, the individual and the group?
6. What is the role of the patron in Renaissance society? How does this affect things?

SECTION 2
The Renaissance Woman

Documents 13.5 and 13.6

Questions on the Renaissance woman follow Document 6. Questions concerning both the Renaissance man and woman follow thereafter.

13.5   Marriage: A Serious Business

Marriage relations in Medieval and Renaissance Europe were not just about love—or rather they were not at all about love. Particularly among the elites of long-standing, blood and family ties were valued more than almost anything else. In the following excerpt, we see some of the honor, prestige, and property that were at stake in marriage negotiations in fourteenth-century Italy.

> Source: "Letters from Alessandra Strozzi in Florence to her son Filippo in Naples" Alessandra Macinghi Strozzi, *Lettere di una gentildonna florentina*, ed. C. Guasti, (Florence, 1877), pp. 394–95, 458–59, 463–65, 475–76, cited in *The Society of Renaissance Florence: A Documentary Study*, ed. Gene Brucker, (New York: Harper and Row, Inc., 1972), pp. 37–40.

MARRIAGE NEGOTIATIONS: THE STROZZI, 1464–65

[April 20, 1464] . . . Concerning the matter of a wife [for Filippo], it appears to me that if Francesco di Messer Guglielmino Tanagli wishes to give his daughter, that it would be a fine marriage. . . . Now I will speak with Marco [Parenti, Alessandra's son-in-law], to see if there are other prospects that would be better, and if there are none, then we will learn if he wishes to give her [in marriage]. . . . Francesco Tanagli has a good reputation, and he has held office, not the highest, but still he has been in office. You may ask: "Why should he give her to someone in exile?" There are three reasons. First, there aren't many young men of good family who have both virtue and property. Secondly, she has only a small dowry, 1,000 florins, which is the dowry of an artisan. . . . Third, I believe that he will give her away, because he has a large family and he will need help to settle them. . . .

[July 26, 1465] . . . Marco Parenti came to me and told me that for some time, he has been considering how to find a wife for you. . . . There is the daughter of Francesco di Messer Guglielmino Tanagli, and until now there hasn't been anyone who is better suited for you than this girl. It is true that we haven't discussed this at length, for a reason which you understand. However, we have made secret inquiries, and the only people who are willing to make a marriage agreement with exiles have some flaw, either a lack of money or something else. Now money is the least serious drawback, if the other factors are positive. . . . Francesco is a good friend of Marco and he trusts him. On S. Jacopo's day, he spoke to him discreetly and persuasively, saying that for several months he had heard that we were interested in the girl and . . . that when we had made up our minds, she will come to us willingly. [He said that] you were a worthy man, and that his family had always made good marriages, but that he had only a small dowry to give her, and so he would prefer to send her outside of Florence to someone of worth, rather than to give her to someone here, from among those who were available, with little money. . . . He invited Marco to his house and he called the girl down. . . . Marco said that she was attractive and that she appeared to be suitable. We have information that she is affable and competent. She is responsible for a large family (there are twelve children, six boys and six girls), and the mother is always pregnant and isn't very competent. . . .

[August 17, 1465] . . . Sunday morning I went to the first mass at S. Reparata . . . to see the Adimari girl, who customarily goes to that mass, and I found the Tanagli girl there. Not knowing who she was, I stood beside her. . . . She is very attractive, well proportioned, as large or larger than Caterina [Alessandra's daughter]. . . . She has a long face, and her features are not very delicate, but they aren't like a peasant's. From her demeanor, she does not appear to me to be indolent. . . . I walked behind her as we left the church, and thus I realized that she was one of the Tanagli. So I am somewhat enlightened about her. . . .

[August 31, 1465] . . . I have recently received some very favorable information [about the Tanagli girl] from two individuals. . . . They are in agreement that whoever gets her will be content. . . . Concerning her beauty, they told me what I had already seen, that she is attractive and well-proportioned. Her face is long, but I couldn't look directly into her face, since she appeared to be aware that I was examining her . . . and so she turned away from me like the wind. . . . She reads quite well . . . and she can dance and sing. . . . Her father is one of the most respected young men of Florence, very civilized in his manners. He is fond of this girl, and it appears that he has brought her up well.

So yesterday I sent for Marco and told him what I had learned. And we talked about the matter for a while, and decided that he should say something to the father and give him a little hope, but not so much that we couldn't withdraw, and find out from him the amount of the dowry. . . . Marco and Francesco [Tanagli] had a discussion, about this yesterday (I haven't seen him since), and Marco should inform you about it one of these days, and you will then understand more clearly what should follow. May God help us to choose what will contribute to our tranquillity and to the consolation of us all. . . .

[September 13, 1465] ... Marco came to me and said that he had met with Francesco Tanagli, who had spoken very coldly, so that I understand that he had changed his mind. They say that he wants to discuss the matter with his brother-in-law, Messer Antonio Ridolfi. ... And he [Francesco] says that it would be a serious matter to send his daughter so far away [to Naples], and to a house that might be described as a hotel. And he spoke in such a way that it is clear that he has changed his mind. I believe that this is the result of the long delay in our replying to him, both yours and Marco's. Two weeks ago, he could have given him a little hope. Now this delay has angered him, and he has at hand some prospect that is more attractive. ... I am very annoyed by this business; I can't recall when I have been so troubled. For I felt that this marriage would have satisfied our needs better than any other we could have found. ...

[Filippo Strozzi eventually married Fiametta di Donato Adimari, in 1466.]

13.6 *On Wifely Duties*

Francesco Barbaro wrote *On Wifely Duties* to his friend and fellow aristocrat, Lorenzo de Medici, on the occasion of the latter's marriage in 1416. He hoped to teach the youth of Florence through de Medici's example and the circulation of his treatise under Medici's auspices. He also wanted to stress the importance of marriage to the maintenance of the aristocratic ruling families of his native Venice in particular and to the Italian city-states more generally.

> **Source:** Francesco Barbaro, *On Wifely Duties*, trans. Benjamin G. Kohl, cited in *The Earthly Republic: Italian Humanists on Government and Society*, ed. Benjamin G. Kohl and Ronald G. Witt, (University of Pennsylvania Press, 1981, © 1978), pp. 189–230, passim.

CHAPTER 1. ON THE FACULTY OF OBEDIENCE

This is now the remaining part to be done here, in which if wives follow me, either of their own free will or by the commands of their husbands, no one will be so unfair as to think that I have not so established the duties of the wife that youth can enjoy peace and quiet the whole life long. Therefore, there are three things that, if they are diligently observed by a wife, will make a marriage praiseworthy and admirable: love for her husband, modesty of life, and diligent and complete care in domestic matters. We shall discuss the first of these, but before this I want to say something about the faculty of obedience, which is her master and companion, because nothing more important, nothing greater can be demanded of a wife than this.

· · ·

If a husband, excited to anger, should scold you more than your ears are accustomed to hear, tolerate his wrath silently. But if he has been struck silent by a fit of depression, you should address him with sweet and suitable words, encourage, console, amuse, and humor him. Those who work with elephants do not wear white clothes, and those who work with wild bulls are right not to wear red; for those beasts are made ever more ferocious by those colors. Many authors report that tigers are angered by drums and made violent by them. Wives ought to observe the same thing; if, indeed, a particular dress is offensive to a husband, then we advise them not to wear it, so that they do not give affront to their husbands, with whom they ought to live peacefully and pleasantly.

· · ·

The wife who is angry with her husband because of jealousy and is considering a separation should ask herself this question: If I put myself in a workhouse because I hate a whore, what could make her far happier and more fortunate than this? She would see me almost shipwrecked, while at the same time she was sailing with favorable winds and securely casting her anchor into my marriage bed?

· · ·

It was considered very good for domestic peace and harmony if a wife kept her husband's love with total diligence. At the olympic games that were dedicated to the great god Jupiter and attended by all of Greece, Gorgias used his eloquence to urge a union of all the Greeks. Melanthus said: Our patron attempts to persuade us that we should all join together in a league, but he cannot bring himself and his wife and her maid—who are only three people—to a mutual agreement (for the wife was very jealous because Gorgias was wildly enamoured of her maid). Likewise, Philip was for a long time displeased with the queen Olympias and Alexander. And when Demaratus of Corinth returned from Greece, Philip eagerly and closely questioned him about the union of the Greeks. Demaratus said to him: "Philip, I consider it a very bad thing that you are spending all your energy in bringing peace and concord to all of Greece when you are not yet reconciled with your own wife and son." Therefore, if any woman wants to govern her children and servants, she should make sure that she is, first of all, at peace with her husband. Otherwise, it will seem that she wants to imitate the very things that she is trying to correct in them. In order that a wife does her duty and brings peace and harmony to her household, she must agree to the first principle that she does not disagree with her husband on any point. But of this enough has been said.

CHAPTER 2. ON LOVE

In the first place, let wives strive so that their husbands will clearly perceive that they are pensive or joyful according to the differing states of their husbands' fortunes. Surely congratulations are proper in times of good fortune, just as consolations are appropriate in times of adversity. Let them openly discuss whatever is bothering them, provided it is worthy of prudent people, and let them feign nothing, dissemble nothing, and conceal nothing. Very often sorrow and trouble of mind are relieved by means of discussion and counsel that ought to be carried out in a friendly fashion with the husband. If a husband shares all the pressures of her anxieties he will lighten them by participating in them and make their burden lighter; but if her troubles are very great or deeply rooted, they will be relieved as long as she is able to sigh in the embrace of her husband. I would like wives to live with their husbands in such a way that they can always be in agreement, and if this can be done, then, as Pythagoras defines friendship, the two are united in one.

• • •

I therefore would like wives to evidence modesty at all times and in all places. They can do this if they will preserve an evenness and restraint in the movements of the eyes, in their walking, and in the movement of their bodies; for the wandering of the eyes, a hasty gait, and excessive movement of the hands and other parts of the body cannot be done without loss of dignity, and such actions are always joined to vanity and are signs of frivolity.

• • •

Moreover, I earnestly beg that wives observe the precept of avoiding immoderate laughter. This is a habit that is indecent in all persons, but it is especially hateful in a woman. On the other hand, women should not be censured if they laugh a little at a good joke and thus lapse somewhat from their serious demeanor. Demosthenes used to rehearse his legal speeches at home in front of a mirror so that with his own eyes he could judge what he should do and what he should avoid in delivering his speeches at court. We may well apply this practice to wifely behavior.

I wish that wives would daily think and consider what the dignity, the status of being a wife requires, so that they will not be lacking in dignified comportment.

• • • •

We who follow a middle way should establish some rather liberal rules for our wives. They should not be shut up in their bedrooms as in a prison but should be permitted to go out, and this privilege should be taken as evidence of their virtue and propriety. Still, wives should not act with their husbands as the moon does with the sun; for when the moon is near the sun it is never visible, but when it is distant it stands resplendent by itself. Therefore, I would have wives be seen in public with their husbands, but when their husbands are away wives should stay at home. By maintaining an honest gaze in their eyes, they can communicate most significantly as in painting, which is called silent poetry. They also should maintain dignity in the motion of their heads and the other movements of their bodies. Now that I have spoken about demeanor and behavior, I shall now speak of speech.

CHAPTER 4. ON SPEECH AND SILENCE

Isocrates warns men to speak on those matters that they know well and about which they cannot, on account of their

dignity, remain silent. We commend women to concede the former as the property of men, but they should consider the latter to be appropriate to themselves as well as to men. Loquacity cannot be sufficiently reproached in women, as many very learned and wise men have stated, nor can silence be sufficiently applauded. For this reason women were prohibited by the laws of the Romans from pleading either criminal or civil law cases.

CHAPTER 8. ON DOMESTIC MATTERS AND THE MANAGEMENT OF HOUSEHOLDS AND SERVANTS

We are interested in the care of our property and the diligence proper to our servants and staff because it is necessary to have both property and servants, without whose help family life itself cannot exist. Surely it is in these two things that the management of domestic matters primarily is involved, for unless a wife imposes her own judgment and precepts on these matters, the operation of the household will have no order and will be in great disarray. Men are naturally endowed with strength of mind and body; both for these and other reasons, they provision their homes by their labor, industry, and willingness to undergo hardships. Conversely, I think we may infer that since women are by nature weak they should diligently care for things concerning the household. For weakness can never be separated from cares nor cares from vigilance. What is the use of bringing home great wealth unless the wife will work at preserving, maintaining, and utilizing it?

• • •

They ought to attend, therefore, to governing their households just as Pericles daily attended to the affairs of Athens.[79] And they ought always to consider how well they are doing so that they will never be deficient in their care, interest, and diligence in household matters. They will surely be successful in this matter if they do what they should do, that is, if they are accustomed to stay at home and oversee everything there.

• • •

So that a wife's duty might be commended to posterity, there were affixed to the bronze statue of Gaia Caecilia, the daughter of Tarquinius, an ordinary shoe and a distaff and spindle, so that those objects might in some way signify that her diligent work at home ought to be imitated by future generations.[81] What neglectful landowner can hope to have hard-working peasants? What slothful general can make his soldiers vigilant for the state? Therefore, if a wife would like to have her maids working hard at home, she should not merely instruct them with words but she ought also by her actions to demonstrate, indicate, and show what they

---

[79] Cf. Xenophon *Oeconomicus* 7.3.5.
[81] Cf. Plutarch *Quaestiones Romanae* 30; *Moralia* 271E.

should be doing. Indeed, there is surely nothing more excellent in household affairs than that everything be put in its place, because there is nothing more beautiful, more useful than order, which is always of the greatest importance. We consider that an army or chorus can be called anything but an army or chorus unless its organization is well preserved.[82] I would have wives imitate the leaders of bees, who supervise, receive, and preserve whatever comes into their hives, to the end that, unless necessity dictates otherwise, they remain in their honeycombs where they develop and mature beautifully. Wives may send their maids and manservants abroad if they think this would be useful to them. But if, indeed, these servants are required at home, they should urge, order, and require their presence. Wives should also consider it their duties to see to it that no harm comes to their husbands' winecellars, pantries, and oil cellars.

. . .

It is now proper to speak, as we have promised, about servants, who, provided they are not neglected, can add great luster to our houses and be useful and pleasant. So they will be if wives will instruct them carefully and if they will not get angry with them before, having warned them, they discover that they have made the same mistakes. I should like that wives, in these matters as in others, follow the example of the leaders of the bees, who allow no one under their control to be lazy or negligent.[88]

. . .

Thrifty wives constantly ought to seek out and appoint sober stewards for the provisions and address them courteously and be generous of them, so that by the great interest of the mistress the industry of the steward daily increases. They should feed their servants so that they will satisfy both their human needs and reward their constant labor. Wives should clothe their servants comfortably as befits the season, climate, and place. Moreover, as Hesiod advises, they should always be careful that servants are not separated from their children and families,[90] for servants will always find a way to stay together with their own family, even secretly. Furthermore, servants will be very grateful if especially good medical care is provided when a member of their family is taken sick. For these acts of humanity, this solicitiousness will make servants very conscientious and hardworking for the household.

. . .

After their offspring have passed their infancy, mothers should use all their skill, care, and effort to ensure that their children are endowed with excellent qualities of mind and body. First they should instruct them in their duty toward Immortal God, their country, and their parents, so that they will be instilled from their earliest years with those qualities

that are the foundation of all other virtues. Only those children who fear God, obey the laws, honor their parents, respect their superiors, are pleasant with their equals and courteous to their inferiors, will exhibit much hope for themselves. Children should meet all people with a civil demeanor, pleasant countenance, and friendly words. But they should be on the most familiar terms with only the best people. Thus they will learn moderation in food and drink so that they may lay, as it were, the foundation of temperance for their future lives. They should be taught to avoid these pleasures that are dishonorable, and they should apply their efforts and thoughts to those matters that are the most becoming and will be useful and pleasant when they become older. If mothers are able to instruct their children in these matters, their offspring will much more easily and better receive the benefit of education.

. . .

Mothers should often warn their children to abstain from excessive laughter and to avoid words that denote a rash character. That is the mark of stupidity, the evidence of passion. Moreover, children should be warned not ever to speak on those matters that are base in the act. Therefore, mothers should restrain them from vulgar or cutting words. If their children should say anything that is obscene or licentious, mothers should not greet it with a laugh or a kiss, but with a whip.

Moreover, they should teach their children not to criticize anyone because of his poverty or the low birth of his lineage or other misfortunes, for they are sure to make bitter enemies from such actions or develop an attitude of arrogance. Mothers should teach their children sports in which they so willingly learn to exert themselves that, if the occasion arises, they can easily bear even more difficult hardships. I would have mothers sharply criticized for displays of anger, greed, or sexual desire in the presence of their offspring, for these vices weaken virtue. If mothers act appropriately, their children will learn from infancy to condemn, avoid, and hate these most filthy mistresses and they will take care to revere the names of God and will be afraid to take them in vain. For whoever has been taught at an early age to despise the Divinity, will they not as adults surely curse Him? Therefore, it is of great importance to train children from infancy so that they never swear. Indeed, those who swear readily because of some misfortune are not deserving of trust, and those who readily swear very often unwittingly betray themselves. Mothers ought to teach their children to speak the truth.

. . .

Therefore, my Lorenzo, your compatriots ought to be stirred by your example and follow you with great enthusiasm, for in Ginevra you have taken a wife who is a virgin well endowed with virtue charm, a noble lineage, and great wealth. What more outstanding, more worthy model could I propose than yours? What more shining, more worthy

---

[82] Cf. Xenophon *Oeconomicus* 1.3.
[88] Cf. Xenophon *Oeconomicus* 7.33.
[90] Probably an allusion to Hesiod *Opera et Dies* 373.

example than yours, since in this outstanding city of Florence you are most eminently connected through your father, grandfather, and ancestors? You have taken a wife whose great wealth the entire world indeed admires but whose chastity, constancy, and prudence all men of goodwill esteem highly. They consider that you are blessed and happy to have her as a wife, and she is to have you as a husband. Since you have contracted such an outstanding and fine marriage, these same men ask God Immortal that you will have the best children who will become very honored citizens in your state. These matters might perhaps seem negligible since I am treating them, but indeed they are, in their own fashion, borne out in your marriage. Thus, surely young men who follow your example will profit more than only by following my precepts; just as laws are much more likely to be observed in a city when they are obeyed by its ruler, so, since your own choice of a wife is consistent with my teachings, we may hope that these precepts will be followed by the youth.

Questions for Documents 13.5 and 13.6:
1. What elements are considered important for a wife in contracting and in maintaining a marriage?
2. What is the role of marriage in Renaissance society? What does marriage have to do with larger concerns? Consider, for instance, the ruling of the state, the extended family, politics, economics, etc.

Questions for Documents 13.1–13.6:
1. What comparisons can be made between the lives and responsibilities of men and women based on these Renaissance documents?
2. Historian Joan Kelly, in an article published in *Becoming Visible: Women in European History* in 1977, asked "did women have a Renaissance?" How would you answer this question based on the documents provided? Be sure to define what you mean by Renaissance.

CHAPTER 14
Of One Church, Many
Protestant Reformation
and Catholic Reformation
(1500–1650)

SECTION 1
Critics of the Medieval Church

14.1 The Trial of John Hus

Not only do official records survive from the trial of John Hus before the Council of Constance in 1415, but Hus's supporters also took notes of the proceedings which resulted in his execution. Below are excerpts from the published reports of one of Hus' followers.

> **Source:** *John Hus at the Council of Constance*, trans. Matthew Spinka, (New York: Columbia University Press, *1965*), pp. 182–209.

On . . . June 8, Master John Hus was again conducted to a hearing in the previously mentioned refectory, where the king presided along with certain cardinals, archbishops, bishops, and other prelates. Lords W. and J. and P. the bachelor, the scribe, were also present there. About thirty-nine articles were read, said to have been drawn from the Master's books. Those that were exactly as stated in the books, the Master acknowledged as his; but those indeed that were not excerpted *verbatim* were read or delivered by a certain Englishman as they appeared in the excerpts and the Master's book. When anything they disliked was contained in the book, the cardinal of C[ambrai] said several times to the king and others: "Look! here it reads worse and more dangerously and erroneously than in the excerpt."

Those articles will follow. A certain person who diligently compared them with the original book, [found that] but few of them were so stated in the book. [*The actual words from his book follows each article.*]

FROM THE ARTICLES DRAWN FROM THE TREATISE "DE ECCLESIA" OF MASTER JOHN HUS

5. "No position of dignity, or human election, or any outward sign makes one a member of the holy Church catholic."

It stands in the book as follows:

". . . What makes one a member of the holy catholic Church is predestination, which is the preparation of grace in the present and of glory in the future, not, how-ever, a position of dignity, or human election, or any outward sign. For the devil [Judas] Iscariot, notwithstanding Christ's choosing and granting him temporary charismatic [gifts]. . . , along with the popular repute that he was a true disciple of Christ, was not a true disciple of His, but a wolf clad in sheep's clothing, as Augustine says," etc.

9. "Peter was not nor is the principal head of the holy catholic Church."

This is how the same stands in the book:

"It is conceded, moreover, that Peter received from the Rock of the Church, which is Christ, humility, poverty, firmness of faith, and consequently blessedness. But that by the words of the Gospel, 'Upon this rock will I build my Church,' Christ should have intended to build the whole Church militant upon the person of Peter is contradicted by the faith of the Gospel, by the exposition of Augustine, and by reason. For Christ was to build His Church upon the Rock which was He Himself, from whom Peter received the firmness of faith, since Christ is the head and the foundation of the whole Church, not Peter," etc. . . .

10. "If he who is called the vicar of Christ follows Christ in life, then he is His vicar. If in fact he walks in contrary ways, then he is the messenger of Antichrist, an adversary of Peter and of the Lord Jesus Christ, and the vicar of Judas Iscariot. . . ."

This does not stand in the book in that form, but is written . . . as follows:

"If then he, called Peter's vicar, walks in the said ways of virtue, we believe that he is truly his vicar and the chief pontiff of the Church he rules. But if in fact he walks in contrary ways, then he is the messenger of Antichrist, an adversary of Peter and of the Lord Jesus Christ. Hence the blessed Bernard[1] in *To Pope Eugenius*, Book 4, writes as follows: 'Among these things you, a shepherd, go forth among the pastures bedecked with gold, clad in multicolored vestments. What does is profit the sheep? If I dare say so, these [pastures] are of great demons rather than of sheep.

---

[1] St. Bernard of Clairveaux was the leader of Western Christianity in the twelfth century. A mystic and reformer, his prestige was far greater than any pope of his era

Not so did Peter act or Paul frisk about!' And further he continues: 'Either deny to the people that you are the shepherd or show yourself to be such. You will not deny it lest he, whose seat you hold, denies you as his heir,' etc. And further: 'In these things you have succeeded not Peter but Constantine.'" Thus Bernard . . . [writes] as follows: 'If in morals he lives contrary to Peter, and if he is avaricious, then he is the vicar of Judas Iscariot who loved the reward of iniquity, selling the Lord Jesus Christ.' "

When this was being read, the presidents looked at one another, smiling and shaking their heads.

To [the reading] of these articles we have already come; but we[2] were late for the first nine, for which reason [they are stated here without] the Master's replies to them.

12. "The papal dignity arose from the Caesars." And further on: "The papal preeminence and institution emanated from the Caesar's power."

. . .

When this article had been read, Master John, rising, said: "That is what I say: that as for the outward adornments and the possession of temporal goods of the Church as such, the papal dignity has its origin from Caesar Constantine; and that later other emperors also confirmed it, as is shown in the *Decretum* distinction 96. But as concerns the spiritual administration and the office of the spiritual governing of the Church, such dignity originates directly from the Lord Jesus Christ." And the cardinal of Cambrai said: "Nonetheless, at the time of Constantine a general Council was held and there that decree was ascribed to Constantine on account of his presence and reverence. Why not, therefore, rather say that the preeminence of the pope emanates from the Council rather than from the power of Caesar?" And the Master said: "Because of the Donation, which, as I said, was granted by Caesar."[3]

17. "The cardinals are not the manifest and true successors of the college of Christ's other apostles unless they live after the manner of the apostles, observing the commands and counsels of our Lord Jesus Christ."

This is according to the text of the book. . . .

When that reading was concluded, the cardinal of Cambrai, who was supreme in the Council, said: "Look! it stands worse and harsher in the book than it was formulated." And he said to Master John Hus:

"You do not observe moderation in your preaching and writing; for you should have adapted your sermons to the need of the hearers. Why was it necessary or useful, therefore, while preaching to the people to preach against the cardinals, since none of them was present there? Rather you should have spoken and preached it to their faces, and not to scandalize the laymen."

And he answered: "Reverend father, I have dealt with such matters because my sermons were attended by priests and other learned men, in order that both the present and the future priests would know beforehand what to guard against."

The cardinal retorted: "You are doing wrong; for by such preaching you wish to destroy the status of the Church."

18. "Apart from the ecclesiastical censure, no heretic is to be turned over the secular courts to be punished by corporeal death."

This proposition does not stand in the book, but they added it themselves; the following is in the book:

"They, the doctors, should be ashamed for their apish and cruel comparison, especially as the Lord Christ, the pontiff of both Testaments, neither would judge a civil suit nor would condemn the disobedient to corporeal death. For as to the first He said, Luke 12: 'Man, who constituted me a judge or divider over you?' As to the second, He said to the woman adulteress, whom the Pharisees declared liable to death according to the law, John 8: 'Neither do I condemn you, etc.' But perchance the doctors would say that this has nothing to do with the case, because the law says: 'He who acts presumptuously, not willing to obey the priest's rule, I mention a case as an example: for it is said in Matthew 18: 'If your brother sins against you, reprove him between yourself and him; if he does not hear you, take him along with you,' etc. And the following: 'Moreover, if he does not hear the Church, let him be to you as a gentile and a publican." Note! to whom did the supreme Lord and pontiff speak? Certainly to Peter, the future Roman pontiff after Him, that he might kindly correct the erring and reprove the disobedient before witnesses, that he might make known the persistently disobedient to the Church, not putting to bodily death the stubbornly disobedient to the Church, but shunning him as a publican and a gentile"; and so forth in the book. . . .

FROM THE ARTICLES DRAWN FROM THE TREATISE WRITTEN AGAINST MASTER STEPHEN PÁLEC

7. "The condemnation of the forty-five articles of Wyclif pronounced by the doctors is irrational and unjust, and the reason alleged by them is fictitious: namely, that none of them is catholic, but every one of them is either heretical, or erroneous, or scandalous."

Is does not agree with the book, but is as follows:

"The forty-five articles are all condemned for this reason, that none of these forty-five articles is catholic, but every one of them is either heretical, or erroneous, or scandalous. 0 doctor! where is the proof? You are a deceiver, falsely making a case you do not prove, etc.; for you show

---

[2] The person who was taking notes of the proceedings arrived late. From article Ten on, he would also record Master Hus's replies.

[3] The Council of Nicea in 325 A.D. did not pass any such decree. The "Donation of Constantine" itself was a forgery of the eighth century, as will be demonstrated by the humanist scholar Lorenzo Valla (1407–1457).

no Scripture to the contrary." And he argued this extensively in the treatise. . . .

The cardinal of Cambrai said: "Master, you told us that you wish to defend no error of Wyclif, and see! here it is now evident from your books that you have publicly defended those articles. And there certainly is stated much that is scandalous and harsh." And the Master responded: "Reverend father! As I said before, I still say that I do not wish to defend either Wyclif's or anyone else's errors. But because it seemed to me to be against my conscience simply to consent to their condemnation, there being no Scripture to the contrary, therefore it did not seem to me [right] to consent immediately to their condemnations. . . ."

Questions:
1. What is John Hus's opinion of the papacy and church hierarchy?
2. What authorities does he use to support his contentions?
3. What does he have to say about the role of secular courts in matters of faith and church discipline?

14.2   Erasmus: A Diatribe Against the Pope

Desidenus Erasmus (ca. 1467–1536), the most renowned of all Northern Renaissance humanists, was Dutch by birth and educated in a school of the Brethern of the Common Life. He was a Biblical scholar, a popular author, and an astute critic of his society and the church, although he ultimately rejected the Protestant Reform. Published anonymously, the following diatribe is directed against Pope Julius II (r. 1503–13), who was known as the Warrior Pope.

> **Source:** Wallace E. Adams, Richard B. Barlow, Gerald R. Kleinfeld, Ronald D. Smith, William W, Wootton, eds. *The Western World To 1700*, (New York: Dodd, Mead & Co., 1969), pp. 372–74.

DIALOGUE: JULIUS LOCKED OUT OF HEAVEN

Persons Of The Dialogue: Pope Julius II, His Genius Or Guardian Angel, and St. Peter
Scene: Before the Gates of Heaven

JULIUS: What's the trouble here? Won't the gates open? I believe the lock as been changed, or else it's jammed.

GENIUS: Better check to see if you've brought the right key. The one for the treasury won't open this door, you know. But why didn't you bring both keys? This is the key of power, not of knowledge.

JULIUS: Why, Hell, this is the only one I've ever used! I've never seen what good the other one was when I've had this one.

GENIUS: Me neither, certainly, except that meanwhile we're locked out.

JULIUS: I'm losing my temper. I'm going to beat on the gate. Hey there! Somebody open this door instantly! What's the matter, nobody here? What's holding up the doorman? Asleep, I suppose; probably drunk.

GENIUS: [*Aside*] This fellow judges everyone by himself.

PETER: It's a good thing we've got a steel door. Otherwise, whoever this is would break down the gates. It must be some giant, or satrap, some sacker of cities. Immortal God! What sewage is this I smell! Well, I certainly won't open the door. I'll just peek out this little barred window and see what kind of monster this is. What do you want? Who are you?

JULIUS: If you knew your business, you would greet me with all the heavenly choirs.

PETER: Rather demanding, isn't he? But first tell me who you are.

JULIUS: As if you couldn't see who I am.

PETER: See? I certainly see a new and never-before-seen spectacle, not to say a monster.

JULIUS: If you are not completely blind, then, I suppose you know this key, even if you don't recognize the golden oak on my coat of arms. And you see the triple crown of the Papacy, besides my cloak, glittering all over with jewels and gold.

PETER: Well, I recognize the silver key, all right, though to be sure there is only one, and it is much different from the keys that Christ, the true Pastor of the Church, once put into my keeping. But how should I recognize that crown, so proud that no barbarian tyrant would ever dare wear it, much less someone wishing to be admitted here? As for that cloak, it does nothing for me. I always kick jewels and gold out of the way, and spurn them like trash. But what's this? Here and there on the key and the crown and the cloak I see the marks of some wretched saloon keeper and impostor, a fellow with my name but not my ways: Simon [Magus], whom I once threw out from the following of Christ for simony.

JULIUS: Well, let these trifles go, if you're wise to them. Now I am, if you don't know, Julius the Ligurian, and if I'm not mistaken you recognize these two letters: P.M. You have learned to read, I presume?

PETER: I guess they stand for *Pestis Maxima*, the Universal Calamity.

GENIUS: Ha ha ha! This riddle-guesser hit the nail on the head.

JULIUS: No, no! *Pontifex Maxi us*, the Pope's title.

PETER: If you were three times *maxi us* and greater even than thrice-great Hermes, you wouldn't be allowed in here unless you were the best of all; that is, a saint.

JULIUS: Well, if it is so necessary to be called a saint, you're being pretty arrogant to delay opening the gate for *me*, when you after all these centuries are only called *sanctus*—saint or holy—but nobody ever calls me anything but *sanctissimus*—most sainted, most holy. There are six-thousand bulls. . . .

GENIUS: Real bull!

JULIUS: . . . in which I am called not only most holy, but by the very name of holiness itself, whenever it pleased me.

GENIUS: By the name of drunkard, too.

JULIUS: I would make 'em call me the Holiest of the Most Holy Lord Julius.

PETER: Well then, go demand heaven from those flatterers who made you "most holy." Let the same followers who gave you your holiness save you. Though I suppose you still think there is no difference between being called holy and being holy.

JULIUS: I'm getting angry! If only I could live again, I'd show you about this business of not being holy and not being saved!

PETER: Oh, there's an indication of a most holy mind! Although I have been watching you narrowly for a long time now, I've seen no sign of sanctity in you—nothing but impiety. Why have you led here this new, un-papal army? Here you have brought with you some twenty-thousand men, and I can't catch sight of a single one who has even a face that is Christian! I see a horrible flood of soldiers with you, smelling of nothing but brothels, drunkenness, and gun. powder. I guess they are some kind of bandits, or rather fiends broken out of Hell to storm Heaven. As for you, the more I look the less

trace of an apostle do I see about you. First of all, what monstrous thing is this, that you wear the garment of a priest and under it you bristle and rattle with bloody armor? And why such belligerent eyes, such a fierce mouth, such a menacing forehead, such proud and arrogant brows? It is shameful to say and painful to see that no part of your body is not spattered with the stains of prodigious and abominable pleasures. Not to mention that even now you are belching and smelling of hangover and drunkenness, and I just saw you [vomit]! The appearance of your whole person suggests that it is not with age and disease but through dissipation that you seem old, withered, and broken.

GENIUS: How vividly he paints him in his true colors! . . .

Questions:
1. How does Pope Julius' conduct in office as described in the dialogue compare with Machiavelli's Renaissance prince?
2. On what grounds did St. Peter exclude Pope Julius from heaven?
3. How do these criticisms of Pope Julius compare to John Hus's condemnation of the papacy?

14.3 Thomas More: *Utopia*

A humanist and a friend of Erasmus, Sir Thomas More was also a valued counselor and chancellor of the Henry VIII, King of England. In 1516, More first published *Utopia* (No Place). It was a book designed to entertain as well as to create a context in which More could safely criticize the prevailing faults and attitudes of European society, including the corruption in royal courts and in the Church. Ironically, it was for standing loyal to that Church that Henry VIII executed Thomas More. In the following excerpt from *Utopia*, the narrator, Raphael Nonsenso, describes the religious ideas of the island he discovered.

Source: Thomas More, *Utopia*, trans. Paul Turner, (New York: Penguin, 1965), pp. 117–24.

Finally, let me tell you about their religious ideas. There are several different religions on the island, and indeed in each town. . . .

On this point, indeed, all the different sects agree—that there is one Supreme Being, Who is responsible for the creation and management of the universe, and they all use the same Utopian word to describe Him: Mythras. What they disagree about is, who Mythras is. Some say one thing, some another—but everyone claims that *his* Supreme Being is identical with Nature, that tremendous power which is internationally acknowledged to be the sole cause of everything. However, people are gradually tending to drift away from all these inferior creeds, and to unite in adopting what seems to be the most reasonable religion. And doubtless the others would have died out long ago if it weren't for the superstitious tendency to interpret any bad luck, when one's thinking of changing one's religion, not as a coincidence, but as a judgement from heaven—as though the discarded god were punishing one's disloyalty.

But when we told them about Christ, His teaching, His character, His miracles, and the no less miraculous devotion of all the martyrs who, by voluntarily shedding their blood, converted so many nations to the Christian faith, you've no idea how easy it was to convert them too. Perhaps they were unconsciously influenced by some divine inspiration, or perhaps it was because Christianity seemed so very like their own principal religion—though I should imagine they were also considerably affected by the information that Christ prescribed of His own disciples a communist way of life," which is still practised today in all the most truly Christian communities. Anyway, whatever the explanation, quite a lot of Utopians adopted our religion, and were baptized. . . .

Of course, many Utopians refuse to accept Christianity, but even they make no attempt to discourage other people from adopting it, or to attack those who do—though there was one member of our congregation who got into trouble while I was there. Immediately after his baptism, in spite of all our to the contrary,. this man started giving public lectures on the Christian faith, in which he showed rather more zeal than discretion. Eventually he got so worked up that, not content with asserting the superiority of our religion, he went so far as to condemn all others. He kept shouting at the top of his voice that they were all vile superstitions, and that all who believed in them were monsters of impiety, destined to be punished in hell-fire forever. When he'd been going on like this for some time, he was arrested and charged, not with blasphemy, but with disturbance of the peace. He was duly convicted and sentenced to exile—for one of the most ancient principles of their constitution is religious toleration.

This principle dates right back to the time of the conquest. Up till then there'd been constant quarrels about religion, and the various warring sects had refused to cooperate in the defence of their country. When Utopos heard how they'd behaved, he realized that this was why he'd been able to conquer the whole lot of them. So immediately after his victory he made a law, by which everyone was free to practise what religion he liked, and to try and convert other people to his own faith, provided he did it quietly and politely, by rational argument. But, if he failed to convince them, he was not allowed to make bitter attacks on other religions, nor to employ violence or personal abuse. The normal penalty for being too aggressive in religious controversy is either exile or slavery.

Utopos made this law, not only to preserve the peace, which he saw being completely destroyed by endless disputes and implacable feuds, but also because he thought it was in the best interests of religion itself. He didn't presume to say which creed was right. Apparently he considered it possible that God made different people believe different things, because He wanted to be worshipped in many different ways. But he was evidently quite certain that it was stupid and arrogant to bully everyone else into adopting one's own particular creed. It seemed to him perfectly obvious that, even if there was only one true religion, and all the rest were nonsense, truth would eventually prevail of its own accord—as long as the matter was discussed calmly and reasonably. But if it was decided by force of arms, the best and most spiritual type of religion would go down before the silliest forms of superstition just as corn is liable to be overgrown by thorns and brambles—for the worst people are always the most obstinate.

So he left the choice of creed an open question, to be decided by the individual according to his own ideas—except that he strictly and solemnly forbade his people to believe anything so incompatible with human dignity as the doctrine that the soul dies with the body, and the universe functions aimlessly, without any controlling providence. That's why they feel so sure that there must be rewards and punishments after death. Anyone who thinks differently has, in their view, forfeited his right to be classed as a human being, by degrading his immortal soul to the level of an animal's body. Still less do they regard him as a Utopian citizen. They say a person like that doesn't really care a damn for the Utopian way of life—only he's too frightened to say so. For it stands to reason, if you're not afraid of anything but prosecution, and have no hopes of anything after you're dead, you'll always be trying to evade or break the laws of your country, in order to gain your own private ends. So nobody who subscribes to this doctrine is allowed to receive any public honour, hold any public appointment, or work in any public service. In fact such people are generally regarded as utterly contemptible.

They're not punished in any way, though, for no one is held responsible for what he believes. Nor are they terrorized into concealing their views, because Utopians simply can't stand hypocrisy, which they consider practically equivalent to fraud. Admittedly, it's illegal for any such person to argue in defence of his beliefs, but that's only in public. In private discussions with priests or other serious-minded characters, he's not merely allowed but positively encouraged to do so, for everyone's convinced that this type of delusion will eventually yield to reason.

• • • •

They pay no attention to omens, fortune-telling, or any of the superstitious practices that are taken so seriously in other countries. In fact they treat them as a joke. But they have a great respect for miracles which aren't attributable to natural causes, because they see them as evidence of God's presence and power. They say such miracles often happen there. Indeed at moments of crisis the whole country prays for a miracle, and their faith is so great that the prayer is sometimes answered. . . .

All their priests are exceptionally pious, which means that there are very few of them—normally thirteen per town, or one per church. But in wartime seven of the thirteen go off with the troops, and seven more priests are ordained as temporary substitutes. When the army chaplains return, they get back their old livings, and the extra priests remain on the staff of the Bishop—for one of the thirteen is given this status—until they succeed, one by one, to vacancies created by the death of the original incumbents.

Priests are elected by the whole community. The election is by secret ballot, as it is for all public appointments, to prevent the formation of pressure groups, and the successful candidates are then ordained by their colleagues. Priests are responsible for conducting services, organizing religions, and supervising morals. It's considered very shameful to be had up before an ecclesiastical court, or even reprimanded by a priest for bad behaviour. Of course, the actual suppression and punishment of crime is the job of the Mayor and other public officials. Priests merely give advice and warning—though they can also excommunicate persistent offenders, and there's hardly any punishment that people fear more. You see, a person who has been excommunicated is not only completely disgraced and with fears of divine vengeance. His physical security is threatened too, for, unless he can very soon convince the priests that he's a reformed character, he's arrested and punished by the Council for impiety.

Priests are also responsible for the education of children and in which quite as much stress is laid on moral as on academic training. They do their utmost to ensure that, while children are still at an impressionable age, they're given the right ideas about things—the sort of ideas best calculated to preserve the structure of their society. If thoroughly absorbed in childhood, these ideas will persist throughout adult life, and so contribute greatly to the safety of the state, which is never seriously threatened except by moral defects arising from wrong ideas.

Male priests are allowed to marry—for there's nothing to stop a woman from becoming a priest, although women aren't often chosen for the job, and only elderly widows are eligible. As a matter of fact, clergymen's wives form the cream of Utopian society, for no public figure is respected more than a priest. So much so that, even if a priest commits a crime, he's not liable to prosecution. They just leave him to God and his own conscience, since, no matter what he has done, they don't think it right for any human being to lay hands on a man who has been dedicated as a special offering to God. They find this rule quite easy to keep, because priests represent such a tiny minority, and because they're so carefully chosen. After all, it's not really very likely that a man who has come out top of a list of excellent candidates, and who owes his appointment entirely to his moral character, should suddenly become vicious and corrupt. And even if we must accept that possibility—human nature being so very unpredictable—a mere handful of people without any executive power can hardly constitute a serious danger to the community. They keep the numbers down, in order not to lower the present high prestige of the priesthood, by making the honour less of a rarity—especially as they say it's hard to find many people suitable for a profession which demands considerably more than average virtues. . . .

Questions:
1. How can the description of the Utopian church be a criticism of the Medieval Church in Europe?
2. Why did the Utopians practice toleration of religious belief?
3. Why were their priests so respected?

SECTION 2
The Protestant Reformation

14.4 Luther's *Ninety-Five Theses*

The *Ninety-Five Theses* is the popular term for the *Disputation on the Power and the Efficacy of Indulgences.* Luther posted these on the Castle church door at Wittenberg on October 31, 1517. When John Tetzel arrived selling indulgences in Luther's parish, chanting slogans that offered years off penance in purgatory for a cash payment, Luther protested against them and took the first steps of the Protestant Reformation. A selection of the Theses below reveals Luther's early position.

> **Source:** *Martin Luther: Selections from His Writings*, ed. and trans. John Dillenberger, (New York: Doubleday & Company, 1961), pp. 489–500. Reprinted with permission from *The Reformation Writings of Martin Luther*, Vol. 1, *The Basis of the Protestant Reformation*, trans. and ed. Bertram Lee Woolf (London: Lutterworth Press, 1953), pp. 32–42, passim.

Out of love and concern for the truth, and with the object of eliciting it, the following heads will be the subject of a public discussion at Wittenberg under the presidency of the reverend father, Martin Luther, Augustinian, Master of Arts and Sacred Theology, and duly appointed Lecturer on these subjects in that place. He requests that whoever cannot be present personally to debate the matter orally will do so in absence in writing.

1. When our Lord and Master, Jesus Christ, said "Repent", He called for the entire life of believers to be one of penitence.

5. The pope has neither the will nor the power to remit any penalties beyond those imposed either at his own discretion or by canon law.

6. The pope himself cannot remit guilt, but only declare and confirm that it has been remitted by God; or, at most, he can remit it in cases reserved to his discretion. Except for these cases, the guilt remains untouched.

20. Therefore the pope, in speaking of the plenary remission of all penalties, does not mean "all" in the strict sense, but only those imposed by himself.

21. Hence those who preach indulgences are in error when they say that a man is absolved and saved from every penalty by the pope's indulgences;

27. There is no divine authority for preaching that the soul flies out of purgatory immediately the money chinks in the bottom of the chest.

28. It is certainly possible that when the money chinks in the bottom of the chest avarice and greed increase; but when the church offers intercession, all depends on the will of God.

32. All those who believe themselves certain of their own salvation by means of letters of indulgence, will be eternally damned, together with their teachers.

35. It is not in accordance with Christian doctrine to preach and teach that those who buy off souls, or purchase confessional licenses, have no need to repent of their own sins.

36. Any Christian whatsoever, who is truly repentant, enjoys plenary remission from penalty and guilt, and this is given him without letters of indulgence.

37. Any true Christian whatsoever, living or dead, participates in all the benefits of Christ and the Church; and this participation is granted to him by God without letters of indulgence.

43. Christians should be taught that one who gives to the poor, or lends to the needy, does a better action than if he purchases indulgences.

45. Christians should be taught that he who sees a needy person, but passes him by although he gives money for indulgences, gains no benefit from the pope's pardon, but only incurs the wrath of God.

50. Christians should be taught that, if the pope knew the exactions of the indulgence preacher he would rather the church of St. Peter were reduced to ashes than be built with the skin, flesh, and bones of his sheep.

62. The true treasure of the church is the Holy Gospel of the glory and the grace of God.

75. It is foolish to think that papal indulgences have so much power that they can absolve a man even if he has done the impossible and violated the mother of God.

76. We assert the contrary, and say that the pope's pardons are not able to remove the least venial of sins as far as their guilt is concerned.

81. This unbridled preaching of indulgences makes it difficult for learned men to guard the respect due to the pope against false accusations, or at least from the keen criticisms of the laity;

82. They ask, e.g.: Why does not the pope liberate everyone from purgatory for the sake of love (a most holy thing) and because of the supreme necessity of their souls? This would be morally the best of all reasons. Meanwhile he redeems innumerable souls for money, a most perishable thing, with which to build St. Peter's church, a very minor purpose.

86. Again: Since the pope's income to-day is larger than that of the wealthiest of wealthy men, why does he not build this one church of St. Peter with his own money, rather than with the money of indigent believers?

90. These questions are serious matters of conscience to the laity. To suppress them by force alone, and not to refute them by giving reasons, is to expose the church and the pope to the ridicule of their enemies, and to make Christian people unhappy.

91. If, therefore, indulgences were preached in accordance with the spirit and mind of the pope, all these difficulties would be easily overcome, and, indeed, cease to exist.

94. Christians should be exhorted to be zealous to follow Christ, their Head, through penalties, deaths, and hells;

95. And let them thus be more confident of entering heaven through many tribulations rather than through a false assurance of peace.

Questions:
1. How do these statements concerning the pope compare to John Hus' opinions (Chapter 14, Document 1)?
2. Why is Luther upset about the sale of indulgences?
3. According to these statements, what is more important in Christian teaching than indulgences?

14.5 The *Ecclesiastical Ordinances* of Geneva

John Calvin (1509–1564), influenced by both Luther's theology and Erasmus' humanism, experienced a sudden conversion in 1533 and became the great leader of a new generation of reformers. In 1541 his Ecclesiastical Ordinances were approved by the citizens of Geneva, allowing him to put his understanding of the church into practice. Reprinted here is part of the central section of the *Ordinances*.

Source: *The Protestant Reformation*, ed. Hans J Hillerbrand, (New York: Harper Torchbooks, 1968), pp. 173–78.

Of the Frequency, Place and Time of Preaching

Each Sunday, at daybreak, there shall be a sermon in St. Peter's and St. Gervaise's, also at the customary hour at St. Peter, Magdalene and St. Gervaise. At three o'clock, as well, in all three parishes, the second sermon. . . .

On work days, besides the two sermons mentioned, there shall be preaching three times each week, on Monday, Wednesday, and Friday. These sermons shall be announced for an early hour so that they may be finished before the day's work begins. On special days of prayer the Sunday order is to be observed.

To carry out these provisions and the other responsibilities pertaining to the ministry, five ministers and three coadjutors will be needed. The latter will also be ministers and help and reinforce the others as the occasion arises.

Concerning the Second Order, Called Teachers

The proper duty of teachers is to instruct the faithful in sound doctrine so that the purity of the gospel is not corrupted by ignorance or evil opinions. We include here the aids and instructions necessary to preserve the doctrines and to keep the church from becoming desolate for lack of pastors and ministers. To use a more familiar expression, we shall call it the order of the schools.

The order nearest to the ministry and most closely associated with the government of the church is that of lecturer in theology who teaches the Old and the New Testament. Since it is impossible to profit by such instruction without first knowing languages and the humanities, and also since it is necessary to prepare for the future in order that the church may not be neglected by the young, it will be necessary to establish a school to instruct the youth, to prepare them not only for the ministry but for government.

First of all, a proper place for teaching purposes must be designated, fit to accommodate children and others who wish to profit by such instruction; to secure someone who is both learned in subject matter and capable of looking after the building, who can also read. This person is to be employed and placed under contract on condition that he provide under his charge readers in the languages and in dialectics, if it be possible. Also to secure men with bachelor degrees to teach the children. This we hope to do to further the work of God.

These teachers shall be subject to the same ecclesiastical discipline as the ministers. There shall be no other school in the city for small children; the girls shall have their school apart, as before.

No one shall be appointed unless he is approved by the ministers, who will make their selection known to the authorities, after which he shall be presented to the council with their recommendation. In any case, when he is examined, two members of the Little Council shall be present.

The Third Order is That of Elders, Those Commissioned or Appointed to the Consistory By the Authorities

Their office is to keep watch over the lives of everyone, to admonish in love those whom they see in error and leading disorderly lives. Whenever necessary they shall make a report concerning these to the ministers who will be designated to make brotherly corrections and join with the others in making such corrections.

If the church deems it wise, it will be well to choose two from the Little Council, four from the Council of Two Hundred, honest men of good demeanor, without reproach and free from all suspicion, above all fearing God and possessed of good and spiritual judgment. It will be well to elect them from every part of the city so as to be able to maintain supervision over all. This we desire to be instituted.

This shall be the manner of their selection, inasmuch as the Little Council advises that the best men be nominated, and to call the minister so as to confer with them, after which those whom they suggest may be presented to the Council of Two Hundred for their approval. If they are found worthy, after being approved, they shall take an oath similar to that required of the ministers. At the end of the year, after the election of the council, they shall present themselves to the authorities in order that it may be decided if they are to remain in office or be replaced. It will not be expedient to replace them often without cause, or so long as they faithfully perform their duties.

The Fourth Order or the Deacons

There were two orders of deacons in the ancient church, the one concerned with receiving, distributing and guarding the goods of the poor, their possessions, income and pensions as well as the quarterly offerings; the other, to take heed to and care for the sick and administer the pittance for the poor. This custom we have preserved to the present. In order to avoid confusion, for we have both stewards and managers, one of the four stewards of the hospital is to act as receiver of all its goods and is to receive adequate remuneration in order that he may better exercise his office.

The number of four stewards shall remain as it is, of which number one shall be charged with the common funds, as directed, not only that there may be greater efficiency, but also that those who wish to make special gifts may be better assured that these will be distributed only as they desire. If the income which the officials assign is not sufficient, or if some emergency should arise, the authorities shall instruct him to make adjustments according to the need.

The election of the managers, as well as of the stewards, is to be conducted as that of the elders; in their election the rule is to be followed which was delivered by St. Paul respecting deacons.

Concerning the office and authority of stewards, we confirm the articles which have already been proposed, on condition that, in urgent matters, especially when the issue is no great matter and the expenditure involved is small, they not be required to assemble for every action taken, but that one or two of them may be permitted to act in the absence of the others, in a reasonable way.

It will be his task to take diligent care that the public hospital is well administered and that it is open not only to the sick but also to aged persons who are unable to work, to widows, orphans and other needy persons. Those who are sick are to be kept in a separate lodging, away from those who cannot work, old persons, widows, orphans and other needy persons.

Also the care of the poor who are scattered throughout the city is to be conducted as the stewards may order.

Also, that another hospital is established for the transients who should be helped. Separate provision is to be made for any who are worthy of special charity. To accomplish this, a room is to be set aside for those who shall be recommended by the stewards, and it is to be used for no other purpose.

Above all, the families of the managers are to be well managed in an efficient and godly fashion, since they are to manage the houses dedicated to God.

The ministers and the commissioners or elders, with one of the syndics, for their part, are carefully to watch for any fault or negligence of any sort, in order to beg and admonish the authorities to set it in order. Every three months they are to cause certain of their company, with the stewards, to visit the hospital to ascertain if everything is in order.

It will be necessary, also, for the benefit of the poor in the hospital and for the poor of the city who cannot help themselves, that a doctor and a competent surgeon be secured from among those who practice in the city to have the care of the hospital and to visit the poor.

The hospital, for the pestilence in any case, is to be set apart; especially should it happen that the city is visited by this rod from God.

Moreover, to prevent begging, which is contrary to good order, **it** will be necessary that the authorities delegate certain officers. They are to be stationed at the doors of the churches to drive away any who try to resist and, if they act impudently or answer insolently, to take them to one of the syndics. In like manner, the heads of the precincts should always watch that the law against begging is well observed.

The Persons Whom the Elders Should Admonish, and Proper Procedure in This Regard

If there shall be anyone who lays down opinions contrary to received doctrine, he is to be summoned. If he recants, he is to be dismissed without prejudice. If he is stubborn, he is to be admonished from time to time until it shall be evident that he deserves greater severity. Then, he is to be excommunicated and this action reported to the magistrate.

If anyone is negligent in attending worship so that a noticeable offense is evident for the communion of the faithful, or if anyone shows himself contemptuous of ecclesiastical discipline, he is to be admonished. If he becomes obedient, he is to be dismissed in love. If he persists, passing from bad to worse, after having been admonished three times, he is to be excommunicated and the matter reported to the authorities.

For the correction of faults, it is necessary to proceed after the ordinance of our Lord. That is, vices are to be dealt with secretly and no one is to be brought before the church for accusation if the fault is neither public nor scandalous, unless he has been found rebellious in the matter.

For the rest, those who scorn private admonitions are to be admonished again by the church. If they will not come to reason nor recognize their error, they are to be ordered to abstain from communion until they improve.

As for obvious and public evil, which the church cannot overlook: if the faults merit nothing more than admonition, the duty of the elders shall be to summon those concerned, deal with them in love in order that they may be reformed and, if they correct the fault, to dismiss the matter. If they persevere, they are to be admonished again. If, in the end, such procedure proves unsuccessful, they are to be denounced as contemptuous of God, and ordered to abstain from communion until it is evident that they have changed their way of life.

As for crimes that merit not only admonition but punitive correction: if any fall into such error, according to the requirements of the case, it will be necessary to command them to abstain from communion so that they humble themselves before God and repent of their error.

If anyone by being contumacious or rebellious attempts that which is forbidden, the duty of the ministers shall be to reject him, since it is not proper that he receive the sacrament.

Nevertheless, let all these measures be moderate; let there not be such a degree of rigor that anyone should be cast down, for all corrections are but medicinal, to bring back sinners to the Lord.

And let all be done in such a manner as to keep from the ministers any civil jurisdiction whatever, so that they use only the spiritual sword of the word of God as St. Paul ordered them. Thus the consistory may in no wise take from the authority of the officers or of civil justice. On the contrary, the civil power is to be kept intact. Likewise, when it shall be necessary to exercise punishment or restraint against any party, the ministers and the consistory are to hear the party concerned, deal with them and admonish them as it may seem good, reporting all to the council which, for its part, shall deliberate and then pass judgment according to the merits of the case.

Questions:
1. Besides setting up the preaching ministry, what else did these *Ordinances* establish?
2. What was John Calvin's position on the separation of church and secular government?
3. What is the method of church discipline described? How does it compare with Hus's opinions (Chapter 14, Document 1)?

14.6 The Augsburg Confession: Defining the Lutheran Faith

In 1530, Emperor Charles V summoned an imperial diet to end the religious disunity caused by the Reformation before beginning military operations against the Turks. Lutheran princes and the officials of imperial cities presented to him the first comprehensive exposition of Lutheran belief. Although this Augsburg Confession firmly stated their doctrinal differences with the Roman Catholic Church, it also emphasized areas of agreement. Signed by princes and magistrates and compiled with the consultation of Luther, this document, written in both German and Latin, was largely the work of Luther's younger humanist colleague, Philip Melanchthon.

> **Source:** *The Book of Concord*, edited by Theodore G. Tappert, (Philadelphia: Fortress Press, 1959), pp. 27–30, 32, 34–46, 95–96.

1. [GOD]

We unanimously hold and teach, in accordance with the decree of the Council of Nicaea, that there is one divine essence, which is called and which is truly God, and that there are three persons in this one divine essence, equal in power and alike eternal: God the Father, God the Son, God the Holy Spirit. All three are one divine essence, eternal, without division, without end, of infinite power, wisdom, and goodness, one creator and preserver of all things visible and invisible. The word "person" is to be understood as the [ancient Christian] Fathers employed the term in this connection, not as a part or a property of another, but as that which exists of itself.

II. [ORIGINAL SIN]

It is also taught among us that since the fall of Adam all men who are born according to the course of nature are conceived and born in sin. That is, all men are full of evil lust and inclinations from their mothers' wombs and are unable by nature to have true fear of God and true faith in God. Moreover, this inborn sickness and hereditary sin is truly sin and condemns to the eternal wrath of God all those who are not born again through Baptism and the Holy Spirit.

Rejected in this connection are the Pelagians and others who deny that original sin is sin, for they hold that natural man is made righteous by his own powers, thus disparaging the sufferings and merit of Christ.

IV. [JUSTIFICATION]

It is also taught among us that we cannot obtain forgiveness of sin and righteousness before God by our own merits, works, or satisfactions, but that we receive forgiveness of sin and become righteous before God by grace, for Christ's sake through faith when we believe that Christ suffered for us and that for his sake our sin is forgiven and righteousness and eternal are given to us. For God will regard and reckon this faith as righteousness, as Paul says in Romans 3:21–26 and 4:5.

VII. [THE CHURCH]

It is also taught among us that one holy Christian church will be and remain forever. This is the assembly of all believers, among whom the Gospel is preached in its purity and the holy sacraments are administered according to the Gospel. For it is sufficient for the true unity of the Christian church that the Gospel be preached in conformity with a pure understanding of it and that the sacraments be administered in accordance with the divine Word. It is not necessary for the true unity of the Christian church that ceremonies, instituted by men, should be observed uniformly in all places. It is as Paul says in Ephesians 4:4, 5, "There is one body and one Spirit, just as you were called to the one hope that belongs to your call, one Lord, one faith, one baptism."

X. THE HOLY SUPPER OF OUR LORD

It is taught among us that the true body and blood of Christ are really present in the Supper of our Lord under the form of bread and wine and are there distributed and received. The contrary doctrine is therefore rejected.

XI. CONFESSION

It is taught among us that private absolution should be retained and not allowed to fall into disuse. However, in confession it is not necessary to enumerate all trespasses and sins, for this is impossible. Psalm 19:12, "Who can discern his errors?"

XIII. THE USE OF THE SACRAMENTS

It is taught among us that the sacraments were instituted not only to be signs by which people might be identified outwardly as Christians, but that they are signs and testimonies of God's will toward us for the purpose of awakening and strengthening our faith. For this reason they require faith, and they are rightly used when they are received in faith and for the purpose of strengthening faith.

XVI. CIVIL GOVERNMENT

It is taught among us that all government in the world and all established rule and laws were instituted and ordained by God for the sake of good order, and that Christians may without sin occupy civil offices or serve as princes and judges, render decisions and pass sentence according to imperial and other existing laws, punish evildoers with the sword, engage in just wars, serve as soldiers, buy and sell, take required oaths, possess property, be married, etc. Condemned here are the Anabaptists who teach that none of the things indicated above is Christian.

Also condemned are those who teach that Christian perfection requires the forsaking of house and home, wife and child, and the renunciation of such activities as are mentioned above. Actually, true perfection consists alone of proper fear of God and real faith in God, for the Gospel does not teach an outward and temporal but an inward and eternal mode of existence and righteousness of the heart. The Gospel does not overthrow civil authority, the state, and marriage but requires that all these be kept as true orders of God and that everyone, each according to his own calling, manifest Christian love and genuine good works in his station of life. Accordingly, Christians are obliged to be subject to civil authority and obey its commands and laws in all that can be done without sin. But when commands of the civil authority cannot be obeyed without sin, we must obey God rather than men (Acts 5:29).

XVIII. FREEDOM OF THE WILL

It is also taught among us that man possesses some measure of freedom of the will which enables him to live an outwardly honorable life and to make choices among the things that reason comprehends. But without the grace, help, and activity of the Holy Spirit man is not capable of making himself acceptable to God, of fearing God and believing in God with his whole heart, or of expelling inborn evil lusts from his heart. This is accomplished by the Holy Spirit, who is given through the Word of God, for Paul says in I Corinthians. 2:14, "Natural man does not receive the gifts of the Spirit of God."

In order that it may be evident that this teaching is no novelty, the clear words of Augustine on free will are here quoted from the third book of his *Hypognosticon* "We concede that all men have a free will, for all have a natural, innate understanding and reason. However, this does not enable them to act in matters pertaining to God (such as loving God with their whole heart or fearing him), for it is only in the outward acts of this life that they have freedom to choose good or evil. By good I mean what they are capable of by nature: whether or not to labor in the fields, whether or not to eat or drink or visit a friend, whether to dress or undress, whether to build a house, take a wife, engage in a trade, or do whatever else may be good and profitable. None of these is or exists without God, but all things are from him and through him. On the other hand, by his own choice man can also undertake evil, as when he wills to kneel before an idol, commit murder, etc."

XIX. THE CAUSE OF SIN

It is taught among us that although almighty God has created and still preserves nature, yet sin is caused in all wicked men and despisers of God by the perverted will. This is the will of the devil and of all ungodly men as soon as God withdraws his support, the will turns away from good to evil. It is as Christ says in John 8:44, "When the devil lies, he speaks according to his own nature."

XX. FAITH AND GOOD WORKS

Our teachers have been falsely accused of forbidding good works. Their writings on the Ten Commandments, and other writings as well, show that they have given good and profitable accounts and instructions concerning true Christian estates and works. About these little was taught in former times, when for the most part sermons were concerned with childish and useless works like rosaries, the cult of saints, monasticism, pilgrimages, appointed fasts, holy days, brotherhoods, etc. Our opponents no longer praise these useless works so highly as they once did, and they have also learned to speak now of faith, about which they did not preach at all in former times. They do not teach now that we become righteous before God by our works alone, but they add faith in Christ and say that faith and works make us righteous before God. This teaching may offer a little more comfort than the teaching that we are to rely solely on our works.

Since the teaching about faith, which is the chief article in the Christian life, has been neglected so long (as all must admit) while nothing but works was preached everywhere, our people have been instructed as follows:

We begin by teaching that our works cannot reconcile us with God or obtain grace for us, for this happens only through faith, that is, when we believe that our sins are forgiven for Christ's sake, who alone is the mediator who reconciles the Father. Whoever imagines that he can accomplish this by works, or that he can merit grace, despises Christ and seeks his own way to God, contrary to the Gospel.

This teaching about faith is plainly and clearly treated by Paul in many passages, especially in Ephesians. 2:8, 9, "For by grace you have been saved through faith; and this is not your own doing, it is the gift of God—not because of works, lest any man should boast," etc.

That no new interpretation is here introduced can be demonstrated from Augustine, who discusses this question thoroughly and teaches the same thing, namely, that we obtain grace and are justified before God through faith in Christ and not through works. His whole book, *De spiritu et litera*, proves this.

Although this teaching is held in great contempt among untried people, yet it is a matter of experience that weak and terrified consciences find it most comforting and salutary. The conscience cannot come to rest and peace through works, but only through faith, that is, when it is assured and knows that for Christ's sake it has a gracious God, as Paul says in Ram. 5:1, "Since we are justified by faith, we have peace with God."

In former times this comfort was not heard in preaching, but poor consciences were driven to rely on their own efforts, and all sorts of works were undertaken. Some were driven by their science into monasteries in the hope that there they might merit grace through monastic life. Others devised other works for the purpose of earning grace and making satisfaction for sins. Many of them discovered that they did not obtain peace by such means. It was therefore necessary to preach this doctrine about faith in Christ and diligently to apply it in order that men may know that the grace of God is appropriated without merits, through faith alone. . . .

It is also taught among us that good works should and must be done, not that we are to rely on them to earn grace but that we may do God's will and glorify him. It is always faith alone that apprehends grace and forgiveness of sin. When through faith the Holy Spirit is given, the heart is moved to do good works. Before that, when it is without the Holy Spirit, the heart is too weak. Moreover, it is in the power of the devil, who drives poor human beings into many sins. We see this in the philosophers who undertook to lead honorable and blameless lives; they failed to accomplish this, and instead fell into many great and open sins. This is what happens when a man is without true faith and the Holy Spirit and governs himself by his own human strength alone. . . .

. . . In keeping with the summons [from the emperor], we have desired to present the above articles as a declaration of our confession and the teaching of our preachers. If anyone should consider that it is lacking in some respect, we are ready to present further information on the basis of the divine Holy Scripture.

Your Imperial Majesty's most obedient servants:

JOHN, duke of Saxony. elector
GEORGE, margrave of Brandenburg
ERNEST, duke of Lüneburg
PHILIP, landgrave of Hesse
JOHN FREDERICK, duke of Saxony
FRANCIS, duke of Lüneburg
WOLFGANG, prince of Anhalt
Mayor and council of Nuremberg
Mayor and council of Reutlingen

Questions:
1. If the papacy and Roman Church had accepted the articles, what effect would it have had on the church hierarchy and institutions?
2. What was the Lutheran attitude toward "good works" and their relationship to faith?
3. How do the writers support their positions on the various issues?

14.7 The Act of Supremacy: The Church of England

Thwarted by the pope's reluctance from getting an annulment of his marriage, Henry VIII (r. 1509–1547) invoked the principle "the king in Parliament can do anything" to validate by legislation his new position as head of the Church of England. The new Archbishop of Canterbury, Thomas Cranmer, granted the king his annulment and Henry married Anne Boleyn.

Source: *Select Documents of English Constitutional History*, ed. George B. Adams and H. Morse Stephens, (New York: Macmillan, 1918), pp. 239–40, reprinted from *Statutes of the Realm* (London, 1810–28) III, 436–39.

ALBEIT the king's majesty justly and rightfully is and ought to be the supreme head of the Church of England, and so is recognized by the clergy of this realm in their Convocations, yet nevertheless for corroboration and confirmation thereof, and for increase of virtue in Christ's religion within this realm of England, and to repress and extirp all errors, heresies, and other enormities and abuses heretofore used in the same: be it enacted by authority of this present Parliament, that the king our sovereign lord, his heirs and successors, kings of this realm, shall be taken, accepted, and reputed the only supreme head in earth of the Church of England, called *Anglicana Ecclesia*; and shall have and enjoy, annexed and united to the imperial crown of this realm, as well the title and style thereof, as all honours, dignities, preeminences, jurisdictions, privileges, authorities, immunities, profits, and commodities to the said dignity of supreme head of the same Church belonging and appertaining; and that our said sovereign lord, his heirs and successors, kings of this realm, shall have full power and authority from time to time to visit, repress, redress, reform, order, correct, restrain, and amend all such errors, heresies, abuses, offences, contempts, and enormities, whatsoever they be, which by any manner spiritual authority or jurisdiction ought or may lawfully be reformed, repressed, ordered, redressed, corrected, restrained, or amended, most to the pleasure of Almighty God, the increase of virtue in Christ's religion, and for the conservation of the peace, unity, and tranquillity of this realm; any usage, custom, foreign law, foreign authority, prescription, or any other thing or things to the contrary hereof notwithstanding.

Questions:
1. On what grounds did Henry claim the right to exercise authority as "Supreme Head of the Church of England?"
2. How does this law change the relationship between church and state government? between England and other European states?

SECTION 3
Reactions to the Reformation

14.8 The German Peasant's Revolt: The Twelve Articles

Luther's stand against pope and emperor coincided with the growing anger and resentment of peasants and urban workers against noble authority. The following year the leaders of the peasants in the southwest German area drew up a manifesto of their demands. Sympathetic to their grievances, yet opposed to social revolution and disruption of public order, Luther urged the peasants to refrain from violence and seek a peaceful resolution. When the nobility disdainfully rejected the Articles, however, a bloody and destructive peasant rebellion erupted that was brutally crushed. Luther sternly approved of the retaliation because of the death and destruction that the rebels' violence had caused.

> **Source:** *Sources of the Western Tradition: Volume I: From Ancient Times to the Enlightenment,* ed. Marvin Perry, Joseph R. Peden, and Theodore H. Von Laue, (Boston: Houghton Mifflin Co., 1995), p 329–30. Reprinted with permission from *Translations and Reprints from the Original Sources of European History,* (1895 series) ed. D. C. Munro (Philadelphia: University of Pennsylvania, 1899), Vol.2, pp. 25–30.

Peace to the Christian reader and the grace of God through Christ:

There are many evil writings put forth of late which take occasion, on account of the assembling of the peasants, to cast scorn upon the Gospel, saying: "Is this the fruit of the new teaching, that no one should obey but all should everywhere rise in revolt, and rush together to reform, or perhaps destroy entirely, the authorities, both ecclesiastical and lay?" The articles below shall answer these godless and criminal fault-finders, and serve, in the first place, to remove the reproach from the word of God and, in the second place, to give a Christian excuse for the disobedience or even the revolt of the entire Peasantry. . . .

The Second Article According as the just tithe [a tax paid in grain] is established by the Old Testament and fulfilled in the New, we are ready and willing to pay the fair tithe of grain. The word of God plainly provides that in giving . . . to God and distributing to his people the services of a pastor are required. We will that for the future our church provost [manager of a feudal estate], whomsoever the community may appoint, shall gather and receive this tithe. From this he shall give to the pastor, elected by the whole community, a decent and sufficient maintenance for him and his, as shall seem right to the whole community. . . . The small tithes,* whether ecclesiastical or lay, we will not pay at all, for the Lord God created cattle for the free use of man. We will not, therefore, pay farther an unseemly tithe which is of man's invention.

The Third Article It has been the custom hitherto for men to hold us as their own property, which is pitiable enough, considering that Christ has delivered and redeemed us all, without exception, by the shedding of his precious blood, the lowly as well as the great. Accordingly it is consistent with Scripture that we should be free and should wish to be so. Not that we would wish to be absolutely free and under no authority. God does not teach us that we should lead a disorderly life in the lusts of the flesh, but that we should love the Lord our God and our neighbor. We would gladly observe all this as God has commanded us in the celebration of the communion. He has not commanded us not to obey the authorities, but rather that we should be humble, not only towards those in authority, but towards every one. We are thus ready to yield obedience according to God's law to our elected and regular authorities in all proper things becoming to a Christian. We therefore take it for granted that you will release us from serfdom as true Christians, unless it should be shown us from the gospel that we are serfs. . . .

---

* This is, tithes of other products than the staple crops—for example, tithes of pigs or lambs.

The Tenth Article In the tenth place, we are aggrieved by the appropriation by individuals of meadows and fields which at one time belonged to a community. These we will take again into our own hands. It may, however, happen that the land was rightfully purchased, but when the land has unfortunately been purchased in this way, some brotherly arrangement should be made according to circumstances.

The Eleventh Article In the eleventh place, we will entirely abolish the due called [heriot, a death tax], and will no longer endure it nor allow widows and orphans to be thus shamefully robbed against God's will. . . .

Questions:
1. What influence did Luther's reformation doctrine have on these Articles?
2. What were their social and political demands?

14.9 A Protestant Woman Argues for Tolerance

In the initial zeal of the Protestant Reformation, women frequently played important roles. Catherine, a cabinetmaker's daughter of Strasbourg (Ca. 1497–1562), married Matthew Zell, an ex-priest turned Lutheran minister. The following selection is from a series of letters she wrote to an angry young Lutheran minister named Ludwig Rabus, whose loathing for the radical protestant movement turned him against the Zells. Now a widow and seeking to vindicate herself, Catherine published the correspondence, consisting chiefly of her own letters.

> Source: *Not in God's Image*, ed. Julia O'Faolain and Lauro Martines, (New York: Harper and Row, Inc., 1973), pp. 203–6.

I, Catherine Zell, wife of the late lamented Mathew Zell, who served in Strasbourg, where I was born and reared and still live, wish you peace and enhancement in God's grace.

From my earliest years I turned to the Lord, who taught and guided me, and I have at all times, in accordance with my understanding and His grace, embraced the interests of His church and earnestly sought Jesus. Even in youth this brought me the regard and affection of clergymen and others much concerned with the church, which is why the pious Mathew Zell wanted me as a companion in marriage; and I, in turn, to serve the glory of Christ, gave devotion and help to my husband, both in his ministry and in keeping his house. . . .

Ever since I was ten years old I have been a student and a sort of church mother, much given to attending sermons. I have loved and frequented the company of learned men, and I conversed much with them, not about dancing, masquerades, and worldly pleasures but about the kingdom of God.

Yet I resisted and struggled against that kingdom. Then, as no learned man could find a way of consoling me in my sins, prayers and physical suffering, and as none could make me sure of God's love and grace, I fell gravely ill in body and spirit. I became like that poor woman of the Gospel who, having spent all she had on doctors to no avail, heard speak of Christ, went to Him, and was healed. As I foundered, devoured by care and anxiety, vainly searching for serenity in the practices of the church, God took pity on me. From among our people He drew out and sent forth Martin Luther. This man so persuaded me of the ineffable goodness of our Lord Jesus Christ that I felt myself snatched from the depths of hell and transported to the kingdom of heaven. I remembered the Lord's words to Peter: 'Follow me and I shall make you a fisher of men'. Then did I labor day and night to cleave to the path of divine truth. . . .

While other women decorated their houses and ornamented themselves, going to dances, wedding parties, and giving themselves to pleasure, I went into the houses of poor and rich alike, in all love, faith, and compassion, to care for the sick and the confined and to bury the dead. Was that to plant anxiety and turmoil in the church of Strasbourg? . . .

Consider the poor Anabaptists, who are so furiously and ferociously persecuted. Must the authorities everywhere be incited against them, as the hunter drives his dog against wild animals? Against those who acknowledge Christ the Lord in very much the same way we do and over which we broke with the papacy? Just because they cannot agree with us on lesser things, is this any reason to persecute them and in them Christ, in whom they fervently believe and have often professed in misery, in prison, and under the torments of fire and water?

Governments may punish criminals, but they should not force and govern belief which is a matter for the heart and conscience not for temporal authorities.

[Urges Rabus to consult the leading reformers on this question and provides him, ironically, with a list.]

. . . When the authorities pursue one, they soon bring forth tears, and towns and villages are emptied . . .

Strasbourg does not offer the example of an evil town but rather the contrary—charity, compassion, and hospitality for the wretched and poor. Within its walls, God be thanked, there remains more than one poor Christian whom certain people would have liked to see cast out. Old Mathew Zell would not have approved of that: he would have gathered the sheep, not destroyed them. . . .

Whether they were Lutherans, Zwinglians, Schwenkfeldians, or poor Anabaptist brethren, rich or poor, wise or foolish, according to the word of St. Paul, all came to us [to the Zells in Strasbourg]. We were not compelled to hold the same views and beliefs that they did, but we did owe to all a proof of love, service, and generosity: our teacher Christ has taught us that. . . .

Questions:
1. What activities did Catherine and her husband engage in?
2. Why did Rabus criticize her and how did she defend herself?

14.10 The Catholic Response: The Council of Trent

The response of the Catholic Church to the Protestant Reformation began, surprisingly, after the election of Pope Paul III (1534–1549), a humanist who immediately appointed his unqualified teenaged grandsons to the college of cardinals. Not only did this action reveal his immoral life, but also his willingness to use his office to increase the wealth and power of his family. Nevertheless, Paul III also appointed able and reform-minded men to offices of authority and called a Church council to deal with the many problems facing the Church. The Council of Trent met intermittently from 1545–1563. Some of its canons and decrees are recorded in the following document.

Source: *Heritage of Western Civilization,* Seventh Edition, ed. John L. Beatty and Oliver A. Johnson, (Prentice Hall, 1991), pp. 452–60.

DECREE TOUCHING THE OPENING OF THE COUNCIL

Doth it please you—unto the praise and glory of the holy and undivided Trinity, Father, and Son, and Holy Ghost; for the increase and exaltation of the Christian faith and religion; for the extirpation of heresies; for the peace and union of the Church; for the reformation of the Clergy and Christian people; for the depression and extinction of the enemies of the Christian name—to decree and declare that the sacred and general council of Trent do begin, and hath begun?

They answered: It pleaseth us.

DECREE CONCERNING ORIGINAL SIN

That our Catholic faith, *without which it is impossible to please God,* may, errors being purged away, continue in its own perfect and spotless integrity, and that the Christian people may not *be carried about with every wind of doctrine*; whereas that old serpent, the perpetual enemy of mankind, amongst the very many evils with which the Church of God is in these our times troubled, has also stirred up not only new, but even old, dissensions touching original sin, and the remedy thereof; the sacred and holy,

oecumenical and general Synod of Trent,—lawfully assembled in the Holy See presiding therein,—wishing now to come to the reclaiming of the erring, and the confirming of the wavering—following the testimonies of the sacred Scriptures, of the holy Fathers, or the most approved councils, and the judgement and consent of the Church itself, ordains, confesses, and declares these things touching the said original sin:

1. If any one does not confess that the first man, Adam, when he had transgressed the commandment of God in Paradise, immediately lost the holiness and justice wherein he had been constituted; and that he incurred, through the offense of that prevarication, the wrath and indignation of God, and consequently death, with which God had previously threatened him, and, together with death, captivity under his power who thenceforth *had the empire of death, that is to say, the devil,* and that the entire Adam, through that offence of prevarication, was changed, in body and soul, for the worse; let him be anathema.

3. If any one asserts, that this sin of Adam—which in its origin is one, and being transfused into all by propagation, not by imitation, is in each one as his own—is taken away either by the powers of human nature, or by any other remedy than the merit of the *one mediator our Lord Jesus Christ, who hath reconciled us to God in his own blood, made unto us justice, sanctification, and redemption*; or if he denies that the said merit of Jesus Christ is applied, both to adults and to infants, by the sacrament of baptism rightly administered in the form of the Church; let him be anathema. . . .

ON THE SACRAMENTS IN GENERAL

Canon I. If any one saith, that the sacraments of the New Law were not all instituted by Jesus Christ, our Lord; or, that they are more, or less, than seven, to wit, Baptism, Confirmation, the Eucharist, Penance, Extreme Unction, Order, and Matrimony; or even that any one of these seven is not truly and properly a sacrament; let him be anathema.

Canon IV. If any one saith, that the sacraments of the New Law are not necessary unto salvation, but superfluous; and that, without them, or without the desire thereof, men obtain of God, through faith alone, the grace of justification;-though all (the sacraments) are not indeed necessary for every individual; let him be anathema.

Canon VI. If any one saith, that the sacraments of the New Law do not contain the grace which they signify; or, that they do not confer that grace on those who do not place an obstacle thereunto; as though they were merely outward signs of grace or justice received through faith, and certain marks of the Christian profession, whereby believers are distinguished amongst men from unbelievers; let him be anathema.

Canon X. If any one saith, that all Christians have power to administer the word, and all the sacraments; let him be anathema.

ON THE MOST HOLY SACRAMENT OF THE EUCHARIST

Canon I. If any one deny, that, in the sacrament of the most holy Eucharist, are contained truly, really, and substantially, the body and blood together with the soul and divinity of our Lord Jesus Christ. and consequently the whole Christ: but saith that He is only therein as in a sign, or in figure, or virtue: let him be anathema.

Canon II. If anyone saith that in the sacred and holy sacrament of the Eucharist, the substance of the bread and wine remains conjointly with the body and blood of our Lord .Jesus Christ, and denieth that wonderful and singular conversion of the whole substance of the bread into the Body, and of the whole substance of the wine into the Blood—the species only of the bread and wine remaining—which conversion indeed the Catholic Church most aptly calls transubstantiation; let him be anathema.

ON THE ECCLESIASTICAL HIERARCHY, AND ON ORDINATION

. . . If any one affirm, that all Christians indiscriminately are priests of the New Testament. or that they are all mutually endowed with an equal spiritual power, he clearly does nothing but confound the ecclesiastical hierarchy; which is *as an army set in array.* . . .

. . . . It decree, that all those who, being only called and instituted by the people, or by the civil power and magistrate, ascend to the exercise of these ministrations, and those who of their own rashness assume them to themselves, are not ministers of the Church, but are to be looked upon as *thieves and robbers, who have not entered by the door.* These are the things which it hath seemed good to the sacred Synod to teach the faithful of Christ. in general terms, touching the sacrament of Order.

ON THE SACRAMENT OF MATRIMONY

Canon IX. If anyone saith, that clerics constituted in sacred orders or Regulars, who have solemnly professed chastity, are able to contract marriage, and that being contracted it is valid. notwithstanding the ecclesiastical law, or vow: and that the contrary is nothing else than to condemn marriage: and, that all who do not feel that they have the gift of chastity; even though they have made a vow thereof, may contract marriage: let him be anathema: seeing that God refuses not that gift to those who ask for it rightly; neither does *He suffer us to be tempted above that which we are able.*

Canon X. If anyone saith. that the marriage state is to be placed above the state of virginity and of celibacy, and that it is not better and more blessed to remain in virginity, or in celibacy, than to be united in matrimony; let him be anathema.

ON THE INVOCATION, VENERATION, AND RELICS, OF SAINTS, AND ON SACRED IMAGES

The holy Synod enjoins on all bishops and others who sustain the office and charge of teaching, that, agreeably to the usage of the Catholic and Apostolic Church, received from the primitive times of the Christian religion, and agreeably to the consent of the holy Fathers, and to the decrees of sacred Councils, they especially instruct the faithful diligently concerning the intercession and invocation of saints; the honour (paid) to relics; and the legitimate use of images; teaching them that the saints who reign together with Christ, offer up their own prayers to God for men, that it is good and useful supplicantly to invoke them, and to have recourse to their prayers, aid, (and) help for obtaining benefits from God, through His Son, Jesus Christ, our lord, who is alone Redeemer and Saviour; but that they think impiously, who denies that the saints, who enjoy eternal happiness in heaven, are to be invocated or who assert either that they do not pray for men; or, that the invocation of them to pray for each of us even in particular is idolatry or that it is repugnant to the word ogf God; and is opposed to the honour of the *one mediator between God and me, Christ Jesus*; or that it is foolish to supplicate, vocally or mentally, those who reign in heaven. Also, that the holy bodies of holy martyrs, and of others now living with Christ. . . . They who affirm that veneration and honour are not due to the relics of saints; or, that these, and other sacred monuments, are uselessly honoured by the faithful; and that the places dedicated to the memories of the saints are in vain visited with the view of obtaining their aid; are wholly to be condemned, as the Church has already long since condemned, and now also condemns.

CARDINALS AND ALL PRELATES OF THE CHURCHES SHALL BE CONTENT WITH MODEST FURNITURE AND A FRUGAL TABLE: THEY SHALL NOT ENRICH THEIR RELATIVES OR DOMESTICS OUT OF THE PROPERTY OF THE CHURCH

. . . Wherefore, after the example of our fathers in the Council of Carthage, it not only orders that bishops be content with modest furniture, and a frugal table and diet, but that they also give heed that in the rest of their manner of living, and in their whole house, there be nothing seen that is alien from this holy institution, and which does not manifest simplicity, zeal toward God, and a contempt of vanities. Also, it wholly forbids them to enrich their own kindred or domestics out of the revenues of the church. . . . It would seem to be a shame, if they did not at the same time shine so pre-eminent in virtue and in the discipline of their lives, as deservedly to draw upon themselves the eyes of all men.

DECREE CONCERNING INDULGENCES

Whereas the power of conferring Indulgences was granted by Christ to the Church; and she has, even in the most ancient times, used the said power, delivered unto her of God; the sacred holy Synod teaches, and enjoins, that the use of Indulgences for the Christian people most salutary, and approved of by the authority of sacred Councils, is to be retained in the Chruch; and It condemns with anathema those who either assert, that they are useless; or who deny that there is in the Church the power of granting them. In granting them, however, it desires that, in accordance with the ancient and approved custom in the Church, moderation be observed; lest by excessive facility. Ecclesiastical discipline be enervated. And being desirous that the abuses which have crept therein, and by occasion of which this honourable name of Indulgences is blasphemed by heretics, be amended and corrected. . . .

Questions:
1. For what purposes did the pope call the Council of Trent?
2. How well did it achieve them?
3. What concessions did the Council make to the doctrinal criticisms of the Protestants?

CHAPTER 15
Absolute Power
War and Politics in Early Modern Europe
(1500–1750)

SECTION 1
The Law and Absolute Power

15.1 The Edict of Nantes

At the end of decades of religious strife, Henry IV of France (r. 1589–1610) decreed the Edict of Nantes, granting religious toleration to the French Protestants, known as Huguenots. This is the first time in European history that a Christian ruler permitted civil liberty as well as freedom of worship to a religious minority.

Source: Sidney Z. Ehler and John B. Morrall, eds. and trans., *Church and State Through the Centuries: A Collection of Historic Documents* (London: Burns and Gates, 1954), pp. 185–88.

Firstly, that the memory of everything done on both sides from the beginning of the month of March 1585, until our accession to the Crown and during the other previous troubles, and at the outbreak of them, shall remain extinct and suppressed, as if it were something which had never occurred. And it shall not be lawful or permissible to our Procurators-General or to any other persons, public or private, at any time or on any pretext whatsoever, to institute a case, lawsuit or action in any Court or judicial tribunals whatever [concerning those things].

We forbid all our subjects, of whatever rank and quality they may be, to renew the memory of these matters, to attack, be hostile to, injure or provoke each other in revenge for the past, whatever may be the reason and pretext; or to dispute, argue or quarrel about it, or to do violence, or to give offence in deed or word, but let them restrain themselves and live peaceably together as brothers, friends and fellow-citizens, on pain of being liable to punishment as disturbers of the peace and troublers of public quiet.

We ordain that the Catholic, Apostolic and Roman religion shall be restored and re-established in all places and districts of this our kingdom and the countries under our rule, where its practice has been interrupted, so that it can be peacefully and freely practiced there, without any disturbance or hindrance. We forbid very expressly all persons of whatever rank, quality or condition they may be, under the aforesaid penalties, to disturb, molest or cause annoyance to clerics in the celebration of the Divine worship, the enjoyment and receipt of tithes, fruits and revenues of their benefices, and all other rights and duties which belong to them; and we ordain that all those who during the disorders have come into possession of churches, houses, goods and revenues belonging to the said clerics, and who retain and occupy them, shall give back the entire possession and enjoyment of them, with such rights, liberties and safeguards as they had before they were seized. We also forbid very expressly those of the so-called Reformed religion to hold prayer meetings or any devotions of the aforesaid religion in churches, houses and dwellings of the above-said clerics. . . .

And in order not to leave any cause for discords and disputes between our subjects, we have permitted and we permit those of the so-called Reformed religion to live and dwell in all the towns and districts of this our kingdom and the countries under one rule, without being annoyed, disturbed, molested or constrained to do anything against their conscience, or for this cause to be sought out in their houses and districts where they wish to live, provided that they conduct themselves in other respects according to the provisions of our present Edict. . . .

We also permit those of the aforesaid religion to carry out and continue its practice in the towns and districts under our rule, where it was established and carried out publicly several distinct times in the year 1597, until the end of the month of March, notwithstanding all decrees and judgments to the contrary. . . .

We forbid very expressly all those of the aforesaid religion to practice it in so far as ministration, regulation, discipline or public instruction of children and others is concerned, in this our kingdom and the countries under our rule, in matters concerning religion, outside the places permitted and conceded by the present Edict. . . .

Books dealing with the matters of the aforesaid so-called Reformed religion shall not be printed and sold publicly, except in the towns and districts where the public exercise of the said religion is allowed. And with regard to other books which shall be printed in other towns, they shall be seen and inspected by our officials and theologians as laid down by our ordinances. We forbid very specifically the printing, publication and sale of all defamatory books, tracts and writings, under the penalties contained in our ordinances, instructing all our judges and officials to carry out this ruling strictly.

We ordain that there shall be no difference or distinction, because of the aforesaid religion, in the reception of students to be instructed in Universities, Colleges and schools, or of the sick and poor into hospitals, infirmaries and public charitable institutions. . . .

In order to reunite more effectively the wills of our subjects, as is our intention, and to remove all future complaints, we declare that all those who profess or shall profess the aforesaid so-called Reformed religion are capable of holding and exercising all public positions, honours, offices and duties whatsoever, Royal, seigneurial, or offices in the towns of our kingdom, countries, lands and lordships subject to us, notwithstanding all contrary oaths, and of being admitted and received into them without distinction; it shall be sufficient for our courts of Parliament and other judges to ascertain and inquire concerning the life, morals, religion and honest behaviour of those who are or shall be appointed to offices, whether of one religion or the other, without enacting from them any oath other than that of well and faithfully serving the King in the exercise of their functions and keeping the ordinances, as has been perpetually the custom. During vacancies in the aforesaid positions, functions and offices, we shall make—in respect of those which shall be in our disposition—appointments without bias or discrimination of capable persons, as the unity of our subjects requires it. We declare also that members of the aforesaid so-called Reformed religion can be admitted and received into all Councils, conferences, assemblies and gatherings which are connected with the offices in question; they can not be rejected or prevented from enjoying these rights on grounds of the said religion. . . .

And for greater security of the behaviour and conduct which we expect with regard to it [the Edict], we will, command and desire that all the Governors and Lieutenants-General of our provinces, Bailiffs, Seneschals asnd other ordinary judges in towns in our aforesaid kingdom, immediately after the reception of this Edict, swear to cause it to be kept and observed, each one in his own district; likewise the mayors, sheriffs, captains, consuls and magistrates of the towns, annual and perpetual. We also enjoin our said bailiffs, seneschals or their lieutenants and other judges, to cause the principal inhabitants from both religions in the above-mentioned towns to swear to respect the present Edict immediately after its publication. We place all those of the said towns in our protection and safe keeping, each religion being placed in the safe keeping of the other; and we wish them to be instructed respectively and by public acts to answer by due legal process any contraventions of our present Edict which shall be made in the said towns by their inhabitants, or to make known the said contraventions and put them into the hand of justice.

We command our beloved and loyal people who hold our Courts of Parliament, "Chambres des Comptes" and courts of aids that immediately after the present Edict has been received, they are bound, all business being suspended and under penalty of nullity for any acts which they shall make otherwise, to take an oath similar to the above and to make this our Edict to be published and registered in our above-mentioned Courts according to its proper form

and meaning, purely and simply, without using any modifications, rectifications, declarations or secret registering and without waiting for further order or commandment from us; and we order our Procurators-General to demand and ensure immediately and without delay the aforesaid publication. . . .

For such is our pleasure. As witness thereof we have signed the present enactment with our own hand, and in order that it may be sure and stable permanently, we have placed and affixed our Seal to it.

Given at Nantes in the month of April, in the year of grace 1598, the ninth year of our reign.

[Signed,]

Henry

Questions:
1. What specific rights did this edict allow the Huguenots?
2. To what extent were they still treated differently from the Catholic majority?
3. How might they become a threat someday to royal authority?

15.2   James I Writes to the House of Commons

James I of Scotland (1566–1625), the son of Mary Queen of Scots, succeeded Queen Elizabeth I on the throne of England. He believed in the divine right of kings; monarchy was instituted by God for the government of his people, making the king responsible only to God himself.

Source: Sources of English Constitutional History: A Selection of Documents *from A.D. 600 to the Interregnum*, ed. and trans. Carl Stephenson and Frederick George Marcham, (New York: Harper and Row, 1972), p. 418.

Mr. Speaker: We have heard by divers reports, to our great grief, that our distance from the houses of parliament, caused by our indisposition of health, hath emboldened some fiery and popular spirits of some of the house of commons to argue and debate publicly of the matters far above their reach and capacity, tending to our high dishonour and breach of prerogative royal. These are therefore to command you to make known, in our name, unto the house that none therein shall presume henceforth to meddle with anything concerning our government or deep matters of state; and, namely, not to deal with our dearest son's match with the daughter of Spain, nor to touch the honour of that king or any other our friends and confederates, and also not to meddle with any man's particulars which have their due motion in our ordinary courts of justice. And whereas we hear they have sent a message to Sir Edward Sandys to know the reasons of his late restraint, you shall in our name resolve them that it was not for any misdemeanour of his in parliament. But, to put them out of doubt of any question of that nature that may arise among them hereafter, you shall resolve them, in our name, that we think ourself very free and able to punish any man's misdemeanours in parliament, as well during their sitting as after—which we mean not to spare hereafter upon any occasion of any man's insolent behaviour there that shall be ministered unto us. And if they have already touched any of these points, which we have forbidden, in any petition of theirs which is to be sent unto us, it is our pleasure that you shall tell them that, except they reform it before it come to our hands, we will not deign the hearing nor answering of it.

Rushworth, *Historical Collections*, I, 43 f.

Questions:

1. Why was James upset with Parliament?
2. What in his letter reveals his opinions about the relationship of Parliament and the monarchy in governing England?

15.3 The Bill of Rights, 1689

James II of England (r. 1685–88) provoked the Glorious Revolution of 1688 by attempting to rule according to the notions of monarchy expressed by his grandfather James I in his letter (Chapter 15, Document 2) and which had cost his own father, Charles II, his head in 1649. Losing nerve in the face of invading forces led by William of Orange, James fled to the French court of Louis XIV. Asserting that the King's flight left the thrones of England and Scotland vacant. Parliament then offered the crown jointly, with certain conditions, to William of Orange and his wife Mary, James II's own daughter. William and Mary accepted those conditions, which are the English Bill of Rights.

> **Source:** William and Mary, St. II, cap. 2, *Statutes of the Realm*, VI, 542–45, in Andrew Browning, *English Historical Documents, 1660–1774*, (New York: Oxford University Press, 1953, VIII, 123-24.

And thereupon the said Lords spiritual and temporal, and Commons, pursuant to their respective letters and elections, being now assembled in a full and free representation of this nation, taking into their most serious consideration the best means for attaining the ends aforesaid, do in the first place (as their ancestors in like case have usually done), for the vindicating and asserting their ancient rights and liberties, declare:

1. That the pretended power of suspending laws, of the execution of laws, by regal authority, without consent of Parliament, is illegal.

2. That the pretended power of dispensing with laws, or the execution of laws, by regal authority, as it hath been assumed and exercised of late, is illegal.

3. That the commission for erecting the late court of commissioners for ecclesiastical causes, and all other commissions and courts of like nature, are illegal and pernicious.

4. That levying money for or to the use of the Crown by pretense of prerogative, without grant of Parliament, for longer time or in other manner than the same is or shall be granted, is illegal.

5. That it is the right of the subjects to petition the King, and all commitments and prosecutions for such petitioning are illegal.

6. That the raising or keeping a standing army within the kingdom in time of peace, unless it be with consent of Parliament, is against the law.

7. That the subjects which are Protestants may have arms for their defense suitable to their conditions, and as allowed by law.

8. That election of members of Parliament ought to be free.

9. That the freedom of speech, and debates or proceedings in Parliament, ought not to be impeached or questioned in any court or place out of Parliament.

10. That excessive bail ought not to be required, nor excessive fines imposed, nor cruel and unusual punishments inflicted.

11. That jurors ought to be duly impaneled and returned, and jurors which pass upon men in trials for high treason ought to be freeholders.

12. That all grants and promises of fines and forfeitures of particular persons before conviction are illegal and void.

13. And that for redress of all grievances, and for the amending, strengthening, and preserving of the laws, Parliaments ought to be held frequently.

Questions

1. What are the practices that Parliament found so unacceptable in James II?
2. In what ways does the Bill of Rights limit the prerogatives of William and Mary?
3. Which of these rights were adopted in the U.S. Bill of Rights? Which ones originated in the medieval relationship between lord and vassal (see Magna Carta, Chapter 9, Document 8)?

SECTION 2
The Practice of Absolutism in France

15.4   Richelieu: Controlling the Nobility

Cardinal Richelieu (1585–1642) was a shrewd and dedicated political leader who accelerated the growth of absolutism in France. He demonstrated tremendous energy, tenacity, and imagination in directing public policy as Louis XIII's chief minister.

Source: *The Western World: Volume I to 1700,* ed. Wallace E. Adams, et al., (New York: Dodd, Mead & Co., 1968), pp. 510–16.

ON THE NOBILITY

After having explained what I consider to be absolutely necessary for the re-establishment of your realm's first order [the clergy], I shall proceed to the second order and say that the nobility must be considered as one of the strengths of the state, capable of contributing much to its preservation and to its stability. But for some time the nobility has been so diminished by . . . the century's misfortunes that it urgently needs to be protected. . . . They are rich only in the courage that leads them to devote their lives freely to the state.

As it is necessary to protect them against their oppressors; it is also necessary to take special care to restrain them from exploiting their underlings. It is very common fault on the part of those born into the nobility to use violence against the common people to whom God seems to have given arms for earning a living rather than for defending themselves. It is very important to stop such disorders by a constant sternness which will make the weakest of yours, although disarmed, as secure in the shelter of your laws as those who are armed.

The nobility has demonstrated, in the recent war, that it inherited the virtue of its ancestors; it is now necessary to discipline the nobles so that they may preserve their former reputation and usefully serve the state. Men who are injurious to the public are not useful to the state; it is certain that nobility which does not serve in war is not only useless, but a burden to the state, and can be compared to a body which supports a paralyzed arm. . . .

As gentry they merit being well treated when they do well, but it is necessary to be severe with them when they fail to do the things which their birth binds them to do. I have no qualms in saying that those who are degenerate in terms of the virtue of their ancestors, and who fail to serve the crown with their swords and with their lives, as well as with the confidence and the firmness that the laws of the state require, deserve to be deprived of the advantages of their birth and reduced to carry a part of the peoples' burden. Since honor should be dearer to them than life, it would be more of a punishment to deprive them of the former rather than the latter. To take away the lives of these persons, who expose their lives every day for a pure fancy of honor, is much less than taking away their honor and leaving them a life which would be a perpetual anguish for them. All means must be used to maintain the nobility in the true virtue of their fathers, and one must also omit nothing to preserve the advantages they inherited. . . . Just as it is impossible to find a remedy for every evil, it is also very difficult to put forth a general expedient for the ends that I am proposing. . . .

It is necessary also to distinguish between the nobility which is at court and that which is in the country. . . . The nobility at court will be notably relieved if the luxury and the unbearable expenditures of court life were reduced. As to the rural nobility, even though it would not receive as much relief by such a decision, because its poverty does not permit it to have such expenditures, it would also feel the effect of this remedy which is so necessary to avoid the ruin of the entire state. . . . Further, your majesty should control the venal provincial governments and the military expenses for which the nobility pays a large enough price with its blood.

If your majesty practiced better regulation of the expenses of his house, instead of maintaining all sorts of people who are received there through their purse, entrance would be barred in the future to those who will not have the good fortune to be born of noble birth. . . . Now, unfortunately, gentlemen can elevate themselves to offices and dignities only at the price of their financial. . . . Further, if your goodness extends itself enough to bestow honors on their children (those who possess the required learning and piety) . . . the nobility will be bound more closely to you, for in removing the necessity of purchasing honors which weighs them down you will give them the true means of maintaining their houses. . . . One will be able to do many other things for the relief of the nobility. But I have suppressed my thoughts on that subject, realizing that they would be very easy to write about but perhaps impossible to put into practice.

THE MEANS OF PREVENTING DUELS

There have been many edicts issued to stop duels, all of them fruitless to the present. Results have been hoped for and waited for, but it has been most difficult to find an effective way to curb this rage. The French scorn their lives in such a way, as experience has made clear to us, that the most rigorous punishments have not always been the best method to stop the frenzy.

The nobility have often thought that there is much more glory in violating rather than obeying your edicts, for they believe such actions demonstrate that their honor is more important to them than their life. Nevertheless, they are in dread of losing their worldly possessions and convenience, without which they could not live happily. . . . The fear of losing their offices, their belongings and their freedom has a greater impact on their minds than the fear of losing their lives.

I have tried not to forget anything which would make it possible for me to suggest some remedy to cure this dangerous evil. I have often tried to determine whether some duels, within the multitude that occur every day, could be reconciled in advance. And I believe there is a marked possibility that by this means we may be able to save France from this madness. In view of the fact that those individuals found justified in engaging in combat could still do so, they should be willing to submit themselves to judges deputized to consider the seriousness of the offense, which would put a stop to the misfortune of duels. There should be few quarrels that could not be settled by compromise beforehand. I believe, along such lines, that one could abolish this barbarism which dictates that every offended man take justice into his own hands and find satisfaction in the blood of his enemies; . . . Unfortunately, the blindness of the nobility is so great that some would ignore the course I have suggested and continue to demand combat to soothe their vanity and give proof of their courage.

The deceased king [Henri IV] attempted this path in 1609, using all the means at his power to make it effective. He deprived the nobility of their properties, their offices, and even the lives of those who fought without permission—but to no avail. This is what has forced your majesty, after experiencing the same conditions at the beginning of his reign, to search for another remedy in his edict of March, 1626. That remedy has had a much greater effect than punishment, for it concentrates on those who value their lives less than their possessions and their liberty.

The best laws in the world are useless, however, if they are not inviolably observed. And because those who commit this offense most often cover the evidence of their duel, it is almost impossible to substantiate their crime. I have no fear in saying to your majesty that it is not enough to punish the participants in confirmed duels through the strictness of your edicts. Even when there has been only unconfirmed information, without full proof of a duel, it is absolutely necessary to apprehend the delinquents and make them prisoners at their own expense, for a long or short period according to the circumstances of their action. Otherwise the uncertainty and negligence which now marks the information your attorney generals ordinarily provide to you, plus the indulgence of the Parlements and the general corruption of the age, is such that every man esteems it an honor to aid those who have fought and then disguised their crimes, thereby rendering your edicts and your most careful efforts useless. It is in such cases that the only sure way to have your laws and ordinances followed is for your authority to pass above the form of the law in order to maintain the law and order necessary to the very existence of a state.

If your majesty orders that all encounters will be considered as duels, and will be punished as such until those who have committed them surrender themselves voluntarily as prisoners, and will be absolved or sentenced according to the law, you will have done all that can probably be done to stem the course of this rage. . . .

THE USES OF PUNISHMENTS AND REWARDS

Punishments and rewards are two quite necessary elements in the conduct of states. It is an ordinary allegation, but more true, and often repeated by all men, that rewards and punishments are the two most important tools of government available in a realm.

It is certain that even though one can make use of no other principle than that of being inflexible in punishing those who fail to serve the state, and religiously reward those who perform some notable service, one will not govern badly, since all men will perform their duty through fear or hope. One should, however, place punishment before rewards, because if it is necessary to eliminate either of the two, it would be better to dispense with the latter than the former.

In the strictest sense good should be embraced for its own sake, for one's love of honor, and no reward is owed to those who perform it. But because there is no duel which does not violate the sense of honor it is meant to uphold, punishment due to disobedience is always required. This obligation is so strict that on many occasions the offense cannot be left unpunished without committing a new one. I am speaking here of actions which injure the state by premeditation and not of the many others which happen by chance and by misfortune, of which princes can and should be indulgent.

Even though to pardon in such cases is a commendable thing, not to punish an offense is a criminal omission because impunity opens the door to license. Theologians and politicians are in agreement on this subject; all agree that while in certain cases it is well for the prince to grant his pardon, it would be inexcusable for officials with public responsibility to substitute lenience for severe punishment. The lesson of experience, for those who have dealt with people for a long time, is that men easily forget favors, remain ungrateful, and become ambitious for further rewards. It is clear that punishments are a much surer means of holding each man to his duty. Men are less likely to forget things that make an impression on their emotions; it is more forceful than reason which has no power over many minds. To be rigorous with those individuals who take pride in scorning the laws and the orders of the state is to serve the public well. One could not commit a greater crime against the public interest than to be indulgent to those who violate it.

Among the several combinations, factions, and seditions which have occurred in this realm during my life,

I have never observed that lenience ever led any mind to naturally correct itself of its evil inclinations. But, on the contrary, it allowed individuals to return to their troublesome ways, and often they were more successful the second time than the first.

The degree of indulgence hitherto practiced in this realm has often put it in very great and deplorable difficulties. Whenever wrongs go unpunished, everyone will completely disregard the laws and take advantage of their position; instead of honorable compliance with the laws, they will consider only what further profit they can obtain for themselves.

If in the past men felt that it was dangerous to live under a prince who rigorously enforced the law, they also were aware that it was even more dangerous to live under a state in which impunity opened the door to every of license. Princes and magistrates who fear they will commit a sin by being too strict can answer to God, but they will only be blamed by wise men if they fail to exercise that authority which is prescribed by the laws. I have often brought this to the attention of your majesty and I urge you again to reconsider this matter carefully, for just as there are princes who need to be turned away from severity in order to avoid unnecessary cruelty, your majesty needs to be diverted from the fault of clemency. This is more dangerous even than cruelty, because such leniency will later require even greater punishments.

The rod, which is the symbol of justice, must not stand idle. I am also convinced that it must not be used so strictly that it is without mercy; but this last quality should not lead to a state of indulgence which authorizes disorders, however small, for those disorders are injurious to the state and may cause its ruin. There are, of course, some men badly enough advised to condemn the necessary severity in this kingdom because it has not been practiced in earlier times. It is only necessary to open their eyes, and make them know that leniency has been too common in the past and has caused the breakdown of law and order, and that the continuation of disorders has demanded recourse to extreme measures. So many of the factions that in the past have ranged themselves against the king have had no other source than excessive royal indulgence. Finally, provided that one knows our history, one can not ignore this truth, for which I can produce testimony straight from the mouths of our enemies. . . .

In crimes against the state, it is necessary to close the door to, pity and scorn the complaints of involved parties, and the cries of an ignorant multitude which sometimes finds fault with everything that is useful and even essential to its well-being. Christians should forget personal offenses, but magistrates are obligated never to forget offenses committed against the public interest. In fact, to let them go unpunished is not to pardon but rather like inviting the individuals to commit the offense again.

There are many people whose ignorance is so immense that they feel it is sufficient to prohibit an evil to remedy it; but they are wrong. I may say in truth that new laws are not as much a remedy for the disorders of states as testimonies to their sickness, and symptoms of the weakness of the government. If the ancient laws had been well executed there would be no need to renovate them or to enact new ones designed to prevent new disorders—which would never have taken place had there existed a strong authority to punish the wrongs committed.

Ordinances and laws are quite useless if they are not followed by vigorous execution. This is so absolutely necessary that while in the course of ordinary affairs justice requires an authentic proof, the same is not true for the state; in such cases, what seems to be conjecture must sometimes be held as sufficiently clear; since the factions and conspiracies which work against the public good are commonly carried on with so much skill and secrecy that there is seldom any proof until after the event, when it is too late to remedy the situation. On such occasions, it is sometimes necessary to begin with direct action and punishment; whereas in all others, as a preliminary to everything else, the facts must be proved by witnesses or irreproachable documents. These maxims seem dangerous, and in fact they are not entirely devoid of peril, but if extreme remedies are not used in the case of wrongs which can be verified only by conjecture, one can only attempt to halt the course of a conspiracy by such innocuous means as the exile or imprisonment of suspected persons.

A man of good conscience and penetrating judicial mind, knowing the course of affairs and the future with almost the same certainty as the present, will protect this practice from abuse. And, if worst comes to worst, the abuses committed are dangerous only to private individuals, which is not too important in comparison to the public interest. However, it is necessary to exercise restraint in order not to open the door to tyranny by these means, which doubtless can be avoided if, as I have said above, one only makes use of mild remedies in doubtful cases.

Punishment is so necessary in regard to the public interest that it is not even proper to compensate a present wrong for a good service performed in the past, that is to say, to allow a crime to go unpunished because the one who committed it had served well on another occasion. This is nevertheless what has been often practiced in this realm in the past. Not only have minor wrongs been ignored in consideration of great services rendered, but great crimes have been ignored for services of no importance, which is completely unacceptable. Good and bad are so different and contrary that they must never be paralleled with one another; they are irreconcilable enemies—if one is worthy of recompense, the other is worthy of punishment, and both must be treated according to their merit. Even when one's conscience could allow a worth-while deed to go without reward, and a notable crime to go unpunished, the needs of the state cannot permit it. Punishment and rewards aim at the future rather than the past; . . .

THE POWER OF THE PRINCE

The prince must be powerful to be respected by his subjects and by foreigners. Power being one of the most necessary things for the greatness of kings and for the prosperity of their governments, those who conduct the principal business of the state are especially obligated to omit nothing which may contribute to the authority of their master.

As goodness is the object of love, power is the cause of fear, and it is most certain that among all the pressures capable of moving a state, fear, grounded on esteem and reverence, has the power to make everyone perform his duty. If this principle is of great efficiency in respect to domestic affairs, it is not less so with respect to external matters. Subjects and foreigners look with the same eyes upon a redoubtable power, and will avoid offending a prince when they know he is in a position to do them harm if he is so inclined.

I have said that the basis of the power of which I speak must be esteem and respect. If such power is based on any other principle it is very dangerous; instead of creating a reasonable fear, it produces hatred for the prince—and princes are never in a worse condition than when they fall into public aversion.

Like a tree with different branches taking nourishment from the same root, the power which makes princes passionately hated or respected is of different kinds: the prince must be powerful through his reputation; and by maintaining a reasonably sized standing army; and by maintaining sufficient funds in his coffers to meet the unexpected emergencies which often occur when one least expects them. And, finally, the prince's power stems from the possession of the hearts of his subjects, as will be clearly shown.

A good reputation is very necessary, for a prince held in high esteem can do more with his name alone than those princes with large armies but a bad reputation. A prince is obliged to be more concerned with the state of his reputation than with his own life, and must be willing to risk fortune and greatness rather than have his reputation tarnished in any way. It is certain that the first weakening of the reputation of a prince, however small it may be, is a dangerous step which may lead to his ruin. . . . History teaches that at all times and in all states princes with great reputations are happier than those who, lacking such an esteem, have surpassed them in strength, riches, and other forms of power.

Those who shape their conduct in accordance with the rules and principles contained in this testament, will doubtless acquire a valuable reputation.

Questions:
1. What role did the nobility play in Richelieu's concept of the state?
2. By what means did he control their behavior and activities?
3. How would you compare Richelieu's concepts of government to the ideas expressed by Machiavelli? Henry VIII? James I?

15.5 Mercantilism: Financing Absolutism

Jean Baptiste Colbert (1619–83), a merchant's son who had served as a financial secretary under Cardinal Mazarin, became Controller General of Finances shortly after Louis XIV took personal charge of the government in 1661. He inaugurated extensive fiscal reforms, but was unable to create a new tax base which could provide a stable income for the crown and a solid foundation for the French budgetary apparatus. Forced to adopt emergency policies to cope with Louis XIV's extravagance at court and in warfare, the economy remained buried in mercantilist regulations and red tape that contributed to the French Revolution of 1789.

Source: *The Western World: Volume I to 1700*, ed. Wallace E. Adams, et al., (New York: Dodd, Mead &Co., 1968), pp. 545–50.

DISSERTATION ON ALLIANCES, 1669

Every nation engages in two types of trading activity: domestic trade, which is carried on within the boundaries of the nation's home territories, and foreign trade, which, with the aid of shipping, is carried on outside the boundaries of the home territories. With respect to domestic trade, almost all nations foster it in the form of goods circulating within the country by means of internal transportation systems. With respect to foreign trade, which is a matter of capital importance, we must understand its structure if we are to have all the information we need for settling the question of alliances.

There are five principal categories of ocean-borne trading:

(1) The movement of goods and wares from one port to another, or from one province to another, for consumption within the kingdom.

(2) The importation from neighboring countries of goods and wares to be sold on the domestic market either as basic living commodities or as luxury items.

(3) The exportation of European wares necessary to the development of the Orient and the importation from the Orient of goods necessary throughout Europe for domestic consumption or for manufacturing processes. Our trade with the Orient is the source of most of our commercial prosperity. It is conducted along two principal sea routes: the first proceeds through the Mediterranean to the Levan-

tine ports of the Turkish Empire; the second extends across the ocean, by way of the Cape of Good Hope, to India.

(4) Trade with the West Indies, of which there are two main streams. The first supplies the Spanish with the products which they need throughout the breadth of their vast empire, stretching from the straits of Magellan to the tip of California Island in the South Sea. These are delivered either to the port of Cadiz, where they are loaded into vessels and delivered to the Spanish colonies where no foreigner is allowed entry, or they are delivered directly to the West Indies, which is a difficult task. In exchange for the merchandise, the same vessels bring back silver from the West Indies and deliver it to the harbor at Cadiz where it is distributed among all the nations which have invested in the enterprise. The other stream is that which delivers similar products and wares to those islands which are held by other European nations and which bring back the sugar, tobacco and indigo that grow there.

(5) Exportation to Northern Europe of all the manufactured wares and agricultural products which are processed in Middle and Southern Europe after having been imported from either the East or the West Indies, and importation from the North of all the market products which grow there: in particular, wood, hemp, ship masts, copper, iron and other shipping materials. It is an established fact that through this exchange, Northern Europe makes all the other exchanges possible, which makes it the most important of all the trade regions.

These different types of trade have always existed in Europe, but when they have been carried out by a single nation, demand has fallen and prices have risen. Thus, trade relations have always drawn more money away from the other parties and have always prospered those who initiate them. Trade with the Near East, which used to include trade with the Far East until the Portuguese sailed around the Cape of Good Hope, was long in the hands of the Venetians. The French and the English enjoyed but a minimal portion of that trade. Subsequently, through exploration and military victories on the coast of Africa, through their business ventures and military successes throughout Asia, not excluding China, the Portuguese have won the biggest part of this trade away from the Venetians and have increased the supply of imported goods. Consequently, consumption is greater and prices have been reduced. Following the example of the Portuguese, the Spaniards have discovered the West Indies which have such an abundance of wealth that there is room for all investors to profit from it.

During the period when these nations dominated foreign trade in the South, the French and the English had a small share of the trade in the North. But for the French this share supplied only an insignificant fraction of their material needs. As for the English, this share provided them with virtually all their needs and in addition met part of the needs of the other northern nations, for the English have always had good trade relations with the North. At first, Bruges was

the principal exchange mart for this trading activity. Then the inhabitants of Antwerp took advantage of their port, facilities and attracted trade there. After the wars between the Spanish and the Dutch, the self-discipline, the moderation and the zeal of the Dutch attracted world trade to Amsterdam and to the other cities of Holland. But they were not satisfied with being the central exchange mart for all Europe and especially for the North. They decided to gain control of foreign trade at its very source. To this end they ruined the Portuguese in the East Indies. They inhibited or disturbed in every possible way the business ventures which the English had established there. They employed and are still employing every means, are exerting every effort, are applying their full resources to assume full control of world trade and to keep it out of the hands of all other nations. Their whole government is based upon this single principle. They know that as long as they maintain their commercial superiority, their power on both land and sea will keep on increasing and will make them so powerful that they will become the arbiters of peace and war in Europe. They can set whatever limits they please upon the law and the design of kings.

As to whether they have the will power and the physical power to become the masters of all trade, there is no doubt at all in the first respect. With regard to their physical power, if we consider their powers in the Near East, in the East Indies, in the neighboring kingdoms and in the North, we can only conclude that they currently occupy first position and need only to maintain that status. In proof of my point, we have been keeping a check on their sea vessels for 4 or 5 years, and we estimate that they possess the incredible number of 15,000 to 16,000.

On the basis of this information, and after a very careful analysis, we can assert definitively that European trade is supported by some 20,000 vessels of all sizes. It is easy to see that this number cannot be increased, inasmuch as the population remains constant in all the nations and that consumer activity remains constant. Of this total of 20,000 ships, the Dutch have 15,000 to 16,000, the English 3,000 to 4,000 and the French 500 to 600.

This, then, has been and remains at present the state of European trade. But before proceeding further, we must note that the naval power of a nation plays an important role in the development of its trading program. In a sense, naval power follows on the heels of trading power because of the vast numbers of sailors and seamen involved, the experience which the captains and other officers accumulate, and the enormous number of ships to which it gives rise. But there is this difference. However superior the Dutch may be to the English in the total number of ships and seamen, they can never excel the English in naval power. The English may have lesser numbers, but they are superior in their experience and their knowledge of sea war and they infinitely excel the Dutch in genuine courage.

As for the French, their naval power and its use are still in the nascent stage. Certainly, therefore, it would be folly for France to try to attain in a few years a power to which the two other nations attained in the one case a century ago and in the other case several centuries ago. One need only consider the limited number of vessels in her merchant fleet to perceive clearly that she can give support to her naval strength only in proportion to that number. This issues from the general axiom that merchant shipping contributes to the strength and substance of all sea power and that no nation can have sea power without having shipping.

With all these factors clearly in mind, we must now return to our original consideration: in the alliance under examination, England is seeking principally to strengthen its trade. This strengthening process can be effected only if England uses more of the vessels belonging to her private citizens and if she increases their number. Such an increase can occur only if England discovers some hitherto unknown trading arenas or by reducing the number of vessels of one of the other nations.

The discovery of a new trading arena is highly unlikely. There is no point even in considering such a tenuous possibility. To be quite frank, such a circumstance could not possibly develop. Even if it should develop, it would not produce a new consumers' market for the products necessary to life and creature comforts. Rather it would offer to one nation and deny to another the means of drawing on those already in use and belonging to a pattern of international consumption that is common to all Europe.

It must be, then, through the reduction in number of the ships of one of the other nations. But that other nation cannot be the French, because there is nothing to be gained from them. In all their ports, both on the Atlantic and on the Mediterranean, they have only 500 or 600 ships which carry a small portion of their wares and goods from port to port, without any trade in the North or elsewhere. We are obliged to conclude, therefore, that England cannot use any more of her subjects' vessels nor can she increase the number without reducing the number of Dutch vessels. Consequently, it is difficult to establish a close alliance when its principal aim would be to increase one's power at the expense of the ally.

The political philosophies of great rulers have always taught that it is not to a weak ruler's advantage to ally himself willingly with a ruler more powerful than he, lest that superior power overwhelm and destroy him. That has happened on numerous occasions. The same political philosophies insist that the weak ruler always work to maintain a balance of power by allying himself to the nearest force in order to hold in check the growth of a third nation.

Applying the same philosophy to the present instance, we see that the Dutch have the most powerful trading system which exists or which has ever existed in the world. The English have a less flourishing system and the French the least flourishing of all. Therefore, reason declares that neither of these two nations may ally itself to the Dutch, for fear that, in the attempt to strengthen their trading power, they would be overwhelmed and completely destroyed. The same reasoning insists that the two nations pool their interests and apply their full might to undertaking a secret war against Dutch trade. They would profit from all the advantages that their location and their power give them to cut the Dutch off from what rightfully belongs to them. We shall outline hereafter several means for accomplishing this.

We should add that trade problems give rise to a continuing battle both in peace and in war among the nations of Europe to see who will win the upper hand. The Dutch, the English and the French are the contestants in this match. Through their zeal the Dutch have amassed sufficient power to fight with 16,000 ships. The English bring 3,000 to 4,000 vessels to the fray, the French bring 500 to 600. It is easy to see who will be victorious. And if the 3,000 to 4,000 align themselves with the 16,000, it is child's play to predict that the 16,000 can lose nothing and that the 3,000 to 4,000 run the risk of keeping on losing and even of being totally destroyed. We should add to these arguments the fact that, in spite of the superior numbers of ships which the Dutch possess in their trade war with the English, the Dutch are a thriftier, more economical people than the English. The former are more industrious, more profit-conscious than the latter. Their government draws its primary financial strength from its trade relations. Since both of these governments shape all their policies in terms of this commercial structure, the English cannot fail to come out second best in such an alliance. These reasons are, of course, quite persuasive in themselves, but there are yet others which must be considered.

It is generally agreed that the English have always demonstrated an instinctive aversion for the French. It is further agreed that this aversion was intensified by the recent war with all its attendant misfortunes. Despite this aversion, however, these kingdoms and their monarchs have remained at complete peace with each other for more than 100 years. This peace was interrupted by the war of La Rochelle which lasted but a few months and once again, subsequently, by the Dutch war. In view of this lengthy period of harmony one may conclude that the two nations can without difficulty live in a mutually comfortable relationship.

It is possible that the citizens of London show a greater hostility to the French now than in the past. But we can assume with a considerable certainty of being right that this hostility is fanned by Spanish and Dutch sympathizers who are in turn abetted by those who favored the recent disorders because they did not want to see the legitimate English government strengthened by such a powerful alliance as one with France. But we may rest assured that this distemper will cool. England has the means to prevent its persisting. What is more, when the alliance is made, the citizens will begin to enjoy its fruits. Thus, the close understanding which has always joined the two nations will be reaffirmed. This is particularly true because in joining forces, the two nations will enjoy real and substantial benefits in the exercise of their trading activities.

We must readily allow that psychologically and temperamentally the English are more akin to the Dutch than to the French. But it is plain to see that if they relish peace and tranquility and if they would not betray their political interests, they can draw no real advantages from an alliance with a people who are ruled by a government of merchants, whose political principles and power function only as an adjunct to their trade relations. Their prosperity will all too easily make the English see what differences separate a republic and a monarchy with respect to their commercial interests, which are the only interests to hold the attention of said republicans. But the alliance and union with the French produces an entirely different effect.

As for any jealousy which the English might feel over French naval power, it could not be a logical jealousy. Control of the earth's land masses lies in the hands of the rulers of those states which are abundantly populated by a naturally courageous and warrior-like people. Control of the seas, however, does not depend on population counts. Control of the sea goes to those who have enjoyed a long and intimate association with the sea. It goes to that nation whose maritime trade relations are elaborate enough to provide a sufficiently large reservoir of sailors from whose numbers a sea force may be formed. It is an established fact that the size of a nation's navy is proportional to that of its merchant marine. But if we are absolutely bound to attribute any jealousy to the English, it would be more logical to suspect that they feel it with respect to the Dutch. Only the Dutch presume to equal England's power in the recent war. Indeed, in view of their continually expanding trade relations, their sea power cannot fail to increase proportionally. As for the mutual aid which nations can bring to each other in their trade relations, the English will destroy themselves if they ally with the Dutch. Everything we have said points to it. An infinite number of examples prove it.

Now that we have given careful consideration to our main point—the advantages to be reaped by the peoples of the two nations—let us consider the interests and the reputations of the rulers of the two nations.

In this connection, there are endless reasons why an alliance with France should be preferable to an alliance with Holland: the blood kinship of the two monarchs; the similarity of their intellects and their personalities; the geographical location of their domains; the similarity of their type of government; the striking dissimilarities of the English monarchy and the Dutch republic; the domestic tranquility which they can bring to their respective nations by a union of interests; their willingness to consider candidly all the advantages and glories which will accrue to them.

To realize this great dream: [1] the monarchs need only join in a close alliance which no subject or no occasion can trouble or interrupt; [2] they need only establish a policy of equal and reciprocal relations between the two nations throughout the breadth of their kingdoms; [3] to this end they need only establish two advisory councils in the two capital cities which will act in common accord, cooperating in every way possible to enhance the quality and extend the scope of the trade relations of the two nations. . . . It would profit the two kingdoms enormously.

Questions:
1. What European nation most impressed Colbert and why?
2. By what steps did he propose that France win commercial supremacy?
3. How does this treatise illustrate Colbert's mercantilist policies?

15.6 The Sun King Shines

In the last years of Louis XIV (r. 1643–1715) at the splendid and magnificent palace of Versailles, the duke de Saint-Simon (1675–1755) began to compile notes describing the King and the royal court. Saint-Simon, a proud aristocrat of ancient lineage, was a gossipy and caustic observer.

Source: Lucy Norton, ed. and trans., *Saint-Simon at Versailles* (New York: Harper and Row, 1958), pp. 245–55, 261, 282.

He was a prince in whom no one would deny good and even great qualities but he had many others that were petty or downright bad, and of these it was impossible to determine which were natural and which acquired. . . . This is not the place to tell of his early childhood. He was king almost from birth, but was deliberately repressed by a mother who loved to govern, and still more so by a wicked and self-interested minister [Cardinal Mazarin], who risked the State a thousand times for his own aggrandizement. So long as that minister lived the King was held down, and that portion of his life should be subtracted from his reign. . . . After Mazarin's death, he had enough intelligence to realize his deliverance, but not enough vigour to release himself. Indeed, that event was one of the finest moments of his life, for it taught him an unshakable principle namely, to banish all prime ministers and ecclesiastics from his councils. Another ideal, adopted at that time, he could never sustain because in the practice it constantly eluded him. This was to govern alone. It was the quality upon which he most prided himself and for which he received most praise and flattery. In fact, it was what he was least able to do.

Born with an intelligence rather below the average, his mind was very capable of development with training and education, for he could learn easily from others [without imitation]. He profited immensely from having always lived among people of the highest quality with the widest knowledge of life, . . .

Indeed if I may say so of a King of twenty-three years old, he was fortunate in entering the world surrounded by brilliant people of every kind. His Ministers at home and abroad were the strongest in Europe, his generals the greatest, and all were men whose names have been handed down to posterity by common consent. The disturbances that rocked the very foundations of the State after the death of Louis XIII [the Fronde uprising] produced a Court full of famous men and polished courtiers. . . . [In the house of

Mazarin's niece] all the most distinguished men and women foregathered every day, making [it] the centre of the Court love-affairs, [and] the gallant intrigues and manoeuvres for ambition's sake—schemes in which birth counted for much, for at that time rank was as much prized and respected as it is now despised. Into this brilliant vortex the King was first launched, and there he first acquired that polite, chivalrous manner which he retained all through his life and knew so well how to combine with stateliness and propriety.... Had he been born into private life, he would still have had a genius for entertainments, pleasures, and flirtations, and would have caused innumerable broken hearts.

Let me repeat. The King's intelligence was below the average, but was very capable of improvement. He loved glory; he desired peace and good government. He was born prudent, temperate, secretive, master of his emotions and his tongue—can it be believed?—he was born good and just. God endowed him with all the makings of a good and perhaps even of a fairly great king. All the evil in him came from without. His early training was so dissolute ... and he would sometimes speak bitterly of those [youthful] days.... He became very dependent on others, for they had scarcely taught him to read and write and he remained so ignorant that he learned nothing of historical events nor the facts about fortunes, careers, rank, or laws. This lack caused him sometimes, even in public to make many gross blunders.

You might imagine that as king he would have loved the old nobility and would not have cared to see it brought down to the level of other classes. Nothing was further from the truth. His aversion to noble sentiments and his partiality for his Ministers, who, to elevate themselves, hated and disparaged all who were what they themselves were not, nor ever could be, caused him to feel a similar antipathy for noble birth. He feared it as much as he feared intelligence, and if he found these two qualities united in one person, that man was finished.

His ministers, generals, mistresses, and courtiers learned soon after he became their master that glory, to him, was a foible rather than an ambition. They therefore flattered him to the top of his bent, and in so doing, spoiled him. Praise, or better, adulation, pleased him so much that the most fulsome was welcome and the most servile even more delectable. They were the only road to his favour and those whom he liked owed his friendship to choosing their moments well and never ceasing in their ambitions. That is what gave his ministers so much power, for they had endless opportunities of flattering his vanity, especially by suggesting that he was the source of all their ideas and had taught them all that they knew. Falseness, servility, admiring glances, combined with a dependent and cringing attitude, above all, an appearance of being nothing without him, were the only means of pleasing him.

Flattery fed the desire for military glory that sometimes tore him from his loves, which was how Louvois so easily involved him in major wars and persuaded him that he was a better leader and strategist than any of his generals, a theory which those officers fostered in order to please him.

All their praise he took with admirable complacency, and truly believed that he was what they said. Hence his liking for reviews, ... and his preference for sieges, where he could make cheap displays of courage, be forcibly restrained, and show his ability to endure fatigue and lack of sleep.... He greatly enjoyed the sensation of being admired, as he rode along the lines, for his fine presence and princely bearing, his horsemanship, and other attainments....

Pride and vanity, which tend always to increase, and with which he was fed continually without even his perceiving it, even from preachers in the pulpits in his presence, were the foundations on which his ministers raised themselves above all other ranks. He was cunningly persuaded that their rank was merely an extension of his own, supreme in him, in them capable of increase (since without him they were nothing), and useful to him, because it gave them as his instruments greater dignity and made them more readily obeyed. That is why secretaries of state and ministers gradually left off their cloaks, then their bands, then their black gowns and simple seemly dress, and finally came to clothe themselves like gentlemen of quality. They then began to adopt the manners and later the privileges of the nobility, rising by stages to eat with the King, their wives assuming, as by right, the same prerogatives as their husbands, dining at the royal table, riding in the royal coaches, and in every way appearing equal to ladies of the highest rank.

Personal vanity of another kind led the King to encourage this behaviour. He was well aware that though he might crush a nobleman with the weight of his displeasure, he could not destroy him or his line, whereas a secretary of state or other such minister could be reduced together with his whole family to those depths of nothingness from which he had been elevated. No amount of wealth or possessions would avail him then. That was one reason why he liked to give his ministers authority over the highest in the land, even over the Princes of the Blood and all others who held no office under the crown, and to grant them rank and privileges to match. That is why any man of consequence who possessed anything which the King had no power either to destroy or maintain was carefully kept from the ministry; he would have been a source of danger and a continual anxiety.

Therein lay the reason for the watchful, jealous attitude of his ministers, who made it difficult for the King to hear any but themselves, although he pleased to think that he was easy for any man to approach. Indeed, he considered that it enhanced his majesty and the respect and fear with which he was regarded, and which he used to snub the most noble, that all men should have access to him only as he passed. Thus great lords and underlings alike might speak freely to him as he went from one room to another on his way to or from mass, or stepped into his coach. The more distinguished might wait at the door of his study, but none dared to follow him inside. In fact, approach to him was limited to those moments. Any matters whatsoever had to be explained to him in a few words, very awkwardly, and always within hearing range of his entourage, or, if one knew him well, one might whisper into his wig, which was scarcely more convenient. His almost invariable answer was, "We shall see" *(Je verrai)*, very useful no doubt as a means of gaining time, but often bringing little comfort.

Private audiences in his study were rarely if ever granted, even when the matter concerned State affairs. Never, for example, to envoys returning or going abroad, never to generals, unless in extraordinary circumstances, and private letters written to the King always passed through the hands of some minister, except on one or two most rare and special occasions.

Nevertheless, in spite of the fact that the King had been so spoiled with false notions of majesty and power, that every other thought was stifled in him, there was much to be gained from a private audience, if it might be obtained, and if one knew how to conduct oneself with all the respect due to his dignity and habits. I, indeed, can speak from experience.

Once in his study, however prejudiced he might he, however much displeased, he would listen patiently, good-naturedly, and with a real desire to he informed. You could see that he had a sense of justice and a will to get at the truth, even though he might feel vexed with you, and that quality he retained all through his life. In private audience you could say anything to him, provided, as I have already remarked, that you said it respectfully, with submissiveness and proper deference, for without that you would have been in a worse plight. With the proper manner, however, you could interrupt him when it was your turn to speak, and bluntly deny his accusations, you could even raise your voice above his without vexing him, and he would congratulate himself on the audience and praise the person he interviewed for ridding him of prejudices and the lies he had been told; moreover, he would prove his sincerity by his subsequent attitude.

It is therefore enough to make one weep to think of the wickedness of an education designed solely to suppress the virtue and intelligence of that prince, and the insidious poison of barefaced flattery which made him a kind of god in the very heart of Christendom. His ministers with their cruel politics hemmed him in and made him drunk with power until he was utterly corrupted. If they did not manage entirely to smother such kindness, justice, and love of truth as God had given him, they blunted and obstructed those virtues to the lasting injury of himself and his kingdom.

From such alien and pernicious sources he acquired a pride so colossal that, truly, had not God implanted in his heart the fear of the devil, even in his worst excesses, he would literally have allowed himself to be worshipped. What is more, he would have found worshippers; . . . From this false pride stemmed all that ruined him.

The Court was yet another device to sustain the King's policy of despotism. Many things combined to remove it from Paris and keep it permanently in the country. The disorders of the minority had been staged mainly in that city and for that reason the King had taken a great aversion to it and had become convinced that it was dangerous to live there.

The awkward situation of his mistresses and the dangers involved in conducting such scandalous affairs in a busy capital, crowded with people of every kind of mentality, played no small part in deciding him to leave, for he was embarrassed by the crowds whenever he went in or out or appeared upon the streets. Other reasons for departure were his love of hunting and the open air, so much more easily indulged in the country than in Paris, which is far from forests and ill-supplied with pleasant walks, and his delight in building, a later and ever-increasing passion, which could not be enjoyed in the town, where he was continually in the public eye. Finally, he conceived the idea that he would be all the more venerated by the multitude if he lived retired and were no longer seen every day. . . . It was then that he first began to attract society to him with fares and diversions and to let it be known that he wished often to be visited. . . .

The frequent entertainments, the private drives to Versailles, and the royal journeys, provided the King with a means of distinguishing or mortifying his courtiers by naming those who were or were not to accompany him, and thus keeping everyone eager and anxious to please him. He fully realized that the substantial gifts which he had to offer were too few to have any continuous effect, and he substituted imaginary favours that appealed to men's jealous natures, small distinctions which he was able, with extraordinary ingenuity, to grant or withhold every day and almost every hour. The hopes that courtiers built upon such flimsy favours and the importance which they attached to them were really unbelievable, and no one was ever more artful than the King in devising fresh occasions for them.

But there would be no end to describing all the different expedients that followed one after another as the King grew older and the entertainments increased or diminished in number, or to telling of the methods he employed to keep so large a Court always about him.

He not only required the constant attendance of the great, but was also aware of those of lower rank. He would look about him at his *letier* and *coucher*, at meals, and while walking through the state apartments or the Versailles gardens, where none but courtiers might follow him. He saw and noticed every one of them, marked very well the absences of those usually at Court and even of those who attended more rarely, and took care to discover the reason, drawing his own conclusions and losing no opportunity of acting upon them. He took it as an offence if distinguished people did not make the Court their home, or if others came but seldom. And to come never, or scarcely ever, meant certain disgrace.

Louis XIV took enormous pains to be well-informed about all that went on in public places, in private houses, society, family business, or the progress of love-affairs. He had spies and reporters everywhere and of all descriptions. Many of them never realized that their reports reached the King, others wrote directly to him, sending their letters by secret channels of his own devising. Their letters were seen by him alone and he always read them before proceeding to other business. There were even some who spoke privately with him in his study, entering by the back way. Through such secret informants, an immense number of people of all ranks were broken, often most unjustly, and without their ever discovering the reason, for the King, once suspicious, never trusted again, or so rarely that it made no matter. . . .

No other King has ever approached him for the number and quality of his stables and hunting establishments. Who could count his buildings? Who not deplore their ostentation, whimsicality and bad taste?

. . . He was entirely ruled by [his ministers], even by the youngest and most mediocre, even by those whom he liked and trusted least. Always, he was on guard against influences, and always believed that he had been completely successful in avoiding them.

Questions:
1. How fairly did Saint-Simon evaluate Louis XIV and the Sun King's court?
2. How did Louis's vanity influence royal policy?
3. In what ways was Louis XIV isolated from reality?
4. How did Louis control the ambitions of the French nobility? How did his methods compare to those of Richelieu?

CHAPTER 16
Europe Reaches Out
Global Voyages and Cultural Encounters
(1500–1750)

16.1   Before Europe: The Zheng He Expeditions

The Muslim eunuch Zheng He (spelled Cheng Ho in the document below) undertook seven expeditions by sea to India and Africa, nearly a century before Columbus sailed the Atlantic. While Columbus sailed with about 100 men, the Chinese crew, all state servants, consisted of thousands of men, ranging from civil officers and soldiers to scribes and cooks. The ships too dwarfed Columbus', with 62 galleons and more than 100 auxiliary vessels. The largest ships each had 9 masts and 12 sails, measured 440' × 180', and weighed 1500 tons. Columbus' three ships had three masts each, were 150' long, and weighed 415 tons all together. A stone tablet, engraved in 1432, commemorates the expeditions, part of which is excerpted below.

> Source: J.J.L. Duyvendak, "The True Dates of the Chinese Maritime Expeditions in the Early Fifteenth Century," *ToungPao* 24 (1938), pp. 349–355; reprinted in Richard L. Graves, et al., *Civilizations of the World: The Human Adventure*, 3rd edition, (New York: Longman, Addison-Wesley Educational Publishers Inc., 1997), p. 573.

The Imperial Ming dynasty in unifying seas and continents . . . even goes beyond the Han and the Tang. The countries beyond the horizon and from the ends of the earth have all become subjects. . . . Thus the barbarians from beyond the seas . . . have come to audience bearing precious objects. . . . The emperor has ordered us, Cheng Ho . . . to make manifest the transforming power of the Imperial virtue and to treat distant people with kindness. . . . We have seven times received the commission of ambassadors [and have visited] altogether more than thirty countries large and small. We have traversed immense water spaces and have beheld huge waves like mountains rising sky-high, and we have set eyes on barbarian regions far away hidden in a blue transparency of light vapors, while our sails loftily unfurled like clouds day and night continued their course, traversing those savage waves as if we were treading a public thoroughfare. . . . We have received the high favor of a gracious commission of our Sacred Lord, to carry to the distant barbarians the benefits of his auspicious example. . . . Therefore we have recorded the years and months of the voyages. [Here follows a detailed record of places visited and things one on each of the seven voyages.] We have anchored in this port awaiting a north wind to take the sea . . . and have thus recorded an inscription in stone . . . erected by the prin-

cipal envoys, the Grand Eunuchs Cheng Ho and Wang Ching-hung, and the assistant envoys.

Questions:
1. How do the Chinese, in this document, perceive their role in these expeditions?
2. How do the Chinese perceive those they meet in traveling?

16.2   From King to King: Letters from Kongo to Portugal

The Portuguese made contact with the kingdom of Kongo in Africa in the 1480s. By the 1490s, King John I of Kongo and some of his nobles were baptized as Christians. He and his successors and the king of Portugal exchanged letters for the next half century. Excerpts from the Kongo kings' letters appear below.

> Source: "Letters from the Kings of the Kongo to the King of Portugal," *MonumentaMissionaria Africana*, ed. Antonio Brasio, (Lisboa: Agencia Geral do Ultramar, 1952), vol. 1: 262–63, 294–95, 335, 404, 470, 488, trans. Linda Wimmer; reprinted in *The Global Experience: Readings in World History*, ed. Stuart B. Schwartz, et al., (New York: Addison Wesley, Longman, Inc., 1997), pp. 240–42.

PORTUGUESE MILITARY AID DURING CIVIL WAR (1512)

And our brother who usurped us, and without justice occupied us, with arms and a great number of people . . . became empowered in all of our kingdom, and lordships, with which when we saw the only solution for our person we feigned sickness; and it being so with us, by a divine inspiration of our Lord, we raised and strengthened ourself, and called up our 36 men, and with them we appeared, and went with them to the main square of the city, where our Father died, and where people of infinite number were with our said brother, and . . . for our Lord Jesus Christ, and we began to fight with our adversaries . . . our 36 men, inspired by grace, and aided by God, our adversaries quickly fled . . . and chaos ensued, and with them witnessing . . . there appeared in the air a white Cross, and the blessed Apostle St. James with many men armed and on horseback, and dressed in white battle garments, and killed them, and so great was the chaos, and mortality, that it was a thing of great wonder.

In this defeat our brother was taken prisoner and with justice condemned to die, as he died, for having rebelled against us; and finally we made peace in our kingdoms . . . as it is today, with the Grace of God . . . and through the miracle made by our Lord, and we send word to the King Dom Emanuel of Portugal . . . and we send to him Dom Pedro our brother, who was one of the 36 men with us . . . and with the letters that the king sent of great works given. . . .

And as the King of Portugal saw the good example . . . followed . . . for the greater growth of our Holy Catholic Faith, he sent by our cousin Dom Pedro and by Simao da Sylva noblemen of your house who came with him, the arms pictured in this card, and the shields with insignias . . . [A]nd as these weapons arrived a cross was seen in the sky, and so the Apostle St. James and all the other Saints fought with us, and with the help of our Lord God we were given victory, and so also as by the King sent us his [men] took part with the said arms. . . .

PROBLEMS IN CONVERSION EFFORTS (1515)

Very High and Powerful Lord,

We the King Dom Alfonso . . . Lord, much holy grace and praise I give to the Holy God the Father and the Son and the Holy Spirit . . . all good and holy things are done through the will of God, without which we can do nothing . . . our faith is still like glass in this kingdom, due to the bad examples of the men who come here to teach it, because through worldly greed for a few riches truth is destroyed, as through greed the Jews crucified the Son of God, my brother, until today he is crucified through bad examples and bad deeds . . . in our time by us who walk crying in this real valley of misery and tears.

. . . [I]n teaching the word of Our Lord [these bad priests] become bad examples and so take the key to the Celestial Kingdom that is the Doctrine of our Holy Catholic Faith, to open the hearts of our simple people . . . and by entering into a life of sin take the key to Hell . . . due to the greed of this world, do not merely take their own bodies and souls to Hell, but guide those most blind with them through their bad examples. I ask of you, Brother, to aid me in establishing our Holy Catholic Faith, because, Lord my Brother, for it were better . . . that the souls of our relatives and brothers and cousins and nephews and grandchildren who are innocent, to see . . . good examples.

. . . I ask you to send stonemasons and house carpenters to build a school to teach our relatives and our people, because Lord, although greedy and jealous men still give bad examples . . . with the Holy Sacred Scripture we may change that, because the world of the Holy Spirit is contrary to the world, the flesh and the devil. . . .

ATTEMPTS TO BUY A CARAVEL (1517)

Very Powerful and Very High Prince and King My Brother

. . . I have several times written you of the necessity of having a ship, telling you to make me one to buy, and I don't know why Your Highness does not want to con-

sent, because I want nothing more than . . . to use it in God's service. . . .

EFFECTS OF PORTUGUESE TRADE (1526)

Lord,

. . . [Y]our factors and officials give to the men and merchants that come to this Kingdom . . . and spread . . . so that many vassals owing us obedience . . . rebel because they have more goods [through trade with Portuguese] than us, who before had been content and subject to our . . . jurisdiction, which causes great damage. . . .

. . . And each day these merchants take our citizens, native to the land and children of our nobles and vassals, and our relations, because they are thieves and men of bad conscience, steal them with the desire to have things of this kingdom . . . take them to sell . . . our land is all spoiled . . . which is not to your service. . . . For this we have no more necessity for other than priests and educators, but [send] no more merchandise . . . nor merchants. . . .

EXPANSION AND REGULATION OF THE SLAVE TRADE (1526)

[M]any of our subjects, through the desire for merchandise and things of this Kingdoms which you bring . . . to satisfy their appetite, steal many of our free and exempt subjects. And nobles and their children and our relatives are often stolen to be sold to white men . . . hidden by night. . . . And the said white men are so powerful . . . they embark and . . . buy them, for which we want justice, restoring them to liberty. . . . And to avoid this great evil, by law all white men in our kingdom who buy slaves . . . must make it known to three nobles and officials of our court . . . to see these slaves. . . .

Questions:
1. How did the Kongo kings respond to the Portuguese early in their relationship? Why?
2. How did this change over time? Why?

16.3 "The Chronicle of Peru: The Incas"

The Incas lived in the Andes mountains, on the western coast of South America from about 1100. Much of what we know about the Incas comes from accounts by the Spanish who destroyed the Inca empire in the mid-1500s. Pedro Cieza de Leon, one such nobleman and soldier, wrote *The Chronicle of Peru* in 1547–1550, immediately after his involvement in the military campaigns against the Incas. Relying on first-hand accounts from the Incas, his "Chronicle" is considered one of the most authoritative accounts available.

Source: Pedro Cieza de Leon, "The Chronicle of Peru: The Incas"; reprinted in *Primary Source Document Workbook to Accompany World Civilizations*, by Philip J. Adier; prepared by Robert Welborn, (New York: West Publishing Company,

1996), pp. 35–36. (Introduction based on Welborn's introduction to the document.)

It should be well understood that great prudence was needed to enable these kings to govern such large provinces, extending over so vast a region, parts of it rugged and covered with forests, parts mountainous, with snowy peaks and ridges, parts consisting of deserts of sand, dry and without trees or water. These regions were inhabited by many different nations, with varying languages, laws, religions, and the kings had to maintain tranquility and to rule so that all should live in peace and in friendship towards their lord. Although the city of Cuzco was the head of the empire, . . . yet at certain points, as we shall also explain, the king stationed his delegates and governors, who were the most learned, the ablest, and the bravest men that could be found, and none was so youthful that he was not already in the last third part of his age. As they were faithful and none betrayed their trusts, . . . none of the natives, though they might be more powerful, attempted to rise in rebellion; or if such a thing ever did take place, the town where the revolt broke out was punished, and the ringleaders were sent prisoners to Cuzco. . . .

All men so feared the king, that they did not dare to speak evil even of his shadow. And this was not all. If any of the king's captains or servants went forth to visit a distant part of the empire on some business, the people came out on the road with presents to receive them, not daring, even if one came alone, to omit to comply with all his commands.

So great was the veneration that the people felt for their princes, throughout this vast region, that every district was as well regulated and governed as if the lord was actually present to chastise those who acted contrary to his rules. This fear arose from the known valor of the lords and their strict justice. It was felt to be certain that those who did evil would receive punishment without fail, and that neither prayers nor bribes would avert it. At the same time, the Incas always did good to those who were under their sway, and would not allow them to be ill-treated, nor that too much tribute should be exacted from them. Many who dwelt in a sterile country where they and their ancestors have lived with difficulty, found that through the orders of the Inca their lands were made fertile and abundant, the things being supplied which before were wanting. In other districts, where there was scarcity of clothing, owing to the people having no flocks, orders were given that cloth should be abundantly provided. In short, it will be understood that these lords knew how to enforce service and the payment of tribute, so they provided for the maintenance of the people, and took care that they should want for nothing. Through these good works, and because the lord always gave women and rich gifts to his principal vassals, he gained so much on their affections that he was most fondly loved. . . .

One of the things which I admired most, in contemplating and noting down the affairs of this kingdom, was to think how and in what manner they can have made such grand and admirable roads as we now see, and what a number of men would suffice for their construction, and with what tools and instruments they can have leveled the mountains and broken through the rocks to make them so broad and good as they are. For it seems to me that if the King of Spain should desire to give orders for another royal road to be made, like that which goes from Quito to Cuzco, . . . with all his power I believe that he could not get it done; nor could any force of men achieve such results unless there was also the perfect order by means of which the commands of the Incas were carried into execution. . . .

Questions:
1. What does the author find to admire about the Incas?
2. What can we learn about Spain from what he says about the Incas?
3. How do you think he could both praise the Incas and participate in their destruction?

16.4   The Jamestown Charter

The colony of Jamestown became the first permanent English settlement in America. Though the colony almost failed, because of disease, hunger, and Indian attacks, it survived with the arrival of new men and more supplies. The following excerpt comes from the letters patent (or First Charter) from the English government in 1606.

Source: "Letters patent to Sir Thomas Gates and others, 10 April 1606," in *The Jamestown Voyages Under the First Charter, 1606–1609*, vol. I, ed. Philip L. Barbour, (Cambridge: Cambridge University Press, 1969), pp. 24–34 passim.

I. 10 April 1606.
Letters patent to Sir Thomas Gates and others.[1]

James by the grace of God &c Whereas our loving and well disposed subiects Sir Thomas Gates and Sir George Somers Knightes Richard Hackluit Clarke *pre*bendarie of Westmin*ster* and Edwarde Maria Winghfeilde Thomas Hannam and Raleighe Gilberde Esquiers William Parker and George Popham Gentlemen and divers others of our loving subiects haue been humble sutors vnto vs that wee woulde vouchsafe vnto them our licence to make habitacion plantaion and to deduce a Colonie of sondrie of our people into that parte of America com*m*only called Virginia and other parts and territories in America either appertaining vnto vs or which are not nowe actuallie possessed by anie Christian Prince or people scituate lying and being all along the sea Coastes

• • • •

and to that ende and for the more speedy accomplishemente of theire saide intended plantacion and habitacion there are desirous to devide themselues into two severall Colonies and Companies the one consisting of certaine Knightes Gentlemen marchauntes and other Adventurers of our Cittie of London and elsewhere

. . . .

and the other consisting of sondrie Knightes Gentlemen merchauntes and other Adventurers of our Cities of Bristoll and Exeter and of our towne of Plymouthe and of other places which doe ioyne themselues vnto that Colonie

. . . .

wee greatly commending and graciously accepting of theire desires to the furtherance of soe noble a worke which may be the providence of Almightie God hereafter tende to the glorie of hys divyne maiestie in propagating of Christian religion to suche people as yet live in darkenesse and myserable ignorance of the true knowledge and worshippe of god and may in tyme bring the infidels and salvages lyving in those partes to humane civilitie and to a setled and quiet governmente doe by theise our lettres Patentes graciously accepte of and agree to theire humble and well intended desires

. . . .

And that they shall haue all the landes woodes soyle Groundes havens portes Ryvers Mynes Myneralls Marshes waters Fyshings Commodities and hereditamentes whatsoever from the said first seate of theire plantacion and habytacion by the space of Fyftie miles of Englishe statute measure all alongest the saide Coaste of Virginia and America towardes the Weste and southeweste as the Coaste lyeth with all the Islandes within one hundred myles directlie over againste the same sea Coaste

. . . .

and

towardes the Easte and Northeaste

. . . .

And

directly into the mayne lande by the space of One hundred like Englishe myles and shall and may inhabyt and remaine there and shall and may alsoe buylde and fortifie within anie the same for theire better safegarde and defence according to theire best discrecions and the direction of the Counsell of that Colonie and that noe other of our subiects shalbe permitted or suffered to plante or inhabyt behinde or on the backside of them towardes the mayne lande without the expresse lycence or consente of the Counsell of that Colonie thereunto in writing firste had or obtained

. . . .

And wee doe alsoe ordaine establishe and agree for vs our heires and successors that eache of the saide Colonies shall haue a Counsell which shall governe and order all matters and Causes which shall arise growe or happen to or within the same severall Colonies according to such lawes ordynaunces and Instructions as shalbe in that behalfe given and signed with our hande or signe manuell and passe vnder the privie seale of our Realme of Englande Eache of which Counsells shall consist of Thirteene parsons [i.e., persons] and to be ordained made and removed from tyme to tyme according as shalbe directed and comprised in the same Instructions and shall haue a severall seale for all matters that shall passe or concerne the same severall Counsells

Eache of which seales shall haue the Kinges Armes engraven on the one syde thereof and hys pourtraiture on the other

. . . .

And that alsoe ther shalbe a Counsell established here in Englande which shall in like manner consist of thirteene parsons to be for that purpose appointed by vs our heires and successors which shalbe called our Counsell of Virginia And shall from tyme to tyme haue the superior managing and direction onelie of and for all matters that shall or may concerne the governmente aswell of the said seuerall Colonies as of and for anie other parte or place within the aforesaid preinctes

. . . .

And moreover wee doe graunte and agree for vs our heires and successors that the saide severall Counsells of and for the saide severall Colonies shall and lawfully may by vertue hereof from tyme to tyme without intervpcion of vs our heires or successors giue and take order to digg myne and searche for all manner of Mynes of Goulde Silver and Copper aswell within anie parte of theire saide severall Colonies as of the saide Mayne landes on the backeside of the same Colonies and to haue and enjoy the Goulde Silver and Copper to be gotten thereof to the vse and behoofe of the same Colonies and the plantacions thereof yielding therefore yerelie to vs our heires and successors the Fifte parte onelie of all the same Goulde and Silver and the Fifteenth parte of all the same Copper soe to be gotten or had as ys aforesaide without anie other manner of profytt or Accompte to be given or yeilded to vs our heires or successors for or in respecte of the same

And that they shall or lawfullie may establishe and cawse to be made a coyne to passe currant there betweene the people of those severall Colonies for the more ease of traffique and bargaining betweene and amongst them and the natives there of such mettall and in suche manner and forme as the same severall Counsells there shall lymitt and appointe

. . . .

Moreover wee doe by theise presentes for vs our heires and successors giue and graunte licence vnto the said Sir Thomas Gates Sir George Sumers Richarde Hackluite Edwarde Maria Winghfeilde Thomas Hannam Raleighe Gilberde William Parker and George Popham and to everie of the said Colonies that they and everie of them shall and may from tyme to tyme and at all tymes for ever hereafter for their severall defences incounter or expulse repell and resist as well by sea as by lande by all waies and meanes whatsoever all and everie suche parson and parsons as without especiall licence of the said severall Colonies and plantacions shall attempt to inhabit within the saide seuerall precinctes and lymittes of the saide severall Colonies and plantacions or anie of them or that shall enterprise or attempt at anie tyme hereafter the hurte detrymente or annoyance of the saide severall Colonies or plantacions

Alsoe wee doe vor vs our heires and successor declare by theise presentes that all and everie the parsons being our subiectes which shall dwell and inhabit within everie or anie of the saide severall Colonies and plantacions and everie of theire children which shall happen to be borne within the lymittes and precinctes of the said severall Colonies and plantacyons shall haue and enioy all liberties Franchises and Immunities within anie of our other domynions to all intentes and purposes as yf they had been abyding and borne within this our Realme of Englande or anie other of our saide Domynions

• • • •

Prouided alwaies and our will and pleasure ys and wee doe hereby declare to all Christian Kings Princes and estates that yf anie parson or parsons which shall hereafter be of anie of the said severall Colonies and plantacions or anie other by his theire or anie of theire licence or appointement shall at anie tyme or tymes hereafter robb or spoile by sea or by lande or doe anie Acte of vniust and vnlawfull hostilitie to anie the subiectes of vs our heires or successors or anie of the subiects of anie King Prince Ruler Governor or State being then in league or Amitie with vs our heires or successors and that vpon suche Iniurie or vpon iuste complainte of such Prince Ruler Governor or State or theire subiects wee our heires or successors shall make open proclamacion within anie the portes of our Realme of Englande commodious for that purpose that the saide parson or parsons having committed anie such Robberie or spoyle shall within the tearme to be lymitted by suche Proclamacions make full restitucion or satisfactin of all suche Iniuries done soe as the saide Princes or others soe complained may houlde themselues fully satisfied and contented and that yf the saide parson or parsons having comitted such robberie or spoyle shall not make or cause to be made satisfaction accordingly with[in] such tyme soe to be lymitted That then yt shalbe lawfull to vs our heires and successors to put the saide parson or parsons having comitted such robberie or spoyle and their procurers Abbettors or Comfortors out of our allegeaunce and protection and that yt shalbe lawefull and free for all Princes and others to pursue with hostilitie the saide Offenders and everie of them and theire and everie of theire procurors Ayders Abbettors and comforters in that behalfe

Questions:

1. Why did these Englishmen want to form colonies in the new lands?
2. Of what advantage was this to England?

16.5 First Contact: The English Describe Pawatah's People

When the English arrived, they recorded their impressions of the countryside and of the people already living in the area, the Pawatah. The description of the Pawatah follows.

Source: "21 May–21 June 1607, Description of the People," in *The Jamestown Voyages Under the First Charter, 1606–1609*, vol. I, ed. Philip L. Barbour, (Cambridge: Cambridge University Press, 1969), pp. 102–04.

15. 21 May–21 June 1607. Descriptin of the People.

A Brief discription of the People.

There is a king in this land called great Pawatah, vnder whose dominions are at least 20th several kingdomes, yet each king potent as a prince in his owne territory. these have their Subiectes at so quick Comaund, as a beck bringes obedience, even to the resticucion of stolne goodes which by their naturall inclinac[i]on they are loth to leave. They goe all naked save their privityes, yet in coole weather they were deare skinns, with the hayre on loose: some have leather stockinges vp to their twisties,[1] & sandalls on their feet, their hayre is black generally, which they weare long on the left side, tyed vp on a knott, about which knott the kinges and best among them have a kind of Coronett of deares hayre coloured redd, some have chaines of long linckt copper about their neckes, and some chaines of pearle, the comon sort stick long fethers in this knott, I found not a grey eye among them all. their skynn is tawny not so borne, but with dying and paynting them selues, in which they delight greatly. The wemen are like the men, onely this difference; their hayre groweth long al over their heades save clipt somewhat short afore, these do all the labour and the men hunt and goe at their plesure. They live commonly by the water side in litle cottages made of canes and reedes, covered with the barke of trees; they dwell as I guesse by families of kindred & allyance some 40 tie or 50 ti in a Hatto[2] or small village; which townes are not past a myle or half a myle asunder in most places. They live vpon sodden wheat beanes & peaze for the most part, also they kill deare take fish in their weares, & kill fowle aboundance, they eate often and that liberally; they are proper lusty streight men very strong runn exceeding swiftly, their feight is alway in the wood with bow & arrowes, & a short wodden sword, the celerity they vse in skirmish is admirable. the king directes the batle & is always in front. Their manner of entertainment is vpon mattes on the ground vnder some tree, where they sitt themselues alone in the midst of the matt, & two mattes on each side, on which they[r] people sitt, then right against him (making a square forme) satt we alwayes. when they came to their matt they have an vsher goes before them, & the rest as he sittes downe give a long showt. The people steale any thing comes neare them, yea are so practized in this art that lookeing in

---

[1] 'The junction of the thighs' (*OED*).
[2] 'Hatto' possibly represents an element cognate with modern Cree *otānow*, 'town', whch appears as the second element in the village name Kecoughtan. It may have been pronounced with a glottal stop or other initial throaty sound which the author recorded with an 'h'.

our face they would with their foot betwene their toes convey a chizell knife, percer or any indifferent light thing: which having once conveyed they hold it an iniury to take the same from them; They are naturally given to trechery, howbeit we could not

Questions:
1. How do the English describe the Pawatah?
2. Why might they describe them as they do? How might the description be distorted by their own beliefs, prejudices, and desires?

16.6   The Experiences of an Indentured Servant

While the men named in the letters patent (Document 4) were men of means (merchants and the like), others also signed on to start a new life in America. Those without money often made the passage as indentured servants, where they gave generally seven years of service to those who paid their passage. After seven years, they were again free men. The following excerpt is from a letter of one indentured servant in 1623.

> **Source:** Richard Frethorne, letter to his father and mother, March 20, April 2 and 3, 1623, in Susan Kingsbury, ed. *The Records of the Virginia Company of London*, (Washington, D.C.: Government Printing Office, 1935), 4: 58–62; reprinted on URL: http://jefferson.village.virginia.edu/vcdh/jamestown/frethorne.html.

LOVING AND KIND FATHER AND MOTHER:

My most humble duty remembered to you, hoping in god of your good health, as I myself am at the making hereof. This is to let you understand that I you child am in a most heavy case by reason of the country, [which] is such that it causeth much sic kness, [such] as the sccurvy and the bloody flux and diverse other diseases, which maketh the body very poor and weak. And when we are sick there is nothing to comfort us; for since I came out of the ship I never ate anything but peas, and loblollie (that is, water gruel). As for deer or venison I never saw any since I came into this land. There is indeed some fowl, but we are not allowed to go and get it, but must work hard both early and late for a mess of water gruel and a mouthful of bread and beef. A mouthful of bread for a penny loaf must serve for four men which is most pitiful. [You would be grieved] if you did know as much as I [do], when people cry out day and night—Oh! That they were in England without their limbs—and would not care to lose any limb to be in England again, yea, though they beg from door to door. For we live in fear of the enemy every hour, yet we have had a combat with them . . . and we took two alive and made slaves of them. But it was by policy, for we are in great danger; for our plantation is very weak by reason of the death and sickness of our com-

pany. For we came but twenty for the merchants, and they are half dead just; and we look every hour when two more should go. Yet there came some four other men yet to live with us, of which there is but one alive; and our Lieutenant is dead, and [also] his father and his brother. And there was some five or six of the last year's twenty, of which there is but three left, so that we are fain to get other men to plant with us; and yet we are but 32 to fight against 3000 if they should come. And the nighest help that we have is ten mile of us, and when the rogues overcame this place [the] last [time] they slew 80 persons. How then shall we do, for we lie even in their teeth? They may easily take us, but [for the fact] that God is merciful and can save with few as well as with many, as he showed to Gilead. And like Gilead's soldiers, if they lapped water, we drink water which is but weak.

And I have nothing to comfort me, nor is there nothing to be gotten here but sickness and death, except [in the event] that one had money to lay out in some things for profit. But I have nothing at all—no, not a shirt to my back but two rags (2), nor clothes but one poor suit, nor but one pair of shoes, but one pair of stockings, but one cap, [and] but two bands [collars]. My cloak is stolen by one of my fellows, and to his dying hour [he] should not tell me what he did with it; but some of my fellows saw him have butter and beef out of a ship, which my cloak, I doubt [not], paid for. So that I have not a penny, nor a penny worth, to help me too either spice or sugar or strong waters, without the which one cannot live here. For as strong beer in England doth fatten and strengthen them, so water here doth wash and weaken these here [and] only keeps [their] life and soul together. But I am not half [of] a quarter so strong as I was in England, and all is for want of victuals; for I do protest unto you that I have eaten more in [one] day at home than I have allowed me here for a week. You have given more than my day's allowance to a beggar at the door; and if Mr. Jackson had not relieved me, I should be in a poor case. But he like a father and she like a loving mother doth still help me.

For when we go to Jamestown (that is 10 miles of us) there lie all the ships that come to land, and there they must deliver their goods. And when we went up to town [we would go], as it may be, on Monday at noon, and come there by night, [and] then load the next day by noon, and go home in the afternoon, and unload, and then away again in the night, and [we would] be up about midnight. Then if it rained or blowed never so hard, we must lie in the boat on the water and have nothing but a little bread. For when we go into the boat we [would] have a loaf allowed to two men, and it is all [we would get] if we stayed there two days, which is hard; and [we] must lie all that while in the boat. But that Goodman Jackson pitied me and made me a cabin to lie in always when I [would] come up, and he would give me some poor jacks [fish] [to take] home with me, which comforted me more than peas or water gruel. Oh, they be very godly folks, and love me very well, and will do anything for me. And he much marvelled that you would send me a servant to the Company; he saith I had been better knocked on the head. And indeed so I find it now, to my great grief and misery; and [I] saith that if you love me you will redeem me suddenly, for which I do entreat and beg. And if you cannot get the merchants to redeem me for some little money, then for God's sake get a gathering or entreat some good folks to lay out some little sum of money in meal and cheese and butter and beef. Any eating meat will yield great profit. Oil and vinegar is very good; but, father, there is great loss in leaking. But for God's sake send beef and cheese and butter, or the more of one sort and none of another. But if you send cheese, it must be very old cheese; and at the cheesemonger's you may buy very food cheese for twopence farthing or halfpenny, that will be liked very well. But if you send cheese, you must have a care how you pack it in barrels; and you must put cooper's chips between every cheese, or else the heat of the hold will rot them. And look whatsoever you send me—be in never so much—look, what[ever] I make of it, I will deal truly with you. I will send it over and beg the profit to redeem me; and if I die before it come, I have entreated Goodman Jackson to send you the worth of it, who hath promised he will. If you send, you must direct your letters to Goodman Jackson, at Jamestown, a gunsmith. (You must set down his freight, because there be more of his name there.) Good father, do not forget me, but have mercy and pity my miserable case. I know if you did but see me, you would weep to see me; for I have but one suit. (But [though] it is a strange one, it is very well guarded.) Wherefore, for God's sake, pity me. I pray you to remember my love to all my friends and kindred. I hope all my brothers and sisters are in good health, and as for my part I have set down my resolution that certainly will be; that is, that the answer of this letter will be life or death to me. Therefore, good father, send as soon as you can; and if you send me any thing let this be the mark.

ROT

RICHARD FRETHORNE,

MARTIN'S HUNDRED

Questions:
1. How does Frethorne describe life in the colony, as it might apply to all inhabitants?
2. How does Frethorne describe specifically the life of an indentured servant?